# ORAL POETRY AND NARRATIVES FROM CENTRAL ARABIA

I

## THE POETRY OF AD-DINDĀN

# STUDIES IN ARABIC LITERATURE

SUPPLEMENTS TO THE
JOURNAL OF ARABIC LITERATURE

EDITED BY

J.E. MONTGOMERY AND R.M.A. ALLEN

VOLUME XVII/I

*Oral Poetry and Narratives from Central Arabia*
Vol. I. *The Poetry of ad-Dindān*

ᶜAbdallah ad-Dindān

P. MARCEL KURPERSHOEK

# ORAL POETRY AND NARRATIVES FROM CENTRAL ARABIA

## I

## THE POETRY OF AD-DINDĀN

*A Bedouin Bard in Southern Najd*

AN EDITION WITH TRANSLATION AND INTRODUCTION

E.J. BRILL
LEIDEN · NEW YORK · KÖLN
1994

This book has been published with financial support from the Netherlands Organization for Scientific Research (NWO).

The paper in this book meets the guidelines for permanence and durability of the Committee on Production Guidelines for Book Longevity of the Council on Library Resources.

**Library of Congress Cataloging-in-Publication Data**

Dindān, 1921 or 2-
[Selections. English & Arabic. 1994]
The poetry of ad-Dindān : a bedouin bard in southern Najd / recorded and edited with translation and introduction by Marcel Kurpershoek.
p. cm. — (Studies in Arabic literature, ISSN 0169–9903 ; v. 17)
Includes Arabic text transcribed in roman script.
Includes bibliographical references and index.
ISBN 9004098941 (alk. paper)
1. Dindān, 1921 or 2- —Translations into English. 2. Dindān, 1921 or 2- —Criticism and interpretation. 3. Dialect poetry, Arabic—Saudi Arabia—Najd—History and criticism. I. Kurpershoek, Marcel, 1949- . II. Title. III. Series.
PJ7820.I47A25 1994
892'.716—dc20 93-39951
CIP

**Die Deutsche Bibliothek - CIP-Einheitsaufnahme**

Dindān, ʿAbdallah Ibn-Muḥammad ad-:
[The poetry]
The poetry of ad-Dindān : a Bedouin bard in southern Najd / recorded and ed. with transl. and introd. by Marcel Kurpershoek. - Leiden ; New York ; Köln : Brill, 1994
(Studies in Arabic literature ; Vol. 17 : Oral poetry and narratives from Central Arabia ; Vol. 1)
ISBN 90-04-09894-1
NE: Kurpershoek, Marcel [Hrsg.]; Studies in Arabic literature / Oral poetry and narratives from Central Arabia

ISSN 0169-9903
ISBN 90 04 09894 1



PRINTED IN THE NETHERLANDS

*To Tonny Scherft, my mother*

CONTENTS

# PREFACE AND ACKNOWLEDGMENTS

In 1989, upon the completion of my tour of duty as a diplomat in the Dutch embassy in Riyadh, I was granted permission by the government of Saudi Arabia to extend my stay in that country for the purpose of conducting research among transmitters of oral traditions of the ᶜTēbah (ᶜUtaybah) and ad-Duwāsir (ad-Dawāsir) tribes in central and southern Najd. The focus of my fieldwork was on orally transmitted poetry and narratives dating back to the pre-modern period in Central Arabia. Yet I decided to partially lift this self-imposed restriction when in Wādi ad-Duwāsir I met the poet locally known by the nickname of ad-Dindān.

In the eyes of his fellow tribesmen Dindān was something of an oddity. No one disputed the fact that he was one of their greatest living poets, a natural talent highly esteemed for his images of life in the desert and especially for his camel descriptions. On the other hand Dindān's stubborn attachment to his old-fashioned bedouin ways, his imperviousness to the lure of modern development and material gain, his solitary existence and headstrong character, were looked upon with a mixture of annoyance, amusement and uneasiness. Perhaps it was for this reason that Dindān aroused my interest: he was a living representative of the same past I was trying to discover through the oral traditions handed down along chains of transmitters. Also, because of his social isolation and desperate resistance to the pressures that gradually pushed him out of his nomadic way of life, Dindān seemed a powerful symbol of a culture that had remained largely unchanged for a thousand years or more but is now rapidly fading. But regardless of his personality and station in life, my primary concern was with Dindān the poet: the more I came to know his work, the more I marvelled at the fact that a poor, illiterate bedouin like him should be able to match the artistry of the great classical and modern literate poets.

From a more pragmatic point of view, the edition of Dindān's poetry seemed a useful addition to the existing body of scholarly work dealing with various aspects of the Najdi tradition. Of course, many poems and fragments in the vernacular of Najd have been transliterated and translated into Western languages. Moreover, numerous anthologies and collections of verse by the present and previous generations of popular Najdi poets, scored in Arabic characters, have been published in Saudi Arabia and other Arab countries. But it occurred to me that if a complete *dīwān* of a living poet, steeped in the conventions and imagery of the 'classical' vernacular tradition, became available in transcribed and translated form, it might contribute to a fuller understanding of the Najdi oral tradition.

The poetic idiom of the Najdi tradition in vernacular poetry, in its Dōsiri dialect version spoken by Dindān, is explained in an extensive glossary included in this edition. The glossary's listing of Classical Arabic words and expressions corresponding or equivalent to Dindān's poetic vocabulary is not only meant to assist the classical Arabist, but also underscores the close historical kinship between this vocabulary and the language of the ancient Arabs. The glossary, the appendix of place names and the detailed table of contents made it possible to dispense with a separate index.

This work would have been impossible without the kind permission of the government of Saudi Arabia and the active assistance of the authorities in Riyadh. In particular, I am grateful for the personal interest taken in my project by the *wakīl* of the Governorate of Riyadh, ᶜAbdallah ibn Bulayhid, who provided me with the necessary letters of introduction and other practical assistance. In al-Khamasīn, the seat of local government in Wādi ad-Duwāsir, my work was greatly facilitated by the hospitality, accomodation and transport put at my disposal by the *amīr* of the Wādi, Muḥammad al-Māḍī.

ᶜAbdallah ad-Dindān, the subject of this book, is illiterate and his wandering, homeless life forces him to keep his possessions to a bare minimum. His *māl*, capital, is a small herd of black camels and the wealth of poetry he carries in his head. Nevertheless, I sent him a copy of the edition that resulted from our association and it is my fervent hope that his literate friends will assure him of my undying admiration and deep gratitude for his patience and co-operation in reciting and explaining his verses to me. He is living proof that illiteracy, utter poverty and social disadvantage are not necessarily a barrier to the creation of true art and that great poetry is not the preserve of any class or group of human beings. Not many bedouins in the true sense of the word remain in Wādi ad-Duwāsir and Dindān is one of them—or rather was, for our association occurred at a time when various circumstances forced him to abandon his wandering life and to put up his camels for sale. As described in this study, Dindān's desperate efforts to continue his nomadic existence were of no avail and against his will he gradually had to settle down in one of the villages of the Wādi. Thus the dwindling tribe of true bedouins lost another of its outstanding members. Perhaps it is no exaggeration to say that with Dindān I caught a glimpse of a world at the moment of its final eclipse.

Among the literate men of the Wādi I should mention ᶜAbdallah Ḥmēr Sāyir ad-Dōsiri, whose anthology *Wāḥat ash-shiᶜr ash-shaᶜbī* (*The Valley of Popular Poetry*) first drew my attention to the work of Dindān and to whom I am grateful for his many explanatory notes to Dindān's verses. I also wish to express my heartfelt thanks to the pre-eminent authority in the field of Najdi poetry and oral culture, Dr. Saad Abdullah Sowayan of the King Saud University in Riyadh, who has been a source of encouragement and valuable advice throughout my venture and without whose concrete assistance in the translation, transcription and interpretation of the materials this work would not have come to fruition. His two major contributions to our knowledge in this field, *Nabaṭi Poetry, the Oral Poetry of Arabia* (1985), and *The Arabian Oral Historical Narrative* (1992), have been my guiding stars from the moment I engaged in this undertaking. For this edition I am especially indebted to the former work's chapter on the prosody of Najdi vernacular poetry and to the latter's comprehensive glossary, as well as to its carefully thought-out and consistent system of phonemic transcription. I hope that Dr. Sowayan will take it as a tribute to his work that I have tried to follow many of the trails he blazed so successfully in this largely unexplored terrain.

Among the colleagues to whom I turned for advice in a later stage of the project I should mention Dr. G.J.H. van Gelder of the University of Groningen, who offered some very helpful comments from the classical Arabist's point of view, Dr. Bruce Ingham of the School of Oriental and African Studies of the University of London, and Professor Dr. Otto Jastrow of the Ruprecht-Karls-Universität in Heidelberg. Their encouraging words after having read an early version of the manuscript greatly enhanced my confidence on the road to the completion of this task. I was also very fortunate to have an editor at E.J. Brill, Peri Bearman, who not only piloted this work to publication with skill and energy, but also gave freely of her own time to correct the English text.

I am grateful to *Asian Folklore Studies*, Nagoya, for permission to include in this work the section on conventionality and originality in the *nasīb* of Najdi poetry, which originally appeared in its special issue devoted to Arab folklore, vol. LII-1, 1993.

For the generous grant which enabled me to publish this edition I would like to express my deep gratitude to the Netherlands Organization for Scientific Research (NWO).

May 1993, Kraainem
Belgium

# NOTE ON TRANSCRIPTION

For the transcription of the poems of ad-Dindān's oral *dīwān*, as well as the two poems with introductory narratives transmitted by the poet, in the vernacular of southern Najd I have chosen symbols which are essentially the same as those used by others who have published Najdi and other peninsular texts in recent times (Sowayan 1985 and 1992, Ingham 1982 and 1986, Prochazka, 1988, Johnstone 1967). The consonant and vowel system of the Najdi dialects does not deviate radically from that underlying the phonetics of Classical Arabic (CA). Apart from differences in vowelling and syllabication (for which the mentioned sources should be consulted), the main differences in comparison with CA can be summarized as follows.

The glottal stop, represented by the CA *hamzah*, has disappeared as a functional phoneme, except when it occurs in initial position. But even there its position is not stable. Also, in many cases the initial glottal stop which is not part of the root has not been maintained. If the initial glottal stop is the first radical of the verb's root it is either dropped, in which case the loss of the *hamzah* may be compensated for by the addition of a final long vowel (*xa̱da, kala*), or it has been preserved as the short vowel of a vocalic onset (*axa̱d*). In many instances, however, it is replaced by *w*, as in *wimar* (for CA *amara*).

If the *hamzah* opens a syllable in non-initial position it changes to *y* (*myah* for *miʾah*, *nāyim* for *nāʾim*), or to *w* if the preceding vowel is *u* (*fwād* for *fuʾād*). A *hamzah* which closes a syllable is dropped and the preceding short vowel is lengthened, if it is not already long (*bīr* for *biʾr*, *rās* for *raʾs*, *manša* for *mansẖaʾ*, *ṭara* for *ṭaraʾ*). Following a diphthong or a long vowel *ī* or *ū* (equivalent to *iy* or *uw*) the *hamzah* is replaced by a doubling of the last *y* or *w* (*nayy* for *nayʾ*, *ridiyy* for *radīʾ*, *mruwwah* for *murūʾah*). The *hamzah* as a medial radical in the verb has disappeared and the glottal stop has been replaced by a lengthening of the preceding vowel, with the result that the verbs concerned have become hollow verbs (*rām* for *raʾima*). In the note on the glossary some further remarks are made concerning the glottal stop and the changes it has undergone in the dialect.

The consonants represented in CA by *ḍād* and *ẓāʾ* have merged into a single voiced interdental emphatic, which is represented by the symbol *ḏ̣*. The voiced velar *g*, pronounced as the Cairene *jīm*, is a reflex of CA *qāf*. In the Najdi dialects *g* and *k* are frequently affricated and pronounced as the dentals *dz* and *ts*, represented by the symbols *ǵ* and *ć*.

Some characteristics of the vowels in Dindān's usage of the Dōsiri dialect, and the replacement of the CA diphthongs *aw* and *ay* by the long vowels *ō*, *ē* and *ā*, are discussed in the chapter on prosody and language of this work's introduction.

It should be pointed out that I have not attempted to give a comprehensive description of the dialect's phonology and other linguistic features. I have assumed that readers who wish to acquire a fuller understanding of the ground rules governing the phonology and morphology would be better served by direct reference to the listed sources than by a rehash of their contents. Therefore this study's section on language focuses in particular on features which set the Dōsiri dialect apart from the dialects spoken in northern Najd and already described in greater detail in the other sources.

Clearly, a good working knowledge of the dialect's phonetics is a prerequisite for the successful transcription of an oral text recorded on tape during a live performance. And, as Sowayan (1985) emphasizes, some familiarity with these phonetic characteristics is also indispensable for the analysis of the metrical structure of Najdi vernacular poetry and its scansion.

In *nabaṭi* poetry, as the poetry in the vernacular of the Najd is called, the hemistich is treated as a continuous sequence of short and long syllables, which implies that word boundaries should be disregarded for the purpose of scansion. This theoretical observation frequently corresponds to the reality of a poet's or a transmitter's practice during rapid delivery. To cite but one example, in the first hemistich of the sixteenth verse of poem no. 6 the cluster *yaṭribillō-ḥan*, as one hears it on the taped record, results from the merger of *yaṭribin la ōḥan* into a single, continuous utterance. Through scansion, based on an analysis of the poem's metrical pattern, one arrives at a sequence of short and long syllables in which this cluster is divided over three different feet and in which the syllabic units straddle two word boundaries. In order to illustrate this the entire hemistich must be scanned: *ḥa rā yir/ ši mā lin yaṭ/ ri bin lō/ ḥa nal ġir māl*.

The technique of scansion is explained in the chapter on metre. The point I wish to make here is that in transcription a balance must be struck between the phonetic realities of the dynamic performance and the demands of a phonemic notation which respects the normal word morphology and makes for a readable text, while leaving the metrical pattern intact. For instance, in the case of *yaṭribillōḥan* I have maintained the elision of the long vowel *ā* of *la* (also because otherwise the metrical pattern would be impaired). Though the remaining *l* has become connected to the following *ō*, the interspacing between *l* and *ōḥan* is a reminder that they must be considered as separate words (and also prevents the subordinator *la*, corresponding to CA *idhā*, from being mistaken for the conditional particle *lo*, corresponding to CA *law*). On the other hand, the transcription does not show the assimilation of the final *nūn* of *yaṭribin* to the following *l* (of *la* with the elided vowel), but maintains the regular inflected form of the third person feminine plural imperfect of the verb. There are sound arguments for doing so, but it is equally obvious that an element of arbitrariness cannot always be avoided in the countless similar decisions which must be made as part of the transcription of an oral text.

In general I have transcribed the feminine suffix in final position as *-ah*, though it is frequently realized with a more centralized vowel, i.e. *-eh*. The suffix of the feminine ending and the third person masculine singular pronominal suffix *-ih* are used in the same poem as an appendix to the rhyming consonant (see p. 98, note 1).

For the phonemic transcription of the taped records I have mainly relied on the above mentioned works, especially on the concise phonological observations and the system of scansion elaborated in Sowayan (1985 and 1992). In addition I have benefited from Prochazka's work on the morphology of verbal forms in the various Saudi dialects (Prochazka 1988). When in the course of transcription any questions arose, I have turned to these works for answers, while keeping in mind the differences between the dialects of northern Arabia and that of the Duwāsir.

The following symbols are used for the transcription of the oral text.

Consonants:

| | | | |
|---|---|---|---|
| ʾ | ء | ṭ | ط |
| b | ب | ḏ̣ | ظ ض |
| t | ت | ʿ | ع |
| ṯ | ث | ġ | غ |
| j | ج | f | ف |
| ḥ | ح | g (affricated *ǵ*) | ق |
| x | خ | k (affricated *ć*) | ك |
| d | د | l | ل |
| ḏ | ذ | m | م |
| r | ر | n | ن |
| z | ز | h | ه |
| s | س | w | و |
| š | ش | y | ي |
| ṣ | ص | ah, at | ة |

Vowels,
Short: *a, e, i, u*
Long: *ā, ē, ī, ū, ō*
Diphthongs: *aw* (mostly monophthongized as *ō* or *ā*), *ay* (mostly monophthongized as *ē*).

Final vowels are always long and therefore are transcribed without macron.

The transliteration of literary Arabic uses the same symbols for the consonants with the following exceptions:

| | |
|---|---|
| th | ث |
| kh | خ |
| dh | ذ |
| sh | ش |
| ḍ | ض |
| ẓ | ظ |
| q | ق |

While it is clearly preferable not to mix the systems used for the transcription of dialect words and the transliteration of literary Arabic, full consistency in the application of this principle is difficult to achieve. For instance, I have chosen to spell the name ad-Dawsarī as ad-Dōsiri, in accordance with the transcription of the tribal *nisbah* throughout the text. Both Mḥammad and Muḥammad occur, depending on the manner in which the rest of the name is spelled. For Arabic words and names occurring in the English text preference is generally given to the spelling used for the transliteration of literary Arabic, e.g. Jikhjūkh instead of Jixjūx. In the appendix of place names I have used the system of transliteration for literary Arabic for names which do not occur in the text of the taped records and whenever I was not sure about the dialect pronunciation of names mentioned by the authors of Saudi geographical handbooks. Where conventional English spellings exist these have been followed, e.g. Mecca, Medina, Saudi etc.

ᶜAbdallah ad-Dindān

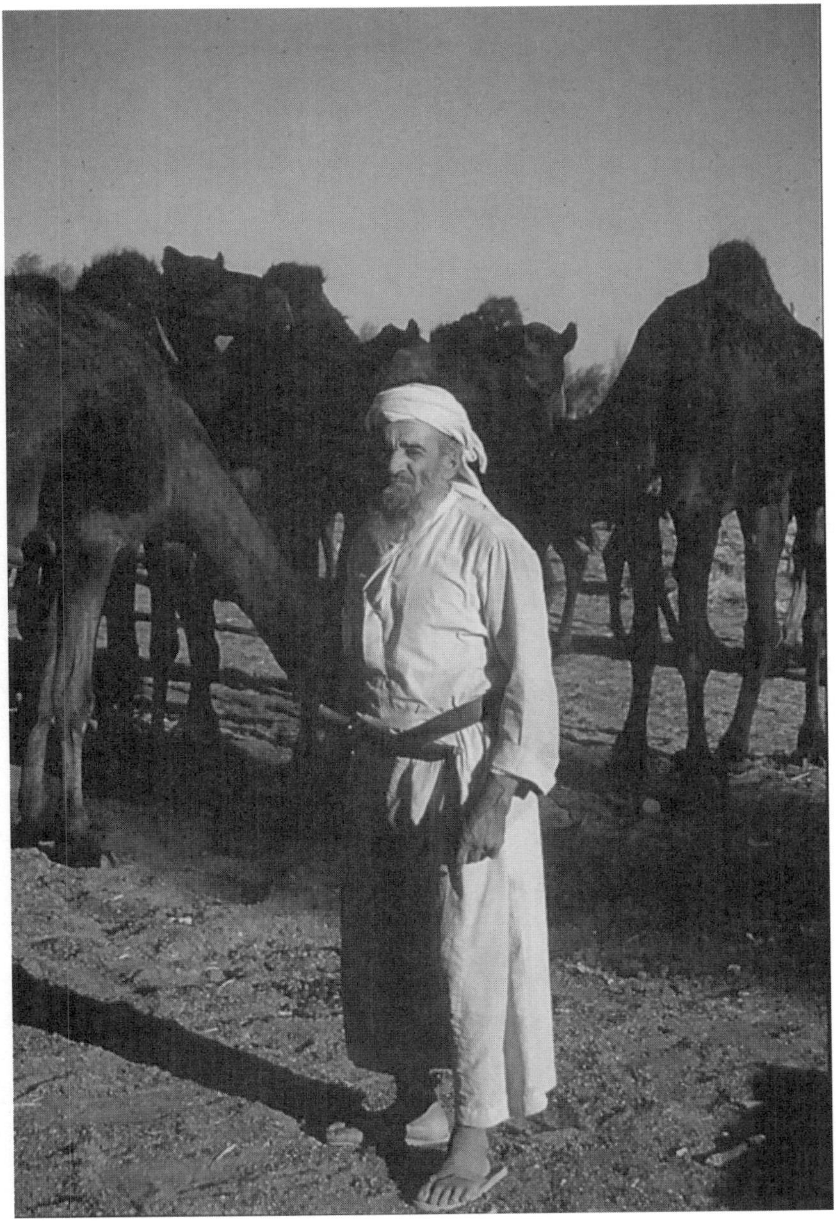

The end of ad-Dindān's existence as a nomad: watering his camels while waiting for buyers at the edge of al-Ldām (p. 14).

# INTRODUCTION

# I. THE POET

## Dindān

### *The Life of a Bedouin Artist*

Three years ago I had the good fortune of spending about six weeks with an old and penniless yet proud and defiant bedouin who is one of the greatest living poets of the Duwāsir tribe in southern Najd. His name is ᶜAbdallah ibn Mḥammad ibn Ḥzayyim of the Ḥarāršah, a subtribe of ar-Rijbān of ad-Duwāsir, but he is generally known by the nickname of ad-Dindān, an onomatopoeia derived from the verb *dandan*, meaning 'to tinkle, to hum a tune, to break into spontaneous verse'.

For Dindān and his colleagues, singing and humming in metre and rhyme is an activity pursued in a spirit of both deadly seriousness and playful contest. Like a group of camel riders traversing the desert, they toss at one another lines of chanted poetry that encourage their mounts to vie neck to neck for speed, as expressed in this verse of Dindān (poem no. 21, v. 6):

*in dandanaw gumt ana alᶜab liᶜb dindāni //*
*w-in ġaṭrifaw bi-l-ġuwāriᶜ gumt aġaddīha*

When others hum the tune, I strike up the merry melody; //
When they ululate the song, I keep the rhyme going.

Indeed, he has identified to such an extent with his poetic gift that neither he nor anyone else calls him by any other name than ᶜAbdallah ad-Dindān. When he follows the custom of oral poets to inscribe their copyright symbol in the first line of a poem (as a painter would sign his name in one of the lower corners of the canvas), this is how he puts it (18/1):

*šarraf aš-šāᶜir ad-Dindān rijmin l-ḥālih //*
*gāl šaffih b-kēfih min ḥasīn al-kalāmi*

The poet ad-Dindān ascended a mountain all alone //
And burst into exquisite verses made to suit his own taste.

The merry, vigorous and somewhat self-willed tone of these verses is characteristic for Dindān, but it is also deceptive. Besides his unshakeable faith in the providence of God, the only sources of comfort

Dindān has in order to relieve the hardships of his existence are the society of fellow-tribesmen, his small herd of camels and, above all, his poetry. And even these pleasures are partly overshadowed by the fact that he lives under a pall of social prejudice and poverty.

When I met him, Dindān was about seventy years old.[1] His situation at that time was not enviable. It was October and he camped on the stubbly ground of some fields about fifteen kilometers west of the built-up area of the Wādi. There his camels pastured on the straw left behind after the wheat had been harvested from the huge circles irrigated by slowly revolving pivots. Dindān did not possess a tent and he used to sleep wrapped in his dirty fur on the ground or in his battered pick-up. For many of his supplies he depended on ᶜUṭrān, one of the most successful breeders of the Duwāsir, whose large herd of famous black camels also foraged on the field. As a hanger-on of ᶜUṭrān's family Dindān occasionally shared their meals and sat down in front of their tent in order to chat with the breeder's older wife over dates, tea and coffee. There was also the younger second wife ᶜUṭrān had just married in Egypt in exchange for ten thousand riyals in the hope that she would bear him sons in addition to the two girls he had by his first wife. He had decked her out in the attire of bedouin women, but there was no way to disguise her broad Egyptian accent and, for local standards, exuberant bearing. For Dindān she remained a stranger in the camp, the daughter of *fallāḥīn* with whom he had nothing in common.

Sometimes ᶜUṭrān would receive visitors, kinsmen from town, for a *d̲ibīḥah*, a meal of roasted sheep. Then a carpet was spread out in front of the tent, a lamp was hooked to the battery of one of the parked pick-ups and four-wheel drive vehicles. After having performed their evening prayers the men would kick off their sandals and sit in a circle on the carpet under the star-studded sky, while all around the camels stumbled among the cars as if attracted by the light and the company. Also, the carpet soon crawled with beetles feeding on the camel dung. This was the *majlis*, the assembly hosted by men of the same kin, each one in his turn, and open to more distant relatives, visitors and friends, which everywhere in Arabia pro-

---

[1] According to the Saudi editor of his poetry, ᶜAbdallah Ḥmēr Sābir ad-Dōsirī, Dindān was born in A. H. 1340 (1921-22) in the town of al-Ldām in Wādi ad-Duwāsir as a member of the Āl Rāšid clan of al-Ḥarāršah al-ᶜYēd̲āt tribe of ar-Rijbān of the Duwāsir; see *Wāḥat as̲h̲-s̲h̲iᶜr as̲h̲-s̲h̲aᶜbī*, Riyadh 1988, ii, 128.

vides the essential environment for the perpetuation of the oral tradition: a largely unrecorded culture of narratives and poems, both contemporary and transmitted from times long gone-by. Told and recited according to time-honoured conventions and practices, this oral literature deals with any subject or theme of common interest and plays a vital role in cementing the sense of a shared identity among and within the tribes and villages of Najd.

On such occasions Dindān's star would outshine all others: the formidable men of ᶜUṭrān's clan would listen spellbound as the destitute, socially maladjusted vagabond of the desert transformed into a cocksure entertainer whose rasping, powerful voice seemed to belie his frail, grandfatherly physique. Yet these fleeting moments of artistic triumph could not change the basic fact that Dindān had increasingly lost control of his destiny as he advanced in age. Since ten years or more several factors had conspired against his continued pastoral existence in the sands, plains and mountainous deserts north and west of the Wādi.

Dindān's most serious handicap was perhaps that he had never married and thus had no sons or sons-in-law on whom he could rely for help with the chores of tending to his camels which he could barely perform himself because of his infirmity. For due to partial paralysis of one leg Dindān was hardly able to walk. Moreover, his unmarried state was something of a social stigma in the eyes of his fellow-tribesmen. In Arabia, and especially in the ultra-orthodox religious climate of the Wādi, bachelorhood is commonly frowned upon and often derided. People would say, only half in jest, 'Dindān is married to his camels.' Still, Dindān was not insusceptible to female beauty; his loving descriptions of camels often occur side by side, and sometimes intermingled with playful, tender verses of love poetry. Generally these verses are couched in the stock images and conventional phraseology of the genre. In some poems, however, one clearly senses that Dindān does not address himself to an idealized female effigy, but to real women of flesh and blood who once stirred his erotic imagination. Contrary to custom, he mentions names of beauties he adored from afar; and perhaps not always so far, as in the chance encounter with a female acquaintance in the mosque of Mecca during pilgrimage (poem no. 29).

The poem about this incident not only confirms the well-known fact that bedouin women are accustomed to act and speak with greater independence than their settled sisters, even with respect to their preferences among the other sex. It also shows that women, or at least some of them, rather liked him. Why then did he not marry? Perhaps Dindān's bitter verses about being rebuffed by his sweetheart's male guardians are more than a mere motif drawn from the repertory of love poetry (poem no. 11). Possibly they are rooted in a real event that thwarted his desire to marry a cousin with whom he had fallen in love. Indeed it is likely that families of some social standing would have been reluctant to wed their daughters to someone notorious for his happy-go-lucky life-style and little means.

### *The Drought*

In my view the most remarkable trait in Dindān's character was his complete lack of social ambition or desire for material advancement. In many respects he lived a life that was not essentially different from that of the bedouins with whom Charles M. Doughty consorted in the desert south of Tayma more than a century ago. The core of Dindān's poetry is an almost static picture of the eternal cycles that dominate the existence of the Arabian nomad. The advent of fortune is heralded by the appearance of clouds on the horizon. If the clouds make good on their promise and the rains fall in heavy downpours on the thirsty desert so that the dry watercourses turn into rushing streams and large pools are left on the ground, the bedouins know they can expect the *rajiᶜ*: the 'return' of the herbage on which their herds can pasture in spring to their hearts' delight.

No great human effort or inventiveness is required from the bedouins in such conditions. The camels and their young will grow big and healthy, putting on layers of fat as reserves against the hard times that inevitably will follow. The bedouins roam the desert at will, sustained by their herds' plentiful milk, without having to toil in order to supply their animals with water and fodder. Nature takes care of itself, so to speak, and gives the nomads a free ride. But these periods of grace only arrive at varying intervals and the state of bliss lasts no longer than a few months. If the rain fails to fall in significant amounts for years in succession, as frequently is the case, hardship is upon them.

Drought and its devastating consequences are a recurrent theme in Dindān's poems. His attitude towards such misfortune is typical for the traditional bedouin outlook. The suffering caused by the *wagt*, the 'time', or *dahar*, 'fate', as they call these barren years, must be born patiently and without bitterness. The bedouins simply must endure, like the seeds of the annuals inside the scorched earth, and have faith in God's compassion and pray that He will bestow on them His mercy by sending the rain clouds. For in the end everything depends on the Lord's inscrutable will. Such is the order of things that determines Dindān's mental outlook.

In 1989 the land of the Duwāsir was in the grip of a drought that had lasted for almost ten years, so I was told. As Dindān says in one of his verses, he and his camels were at their wits' end (poem no. 12). All that was left to him and other bedouins was to reminisce nostalgically about their halcyon days: the period which they had come to remember as the short, but golden reign of King Khālid. Not only did the desert blossom in those days, the abundant rains also coincided with the *ṭafrah*, the (second) oil-boom. A flood of oil-dollars, converted into riyals, swept the country like the *sēls*, the torrents ripping up the bottoms of the gullies after heavy rains. And, as Dindān says in his verses about the imaginary downpours he likes to picture in his mind, *ma gaᶜad wādi*, 'not a wadi missed out' on God's bounty.

In the time of King Khālid the bedouins may not all have become millionaires, but without exception they did receive a fair share of the windfall. This was a true *ribīᶜ*, luscious spring pasture, the land of milk and honey of their dreams. Many of them took the opportunity to build a large house in one of the existing villages and towns or in the *hijar*, the new settlements, and to purchase new vehicles and *wiyyat* (sing. *wāyit*), the sturdy Mercedes trucks mounted with a big watertank that facilitated the task of catering to the needs of their herds. Fodder for the camels was cheap and plentiful: a fifty-kilo bag of barley cost only eight riyals. It is true that the milk of camels only acquires its delicious taste and richness of ingredients when the animals graze on the various plants, grasses and bushes of the desert, especially the saline *ḥamḍ*-plants. But breeders who prefer to keep their herds close to the Wādi depend on this cheap supply of barley, *nxālah*, ground chaff of wheat which is fed to the animals admixed with water, and *birsīm*, clover. In the dry season or in times of drought barley becomes the main staple for the vast majority of herds, even for the bedouins who would prefer to pasture their camels in the desert.

During the reign of King Khālid the camel-breeders, already favoured by the abundance of fodder, also prospered commercially. The big-bodied, black camels of the Duwāsir were in great demand everywhere in the country on account of their copious produce of milk. In those days it was not unusual for good camels to be sold for one hundred thousand riyals or more per head. ᶜUṭrān, Dindān's host, made a fortune which he invested in real estate and the acquisition of a plantation of date palms. Everyone in the Wādi knows the story of the camel dealer who made an offer of three hundred thousand riyals for one of ᶜUṭrān's champion studs. ᶜUṭrān turned the offer down and the next day the stud was dead: it was whispered that the dealer possessed a 'strong eye' and had vented his resentment by unleashing at the stallion one of his murderous glances.

In 1989, however, this period of ease and plenty was already a fading memory for the bedouins. On the other hand Dōsiri families and companies that had invested in wheat-growing were still making large profits. Deep under the Wādi runs one of the country's huge aquifers, a vast reservoir of fossil water. Thanks to this almost limitless supply of water the size of the traditional agricultural area, the old palm gardens, had increased manifold. The circular fields, irrigated by pivots, had extended in all directions, especially towards the west, with the exception of the north where the hard, dull green of the palm-trees abruptly ended in the whitish yellow of the sandhills that have shielded the Wādi from that side since time immemorial. The high fixed price paid by the government (about eight times the price of the world market) and the subsidized supply of seed-corn, the favourable loans for the purchase of equipment, water pumps and so on, and the cheap imported labour turned agriculture into a huge money-making machine for those who had access to it and knew how to use it.

Simple nomads like Dindān did not belong to that category. Dindān had nothing like the influence, connections and *savoir faire* needed even to make a modest start in the agro-business, nor did he have the inclination to do so. Like many others, he preferred to stick to the way of life he had inherited from his ancestors. The drought, the drop in the prices paid for camels to one-tenth or less in comparison with those of a decade before, the rise of the price of a fifty-kilo sack of barley from eight riyals in the good old days to twenty-four and a half—these were difficulties Dindān faced calmly and with brave fatalism.

It seemed to escape Dindān, though unconsciously he may have been aware of it, that this spell of hardship was of a different nature than previous droughts and that this time the socio-economic tide was running against him and other small breeders in a more fundamental way. In pre-modern days most inhabitants of the peninsula were accustomed to their condition of semi-permanent poverty and want. The effects of drought, locusts and other natural plagues were felt in equal measure by nomads and the settled population. The development of wheat-growing as the mainstay of the Wādi's economy has changed this. A new class of entrepreneurs and owners of large estates, mostly grafted onto the traditional families of tribal grandees, has financially profited from the modern development of the country's economy. But those who, like Dindān, failed to seize this opportunity and continued to cleave to their old ways have become increasingly marginalized—perhaps definitively so. In 1989 the pressures of these inexorable economic forces had become so great that some of the small breeders could no longer avoid taking the step any bedouin would try to postpone as long as possible: driven by utter desperation they were beginning to sell off their camels.[2]

### *Dindān's Bedouin 'Unruliness'*

In the course of the two months of my sojourn in the Wādi it gradually became clear to me that this was the general economic backdrop against which Dindān's plight had to be seen. But other, more personal factors were involved as well. Dindān was not only out of tune with his time in an economic sense. His *faits et gestes* in pursuit of old-fashioned tribal ideals, his reckless disregard for the consequences of his acts in defiance of established authority and religious orthodoxy as now understood in the Wādi, all contributed to his local notoriety. In this regard at least two examples of Dindanesque behaviour stood out in local memory.

About fourteen years before my arrival Dindān was encamped, together with some fellow-tribesmen, at the well of al-Ǵīʿah in the proximity of some rocky elevations, the Jazla mountains. This area, west of the Wādi, used to be one of Dindān's favourite haunts. On those peaks he composed many a poem and al-Jazla is among the mountains he singled out for special mention in the verses imploring the Lord to bless specific locations by releasing rains on them. The

---

[2] Towards the end of 1989 one horror story that circulated in many a *majlis* of the Wādi was about a bedouin who, unable to cope with the costs of feeding his camels, had been forced to sell his small herd of twenty-five animals for the paltry sum of 900 riyals each.

ownership of the well was in dispute. In spite of the modern development of Saudi Arabia, the possibility of recourse to courts and administrative or political arbitration, tribal quarrels over title and access to wells continue unabated in the breadth and width of the Arabian deserts.[3] But unlike the situation in the old days, before the writ of Riyadh ran supremely among the tribes, these disputes are no longer fought out with armed force. Normally the status quo is maintained, while the underlying contention keeps simmering at the level of political manoeuvring, mutual animosity and verbal hostility.

But occasionally tempers get so short that small-scale violence breaks out. This happened at al-Ǵīᶜah when one morning the Duwāsir encamped close to the well were attacked by a band of armed Gḥaṭān from one of the tribe's southern sections settled in the adjoining Wādi Taṯlīṯ. The Duwāsir took cover and fired their semiautomatic weapons in defence. Two men were fatally hit before the Gḥaṭān decided to call it a day. In itself there was nothing remarkable about this minor incident. The more significant part of it was the poetic aftermath which showed the lingering strength of the old tribal spirit.

Like other tribes, the Duwāsir are aware that this kind of lawless behaviour is not tolerated by the government and its local authorities. Since the time of King ᶜAbd al-ᶜAzīz political and religious pressure, backed up by the overwhelming might at the disposal of the centre, have taught the tribes to abandon their raiding habits and not to take the law into their own hands. But even seventy years or more of central control have not been sufficient to erase completely the legacy inherited from centuries of tribal chauvinism. A small spark, like the shoot-out at al-Ǵīᶜah, is sometimes enough to rekindle the bellicose tribal spirit—a spirit that is kept alive in the oral traditions about the tribes' proud and warlike past.

The customary medium, as it always has been, for giving expression to these sentiments is poetry. At the occasion of the confrontation at al-Ǵīᶜah ᶜAbdallah Ḥmēr, the author of an anthology of Duwāsir poetry, including that of Dindān, was moved by the surge of tribal feeling caused by this incident to celebrate the feat of his

---

[3] For instance, Sowayan, *The Arabian Oral Historical Narrative*, Wiesbaden 1992, 99, paragraph 075, refers to a recent dispute between ᶜAnazah and aš-Šarārāt about the possession of wells.

kinsmen in an ode running to about 130 lines. At least, this is what I was told, for the victory song was never recited to me. As one of the leading local intellectuals, an employee in the department of education and a one-time religious emissary, ᶜAbdallah knew exactly where the government would draw the line. So, once the first exitement was over, he withdrew his work from circulation, i.e. he no longer recited or mentioned it in any of the *majlis* he frequents almost daily in the various parts of the Wādi where he is welcomed as an esteemed visitor thanks to his lively conversation, broad culture and irreproachable moral stature.

The similarities and differences between the reactions of ᶜAbdallah Ḥmēr and Dindān to the situation are telling. As a perfectly adjusted individual ᶜAbdallah demonstrated the right kind of tribal "patriotism" and loyalty at a moment when no one could be blamed for not remaining immune to the general commotion. At the same time he soon returned to the behaviour one might expect from a sensible, rationally controlled member of the local elite by falling in rapidly with the official line. In short, he never exceeded the bounds imposed by correct opinion on the expression of his loyalties—not by remaining cool when tribal tempers flared nor by violating the norms of conduct prescribed by the authorities.

Dindān, on the contrary, had no such inhibitions and allowed himself to be carried away completely by the wave of tribal pathos provoked by the incident. First, he was one of the handful of men who actually took part in the fighting on that day. He sprayed the Ghaṭān with fierce bursts from his Kalashnikov gun and was hit in the shoulder by an enemy bullet. Then he composed two *razaf*s, war songs, and put them into circulation in disregard of the government decree banning such poetic activities which might further fan the flames of tribal passion (poems nos. 30 and 31).[4] For his role in the incident and its sequel Dindān was jailed for four months.

Another example of behaviour that rattled the conscience of the Wādi was a poem in which Dindān replied to the presumptuous claims of one of his rivals in the local circuit of oral poets. Most of

---

[4] In CA *razf* means 'hurrying, moving quickly'. In the vernacular of Najd it has the meaning of 'swinging the sword' (in the traditional sword dance). Therefore, Dindān's two poems in this genre were probably meant to be sung by the participators in sword dances celebrating the "victory" over Ghaṭān. In this respect the *razaf* may be akin to the Yemeni *razfah*, verse chanted at tribal dances, see Caton, Steven C., *'Peaks of Yemen I Summon'*, Berkeley-Los Angeles 1990, 45-47, 68.

the poem consists of an unobjectionable emotional prelude and a lengthy description of an excellent riding camel. The part that outraged local orthodox opinion and made a shiver of superstitious fear run down the spines of the less educated were a number of verses wedged between these two sections (verses 8-17 of poem no. 9, see also pp. 60-62).

From a literary perspective, one may feel that in passages as these Dindān's art rises to its greatest heights. For in these furious outbursts of emotion—whether caused by wounded pride, despair, sadness or resignation to his fate—Dindān achieves an expressiveness that in effect surpasses the level attained by a poet who merely has mastered all the techniques of the poetic craft. And in Dindān's defence one might reply to his local detractors that he certainly was not guilty of blasphemous intent. My conjecture is that in these verses Dindān followed the habit of Duwāsir poets to slug it out in an imaginary arena—though it is not always easy to determine whether these diatribes are mostly launched in a spirit of jest or in one of serious contest. In any case, the appetite for poetic conquest and the boastful inflation of one's own ego to outsized proportions seem to be an integral part of the constant sniping between the local rivals. Dindān's portrayal of his own work or his talent for poetry as an unassailable fortress of fabulous dimensions seems to fall within the same category (poem no. 25).

The use of hyperbole, including the imaginary assumption of divine attributes, should probably be seen in that light. In the passage declared inappropriate by the arbiters of local taste, Dindān carried this stylistic device to its extreme. By extending his imagination to the furthest removes of the universe, gobbling up the entire creation, wrapping himself alternatively in the cloaks of the day and the night and so on, he might have wished to outstrip the claims of his competitors or to state that poetry, like magic, may transcend the limitations of humdrum reality. To religious ears in the Wādi, however, this innocent game of hyperbole clearly went beyond the pale of propriety.

## *The Twilight of a Nomad's Career*

It so happened that I made Dindān's acquaintance at a moment when the various adverse currents at work against Dindān had joined forces and were about to unleash their final onslaught on the poet. As I sat down with Dindān on the stubbly field for a first recording session, I noticed that he seemed absent-minded and that his gaze constantly swerved to the undulating line of sand that glowed in a warm reddish hue as the rays of the sun began to slant in the late afternoon. Later I learned that his herd of twenty-four camels had not returned from the sands as was their wont. Dindān had been unable to chase his camels by car because his rickety Datsun pick-up had finally refused service in protest against persistent maltreatment. An inspection under the hood showed a clump of sand and grease, barely recognizable as an engine. The battery was empty and so was the sump: the dipstick was dry except for a tarry clot of coagulated oil at its very tip. *Sawāgti ṣhabah*, 'I don't drive well,' he freely admitted, explaining that the battered condition of his car was the result of numerous collisions with trees and other natural obstacles in the desert. Also, a pursuit of the eloped camels on foot was excluded because one of Dindān's legs had become partly paralyzed by arthritis in the knee—according to popular belief this was the punishment of heaven for the brazen, ungodly verses in poem no. 9. In consequence Dindān had to give up camel riding and could only walk, or rather limp, with the help of a stick.

A few days later Dindān's cousins tracked down the animals at Jikhjūkh, a well in the desert more than two hundred kilometers from the Wādi. In the meantime I saw to it that the engine of Dindān's pick-up was overhauled in a workshop. And then Dindān disappeared. A few weeks later I traced him to another stubble field near the village of al-Far$^{c}$ah, at the western edge of the Wādi's palm gardens. There his twenty-four camels eked out a meagre existence among hundreds of others, some owned by poor bedouins like Dindān and the majority tended by Sudanese herdsmen in the employ of Dōsiri breeders.

This time Dindān had struck up a friendship with a family of Sbē$^{c}$ (Subay$^{c}$) bedouins who had pitched their 'house of hair' at the foot of the first sand-hills. The bedouins and herdsmen shared their food with him and occasionally gave him a hand in taking care of his animals. But it was clear that Dindān's existence as a free-roaming nomad was rapidly drawing to a close. He complained that there was no longer a drop of milk in the udders of his enfeebled camels. Dindān himself seemed at the end of his tether. He no longer had the force to drag the fifty-kilo sacks of barley from the pick-up's platform. A passing bedouin had to lend him a knife to rip open the sacks. Then the starving animals almost trampled him as he emptied part of the sack into a trough cut out of the tube of an old tyre. With great difficulty he lugged the sack some distance to fill another trough for the younger and weaker animals. And even worse, the herds would have to leave soon because the fields were to be sown for the winter crop. A retreat into the desert was not a luring prospect, since the drought had left only the branches of the acacia-trees for the camels to nibble on. So the Sbē$^{c}$ decided to drive their camels and flocks of sheep and goats back across the desert to al-Khurmah in their own tribal area.

The tiresome and time-consuming hunt for Dindān's camels had convinced his cousins that something had to be done about the situation of their ailing uncle. Their own economic circumstances had become somewhat straitened of late. Over the years they had willingly paid for the two sacks of barley Dindān needed daily as a bare minimum for his camels' subsistence. But the weight of this subsidy began to make itself felt in their reduced budget. So they told their uncle that they were loath to go on hunting for his camels. In their opinion it had become obvious that Dindān had become physically unfit for his "hobby". Therefore the cousins generously offered him a permanent lodging in the house of one of them, a laid-off truck-driver. In addition they suggested that Dindān sell off his herd and use the proceeds to open a small shop in sweetmeats, biscuits, cola and other refreshments.

Dindān protested, but he knew that he had little choice. He moved in with his cousin and notice was served to fellow-tribesmen that his camels were for sale. Nevertheless Dindān continued to drag his feet. He turned down an offer of two hundred thousand riyals for the entire herd, saying that each one of the twenty-four camels was worth that price. His cousins were horrified by this foolhardy rejection of good fortune: in their view he should have considered himself lucky even with a quarter of that amount. At that juncture they decided to press home their arguments by cutting off the subsidy for his camels' barley.

In those weeks I used to meet Dindān at the place where he had penned his herd, a dreary wasteland at the northern edge of the slums of al-Ldām, mainly inhabited by the descendants of the Wādi's former slave population. In return for some help with his chores and occasional gifts of barley—in violation of the strict orders I received from his cousins not to prolong the agony by substituting for their subsidy—Dindān consented to submit to my questioning.

Reciting poetry was easy to him. The verses flowed from his lips in an uninterrupted stream, hundreds of them, for great lengths of time, and yet he showed no visible signs of fatigue. But like most of the other illiterate poets and transmitters, the effort to explain his verses to a foreigner like me soon left him utterly exhausted. Though he agreed to undergo this ordeal patiently enough, it was never long before his forehead became beaded with sweat, his mind began to wander and his answers became incoherent. If pressed by repeated questions he clammed up completely, like an overheated engine. No amount of cajoling or entreaties would make him budge once he had reached that stage. Putting the finishing touches to our work was therefore a slow and painful process I had to spread out over many sessions, while being careful to avoid that Dindān's growing distaste for this kind of work would bring it to a premature halt.

Each afternoon, after the *ᶜaṣr* prayers, Dindān would feed his camels and fill a big metal trough with water he illegally tapped from an underground pipe belonging to the municipality. While nearby a group of black boys, the descendants of the Wādi's former slave population, played soccer and some curious idlers gathered around us, I would invite Dindān to sit down in the shade of his pick-up and gently try to elicit from him an answer to my questions. In this way our association drew to a close. How Dindān provided for his camels I do not know. Once we called on the first editor of his work and fellow Rijbāni ᶜAbdallah Ḥmēr, whom Dindān wished to visit because, as he said, they had not met for years. But, as it turned out, there was another reason involved as well: Dindān lost no time before telling ᶜAbdallah that he was in urgent need of money and asking him whether he knew anyone who might be interested in buying his Kalashnikov sub-machine-gun.

As our sessions came to an end the camels were still cooped up in their pen, waiting for a buyer. So far only one young male had been sold. The camel's forelegs were tied together and the poor beast was therefore unable to compete with the others for a place round the piece of rubber filled with barley. But Dindān apparently felt that the animal, having been sold, was no longer of his concern.

By the time I left the Wādi the fate of Dindān and his camels had not yet been decided. Although Dindān had effectively been made his cousins's ward, he still wriggled to escape from the inevitable and had not abandoned all hope of retaining his herd. Even in the undignified surroundings of their pen, the camels were the one attribute that continued to link Dindān, albeit tenuously, with his past as an independent, proud and headstrong bedouin. Yet the outcome, it seemed, could hardly be in doubt, for no one was willing to shoulder the burden of keeping Dindān in his nomad's business.

The last I saw of Dindān was when we returned from the pen and I dropped him at a mosque at the far end of the yard and garden of his cousin's house. I helped him out of the passenger seat of the pick-up the authorities in the Wādi had put at my disposal and handed him his stick. We shook hands and we said farewell. *In šа llah ma tšūf šarr*, 'so the Lord wishes you will fall upon no evil,' he mumbled and, without once looking back, he hastened away in a crooked shuffle for fear of being late at evening prayers.

## The Poet and His Art

### *The* Dīwān

My search for local traditions in Wādi ad-Duwāsir with the help of some local acquaintances covered, albeit in a very imperfect way, the area from the village of al-Farᶜah in the west to at-Tamrah in the east. In this rather superficial sweep I came across a good number of mostly old and very old illiterate men whose memories turned out to be valuable depositories of pre-modern poetry and narratives. Also, I met several middle-aged men—mostly government employees and businessmen who had been exposed in various degrees to formal education—who wrote poetry in a modified dialect. The idiom in which they composed their verses is partly derived from the old, pre-modern tradition of Najdi oral poetry, overlaid with elements and themes borrowed from the new linguistic, cultural, economic, social and ideological environment. For instance, a poet like ᶜAbdallah Ḥmēr prefers to stress the proud past and present of the Duẉāsir collectively rather than that of his individual tribe and village (incidentally this is true for Dindān as well). I was less interested in this more recent type of poetry, at least for the purpose of my research.

In addition I came in contact with a small number of poets who either were so old that their formative years dated back to a period well before the beginnings of modernity in the Wādi or were bedouins who had remained outside the mainstream of development and continued the way of life inherited from their ancestors. The only representative of this latter category with whom I associated for a protracted period of time in order to systematically record and annotate his work was Dindān.

As I set out in some detail in the preceding chapter, Dindān had stayed very much aloof from more recent trends and currents in the area. Scorning the opportunities for bedouins to exchange the hardships of a nomadic life-style for a more comfortable settled existence, he continued to wander with his small herd of camels in the Haḏb—the variegated scenery of sand drifts, immense plains, craggy mountains and rocky outcrops intersected by steep torrent beds and wooded wadis north of Wādi ad-Duwāsir—and other surrounding deserts to the west and southwest. Thus Dindān had remained a *fiṭri*, a 'natural man', with an amazing knowledge of the ancient lore of the bedouins. His poetry bears witness to the fine distinctions the terminology of these nomads makes between the various seasons, the physiognomy of the different kinds of terrain and the effects on it produced by rain or drought, the characteristics of camels and other natural phenomena.

In many respects Dindān's outlook and experience in life are not far removed from the portrayal we find in the pre-Islamic and early classical poetry of Arabia. And it is interesting to note that many lexical items and semantic connotations in this vernacular poetry are more akin to the ancient vocabulary, as stored in the vaults of the great classical dictionaries, than to the "correct" modern standard Arabic (a fact I have underscored by frequently adding the corresponding or comparable classical items between brackets in the glossary to this edition).

Dindān's poetic idiom can therefore be called "archaic", as long as one keeps in mind that he is not consciously harking back to the classical tradition. Rather his work seems to corroborate the thesis that in many regards the Najdi tradition is closely related to the ancient Arabic poetry and therefore might be considered one of its distant, but linear descendants.[5] But in stressing the parallels and similarities one should not lose sight of the important differences that have resulted from a process of evolutionary change during the thousand or more intervening years. References to these parallels and differences will be noted in the course of the discussion of

---

5 See the chapter 'Nabaṭi Poetry and the Classical Literary Tradition' in S.A. Sowayan's *Nabaṭi Poetry*, Berkeley-Los Angeles 1985.

thematic, linguistic and prosodic aspects of Dindān's *dīwān* and in the glossary.

Though we spent many days together, I learned very little about Dindān's earlier life and the only excuse for this regrettable omission is that my time and energy were wholly absorbed by the collection and interpretation of the oral material. Moreover, any questions outside the sphere of his immediate interests and poetry met with reticence or at best a very lapidary response on Dindān's part. Thus all he told me about the way in which he mastered his craft was that as a boy his imagination was captured by the poetry routinely recited in the men's compartment of the bedouin tents. Apparently without any special effort Dindān soon became a poet in his own right.

It seems that Dindān never derived any material gain from his talent for the art of poetry. As mentioned earlier, the idea of seeking pecuniary rewards in life was far from his true bedouin ethos. Yet he might easily have supplemented his negligible income and found the wherewithal to shelter himself and his camels from indigence if he had deigned to cater to the taste of the rich and powerful for poetic adulation, as always had been the custom in Arabia. In his choice not to pursue social or material advantages with his gift for poetry Dindān was not motivated by any objections of principle. Deeply rooted in the natural rhythm of life in the desert and rather coy and abrupt in personal contact, Dindān was temperamentally unfit for the kind of diplomacy and manoeuvring involved in eliciting the financial favours of considerable personages. This explains the complete absence of any panegyric poems or passages of this kind in his work. Both in life and art Dindān always stayed true to himself and his bedouin origins.

It should be noted at the outset of the analysis and discussion of Dindān's work that this edition does not include all that Dindān spoke in metre and rhyme. I suspect that there is a considerable amount of doggerel and scurrilous satire he preferred to keep to himself. Rather these are the poems which in Dindān's opinion, if not in the opinion of other Duwāsir, are "fit to print". Though Dindān composed and stored these poems exlusively in his head—his breast, he would say—, without any exterior aid, the recension of this oral poetry is as well defined and fixed as its scriptural counterpart. Many poems I recorded more than once and I never found the slightest difference or any omission in the verses. On one occasion only, when he was tired, did one poem become entangled with another.[6] He then decided to stop and set the record straight at the next session.

If there were any of his verses in the anthology published by Ḥmēr that were missing in my recordings and I drew his attention to the discrepancy, Dindān most emphatically denied that he had said those verses, stating by implication that these were of the editor's making (see the chapter on the Ḥmēr edition). In some cases Dindān nevertheless would generously add that these unauthorized, supposititious verses also contained a good deal of 'truth'.

The prosodic characteristics of Dindān's work will be discussed separately. Suffice it to mention here that both the regularity and great diversity of metres used by Dindān is further testimony to the high quality of his workmanship. Also, the prosodic analysis fully bears out the conclusions arrived at by S.A. Sowayan in the chapter dealing with prosody and language in his *Nabaṭi Poetry*.

Finally, for the sake of completeness I have included in this edition two poems and their narrative introduction I recorded from Dindān in his capacity as a transmitter. One is an old *qaṣīdah* of more than fifty verses attributed to a woman of the tribe of Ziᶜb who is said to have found refuge with the Duwāsir when her own tribe was annihilated by the S͟harīfs of Mecca. According to the legend, the powerful clan of Āl Bu Sabbāᶜ in Nazwah trace their pedigree to her son. The other poem tells how Ibn K͟hwēr, in distant times a sheikh of the Āl Bu Sabbāᶜ, rescued the daughter of his *giṣīr*, protected neighbour, and her camels from a raiding party of Sbēᶜ.

In the recording of these two transmitted pieces the greatest difficulties occurred in the narrative introductions. In startling contrast with Dindān's versatility and firm grip in poetry, his narrative style was rather hesitant and confused. He did not seem to appreciate that in order to be comprehensible to the uninitiated a narrative should be structured in a certain way (sequence of events, transitions, the syntactic arrangements of the narrative blocks etc.) or that an explanation of the circumstances surrounding the dramatic events and other information essential to the story's intelligibility should be furnished. In the event I recorded each narrative section

---

6 Poems nos. 6 and 24: after verse 26 of poem 6 he continued with verse 10 of poem 24 (a poem with the same metre, but a different rhyme) apparently because of the similarity of the preceding verses and the fact that the addressee in both poems is the poet ᶜBēd ibn Ḥamdān.

twice and in addition took it down at his dictation. From these versions I collated the short narratives presented in this edition.

*Dindān's Ethos as a Bedouin and Poet*

Although Dindān told me very little about his personal history, his experience in life or his views, some insight in his mental outlook can be gleaned from the poetry itself. Before addressing the more literary aspects of his poetry it might therefore be useful to dwell for a moment on some elements in the verses that offer a clue to his ethos as a bedouin and poet.

By any measure Dindān is a very religious person. Not only is he very compunctious about performing his religious duties, like praying and fasting, in his poetry he also shows himself a man deeply imbued with the spiritual values of Islam. In more than half of his poems Dindān addresses himself to God, asking for the Lord's compassion and means of subsistence for himself and his camels and affirming his deep faith in His providence, omnipotence and justice. When Dindān turns to God it is to pray for fortitude in the face of hardship and suffering and to draw comfort and hope from the certainty that his cheerful surrender to the Lord's decree will in the end bring its reward.

Certain prevalent concepts in the world view of the bedouins—like *ad-dahar*, adverse fate, and *ad-dinya* in the sense of 'the vicissitudes of life', 'the world', as more or less independent, blind forces—can be traced to pre-Islamic times. As Dindān's poetry illustrates, these concepts have been subsumed in the creed of the now more thoroughly "Islamicised" bedouins of Saudi Arabia.

Besides these expressions of religious sentiment, and sometimes intermingled with them, a popular theme in the Najdi tradition is the *fakir* (the classical *ḥikam wa-naṣāʾiḥ*): homespun wisdoms and precepts, often covered with a patina of religious righteousness, reflecting popular prejudices, beliefs and attitudes.[7] Related to this theme, and also that of the *mufākharah*, boastful panegyrics, is the idea of *ʿirḍ*, honour.

---

[7] Some of Dindān's verses on the theme of the 'times' or the 'world', like verses 11 and 12 of poem no. 21, correspond closely to the classical *zuhd*, in which the poet gives expression to his ascetism and puts a mental distance between himself and the world in its material aspect. Cf. G.J.H. van Gelder, *The Bad and the Ugly*, Leiden 1988, 120, for a discussion of the way in which the poetic modes of *zuhd*, *hijāʾ* (invective poetry), and *ḥikam* sometimes blur at their interface.

In Islam the concept of *ʿirḍ* lost its original character as the guiding ethical principle it used to be for the Arabs in the pre-Islamic period, the *jāhilīyah*. 'No longer capable of being the cause of boastfulness (Islam opposing *taqwā*, "godliness, piety", to *ḥamīyah*, "tribal pride, ardour"),' *ʿirḍ* became 'connected with religion or with a moral principle emanating from religion.' However, as Bichr Farès also points out in his article on *ʿirḍ* in the *Encyclopaedia of Islam*, 'among the modern bedouins we still find *ʿirḍ* with almost all its pre-Islamic force.'

Dindān, being a pure bedouin, but one who lives in constant interaction with the settled majority of his tribe, was strongly influenced by the rigorously orthodox practices and beliefs of the Duwāsir population in the Wādi. *Ya-rabb ʿinna ʿala t-tagwa wi-l-īgāni*, 'O Lord, help us to be devout and steadfast in faith,' is his prayer in poem no. 21. Yet in the same poem and elsewhere one finds many elements more closely akin to the old *ḥamīyah* than to the Islamic *taqwā*. Indeed, as will be demonstrated in the chapter listing some of the differences between Dindān's work as I recorded it and the edition of Ḥmēr in *Wāḥat as͟h-s͟hiʿr*, it is interesting to note that Ḥmēr, being an educated settled member of the tribe, systematically censored the passages which to the orthodox ear smacked too much of the old "ignorance". This reflects the fact that among the Duwāsir, converted to Wahhābī orthodoxy from their semi-heathenish practices only two centuries ago, there persists an amount of tension between their neophyte Islamic fervour and the lingering presence of the old tribal ethos.

As Farès puts it, the various elements connected with the notion of *ʿirḍ* may be classed under three headings: the tribal group, the family and the individual. The direct references, and most of the implicit ones, in Dindān's work to his *ʿirḍ* fall within the last-mentioned category. More precisely, they seem related to his pride in his pre-eminence as a poet. It would appear that some of his more furious outbursts, invariably resulting in some of his most gripping verses, are a reaction to what he perceived as challenges or insults directed against the integrity of that position. Such attacks—presumably by rivals in the local circuit of oral poets, persons harbouring a grudge against him or simply scoffers wishing to rouse the poet's quick ire—wounded his sensibility and pride, *ʿirḍ*, and left the poet steaming with rage.[8]

---

[8] Cf. verse 1 of poem no. 27.

The vehemence of Dindān's response to such slights comes out best in the magnificent seventeen verses of the prelude and its immediate sequel of poem no. 9 (see also p. 12 and pp. 60-62). Here Dindān rises to truly great poetry when he moves from a description of the bitterness that spoilt his taste for life to a vivid portrayal of the almost supernatural force of the poetic inspiration as it erupts from his burning temper and on to the Titanic passage that more than anything contributed to his local notoriety. The last two verses of this passage (verses 16 and 17) show a mixture of Islamic feeling and an unrestrained desire to completely crush his opponent, without giving a hoot for the rest of mankind's opinion, which is remarkable for its marriage of religious and bedouin elements. But interestingly, the fencers in these poetic duels seem to obey the rule that only one's individual qualities as a poet are a legitimate target for their rapiers. Unlike his colleagues in Arab antiquity, Dindān does not seek to crush his opponents by dragging in their social standing or by impugning their ancestry. Explicit *ad hominem* attacks are not found in Dindān's work.

The approach is somewhat different in the equally interesting poem no. 25. This poem can be seen as an allegory for the poet's prowess and as such it also belongs to the category of *mufākharah*. In the prelude the poet likens the powers and vastness of his *kalām* ('speech', but in the parlance of the Najdi tradition a synonym for poetry) to the seas, swarms of locusts and the number of grains of sand in the high dunes. At this point the poet stirs the interest of his audience with a composite riddle and then proceeds to paint a vision of an impregnable fortress of fantastic dimensions where his honour as a poet is secure and safe. Step by step the verses trace the construction of the fortress until the final touch is put on it by the embellishment of its embattlements with the moon and the sun, as beacons for travellers, and the guard post for the Angel of Death. From this unassailable vantage point Dindān sets out to teach his rivals among the local poets a sharp lesson in the moral and artistic requirements that must be fulfilled before a man may consider himself a member of the guild.

A third example is poem no. 21. This poem does not deal with a poetic challenge, but with the calumnies or evil talk (*harjah*, which may or may not have been verse) spread by a man called by name, Gabbāni. Again, the prelude speaks about Dindān's sleeplessness and his rancorous feelings, but also about his determination to defend his violated honour with all his might. He states that nothing will be able to silence his voice as a poet and he sends up a prayer to God. This prayer then slides into a meditation about the fickle nature of fate and the changeability of the *dinya*, the world, which turns good into bad and perversely favours the fortunes of good-for-nothings and prattlers over those of worthy and wise men. In this roundabout way Dindān arrives at the moral counsel bequeathed to him by his father.

In a dozen verses of *ḥikam*, maxims and wise sayings, Dindān sums up the basic concepts that govern his attitude towards his fellow men. The guiding principle is, in essence, that one should be as tolerant as possible, drawing a veil over the other's lapses and extolling his virtues. Unless, that is, the other acts from evil intent and schemes to undermine or pierce the sanctuary of one's honour. In that case one should not shirk his duty and fight back tooth and nail. For if one appears ready to compromise on his honour, people will consider him a weakling and coward. Since it is worse than death to be held in such low esteem by public opinion, a true man counter-attacks and in his turn seeks to destroy the reputation of his adversary: 'With his right hand a man whitens his face' (verse 26), i.e. noble, warlike deeds are the means by which a man keeps his honour intact and untainted. Add to this that a valiant man never proves himself at the expense of his own kin, but is always in the forefront with those who ward off the external threats. In living by these rules, a man should be as patient and enduring as a camel drawing water, even though the wooden supports of the pack-saddle to which the bucket's rope is attached are pressing against his flanks and causing him excruciating pain.

This is the moral bequest Dindān received from his father and, so he ends, 'the customs we inherited from our ancestors we will never forsake.'

### *The Composition of Oral Poetry: Building with Modules*

In its appreciation of classical Arabic poetry Western scholarship has frequently remarked upon its purported lack of overall coherence: the absence of stylistic or thematic elements tying together the verses into a unique artistic unity, a poem that is more than the sum of its individual verses.[9] Faced with examples of the Najdi oral tra-

---

9 See on this subject G.J.H. van Gelder, *Beyond the Line. Classical Arabic Literary Critics on the Coherence and Unity of the Poem*, Leiden 1982.

dition in poetry these students of literature would perhaps come to the conclusion that the purported structural "weakness" of ancient classical poetry also applies to its distant relative that has survived to this day.

The first observation one should make with regard to this kind of criticism is that it does not take into account the cultural context and the artistic frame of reference within which an oral peninsular poet like Dindān operates. Western concepts of organic unity as applied to poetry are totally alien to Dindān. Like his audience he has been nurtured in the Najdi tradition of poetry and narration to the exclusion of any other literary influence. Accordingly the sole yardstick by which he and his audience measure his performance in this field is the standard provided by the living oral culture as it exists in the Wādi. The world outside Saudi Arabia is hardly of concern to them. Strange as it may seem to a Western public, during my stay in the Wādi Dindān and his uneducated fellow-tribesmen made it unequivocally clear to me that they were completely indifferent to the prospect of Dindān's poetry, or that of any other Dōsiri, circulating in translation in distant countries.

The second observation arises from an impression one gathers from a closer analysis of the relationship between the various poems of the *dīwān* as a totality, i.e. as distinct from the relation between the verses in any single poem. In other words, the question is what would be the results if one were to study Dindān's entire poetic output, his *dīwān*, as if it were one organic whole or superpoem—of course without losing sight of the fact that each individual poem is the product of a single act of creation. In that case it will appear that the oral poem and its segments are closely linked to a larger continuum extending beyond the *dīwān* into the vast sea of the Najdi tradition in poetry. It is only natural that in this environment qualities like the uniqueness and unity of the individual poem do not receive the same emphasis as in the Western tradition. The dynamic dimension of this poetry's mode of existence, including its functional side and the peculiarities of oral composition, equally militates against the pursuit of such ideals. Drawing the circle even wider one may add that these characteristics of cultural expression faithfully reflect a social situation in which the collectivity is always present as a determining factor.

One might begin a reading of the *dīwān* in this spirit by taking the first example that presents itself: the first and second poems of this collection are not only in the same metre and almost the same rhyme (the only difference being that the second hemistichs of the first poem rhyme on *-āli* and those of the second one on *-ādi*), they are similar even in their thematic structure and on the level of motifs. There is a considerable difference in length, however, for the second poem has more than twice the number of verses compared to the first one. But even with regard to length one notes that the thematic development runs parallel for about thirteen verses. At that point the first poems stops or is broken off, while the second continues and reaches a length of twenty-seven verses. The second half of the second poem adds a thematic development not found in the first poem: a section of *mufākharah*, boastful praise for the tribe of the Duwāsir.

Here one might raise a question from the point of view of Western esthetics: Why does Dindān repeat himself to the extent of almost duplicating one poem in the next? To begin with one might reply that repetition and the accumulation of similar stylistic and thematic matter are characteristic for literary techniques worldwide. In this particular case, however, I would add that the core of both poems is a request or prayer to God for rain. One can easily understand why something that is a major concern to a bedouin like Dindān should also be a central and recurrent theme in his poetry. As will be discussed later, this "rain poetry" has a ritualistic character and strongly religious overtones. The recurrence of poems and passages on this theme that are very similar in content and form may therefore simply reflect that Dindān composed such a "prayer" each time the hardships caused by drought impelled him to do so. This would explain the repetition in functional terms.

But repetition is also an intrinsic feature of this poetry's structure: the relationship between the constituent parts of the individual poems, between both these parts and poems on the one hand and on the other the totality of Dindān's *dīwān* as well as the Najdi tradition as a whole, as mentioned before. An analysis of Dindān's poems will show that they are built from certain thematic blocks which are also used in the construction of other poems. Within each poem these blocks as a rule are cemented together by standard formulas or markers of transition that announce in a manner easily recognizable to the audience the nature of the block that follows. When studied in more detail it also will appear that each type of block from which the poem is constructed—whether the emotional prelude, the description of the camel or any other section—is itself composed of certain recurring features. The sequence of these features (imagery, vocabulary, motifs, phraseology etc.) corresponds closely from one thematic block to another of the same type. The thematic matrix on pp. 30-31 gives an overview of the distribution of the various sections or modular blocks and the motifs within these sections.

Widening the circle to include the work of other Najdi poets, as will be done in the section on the *nasīb* in Najdi poetry, one finds that Dindān for his "building materials" draws on a huge "warehouse": a store of themes, stock phrases and recurrent images, similes and techniques that together form the common inventory of the Najdi tradition in poetry as it has evolved over centuries of practice and as Dindān came to know it through the discourse of the men in the Arabian *majlis*.

When viewed in the context of the *dīwān* as a whole, the individual building-blocks making up a poem may be seen to be part of a comprehensive structure based on the use of certain modules. Hence one might speak of the modularity or modular structure of this poetry. If rhyme and metre are very similar, as in the first two poems of the *dīwān*, one might without difficulty substitute one module, or individual verses of such a building-block, for the other. One might shift the prelude, i.e. the first three verses, from one poem to the other; or the prayer for rain (the next three or four verses); the camel description (seven verses); and add the long *mufākharah*, the boastful panegyrics, of the second poem to the first. Thanks to the standard repertory and the well-marked formulas of transition, all this could be achieved without any difficulty. Indeed, the only person in the world who would be able to detect the exchange and substitution is Dindān himself.

Admittedly, this is a somewhat extreme example. Few, if any, poems in the *dīwān* bear such a close resemblance to one another as the first two (the order of the poems is the one of recording). Yet in a concentrated form this example brings out a general pattern in the *dīwān* and therefore it may be helpful in gaining a better understanding of the issue at stake.

The sequence of the modules, that is, the order in which the building-blocks are stacked on top of one another (or are strung together, the choice of metaphor can be left to one's taste), by and large obeys the logic of the conventions governing Najdi oral poetry. It is probably not coincidental that this conventional order corresponds to a great extent to that of early classical Arab poetry. As a rule a poem by Dindān opens with an emotional, melancholy prelude, the equivalent of the classical *nasīb*, in which the poet pictures himself standing on a lonely mountain peak where he feels free to release his pent-up sorrow or fury in an outburst of rage and grief and goes on to describe in striking similes how he is seized by inspiration as the first stage in the process of artistic creation.

Then the poet may offer up a prayer to God and launch into a depiction of imaginary downpours and floods rushing off the mountains and inundating the plains. Descriptions of camels, camel riding (and its modern variant, the motorcar), the journey of the messenger and love lyrics are alternative or additional modular elements. So are the *ḥikam*, scenes of warfare and raids and their corollary, the boastful panegyrics on one's own tribe and kin. Here the poem may end rather abruptly, or it may be wound up with a section of *madīḥ*, laudatory verses addressed to friends or kinsmen to whom the messenger is to deliver the poet's greetings, along with the poem itself, and the usually terse message contained in that elaborate envelope which is the poem.

In the great majority of cases the sequence of modular sections is a natural flow that produces a satisfactory esthetic impression. Poem no. 12, for instance, seems to answer fully to the Western concept of artistic unity. The development of its sections follows an emotional curve, ranging from the elegiac mood of the prelude, despair at the drought, resignation to the Lord's decree, a reaffirmation of faith, a description of nature's revival after rain and on to a joyful ode on the poet's sweetheart and the delights of her charming conversation. Thus the poem's twenty-seven lines reflect how the poet succeeded in curing himself of sorrow through the power of his imagination that made him enter a world of plenty and love, a true spring season called to life in the poet's mind.

This poem's high level of integration, the smoothness of transition from one theme to another and the arrangement of the modular blocks in a mutually reinforcing way are not achieved everywhere in Dindān's work. For the purpose of my argument, however, the exceptions are especially interesting, because they provide further evidence as to the manner in which an oral poet composes his work. Three examples may be cited as cases in point. In poem no. 6 a prelude of eight verses gives a dramatic picture of the poet's mental torment, but the following sections lack the normal reference to the cause of this suffering (drought, unrewarded love, wounded pride because of another poet's insults etc.). The same observation can be made with regard to the rancorous feelings expressed in the single preludial verse at the outset of poem no. 8. The remainder of the poem—eight verses of camel description, two about the cleverness of the rider and two with words of praise for the destinee of the poem—does not give a clue as to the cause of the poet's anger. In poem no. 14 the prelude is couched in the phraseology normally reserved for love lyrics. Hence one is left with an impression of *non sequitur* when the poet proceeds not in the *ġazal* mode, but with a prayer for rain.

These minor disjunctions seem to corroborate the theory that the poet, while setting out to compose with a global idea of the result he wants to achieve in terms of the poem as a whole, nevertheless constructs each module or section relatively independent from his work on the others. It is true that to some extent this also applies to the way in which many literate authors go about their composition. But the difference is that for the oral poet it is more difficult to rework any previously composed section in order to remedy incongruities in the light of what followed. Moreover, the poetic material for the themes, the themes themselves, the arrangement of the themes in sections and the transitions between these sections are standardized or "prefabricated" to a considerable degree. One might compare the Najdi oral culture to a "do-it-yourself" store from which oral poets can draw freely in order to construct a house of their own liking. The ready availability of this material and the modular technique of composition enable the poet to concentrate on the assembling of one section and to move on to the next once he has securely locked the preceding one in his memory without having to deal with the complexities of first designing an overarching structure into which each constituent part finds its proper place. At the same time the use of this technique explains why these poems are somewhat loosely constructed, at least to Western taste, and why sometimes themes are found adrift without even the moorings provided by conventional sequence.

To subscribe to this view of the structure of Dindān's work by no means belittles or reflects negatively on his or any other Najdi poet's artistic merits. It simply underlines the fact that these poets avail themselves of the conventional repertory and the modular technique because in their situation these are the materials and tools most suited to the process of oral composition and the achievement of the desired impression on the audience during performance.

# II. THE POETRY

## General

### *The Themes of the* Dīwān

Leaving aside the war songs of nos. 30 and 31, Dindān's collection of oral poetry numbers 548 verses spread over twenty-nine poems. As a quantitative illustration of the position of the various themes in the *dīwān*, this total number of verses can be subdivided as follows:

- Sentimental introductory verses corresponding to the classical *nasīb*: 134.[10]
- Description of the camel's physique and qualities: 179.
- Description of thunderstorms, rain and its effect on the parched desert: 62.
- Love poetry (*ġazal*): 54.
- Supplications and praise to God: 45.
- The remaining 74 verses are devoted to familiar themes like moralizing maxims, and conventional wisdom (*ḥikam wa-naṣāʾiḥ*); glorification of the poet's tribe (*mufākharah*); description of the itinerary the messenger has to follow (*ar-riḥlah*); greetings to the addressee and verses said in his praise (*madīḥ*).

---

10 In the thematic matrix I have included under the heading of the *nasīb* riddles (*alġāz*), the *aṭlāl* motif and extended similes of the *ya-tall galbi* type, as explained in what follows.

## *Thematic Matrix*

| VERSES ↓ POEMS → | 1 | 2 | 3 | 4 | 5 | 6 | 7 | 8 | 9 | 10 | 11 | 12 |
|---|---|---|---|---|---|---|---|---|---|---|---|---|
| *Nasīb* | | | | | | | | | | | | |
| Total | 3 | 2 | 3 | | 4 | 8 | 1 | 1 | 17 | 2 | 4 | 7 |
| Mountain scene | 1-2 | 1-2 | 1 | | 1-2 | 1 | | 1 | | 1 | 1 | |
| Complaint heart/eye | 3 | | 2 | | 3-4 | 2-3<br>5-6 | | 1 | 2-4 | | 2-3 | 2-7 |
| Extended simile of *ya-tall galbi* type | | | 3 | | | 7-8 | | | | | 4 | |
| Deserted camp (*aṭlāl*) | | | | | 4 | | | | | | | |
| Poetry/creative process | | | | | | 1,4,<br>6 | 1 | | 1<br>5-9 | 1-2 | 1 | 1 |
| Poet's self-assertion | | | | | | | | | 10-17 | | | |
| Riddles (*ġaṭuw*) | | | | | | | | | | | | |
| Prayers/afirmation of faith | 4 | 3-4 | 4-7 | | | 9-13 | | | 5 | 3-4<br>14 | | 8,19<br>13-18 |
| Fickleness of the world, fate (*ad-dinyā*) | | | | | | | | | | | | 18 |
| Maxims, wise sayings (*fakir*) | | | | | | | | | | | | |
| Rainfall | 4-6 | 4-7 | 7-14 | | | | | | | 5-10 | | 19-22 |
| Effects of rain | 7 | 8 | 15 | | | | | | | 11 | | 23-24 |
| Camel Herds | 8-13 | 8-14 | 15-22 | | | | | | | 11-13 | | 8-13 |
| The itinerary (*al-irćāb*) | | | | | | | | | | | | |
| Riding camel/motor car | | | | 1-22 | 5-12 | 14-31 | 2-16 | 2-9 | 18-33 | | 5-12 | |
| Praise for messenger | | | | | | 32 | | 10-11 | | | | |
| Love lyrics (*ġazal*) | | | | | | | | | | | 13-22 | 24-27 |
| Horse/war scene | | 15-22 | | | | | | | | | | |
| War song (*razaf*) | | | | | | | | | | | | |
| Tribal boasting (CA: *mufākharah*) | | 23-27 | | | | 11-13 | | | | | | |
| (Address to) destinee | | | | | | 33-34 | | 12-13 | 34-36 | | | |

It should be emphasized that the classification of the verses under these headings is only intended to give an approximate idea of the distribution of the various motifs in the *dīwān*. While referring to this matrix one should keep in mind that there is considerable overlap between the motifs and that often verses might be classed under more than one heading.

| 13 | 14 | 15 | 16 | 17 | 18 | 19 | 20 | 21 | 22 | 23 | 24 | 25 | 26 | 27 | 28 | 29 | 30 | 31 |
|---|---|---|---|---|---|---|---|---|---|---|---|---|---|---|---|---|---|---|
| 2 | 5 | 3 | 4 | 7 | 1 | 21 | | 7 | | 13 | 2 | 15 | 1 | 1 | | | | 1 |
| 1 | 1 | | | | 1 | 1 | | | | 1 | 1 | | | 1 | | | | |
| | 3-5 | 1-3 | 1-4 | 4-7 | | 2-3 | | 1-3<br>7 | | 2<br>5-7<br>12-13 | 2 | | | | | | | |
| | | | | | | 4-9<br>10-14<br>18-24 | | | | 7-9 | | | | | | | | |
| | | | | | | | | | | 3-4<br>10-11 | | | | | | | | |
| 2 | 2 | | | | 1 | | | 4-6 | | 1 | | 3-6 | 1 | | | | | 1 |
| | | | | | | | | | | | | 11-17 | | | | | | |
| | | | | | | | | | | | | 7-10 | | | | | | |
| 2-4<br>18-22 | 6-9 | | | 1 | 2 | | | 8-10<br>19 | | | | | 29-30 | 2 | | | 1-2<br>27 | 12-14 |
| | | | | | | | | 11-18 | | 4 | | | | | | | | |
| | | | | | | | | 7<br>20-32 | | | | 18-20<br>22 | | | | | | |
| 4-11 | 9-20 | | | | 2-9 | | | | | | | | | | | | | |
| 12 | | | | | 10-11 | | | | | | | | | | | | | |
| 12-17 | | | | | | | | | | | | | | | | | 20-21 | |
| | | | | | | | | | | | | | 11-13 | | | | | |
| | | 4-5 | 5-11 | | | | 1-6 | | 1 | 13-15 | 3-9 | 1 | 2-10 | 3-14 | | | 23 | |
| | | | | | | | | | | | | | | | | | | |
| 18 | | 6-12 | 12-13 | 8-12 | | 15-17 | | | | | 11-17 | | | | 1-7 | 1-8 | | |
| | | | | | 12-19 | | | | | | | | | | | | | |
| | | | | | | | | | | | | | | | | | 1-27 | 1-14 |
| | | | | | 19-25 | | | 27-32 | 2-9 | | | | | | | | 9-12<br>14,25 | |
| | | | | | | | | | 2 | | 10 | 2<br>21 | 14-30 | | | | 24-26 | 2 |

*The Object of the Poem*

A modern Western poet might raise his eyebrows in astonishment when asked why he expresses himself in verse, for in the West it is commonly assumed that a deep chasm lies between the mundane pursuits of the general public and the modern poetic sensibility that seeks to carve out its own truths for no other reward than the admiration or respect of the like-minded. In Arabia, however, this question is not considered rude at all. Many times I myself was asked what profit (*fāydah*) I derived from my endeavours. Even today the *qaṣīdah* in its most crude form—a stratagem to elicit financial reward or other favours—is still widely practised in Saudi Arabia.

Dindān, as his sorry socio-economic state testifies, never stooped to that level. The names that one finds in the sections of his poems corresponding to the classical *madīḥ* are those of fellow poets he is in poetic correspondence with and friends who are in jail or other sorts of trouble. The poems featuring the *aṭlāl* motif (the description of the poet's melancholy mood as he chances upon the traces of a deserted encampment once inhabited by the tribe of his beloved), as a prelude to memories of deceased friends, fall into the same category.[11]

In six poems the sufferings of the poet are set in the *ġazal* context of unrequited love.[12] In two poems he reacts to smears against his honour.[13] In eight poems the charged emotional state described in the *nasīb* is directly linked to the disastrous effects a prolonged drought has for the bedouins and their herds.[14] The core of these poems is a request for rain. Some take the form of fervent prayers to God to send down his bounty and save the bedouins from *ad-dahr*, the remorseless fate that oppresses them, a distinctly pre-Islamic concept, though it is not recognized as such by the naturally devout Dindān. These poems, for all their vivid descriptions of scenery and bedouin life, are primarily an attempt to communicate with the supernatural, and as such might be classed as being in the domain of rite and private devotion.[15]

From this it becomes clear that Dindān sings his verses neither in

---

[11] Musil observes that 'the Rwala have many songs in which the solitary wayfarer speaks to the old camping place'; see *The Manners and Customs of the Rwala Bedouins*, New York 1928, 78-85.

[12] Poems 11, 15, 16, 17, 19, 24.

[13] Poems 21 and 27.

[14] Poems 1, 2, 3, 10, 12, 13, 14, 18.

[15] See pp. 25 and 63.

the hope of immediate financial reward nor exclusively for entertainment or art's sake. For him poetry fulfils many other functions as well: it conveys messages and greetings to friends and beloved ones, prayers to God, affirmations of both individual and tribal self-esteem, and words of retaliation for attacks upon his honour. In addition to these external functions, many poems also serve an internal, psychological purpose which is closely related to the feelings expressed in the *nasīb*. Like the classical *nasīb*, these introductory verses are characterized by their melancholy and emotional tone and their expression of a sense of loss and separation from an ideal state (be it the separation from the poet's sweetheart, kin, friends, or his own youth) and suffering (be it the effects of drought, want, a slight, a fellow poet's scoffing, etc.).[16] At the same time the *nasīb* makes clear that the verses that follow are the antidote for the disease, as when he says (26/1):

> I was roused to speak my mind—with God I seek refuge from Satan—//
> In words that give relief from the heaviness of my heart.

It is entirely consistent with Dindān's bedouin way of life that the therapeutical aspect of his poetry normally takes the form of an imaginary drenching, a description of himself or a *jēš* (a group of mounted men) riding fast camels at a lively pace, or a bitter diatribe against his satirizer. Thus the poem closes the circle of loss, grief, compensation, and restored mental equilibrium.

## The *Nasīb*: Originality and Conventionality[17]

### *The* Nasīb *in Najdi Poetry*

Though Western esthetic concepts, like the one of 'organic unity', are not immediately relevant to the Najdi tradition in poetry, a dis-

---

16 Cf. Wagner, *Grundzüge der klassischen arabischen Dichtung*, Darmstadt 1988, i, 85, 87.

17 This chapter was published earlier in *Asian Folklore Studies*, 52/1 (1993), 33-74. Although it does not deal only with Dindān, I have included most of the article in this edition as it will give non-specialists among the readers an opportunity to view Dindān's poetry side by side with that of other poets and thereby to get a clearer idea of Dindān's position in the context of the Najdi tradition as a whole. Its source of inspiration was S.A. Sowayan's landmark contribution 'al-Muᶜānāt wa-l-ibdāᶜ fī naẓm al-qaṣīdah an-nabaṭīyah' (1987). It should be noted that, for reasons I am unable to explain, the poems by Dindān are metrically much more varied

cussion on the question why this is so may help us to clarify important aspects of this poetry's mode of existence: the structure and function of this poetry as well as the techniques of composition proper to its oral character. Similarly, the questions raised if one tried to apply another Western artistic concept, that of originality, to this poetry might enable us to gain a better understanding of the interaction between the conventions of the tradition and the poet's individual genius, especially on the level of imagery and similes. The obvious choice among the various sections of the poem for an assessment of this kind are the introductory verses which may be taken to represent the equivalent of the classical *nasīb*.

As in the classical Arabic *qaṣīdah*, a melancholy, elegiac mood is predominant in the *nasīb* of Najdi vernacular poetry (also called *nabaṭi* poetry). Also, in many poems the classical motifs are still present, such as the *aṭlāl* scene and the complaint about the contrast between the poet's physical age and his young, amorous heart.[18] In the formal scheme of the poem the introductory verses describe or hint at the emotional impulse that set the creative process in motion and provide, as it were, the justification for what follows. Thus the *nasīb* is at once an integral part of the poem and the statement of its *raison d'être*. But in reality this function of the prelude is less important than the fact that it offers a lyrical poet like Dindān ample scope to develop the motifs closest to his poetic soul.

In the Najdi tradition the highly charged state of mind in which the poet's inspiration wells up, like ecstasy seizing an oracle, becomes itself a major dramatic theme in the poem. In the prelude the poet describes the wounded feelings and the mental pain he has been careful to conceal from the public eye. He pictures himself in the solitude of the desert or mountains as he gives free rein to his emotions and his state of mental turbulence portends the advent of inspiration. Finally, there is an element of *mufākharah* as the poet boasts how he mastered the raw, refractory material yielded by the volcanic outburst of inspiration, subjugated it to his will and strung it out in

---

than those by others cited in this chapter. The long metre--v---v--v--(an adaptation of the classical *aṭ-ṭawīl*) is used in fifteen of the eighteen fragments by other poets (and in all of the four fragments chosen from Ibn Sbayyil's *dīwān*), the remaining three being *al-basīṭ* (two) and *aṭ-ṭawīl* (one). In Dindān's work this long metre is used in four poems (cf. the matrix of scansion on pp. 92-95).

[18] Already in the classical *nasīb* complaints about the poet's old age developed into an independent theme, cf. Wagner, E., (1988) i, 99-100.

verses like as many polished beads. About half of Dindān's poems contain explicit references to his poetic tastes and to the creative process and include boastful passages about his pre-eminent position among his fellow artists. These references vary in length and elaborateness from one line to an entire poem of twenty-two verses (no. 25). Taken together they present a fairly comprehensive picture of Dindān's conception of the nature of poetry and of his own relation to it. Moreover, these passages often are remarkable for the richness of the imagery and extended similes that translate these surges of emotion into dramatic scenes from the life of the bedouins and villagers.

The procedure I have adopted for the purpose of this chapter is the following. First, the place of the *nasīb* in the overall structure of the poem is discussed. Then the main motifs featuring in the *nasīb* itself are illustrated with fragments taken from the work of Dindān and other poets. The core of the chapter is a discussion of the extended simile, a stylistic device that allows the Najdi poet to display his art to the full. Dindān's imagery in this and other parts of the *nasīb* is compared to that of other Najdi poets. Samples from their poetry show the degree to which these poets draw on a common store of motifs, images, and phraseology on the one hand and, on the other, illustrate the individual touches by which an accomplished poet seeks to distinguish himself within the context of the tradition. The chapter is rounded off with a conclusion offering some general thoughts on the subject.

For examples from the work of other poets than Dindān I have relied primarily on four contemporary Saudi collections of oral poetry, all answering to relatively high editorial standards and containing good samples of lyrical verse by a generation of illiterate poets preceding Dindān. One such predecessor is ᶜAbdallah ibn Sbayyil (d. 1938), a poet renowned in the entire Arabian desert, who lived in Nifi, a small town in the High Najd (*ᶜĀliyat Najd*) situated in the territory of the ᶜTēbah tribe.[19] Very similar in content and form is

---

19 Sbayyil, Muḥammad ibn ᶜAbd al-ᶜAzīz ibn, *Dīwān Ibn Sbayyil*, Riyadh 1988, and al-Faraj, Khālid ibn Muḥammad ad-Dōsirī, *Dīwān an-Nabaṭ*, Damascus 1952. The latter is one of the earliest and best collections of Najdi poetry, including the *dīwāns* of other, predominantly lyrical, poets as well. The former is a more recent collection by one of the poet's grandsons. Where the text of both editions varies slightly I have generally followed the former edition. For my interpretation of the verses I am indebted to the poet's cousin Ḥmūd ibn ᶜAbd al-ᶜAzīz ibn Ḥmūd ibn Sbayyil, a retired judge living in Riyadh.

the poetry of Fhēd al-Mijmāj, a poor agricultural labourer and a contemporary of Ibn Sbayyil who lived in the village of al-Aṯlah, not far from Nifi. The same applies to Mašᶜān al-Htēmi, a bedouin who wandered in the deserts of Najd about a century ago, and to ᶜBēd ibn Hwēdi ad-Dōsiri, an agricultural labourer who was born in the small town of aš-Šaᶜra, east of Nifi, and who lived in the same period and circumstances as the others just mentioned.[20] Finally, I have made use of an anthology of verse by poetesses of the Arabian desert.[21]

## *Relation of the* Nasīb *to Other Parts of the Poem*

In Dindān's poetry the introduction, whatever its length, is usually well defined by its content and the formula of transition that sets it apart from the main theme.[22] In many poems this transition from one section to the other is marked by a form of address. Once the poet has concluded his introduction he turns to the immediate addressee of his words. If he addresses himself to God (as in eleven of the poems) with the vocative *ya-llāh*, this is usually followed by *ṭālibk lēlin* or *bi-lēlin* 'I request You to send a night (of clouds and rainfall)' and a description of clouds, thunder, rain, and torrents rushing through watercourses (as in eight of the poems).[23] In the case of the

[20] Samples of the latter three's poetry are taken from Junaydil, Saᶜd ibn ᶜAbdallah ibn, *Min aᶜlām al-adab a͟sh-s͟haᶜbī, s͟huᶜarāʾ al-ᶜĀliyah*, Riyadh 1980-81. Ibn Junaydil is an authority in the field of geography and popular culture whose intimate acquaintance with these subjects stems from the fact that as a young man he used to travel widely on camelback as a trader in agricultural equipment.

[21] Raddās, ᶜAbdallah ibn Muḥammad ibn, *S͟hāᶜirāt min al-bādiyah*, Riyadh 1984-85. Ibn Raddās (born in 1924 or 1925) collected these poems in the course of his travels as an inspector for the Ministry of Labour, see al-Bilādī, ᶜĀtiq ibn Ġayt͟h, *Nasab Ḥarb*, Mecca 1984, 271-272. He is now retired and lives in Riyadh.

[22] Apart from the six poems devoted to a single theme (poems 4, 20, 28, 29, 30, 31), only one of the twenty-five poems does not begin with such an introduction: poem no. 22 opens with *rāćib illi* (O rider of) followed by one line of camel description, and the *naṣṣah* (steer her to) immediately ushers in the *mufāk͟harah*. Poem no. 25 opens with *ya-nidībi* (O my messenger) and one verse of camel description, followed by *naṣṣah* and one line of *madīḥ* addressed to the recipient. In verses 3-10 of this last poem Dindān boasts of the inspirational resources at his command and presents his audience with a composite riddle. Verses 11-17 describe the poet's construction of an unassailable fortified palace guarded by the angel of death, which can be read as a highly original metaphor for Dindān's own art. See Sowayan (1987), 87, on building as a metaphor for composing poetry. In the thematic matrix these verses have been included as part of the introductory section.

[23] This formula, a prayer addressed to God (*ya-llāh ṭalabtak*), is also used in connection with other requests, e.g. for camels or forgiveness and paradise, see Musil (1928), 285 and 323.

poet turning to the messenger, the words *ya-rāčbin* 'O rider (of a camel or car of such and such qualities)' or *ya-nidībi* 'O messenger of mine' are invariably followed by a description of the mount or vehicle (as in twelve poems). Both *ya-llāh* and *ya-rāčbin* occur in two of the poems (nos. 6 and 9).

Generally the description of the camel and the journey ends in a phrase beginning with *tanṣa* 'you head for', *naṣṣah* 'steer (the camel) towards', *lya jan*, *lya lifan* 'when (the she-camels) have arrived at' etc., followed by greetings to the final addressee, a terse indication of the message, and words of praise for its recipient and his tribe or kin.

In four poems (nos. 11, 15, 16, 24) the address to the messenger (or the mount in the case of no. 15) and the connected description of the camel or car separate the *nasīb* from the love lyrics of the *ġazal* section, in no. 24 with the addition of words destined for the *mamdūḥ* to whom the messenger is to report on the lovelornness of the poet. In two poems (nos. 17 and 19) the *ġazal* section immediately follows the *nasīb*, the transition being marked by the formula of transition: *min ᶜana (ġaḏḏ an-nahad)* 'all this because of (one with luscious breasts etc.)' and *ᶜalēk ya-* 'for your sake (O beauty of such and such traits)'.[24] In Najdi poetry a direct transition from the *nasīb* to *ġazal* is generally signalled by some formula of this kind.

In poem no. 15 Dindān speaks to his young riding camel (*bakriti*) and in no. 17 he asks God to punish a dove whose cooing renewed his pangs of love. Poems nos. 19 and 23 (on the *aṭlāl* theme, the lament on the site of an abandoned encampment, which is closely related to the *ġazal*) consist almost entirely of a soliloquy by the poet. The latter one, however, ends in an address to the censurer and claims that only a ride on a spirited camel will cool the inflamed heart, in verse reminiscent of Imruʾ al-Qaysʾ *fa-daᶜ dhā wa-salli al-hamma ᶜanka bi-jasratin* 'leave that subject and dispel your worries on the back of a strong she-camel.' Unlike most of Dindān's poems, which fall into two, three, four, or more sections separated by more or less standardized markers of transition, these two are mainly made up of only one section, the *nasīb*, but one that has grown into a full-fledged poem in itself.

---

24 This marker *min ᶜana* frequently occurs in the poetry of the Duwāsir in addition to such formulas as *ᶜalēk ya-* or *ᶜala allaḏi* 'for one who', commonly used by poets who lived in central Najd.

### *Parts of the* Nasīb

It would be difficult to subdivide the *nasīb* into constituent parts that are as well defined as is the *nasīb* in relation to the other parts of the *qaṣīdah*. However, the following motifs may be bracketed together for the sake of convenience: a scene on a lonely mountain; a description of the process of poetic inspiration; the suffering of the heart and its adjunct, the extended simile belonging to the category of *ya-tall galbi* 'how the strings of my heart are being pulled'.

*The Lonely Mountain Scene*

Though the poet's ascent of an elevation in order to look out over the surrounding desert is a motif not unknown in classical poetry, it seems to be of considerably more frequent occurrence in the vernacular poetry of Arabia.[25] As the poetess Nūrah al-Ḥmūd said:[26]

> *rāᶜi l-hawa dāymin fi rās mirgāb //*
> *wi-lya ᶜtala margibin tūḥi ǵinībih*

> The lovelorn can always be found on his look-out; //
> When he has climbed to its top you hear his wailing.

But even among his fellows Dindān strikes one as a particularly assiduous climber of mountains, as no doubt he was before one of his legs became nearly paralyzed by arthritis. In the solitude of a mountain peak, its craggy rocks lashed by violent winds and dust storms and frequented by no other living beings except falcons, the poet can give free rein to his feelings. There the psychic forces raging inside him are brought into the more immediate presence of the supernatural and the awesome power of nature. Under such circumstances the poet must be prudent that his inspiration does not come from the wrong source (24/1):

> From the look-out post I climbed I curse Satan, //
> Feeling out of sorts on these lofty crests.

Half of Dindān's poems open with such a mountain scene. The poet states that he has climbed to the pinnacle, referring to himself either in the first or third person. In the latter case the subject of the verb

---

[25] On this motif see Sowayan (1987), 96-100. Verbs used for 'to climb' are *ḏabb, riga, bida, šarraf, naṭṭ, taᶜalla, ᶜadda*. Also see Sowayan (1987), 96-100, for the mountain or look-out (*rijim, nāyif, mašraf, margab, mirǵāb, ḥaja, majdūr* etc.) and adjectives indicating its shape (*mdamlaj, mgawwar, maḏrūb, malmūm* etc.).

[26] Ibn Raddās (1984-85), i, 65.

is *an-naššād*, *aš-šāᶜir* (the poet), or his proper name. The ascent is made in the early part of the morning (*aḏ-ḏaḥa*).[27] Once his tumultuous mood has subsided and the poet begins his descent, he is in a state of physical and mental exhaustion and wishes he had never embarked on the climb (2/2):

> A rock from where one has an unbounded view over the other landmarks; //
> There sorrow welled up in me with renewed force: Wish I hadn't climbed that peak![28]

He feels that the mountain has tricked him into this enterprise,[29] but his excuse is that he really had no choice (14/1):

> I climbed the peak of a lofty mountain against my wish, //
> Driven to that high vantage point by the poetic urge.

*The Inspirational Process*[30]

On top of the mountain the poet is overcome by conflicting emotions. His suppressed fury bursts forth and he is so agitated and desperate that his mind clouds over and he almost goes berserk (8/1):

> I climbed a mountain in a state of mounting fury, //
> Till my mind clouded over and I groped for words.

It is in this extreme condition that his inner self is stirred sufficiently for the verses to well up (10/1-2):

1. After sunrise the poet climbed to a high ridge, //
   A mountain that brought me into a pensive mood.
2. From every nook and cranny the verses marched up to me, //
   Though the Lord loves moderation in everything.

The involuntary nature of this process is stressed over and over again (11/1):

---

27 Similarly a Dōsiri poetess: *ana bādyah wagt aḏ-ḏaḥa rās rijmin bān*, Ibn Raddās (1984-85), ii, 147.

28 Cf. Musil (1928), 178, *naṭṭēt ana l-mirgāb allah yixūnih* 'I ascended the lookout—may God deceive him (i.e. the mountain)!'

29 *min ġarrih* 'because of his deception'.

30 See Sowayan (1985), 91-100, the chapter 'Composition: The Poet's Viewpoint' and Sowayan (1987). Similarly, the process of composition and its accompanying mental state are a common theme in Yemeni tribal poetry, cf. Caton (1990), 37-39.

I climbed a mountain soaring up four hundred and eighty thousand feet high. //
There he who vowed to abstain from all rhyming broke his fast.

One verse calls forth the next and before long the poet is almost swept away by the flood of his own inspiration. From everywhere the verses come hurrying to him and press around him like camels crazed with thirst (6/4):[31]

No sooner did I chant one verse, than others came like camels rushing to a well //
And pressed around me, lowering their big heads to the water.

Or like hosts of young wingless locusts crawling, pushing, and riding on one another's backs, swarms of locusts in the sky or grains of sand in the high dunes (25/4-6):

1. Or swarms of Tihāmah locusts that darken the sky; //
   No sooner than winter has turned its back,
2. Their whirling columns are seen from Kuwait to Tihāmah. //
   Count those numbers and you'll know how much I have to say.
3. Also, count the grains of sand in a dune, not skipping one of them, //
   But make sure you do your counting right during a dark, moonless night.

Visions undreamt of unfold as the inspiration bursts forth. But in this crucial moment the poet does not let himself be overpowered, and thanks to his mastery of the art moulds his thoughts in eloquent verses that obey the laws of rhyme and metre (7/1):

Bring the pen, for I have verses to say;[32] //
I am not one to mangle them, nor do they turn out flawed.

Indeed, the verbs used for 'composing poetry' all imply a firm grip of the professional requirements.[33] Thus the emotions are brought under control and translated into verse:[34]

*yigūl Maš<sup>c</sup>ān al-Htēmi tifalham //*
*gāfin rijas bēn aḏ-ḏlū<sup>c</sup> al-maġālīǵ*

---

[31] See also Sowayan (1987), 76.

[32] 'Bring the pen' etc.: an appeal to an imaginary scribe is a stereotyped motif in oral Najdi poetry.

[33] Examples are *ysanni<sup>c</sup>, yfaṣṣil, yǵaddi*. Sowayan (1987), 87, and Sowayan (1985), 94: *y<sup>c</sup>addil, ywallif, yāzin, y<sup>c</sup>asif, yanḥat, yṣaxxir, yanjir, yabni, yiṣūġ*.

[34] Ibn Junaydil (1980-81), 105. *gāf* (lit. 'rhyme'), *ǵīl, timāṯīl, nišīd, giṣīd* etc.

> This is the poetry said by Mašᶜān al-Htēmi //
> Verses that raged between the walls of his ribs.

The result is as delicious as camel's milk,[35] true poetry that lends itself to being sung (31/1):

> The poet ad-Dindān set his thoughts to a tune, //
> Moulding each verse so as to express its meaning with eloquence.

*The Suffering of the Heart*

The poet who stands brokenhearted on top of the mountain feels a surge of emotion pressing inside him, straining to be released. But his attempts at restraint only increase the fury of the emotions and the poet's mental pain (12/3-4):

1. Distress clouded my mind and palpitated in my breast, //
   As if cupping glasses were tapping my heart's arteries.
2. In the open desert I felt as if hemmed in by walls, //
   While the winds of moodiness tugged at my heart.

And (19/1-3):

1. ᶜAbdallah ad-Dindān climbed the high cliffs //
   Of a mountain soaked with rain by heavy clouds.
2. There I gave free rein to the feelings pent up between my ribs, //
   And, disconsolate, I burst out in tears.
3. If only people knew what secrets I kept hidden: //
   My attempts at restraint put me through the pains of death.

At the centre of the forces unleashed during the creative process is the heart.[36] It is roasted by flames until it becomes cooked to perfection.[37] Violent, hot winds wither the heart's green sprouts. The

---

[35] E.g. Ibn Junaydil (1980-81), 101:
1. *wi-bdaᶜt gāfin fāhmih ma taᶜarwaj //*
   *w-killin ᶜala gāf al-Htēmi šifāwi*
2. *yišdi l-darr illi waladha ydarrij //*
   *lya jāt min nabt aš-šiᶜīb al-frāwi*
1. My verses do not limp, for they were composed with skill; //
   My poetry is popular with audiences everywhere:
2. Sweet as the milk of one that gently nudges on her calf, //
   When she returns from grazing in a broad valley.

The comparison of charming conversation and poetry to the sweet taste of camel milk is a recurrent simile in Najdi poetry.

[36] *galb al-ᶜana, al-galb al-mᶜanna, galb al-xaṭa* 'the unreasonable, enamoured, afflicted heart'.

[37] *nijāḥ* 'the state of being well-done, completely cooked'.

heart is likened to the dry bed of a watercourse after a long drought or to a shallow pool of rain-water from which foam and dust are blown by the desert winds. Sometimes it seems as if the heart is being plucked out of the breast by a pair of pincers. In the *ġazal* sections one also finds the familiar dialogue between the poet's heart and his common sense, with the latter upbraiding the former for its persistence in delusion.

In the end, the secret thoughts, worries and sorrows the poet tried his utmost to suppress can no longer be contained in the cage between his ribs, and they pour forth.[38] This moment is heralded by the appearance of tears that stream from his sleepless and miserable eyes like water pouring from a bucket or gushing from a well after the sand and debris clogging it have been scraped away.[39]

### *The Extended Simile in the* Nasīb

The comparison of a tearful eye to a bucket from which water splashes when it is drawn from a well by a camel was already dear to the early classical poets.[40] Often this motif is amplified in an extended simile with detailed descriptions of the technique of irrigation. By far the most famous example is the seven verses on this topic by Zuhayr ibn Abī Sulmā, but there is no dearth of this simile in the work of other classical poets as well. Since socio-economic conditions in Arabia remained largely unchanged until the second half of this century, including the methods used to draw water, it is not surprising that the vernacular oral tradition has retained and refined this motif.[41]

The extended simile is announced by formulas like *ya-tall galbi* 'ah, how my heart is being pulled', *ya-lajjiti* 'ah, how my heart

---

38 *hawājīs, ruwābiᶜ* 'worries, concerns one tries to keep to himself'; *bēn as-sarājīf, ṣindūg al-ḥaša* 'the room between the ribs' that is pictured as a cage imprisoning the emotions; *sadd, ćinīn* 'what is hidden there, contained by the walls'; *bāḥ, bayyaḥ*, passive *bīḥ*, 'to appear, to become exposed to public scrutiny' is said when the poet is forced to give himself away.

39 *fōḥ figr al-bīr la ḥirrik difīnih* (16/4) 'like a well whose sand-filled bottom is scraped up'; *fawwaᶜat bi-l-jamm l-azrag ma tmāḥi* (17/7) 'the limpid water came gushing to the surface and did not require someone to tug at the rope in order to make sure that the bucket was full or to descend into the well in order to scoop it up in case the well was almost dry.'

40 Cf. Wagner (1988), i, 72, 97-98.

41 For the extended simile in *nabaṭi* poetry, as the vernacular poetry of Najd is called, and some beautiful examples see also Sowayan (1985), 113-117.

clamours', *ya-mall galbin* or *mall galbin* 'how much suffering from a heart', *ya-wijūdi* 'ah, how I am pained', *ya-wanniti* 'ah, how I cry, lament'. In all these cases Dindān's poems open with a mountain scene. In other sources one also finds: *ya-jarr galbi* 'ah, how my heart is being tugged at', *ya-ḥann galbi* 'ah, how my heart is moaning and whining', *fariy galbi* 'how my heart is torn', *zō$^{c}$ galbi* 'how my heart leaps, flutters'.

In these, the most poetical sections of the *qaṣīdah*, each poet in his own way employs the standard repertory of images familiar to his audience in order to paint his heart's distress in the most vivid colours. An idea of this interplay between real emotion, the conventions of the *nasīb*, and the poet's ability to add individual touches might be gained from the following examples of Dindān's and other poets' use of the extended simile.

*Labour at the Well*

The strain on the poet's heart implied in the formula *ya-tall galbi* 'how severely my heart is being pulled' can be visualized in many ways. Thus one finds as the second part of the simile a description of a falcon flapping its wings in an effort to escape from the *sbūg*, the leather loops that keep it tied to its padded perch when it spies a flock of bustards.[42] Or, in a reversal of roles, the comparison is made with a falconeer waving his arms in the hope of luring back a falcon that flew away to join its own brethren in freedom.[43]

However, as a motif in the *nasīb* of Najdi poetry nothing equals the popularity of the *sāni* and the *sānyah*, the labourer and his camel that draw water from the well. One can think of various explanations for this, but certainly the sight of a camel being urged on relentlessly as it paces up and down the same path and heaves mightily at the ropes must have struck the imagination as a powerful metaphor for the condition of one ridden by the devil of poetry. As $^{c}$Bēd ibn Hwēdi said in a variation on the Arab adage *sayr as-sawānī safar la yanqaṭi$^{c}$* 'the course of the beasts that draw water is a journey that does not end':[44]

---

42 E.g. Ibn Raddās (1984-85), i, 58.
43 E.g. al-Faraj (1952), 210.
44 Ibn Junaydil (1980-81), 151.

*yigūl al-mwallaᶜ wa-r-ruwābiᶜ tdīrih dēr //*
*ćima dēr miᶜwādin ᶜala ma baġa s-sāni*

These are the words of one infatuated, as he's driven in circles by worry //
Like a camel drawing water from a well goes back and forth at the driver's directions.

Unlike the classical poets, who compare the eye's tears with the water drawn in buckets from a well, Dindān builds his simile on a comparison between his torn heart (*ya-tall galbi*) and the strain on the bucket's rope, and hence on the camel, as a result of the driver's cruelty, indifference, or inexperience (6/8):

Or is it torment like that of a leather bucket hoisted by a clumsy youngster, //
And ripped open by sharp stones protruding from the sides of the well.

In a similar vein ᶜAbdallah ibn Sbayyil says:[45]

1. *ya-tall galbi tallat al-ġarb li-ršāh //*
   *ᶜala zaᶜāᶜin ḥāylin ṣaddarat bih*[46]
2. *sawwāgha ᶜabdin d̲arabha bi-miḥdāh //*
   *imm amrisat bi-ršāh walla wiṭat bih*[47]
3. *ćannik ᶜala sōgah thimmih w-tanxāh //*
   *la ᶜawwad allah sāᶜtin ᶜarrifat bih*
4. *ly agfa b-ha ćann aṭ-ṭimāmīᶜ tašᶜāh //*
   *ćann ad-daluw ṭērin lya nazzaᶜat bih*[48]
5. *lēn immazaᶜ ġarbih ᶜala ḥadd ᶜargāh //*
   *w-jīlān bīrih bi-l-msūḥ lᶜabat bih*[49]

1. Ah, my heart is being pulled like a bucket by its rope, //
   By a vehement she-camel, barren of womb, that struggles down the path,
2. Beaten with a stick by its driver, a slave: //
   Either the rope slips off the roller or she steps on it.
3. He drives her as if you were encouraging him or shouting him on in battle; //

---

[45] Al-Faraj (1952), 206-207 and Ibn Sbayyil (1988), 131. Junaydil, Saᶜd ibn ᶜAbdallah ibn, *as-Sānī wa-s-sāniyah*, Riyadh 1987-88, contains much relevant information on this and other poems dealing with the technique of drawing water.

[46] See also Ibn Junaydil (1987-88), 37, 79, 94.

[47] Ibn Junaydil (1987-88) gives *lya razz miḥdāh* 'when (the slave) raises his stick'. *amras* 'to slip off the waterwheel' (said of the rope holding the bucket), Ibn Junaydil (1987-88), 100 (cf. CA *imrās*). See also Ibn Junaydil (1987-88), 31, 38, 99.

[48] Ibn Sbayyil (1988) has *tanxāh* and al-Faraj (1952) *tanḥāh* instead of *tašᶜāh*, which is given by Ibn Junaydil (1987-88), 38.

[49] See also Ibn Junaydil (1987-88), 38, 83-84, 100.

Cursed be the hour she came to know him.
4. When he chases her down the path like a camel hurried on by raiders, //
 She pulls so hard that the bucket comes flying up the well like a bird,
5. So that its leather became torn at the wooden crosspieces over its mouth, //
 As it banged and scraped against the stones covering the well's shaft.

There is a difference between the drawing of water for the purpose of watering the camel herds and for irrigation. The first is a relatively simple operation carried out with a minimum of equipment, as described in these verses of Ibn Sbayyil:[50]

1. *ya-tall galbi tallatēnin mn agṣāh //*
 *tall al-wrād illi ḥyāmin wrūdih*
2. *yamm aṭ-Ṭwāl illi ᶜdūdih mṭawwāh //*
 *yrūᶜ jaḏḏābah mijāḏib ᶜdūdih*[51]
3. *ᶜala giᶜūdin ma ysāniᶜ bi-mamšāh //*
 *mistaṣᶜibin ma yitbaᶜ illi yigūdih*
4. *la gāl ya-rāᶜi l-jimal zād bi-xṭāh //*
 *imma ngaṭaᶜ walla tiṣarram ᶜamūdih*[52]

1. Ah, how my heart is being pulled again and again from its roots, //
 Like the strain on the ropes of a well circled by camels crazed with thirst,
2. Towards aṭ-Ṭwāl, deep wells with walls made of stone, //
 That pose a daunting challenge to those who draw the water,
3. Let alone with a young male camel that does not obey directions, //
 An unruly beast that does not follow the man leading it.
4. If the man at the well shouts, 'Halt the camel!' it only increases its pace, //
 Either cutting the rope or breaking the poles of the hoist.

Two factors combine to put a severe strain on the rope: the depth of the well and the unruly behaviour of the young male camel that has not gone through the kind of training (*ᶜsāf*) that a regular *sānyah* receives before being put to work. Also, unlike the trained *sānyah*,

---

[50] Al-Faraj (1952), 168-169 and Ibn Sbayyil (1988), 120.

[51] *aṭ-Ṭwāl* 'the long ones', the name of some wells on the caravan road from Kuwait, Ibn Junaydil (1987-88), 38. Obviously these are the Ṭwāl wells in the possession of the Mutair tribe (see Ingham, Bruce, *Bedouin of Northern Arabia*, London 1986, 23-24, 32).

[52] This verse is explained later in the text on basis of Ibn Junaydil (1987-88), 41-42.

this camel pulls the rope towards an undefined point, only halting when the driver hears the shout of the man at the well who catches the bucket and empties it into the trough (*ḥōḏ*). This shout—*ya-rāᶜi l-jimal* 'O driver of the camel!' or *ᶜawwid* 'return!'—is a sign that the bucket has reached the top of the well, but in this case the wayward camel continues to pull despite all efforts to stop it and thus plays havoc with the equipment, either breaking the rope or one of the two stout poles that support the wooden roller (*maḥālah*) over which the rope (*ar-rša*) runs.

What especially captured the imagination of the poets is the terror felt by the *sānyah* for the slave who mercilessly drives her on. The fate of these camels—toiling like prisoners condemned to forced labour under the supervision of a camp bully—may have appeared especially gruesome to the poet when compared with that of camels pasturing freely in the desert. In any case, this master-slave relation, in which the master is himself a slave, is a recurrent motif in these sections. As described by Ibn Sbayyil, the driver's misguided zeal only results in the rapid exhaustion of the animal and damage to the equipment, thus necessitating time-consuming repairs. Similar scenes of cruelty were translated into gripping similes by other poets like Masᶜān al-Htēmi:[53]

1. *ya-wanniti wannat ṯalāṯin halāyim //*
   *min nasfihin xiḏr al-jmām ad-dagārīg*
2. *sawwāghin ᶜabdin maᶜa l-lēl yajham //*
   *w-anjaḥ miṣāxifhin b-rūs al-misāwīg*

1. My groans are like those of three gaunt she-camels, //
   Worn from drawing the well's copious greenish-blue water.
2. Their driver is a slave who starts working towards the end of night, //
   Raining blows with his stick on their bodies' tender parts.

And ᶜBēd ad-Dōsiri:[54]

1. *o tall ḥabl as-sānyah ᶜigb l-iᶜlāg //*
   *sawwāgha nāsin manāṭīg dīnih*
2. *lya jat maᶜa s-sanda f-la hīb tinsāg //*
   *la šakk bāgin hēniha llah yihīnih*

---

[53] Ibn Junaydil (1980-81), 105.
[54] Ibn Junaydil (1980-81), 143-144.

1. Or like the bucket's rope is straining at the she-camel after it has been joined to the saddle, //
A camel driven by a slave forgetful of his religion's prescriptions.
2. Doesn't he know that she should not be urged on as she makes her way back to the well up the tow path? //
But he is bent on humiliating her, may God punish him!

As Ibn Junaydil points out, on their return from the lower end of the tow path (*maṣabb*) after the bucket has been drawn from the well and emptied into the reservoir (*al-lza*) the camels are allowed to walk back up the slope (*sanda*) toward the turning point at the well (*mᶜaddal*) at an easy pace in order to let them recover somewhat from the exertion. Therefore the stick (*miswigah*) is only used to spur them on while they are drawing up the heavy bucket on their way down the slope. To beat the camel on its return towards the well is considered an outrage.[55] And under no circumstances should the camel be hit on her tender parts—such unethical treatment is also likely to result in the mishaps described in Ibn Sbayyil's poem. Of course the likelihood that the slave loses his temper is greater if the camel has not been well trained, or for some other reason behaves in a recalcitrant way:[56]

*wa-tall galbi tall ġarb an-nuwāᶜīr //*
*ᶜala t̲alāt̲in ḥīl fi hinn zarga*

Ah, my heart is being torn like a bucket dangling from the wooden poles, //
Drawn by three sterile she-camels, one of them an unruly white.

Here the disturbing factor is the presence of a *zarga*, a white animal with a few black hairs that is notorious for its impetuousness and unruliness and for shying at the least thing.[57] These qualities make a camel unsuited for labour requiring docility and a steady, regular effort.

*Clamour of the Heart*

Similes announced by the formula *ya-lajjiti* etc. generally refer to sounds, especially noises of distress, confusion, and anxiety, as in the following verses by Mašᶜān al-Htēmi:[58]

---

55 Ibn Junaydil (1987-88), 39, 99.
56 Ibn Raddās (1984-85), i, 184.
57 Musil (1928), 329, 334; Junaydil, Saᶜd ibn ᶜAbdallah ibn, *K̲hawāṭir wa-nawādir turāt̲hīyah*, Riyadh 1987, 168.
58 Ibn Junaydil (1980-81), 100.

1. *ya-min li-galbin sajj fi marbiᶜih lajj //*
*lijlāj ahal sūgin tibīᶜ al-kisāwi*
2. *lajjat maḥāl al-bīr yōm ytidāraj //*
*tiǵbil w-tiǵfi bih t̲alāt̲in ᶜadāwi*
3. *sawwāgha ᶜabdin lya gām yanhaj //*
*ᶜabdin ḥalāl al-gōm ma hūb yāwi*[59]

1. What to do with a heart distracted by love and raging inside its breast, //
Like the clamour of market vendors selling cloth?
2. Or the screams of wooden rollers turning rapidly above the well //
As three sturdy camels pace back and forth towing the rope,
3. Once their driver, a slave, begins to rush them up and down: //
May that merciless fellow be captured and taken away as the enemy's booty!

In this example a third element has been added to the motif of the slave driving three camels: that of the wooden wheel (*al-maḥālah*) over which rolls the rope that joins the bucket to the camel saddle (*ćitab*) especially made for this purpose.[60] The *maḥālah*, together with the elongated bucket (*ġarb*), the wooden crosspieces tied over the mouth of the bucket (*ᶜarqāh*), and the rope (*ris̲h̲āʾ*), are part of the vocabulary that has remained virtually unchanged since the time of Zuhayr ibn Abī Sulmā.

In the period called *aš-šarbah*, when the wheat fields are in need of constant irrigation, the clamour of the sqeaking wooden water-wheels used to sound almost all night long and disturb the sleep of the village folk.[61] In poetry this noise (*lajjah, lijlāj*) is compared to the mayhem of the stormy emotions inside the poet's heart, a connection made explicit in this verse by Fhēd al-Mijmāj:[62]

*ᶜalēh maḥḥāl aḏ-ḏimāyir zalāzīl //*
*tjūḏ min figdih w-min šidd fargāh*

For her sake the wooden wheels of my inner self are shaking and squeaking, //
Twisting about because of her absence and the pain of separation.

---

[59] *ma hūb* 'he is not' (followed by the predicate), the particle of negation *ma* and a contraction of the personal pronoun *hu* and the emphatic *b-*.

[60] Ibn Junaydil (1987-88), 45-46.

[61] *aš-šarbah* 'a period of one month and ten days in late spring when water for the irrigation of the fields has to be drawn day and night', Ibn Junaydil (1987-88), 105-107.

[62] Ibn Junaydil (1980-81), 48.

Similarly Dindān says (6/7):

> My heart whined like the squeaking of the wooden wheels suspended above a well //
> While well-trained camels briskly draw its water.

The simile is further enriched by the fact that the sound of the *maḥālah* is sometimes directly connected to the monotonous songs chanted by the camel-driving slave or labourer in order to stay awake at night and to relieve the tediousness of his work:[63]

1. *ya-lajjiti lajjat maḥāḥīl ᶜabbāb //*
   *saggāyhin b-aṣwāthin miᶜijbātih*
2. *ṣaddar ᶜala ᶜirbin marājīᶜ w-asbāb //*
   *rasm aš-šaḥam bi-ḏhūrhin ćālyātih*

1. Ah, my screams are like those of the waterwheels turning above an abundant well, //
   Singing in voices that cheer up the man in charge of the irrigation.
2. Down the tow path he leads camels, some of them old hands and some new to the job, //
   The spring pastures having covered their backs with layers of fat.

As Ibn Junaydil explains, the noise made by the *maḥālah* becomes louder as the bucket becomes heavier with water and the tension on the rope increases. Sometimes the driver of the camels on the tow path (*masna*) used to hammer a small, tapered piece of fig-tree or desert-plum (*sidr*) wood into one of the cracked ends of the axis on which the roller turns. As a result the *maḥālah* did not turn as smoothly as before and a bucket of smaller size had to be attached to the rope. But the advantage gained was a sound that, though far from melodious, was regular enough that the labourer could tune into it with his own chanting and thus find some distraction from the boredom of his work. Such a roller was called *maḥālat al-jāhūš*.[64] Another enlivening touch was added by the gay colours painted on the *maḥālah*:[65]

> *lya girrbat Ḏirwah w-bint al-Jahāmah //*
> *maḥḥālha mitl al-bniyy al-maxāḏīb*
>
> When Ḏirwah and bint al-Jahāmah were brought to the tow path, //

---

63 ᶜBēd ibn Hwēdi in Ibn Junaydil (1980-81), 167.
64 Ibn Junaydil (1987-88), 76.
65 Mḥammad ibn Salmān in Ibn Junaydil (1987-88), 75.

The turning waterwheels resembled the hands dyed with henna of gesticulating young ladies.

One rare adaptation of the *maḥālah* motif appears in these verses by the poetess Waḏḥa al-Mašʿān of Ḥarb, a tribe through whose territory the Mecca-Medina stretch of the Ḥijāz railroad ran:[66]

1. *al-galb ćannih bi-l-misāmīr masmūr //*
   *sumr al-ḥadīd mjawwdīn fi ḏbābih*
2. *walla ćima lajjat maḥāḥīl bābūr //*
   *tsūgih al-kiffār sōg ar-ribābah*[67]

1. My heart squirms as if it has been spiked with nails, //
   As if the dark iron were riveted onto its arteries;
2. Or like the rattling sound made by a steam engine's wheels, //
   Driven by the infidels as one plays a one-stringed fiddle.

*Sound of Distress*

A different kind of *lajjah* is that of suffering camels. The *xalūj*, a she-camel bereft of her young, is an obvious example:[68]

*ya-lajjiti lajjat xalūj al-miṣāgīr //*
*illi ʿala bawwin tizāyad ḥnāha*[69]

Ah, my moans are like those of a she-camel bereft of her young, //
As she stoops again and again over the stuffed skin of her slaughtered calf.

The groans of thirsty camels suffering the torments of Tantalus as they crowd around a desert well, unable to reach its water in the absence of a herdsman, provided the poets with another simile for the anguished voices inside them. Take this scene of sheer terror that a pure bedouin like Dindān may have derived from his own experience (19/4-9):

1. I moan and groan like a herd of camels standing with bent necks, //
   Looking over the brink of the well for more than three days,
2. Their humps sagging, gone whatever remained from grazing on the *xazārīf*-plants; //
   And then, on the fourth day, heard the shouts of the herdsmen.
3. Once covered with fat, they now look like shrivelled thongs: //

---

[66] Ibn Raddās (1984-85), i, 339.

[67] *ribābah* 'one-stringed violin', see Sowayan (1985), 138-140 on singing and musical accompaniment.

[68] Siʿīdah aṯ-Ṯaʿliyyah in Ibn Raddās (1984-85), i, 369.

[69] See glossary under *bww*.

Cruel thirst robbed them of the strength they gained from spring's pastures.
4. Like a bundle of dead acacia-wood they trudge along //
At the time of Canopus' eclipse when the great heat sets in.
5. Disgusted by the foul smell of the water poured into the trough, //
The animals groaned so pitifully as to make a happy fellow turn grey.
6. When he stirred the filth on the water with a ladle, //
The man scooping up the water inside the well fainted, overcome by the stench.

For *lajjah* the poetess Waḏḥa al-Mašʿān al-Ḥarbiyyah substituted *ya-ḥann galbi*, a formula closer to the sound usually associated with camels, but otherwise the simile is the same:[70]

1. *ḥann galbi ya-ʿAli ḥannat al-xūr //*
*tawāridan ʿēnin ǵilīlin šarābah*
2. *ila ṣifaghin ya-ʿAli tāyih aš-šōr //*
*tijāwiban yašdin ginīb aḏ-ḏyābah*

1. My heart, ʿAli, groans like camels rich in milk, //
When they come to a well holding but a little water,
2. Because, ʿAli, some half-wit has led them astray (from the road to the right well), //
Their moans mingling like wolves responding to one another's howls.

With these verses Waḏḥa began a poem lamenting a loved one who had fallen victim to smallpox. Dindān's more playful comparison with the sound of a mortar as the coffee-beans are being pounded shows that the poet's complaints about his grieving heart need not always be taken as literally (23/7-9):

1. Woe unto a heart that struggled to conceal its bitterness! //
Like a mortar made of copper, it rings out when beaten.
2. When its rim is struck with force it screams and whines, //
And when its bottom is pounded its ribs raise a clamour.
3. If it begins to purr, then knock it merrily, //
But if it howls in terror, the company groans in sympathy.

*Terrors of the Chase*

Whereas the previous similes dealt with more or less static scenes, descriptions taken from the repertory of raiding, war, and perilous desert crossings add a measure of excitement to the terror and an-

70 Ibn Raddās (1984-85), i, 339.

guish, as in the following opening of one of Ibn Sbayyil's poems:[71]

1. *ya-tall galbi tall rakbin l-šimšūl //*
*rabᶜin mišāćīlin ᶜala kinnasin ḥīl*
2. *šāfaw warāhum mišᶜal aš-šēx mašᶜūl //*
*yōm ibrahazz al-lēl šāfaw rijājīl*
3. *šāfaw warāhum zōl w-agfaw ćima l-jōl //*
*jōl an-naᶜām illi tigāfan miḏālīl*
4. *yōm ixṭafōhin rawwaḥan ṭiffaḥ jfūl //*
*ćannih yramma min taḥathin hadāmīl*
5. *o tall ḥiṣn msarrib al-gēḏ bi-ḥlūl //*
*ćaṯḥ an-njūm w-fāxatōh az-zimāmīl*
6. *fi māgiᶜin ma bēn gātil w-magtūl //*
*ṭāḥat ḥḏāha wa-l-mawārid midāhīl*[72]
7. *xamsin misīrathin wala ṭālaᶜan zōl //*
*w-hādann ᶜigb mlāfaḥ al-ᶜirf wa-ḏ-ḏēl*
8. *tišāwaraw ma bēn ᶜāḏil w-maᶜḏūl //*
*wa-l-ᶜidd l-adna ḥāl dūnih maḥāwīl*
9. *taxayyaraw min ṭayyib al-fōd ziᶜjūl //*
*wa-l-mingaṭiᶜ xallōh miṯl al-maxāyīl*

1. Ah, my heart is straining like mounted men hurrying a small camel herd, //
A group of proud warriors riding strong, barren she-camels.
2. Looking behind them they saw that the sheik's torch had been lighted, //
And when the night sky paled they descried warlike men chasing them.
3. They saw the men's silhouettes behind them and flew away like a flock, //
A flock of fleeing ostriches racing after their shadows,[73]
4. A herd snatched and driven away in a mad, panicky gallop, //
As if scared by someone throwing rags under their legs.
5. Or is it like the strain felt by horses in the quivering heat of full summer //
And the dust stirred up by the heavenly constellations, while the men leading the camels with the supplies missed the rendezvous.
6. In a dangerous land where an encounter means a battle for life or death //
They lost their horseshoes, whereas the enemy was camped in force around the wells.

---

[71] Al-Faraj (1952), 198-199 and Ibn Sbayyil (1988), 110-111.

[72] *midhāl* pl. *midāhīl* 'places frequented by man or animals', i.e. the watering places were crowded with enemy tribes and were inaccessible to them.

[73] Hunters approach their prey with the low sun in their back. Therefore the ostriches flee *miḏālīl*, in the direction of their shade, away from the sun (CA *ẓill* 'shadow').

7. Their fourth day without water and without seeing a living soul, //
 Until they became strangely quiet and no longer shook their manes or waved their tails.
8. Reproaches flew back and forth as the men took counsel, //
 And, knowing that a waterless desert separated them from the nearest well,
9. Each of them took a strong animal from the best of the booty //
 And the rest were left behind like so many scarecrows in the desert.

The first part of this *nasīb* likens the pull at the heartstrings to that felt by a group of camel rustlers who have snuck up to another tribe's camp at night, unfettered a number of camels, and made off. As they rode off in the darkness and looked back they saw the light of a flame in the distance, telling them that the inhabitants of the camp had discovered the theft and were on their trail with the help of a big torch. At the time Ibn Sbayyil composed this poem his audience was as familiar with the "technical" vocabulary of raiding as it was with that of the *sānyah*, and therefore the poet could afford economy of detail: a few deft strokes on the canvas were sufficient to evoke in the mind of the listeners all the associations required to fill in the background. What these associations were one can glean from the available sources, as in the information given by Mūhiǵ al-Ġannāmi al-ᶜTēbi to the German scholar J.J. Hess (Mūhiǵ's account of such a nocturnal chase bears an uncanny resemblance to another poem by Ibn Sbayyil that opens in a similar fashion).[74] Here are Dindān's variations on the motif of the hot pursuit (19/18-24):

1. Ah, the pull at my heart is like that felt by mounted men returning from a raid, //
 As they plunge over the ridge of a low hill.
2. They heard the alarm cries and the sound of shots fired at them, //
 And, no mistake, they saw clouds of dust thrown up by snorting steeds.
3. The horsemen overtook them, singing war songs, //
 While vying for their kill, everyone saying 'My quarry!'
4. The raiders kicked the necks of their fleet camels, //
 And helter-skelter rushed down from the crest of the stony hill.
5. Were it not for the dark of night that covered the winding trails, //
 None of them ever would have touched his camel's belly girths again.
6. The pursuers outflanked the raiders, then took them in their horses' breasts, //

---

[74] Hess, J.J., *Von den Bedouinen des Innern Arabiens*, Zürich-Leipzig 1938, 41-42; al-Faraj (1952), 213.

And stabbed them with the points of their spears in the neck,
7. Until the fiery among them became as meek as lambs, //
And the intractable as tame as camels trained to draw water.

The second motif in Ibn Sbayyil's introduction, marked by a repetition of the *tall* formula, involves another risk connected with raiding: that of getting lost in the desert. On major raids over long distances the men owning horses used to detach themselves from the *zimāmīl* (the men leading the camels transporting the water, fodder, and other supplies) as they neared the enemy camp in order to carry out the attack and seize the booty. The purpose of this tactic was to forestall the possibility of the slower pack camels falling prey to a counterattack on horseback by the other tribe. The *zimāmīl* would take a different route and, at a predetermined location, await the return of the fighting men with the captured herds. As described in great detail by Sowayan (1992), it often happened that one or the other of the two parties went astray and missed the rendezvous.[75] If this happened the horse riders were in immediate danger, especially in summer, since horses are not able to go for more than a few days without water. The poem tells us that in this case the horses had not been watered in four days and thus their fate was sealed. Accordingly the men, after some deliberation and quarreling over who was to blame for the error in desert navigation, decided that only a forced march to the nearest well on the fittest of the captured camels offered them any chance of survival. The horses and the rest of the camels were left behind to face a certain death.[76]

### *The Pain of Defeat*

A related motif is that of the pain and terror felt by a man who has fractured a bone on a raid or journey, or by one wounded in war and abandoned in the desert. The formula marking the beginning of the simile is either *wannah* 'crying, moaning' or *wajd* 'pain, suffering':[77]

*wannēt ana wannat illi ṭaggih aṭ-ṭāyif //*
*walla kisīrin ᶜala l-ᶜērāt tūmi bih*

---

[75] A similar tale is told by Musil (1928), 654.
[76] Cf. Ibn Raddās (1984-85), i, 59 and 303 for a similar treatment of the motif.
[77] ᶜAmša al-Mašᶜān in Ibn Raddās (1984-85), i, 354.

Ah, my cries are like those of one suffering from a bout of anxiety, //
Or one who has fractured a bone and is swaying back and forth on the back of hardy camels.

And Ibn Sbayyil:[78]

1. *ya-wanniti wannat ṭiᶜīn aš-šiṭīrah //*
*fi sāᶜtin yūxaḏ ṭimaᶜha ᶜšāwah*
2. *xilli nahār al-kōn wasṭ al-kisīrah //*
*ma lih walad ᶜammin wala lih danāwah*
3. *w-la yiᶜarf aṭ-ṭāliᶜ min ayyah ᶜašīrah //*
*min kill badwin nawwhum bi-l-ᶜatāwah*

1. My moans are like those of one wounded by a sharp blade, //
When the robbers are despoilt of their booty by one stronger than them,
2. Left behind on the field of battle amidst the fallen, //
Without a kinsman or a relative anywhere near,
3. And no way to know from what tribe hails the man approaching him //
From among the bedouins who make oppression their trade.

Again, the feelings of animals are treated with no less sympathy than those of man, as in the following verses by Ḥwēd ibn Ṭihmāj al-ᶜIḏyāni al-ᶜTēbi about an unfortunate wolf:[79]

1. *o wajd sirḥānin jara lih ᶜaṯābīr //*
*min al-hajaf wa-l-jūᶜ jarr al-ginībi*
2. *ma yimriḥ al-maḏhūb yaṯᶜa d-duwāwīr //*
*w-ᶜaddōh ḥirrās al-ᶜarab wa-l-ćlībi*
3. *yalwi b-hum lēn aṣbaḥ aṣ-ṣibḥ ya-Mnīr //*
*ṯumm inhazam sāriḥ ḏiᶜīf an-niṣībi*
4. *w-ᶜitānih at-taffāg b-umm al-misāmīr //*
*wa-hwah maᶜa l-mixwāᶜ yihḏib haḏībi*
5. *w-ṯārat w-ġaddāha wiliyy al-migādīr //*
*wi-lya ann ᶜaḏm as-sāg ġādin ḥaṭībi*

1. Or like the pain of a wolf whose luck ran out, //
And howls from hunger and exhaustion.
2. Instead of lying down for the night he is on a rampage around the tents: //
In spite of the resistance put up by the bedouins' guards and dogs,
3. He kept circling around them until the new day dawned; //
Only then did the wretched animal scamper away.
4. The gunman took aim at him with his rifle, //

[78] Al-Faraj (1952), 182 and Ibn Sbayyil (1988), 58.
[79] Ibn Junaydil (1980-81), 229-230.

While he ran down a patch of low ground at a fast trot.
5. The gun fired and, guided by the Lord of Destiny, the bullet hit home, //
And behold, the bone of the wolf's leg was smashed to pieces.

These fragments offer no more than a glimpse of the rich imagery displayed by the representatives of the oral Najdi tradition. The number of examples illustrating their virtuosity in describing the dog's life of the poet's heart could be expanded *ad infinitum*. In the hands of a poet like Ibn Sbayyil these similes are moulded to suit the delicate and playful mood of his work. Others find in the convention the means to express in a personal manner a true sense of loss, like the ᶜTēbah poetess ᶜAmša al-Mašᶜān who weeps over the death of her first infant son in a dirge opening with this complaint:[80]

1. *ya-jarr galbi maᶜ Dḥayyim yijirrih //*
*jarr ar-rša min fōg ᶜūj al-luwāḥīf*[81]
2. *wa-s-sadd minni bāḥ wa-š-širb murrah //*
*wa-l-murr ma yibri l-glūb al-muwālīf*[82]

1. Ah, how my heart is being pulled because of Dḥayyim, //
Like the rope is pulled over the roller between the slanting poles.
2. The emotions I tried to repress have burst forth; bitter is my cure, //
But bitter herbs do not cure the hearts of those who love.

The traditional similes offer a vehicle for the expression of a wide range of emotions and moods, from this mother's lament captured in metre and rhyme to the jocular verses of poets who merely wish to frolic in the playground of convention.

## *Conclusion*

Though this survey presents only a very incomplete picture of this vast and largely unexplored subject, one can nevertheless draw some conclusions from the foregoing.

### *The* Nasīb

Within the *qaṣīdah*, as it has developed in the oral tradition of Najd, the *nasīb* (the introductory section) still represents a distinct segment

---

80 Ibn Raddās (1984-85), i, 360.
81 Dḥayyim is a pet name for ᶜAbdu r-Raḥmān.
82 *al-glūb al-muwālīf* 'the affectionate, tenderly loving hearts' (CA *maʾlūf*). In the Najdi dialect the initial glottal stop of the first radical of the root *hamzah* usually changes to *w*, see Sowayan (1985), 151.

that is set apart from the other sections by its emotional content and recurring motifs and similes, as well as by certain stylistic markers. Some of the motifs, images, and vocabulary proper to the classical *nasīb* have been retained almost unaltered. But whereas a melancholy, plaintive mood continues to be characteristic for the prelude, the tendency in Najdi poetry is towards greater self-reflexiveness; to a degree unknown in ancient times, the inheritors of the classical tradition dwell on the creative process itself and its accompanying psychological condition.

*The Tradition*

In composing, the poets make use of a common store of themes, motives, stock images, phraseology and prosodical options that together constitute the heritage of Najdi poetry. That this living tradition encompasses many "archaic" elements should not be surprising, for due to its natural barriers Najd remained sealed off from the outside world until the early part of this century. As a result its socio-economic situation remained virtually unchanged for more than a thousand years. Thus the sense of alienation an eighth-century *muḥdath* poet in Baghdad might have already felt regarding his early models was not experienced by the Najdi poets until the first part of this century: for them the inherited repertory continued to correspond to the facts of their daily life. Indeed, the Najdi poets cited in this article are much closer to the spirit and imagery of pre-Islamic poetry than were the urban poets in the early centuries of Islam.

*Art and Nature*

Of course one can only speak in relative terms about matching art and nature. Literature often tends to play by its own rules, with a sovereign disregard for facts outside its domain. In Arabia this tendency has become even more pronounced as the modern development of the country rapidly widened the gulf between the literary reality of Najdi poetry and the socio-economic environment in which the poets live. Nowadays the old vocabulary of war, raiding, animal husbandry, and agriculture mainly survives through the continuing popularity of pre-modern poetry. Also, the later poets, especially those living in the conservative tribal society, have been slow to respond to the changed situation. The work of Dindān, for example, is remarkably close in expression and imagery to that of

Ibn Sbayyil, though the two men are separated by a three-generation gap that coincided with the modern transformation of the country. This can be explained in part by the fact that Dindān remained wedded to the life-style of his ancestors and preferred to pay the price of economic marginalization rather than give up his nomadic existence in the desert with his small herd of camels.

Yet it is true that even a bedouin like Dindān only knows from hearsay many poetic elements of which Ibn Sbayyil and his contemporaries had (or might have had) firsthand experience. For instance, Dindān and other poets continue to compare the speed of fleet camels to that of fleeing ostriches, an animal that had already been hunted to extinction in Arabia by the the time they grew up. An interesting example of Dindān's use of archaic imagery for a practical purpose is found in poem no. 26. The poem is addressed to friends who have been jailed in Riyadh. One line of *nasīb*, including the pious formula 'I seek refuge with God from Satan', is followed by a description of the camel and the landmarks on the way of the messenger, though nowadays no one in Saudi Arabia uses the camel as a means of transportation. Then comes a lengthy address to the friends behind bars. The eulogy of these men is phrased in the epitheta of pre-modern heroism, like 'a clan famous for drenching the tips of their spears in enemy blood'. This speaks for the fact that, as in the classical period, the tradition perpetuates itself and continues to hold sway over the poets long after the conditions in which it originated have fundamentally altered.

Although the Najdi tradition is still overwhelmingly rooted in ancient lore, there are signs that it also tries to adapt itself to the new environment. Thus the description of cars travelling at great speed through the desert has become widespread. Poem no. 16 may be referred to as an example. But in spite of the poets' efforts to animate their descriptions by imparting a camel-like inner life to the cars, this substitution for the old camel description can be no more than a surrogate. The disjunction between the world of the oral tradition and the reality of contemporary Arabia cannot be remedied merely by the introduction of such modern adaptations, nor can this tradition's decline in Saudi Arabia be brought to a halt by such means.

Like most of the imagery in the similes, the survival of the ostrich in modern poetry is surely an archaism, but matters are sometimes less clear-cut. For example, an established motif both in ancient Arabic poetry and in its linear descendant, the oral tradition of the

Najd, pictures the poet standing on top of a mountain or hillock and watching in desperation as the caravan carrying his beloved disappears in the distance. In Dindān's case this is not a stereotyped prelude, but part of the reality he lived. When he felt the urge to compose a poem he did indeed climb one of the rocky ridges and conical basalt peaks in the desert around Wādi ad-Duwāsir. In doing so Dindān followed in the literary traces of countless Najdi poets before him, but not all of his predecessors necessarily matched poetry and reality as neatly as did Dindān. It seems likely that most of them composed their mountain verses in more comfortable quarters. And even Dindān's poetic mountaineering may have been another example of nature following literature.

The same holds true for Dindān's use of the *aṭlāl* motif. There can be no doubt that he felt genuine sorrow about the passing away of fellow-tribesmen and was reminded of the happy hours he had spent in their company when he came across the traces of one of their former camps.[83] Nevertheless, his verses on the subject are distinctly literary and traditional in character. Yet another example is the cooing of the dove that awakened the poet's nostalgic memories of his former romancing. No doubt he often heard the cooing of a dove while slumbering in the shade of a tree, but the poetic tradition was no doubt the determining factor in his choice of this particular motif rather than that of the warbling of a lark or other bird found in the desert.

### *Convention and Originality*

In a traditional society like that of the Najd, the concepts of convention and originality cannot be applied in the same way as they are in the West. Outside the circles of the urban literate elite, poetry in Arabia is still an art to be enjoyed orally and collectively. Therefore poetry must answer to certain expectations of the audience, based on the audience's previous experience, in order to be understood and appreciated. For the poet to step too far outside the bounds of tradition would be tantamount to poetic suicide. The Najdi poet is imbued with this tradition from the first day he sits in the *majlis* (the circle of men assembled on the carpet to discourse freely on any sub-

---

83 One of the early developments of the *aṭlāl* motif was that the classical poets extended it to include a lament about the forced departure of their own tribe due to war, Wagner (1988), i, 99.

ject of common interest while sipping tea and coffee), and feels the lure of rhyme and metre when listening to the poetry that is routinely declaimed on such occasions.

Yet within the bounds of tradition there is ample room for each Najdi poet to choose and elaborate in order to imprint his work with the stamp of his own individuality. As the samples presented in this chapter demonstrate, originality in this type of poetry can be understood as the incorporation of individual touches to the treatment of any given theme or motif (such as raiding, drawing irrigation water with the help of a camel, and in the case of Dindān, the life of a nomad in the desert). Only an artist with a sound knowledge of the traditional environment underlying these themes and motifs, and a keen eye for its possible application in poetry, will be able to do so. Craftsmanship and originality in this sense are the qualities most highly regarded by the audience. Thus the interaction of the poet, the audience, and the environment sustain the vitality of the tradition.

*Originality?*

Nevertheless, the material in the existing collections and my own data certainly show departures that seem highly original and innovative. But even in these cases the Western concept of artistic originality cannot be applied without qualification. For instance, the poetess who replaced the screaming of the wooden waterwheels suspended above the well with that of the iron wheels of a steam engine, both called *maḥāḥīl*, may have borrowed this innovation from another poet in her own tribe or any other located in or near the area crossed by the Ḥijāz railroad. One poet or poetess must have been the first to introduce this image, but it is in the nature of oral poetry that one will never know for certain who was the ''inventor''.

Some of these departures raise even more complex questions, as in the following intermediate section wedged between a traditional *nasīb* (a complaint of the heart) and an equally traditional camel description in Dindān's poem no. 9:

1. Where can I turn for a tongue, other than the one I already have, //
   To help me express what this one is incapable of saying?
2. God I praised the day I recovered my poetic bearings //
   And my heart broke out in sobs after suffering in silence for a year.
3. The verses dictated to me by the Merciful I understood, //

As they responded to one another's melody and marched on me in battle array.
4. Everything imaginable occurred to me at once, strange as it seems, //
While my breast boiled over like coffee in a pot made in al-Aḥsāʾ.
5. Earth and sky I gobbled up, but for me it wasn't even chicken feed, //
With the throne of heaven thrown in, it's but a poor chunk.
6. Gulping down the seas didn't quench my thirst, //
But then I'd drain the oceans in one sip.
7. If all mountains were ground into kohl, it would not even cover the corners of my eyes, //
Nor would all trees provide enough sticks to smear it with.
8. After supping on sun and moon my stomach still rumbled with hunger, //
And now there is nothing else left to eat, poor me.
9. I swallowed the years and smashed Satan's banner; //
I imbibed the winds and the jinn prostrated themselves for me;
10. As a cloak of coarse wool I threw the day around my shoulders, //
And I wrapped myself in the dark of night as in a furred mantle;
11. I gathered the stars, as well as all the spite I could muster, //
With the intention of silencing them for good, that rabble!
12. To God, the mighty Lord I entrust myself, //
And as for the rest of mankind, I don't give a damn.
13. O rider of mounts left unimpregnated since the summer, //
Fully grown she-camels, so lean as to resemble the curved grip of a cane;

There can be no doubt as to the great poetic force of this passage. That, however, was not the issue at stake in the Wādi. As mentioned earlier, these particular verses scandalized public opinion in the local community and, according to popular belief, brought upon Dindān divine wrath in the form of the partial paralysis of one of his legs. The poet (and the poem itself) say that the lines were spoken in response to a verbal assault by a rival poet. Unfortunately, I never learnt which poems elicited this and other furious eruptions of hyperbole from Dindān. The lack of comparable material makes it impossible to tell at this stage whether they are truly original departures or whether they fit a local convention. One possibility is that these verses are part of more or less established patterns of local poetic exchange in which each poet tries to overwhelm his opponent by making fantastic claims for his own poetic prowess. If this is true, then either Dindān took unusual freedoms with the rules of these contests or this particular circuit of poets itself operates in some respects on the margins of local society.[84]

This example also shows that published materials alone cannot provide a basis for well-founded judgments on these questions, since verses that are likely to jar on religious or other sensibilities do not appear in print. If anything, the conclusion must be that our understanding of the interrelationship between the individual poet and the tradition of which he partakes will remain sketchy until further research fills in the white spots of what is still very much a huge *terra incognita*.

## The Main Themes

### *Prayers for Rain*

Prayers to God to send his rainclouds and to drench the scorched earth so that nature can spring to life again are at the core of eight poems. These sections are heralded by formulas like *ṭālibk lēlin* 'I ask You for a night', *ya-llah b-lēlin* 'O God send us a night (of clouds and rain)' or *ᶜasa rizīn* 'I wish for clouds heavy with rain'. These formulas are followed by verses depicting the transformation of the land when the clouds burst open and shower their gifts of water on the plains, mountains and sands of the desert. The poet specifies by name the favourite haunts he wishes to receive their share (the Jazla mountain overlooking the well Dindān and his friends defended against Ghaṭān is mentioned in five poems). In the shapes of the clouds the poet detects many kinds of heavenly herds and game: the upright, towering white fronts of the cumulus clouds that sail through the sky trailing their black mass are compared to the white heads of the otherwise black Najdi sheep; the low driving racks in advance of the front are like gazelles darting away; and the downward curve of the fringes are likened to the necks of black camels bending to a pool of water.

*Yissi, siga dār, midāhīl* 'may the rain irrigate, drench the range' (of such and such a camel, palm gardens, tribe, loved one) is a way for

[84] In the sectional sequence of the poem this passage occupies an intermediate position between the *nasīb* proper and the camel section introduced by the marker *ya-rāčbin*. It could be considered both as a prolongation of the self-reflexive motif describing the creative process and as an independent section of *mufākharah*, viz. a celebration of the composer's poetic skills.

the poet to express his special favour or affection for the places and beings he holds dear. Alternatively, the transition towards the next section is made by the formula *yafraḥ, tafraḥ bh* 'he (the owner of palm-trees), she (the she-camel) is happy, joyful' (because of the *xēr*, the blessed gift of the clouds). For persistent, abundant rains (*wabil, waddān*) allow the thirsty soil to recover (*tirjiᶜ ad-dār*), bring a promise of good pasture for the exhausted, lean camels and give some relief to the owners of date palms from the incessant toil involved in the irrigation of the trees.

In these sections Dindān conveys a sense of the majesty and rugged scenic beauty of the desert around the Wādi. At the same time he paints his dream of that elusive paradise of the bedouins: an eternal *ribīᶜ*, spring pastures, in which the *xēr*, the 'good' is always plentiful. In one of his most exquisite poems, no. 12, composed when Dindān and his herd were severely struck by drought, the atrocious heat in which body and soul of both men and animals wilt and languish is contrasted with this land of milk and honey. The juiciness and soft surface of the greenery that sprouts in the traces of the rain stir up associations with the fragrance and smooth skin of young bedouin women. So the resuscitating powers of rain, the cornucopia of spring, and the lustfulness of all beings amidst this plenty is called forth in the poet's imagination as a spell against the desolation of the drought.

In poem no. 12 the transition from the infernal reality to the paradisiac dream—a contrast built on the use of sets of antonyms associated with drought and the spring season of plenty—is made by way of a prayer to God and a meditation on his wisdom. The devotional character of these rain poems is even more prominent in two other poems (nos. 10 and 13). Here the core of the poem, the request for rain and its imaginary fulfilment, is wedged between fervent invocations of God's bounty and his protection from the strokes of fate. Standing on the mountain top the poet feels the verses stirring inside him and sends up his prayer (13/2-4):

1. He (the poet) pronounced 'in the name of the Lord' before striking up his song, //
   And prayed to God before he began composing his verses.
2. Truly, countless were the entreaties I sent up. //
   My need was great and so was the hope I placed in His munificence.

3. O God, send us a night whose clouds are not dispersed by the winds, //
Making good on their promise with floods that rip up the bottoms of the gullies.

And ends thus (13/19-22):

1. Scorched by drought and villagers who raised the price of our staples, //
We suffered at the hands of money-lenders and their cunning.
2. May God free us and all noble souls from hardship. //
He bestows His bounty lavishly and sends down to us His blessings.
3. O Beneficent One, open one of the gates of Your throne for the flow //
Of sustenance that softens the hard, shrivelled livers;
4. He decrees the good, His is the reign and the last day. //
God's commands we must obey, He who speaks the true words.

*The Camel Section*

Camels play a central role in Dindān's life: in a sense they are his *raison d'être*. His entire existence, his pride, independence and status as a bedouin are predicated on his overlordship over his small herd. Unlike most Arabian nomads, Dindān did not choose of his own volition to switch to a semi-nomadic or fully settled life in which camel husbandry plays only an accessory part. His camels are his *māl*, all he owns in the world. He would never dream of selling them. Even when fate had pushed him with his back to the wall his fellow-tribesmen predicted that Dindān would rather die, stretched out on the ground in view of his herd, than surrender and sell his animals.

Almost a third of Dindān's poetry is devoted to descriptions of camels. These sections may be classed under two different headings: the camel as a mount and as a herd animal kept mainly for its milk. It is in his vivid descriptions of the milch camels that Dindān succeeds best in conveying his genuine feeling and deep affection for his animals. Invariably camel sections of this sort occur within the context of poems in which he sends up his entreaties to God for rain.

*Tafraḥ bh* 'she rejoices (at the rain)' or *siga, yissi* 'may (the clouds) water (the well, tribal range, haunts of such and such a camel)', are the formulas marking the transition to passages in which Dindān seems to caress his animals with a loving glance. *Ya-zīnha* 'how beautiful they are', he exclaims when he beholds them and asks God to provide for them with His *xēr* 'good', i.e. 'lush pastures', and to grant them a long and happy life.

In poems nos. 2 and 3 Dindān singles out a huge black she-camel (*malḥa, sōda*). She is affectionately attached to her master, even for a moment forgetting her calf when he calls her, and he in his turn is touched by her beauty, strength and bossy behaviour. Like a stud, her alert face and lively eyes are in all directions. On the day the herd returns from its pasture in the desert to be watered she impetuously plunges to the fore, poises herself at the trough in which the herdsman pours the water, shoves and kicks at her neighbours, and refuses to budge one inch as long as the trough is not empty. Her aggressive demeanour causes additional trouble to the *gallāṭ*, the man who comes to the well to draw water for the herd. But her rambunctious vitality and coquettish, swaying gait are his delight and he is more than ready to forgive her for any inconvenience she caused him. And indeed one day at the edge of al-Ldām, Dindān pointed to a black female with some silvery hairs glistening on her neck, an aged *prima donna*, when I asked him who was his sweetheart among his camels.

These are the camels of the herd (*ṭarš*), she-camels whose udders are netted in a thick mesh made of camel wool tied across the hip and under the tail (the *šamlah*) to prevent their young from sucking their milk. The description of these camels in the context of the rain poems makes it clear that to the poet they are a symbol of fertility.

In contrast, the sections featuring the camel as a riding animal are more closely related to the world of manly virtues (such as endurance of hunger, thirst and fatigue), the courage to venture into daring undertakings (such as the crossing of vast, waterless deserts), and qualities like strength and speed. Within the poem these sections are generally set in the context of the poem's address to the messenger who is to carry the poem to its destinee. Therefore they are mostly preceded by the transitional formula *rāčib illi* 'O rider of one (camel or motor car of such and such qualities)' or *ya-nidībi* 'O messenger of mine'.

Four poems are completely, or almost so, devoted to the joys of camel riding and descriptions of the mount (4, 7, 20, 27). One of these, no. 4, has become quite famous among the Duwāsir. Unlike the double rhyme of the other poems (i.e. one monorhyme for each of the two hemistichs being maintained throughout the poem), it is a strophic poem, rhyming according to a varying scheme in which only the rhyme of the last two syllables of each fourth hemistich is a recurrent one: AAAX, BBBX and so on. The metre of this poem consists almost exclusively of long syllables. Dindān called this type of prosodic arrangement a *mrawba*ᶜ (in reference to the rhyme scheme). The poem shows no thematic development nor the usual wealth of imagery; rather it is a poem of sheer movement, an impression strengthened by its pounding cadence and varied rhyme. Its sole function is to convey the delight the rider of this camel takes in his spirited mount as he seeks to control her wild surges and *ṣalf*, a mount's tempestuous nature and caprice the rider must vanquish and subdue to his will if he is not to be thrown off together with his gear. Therefore this poem might be considered as an independent development of the classical consolation motif. In its integrated form this same motif occurs at the end of poem no. 23, where the poet seeks to cool the flames of his amorous heart and to find diversion from his lovesickness in the excitement of a fast excursion on camel-back.

In general, however, the camel descriptions following the formula of transition *ya-rāčbin* are of a more conventional character. It would be tedious to sum up here the descriptions of the different parts of the camel's body and the accompanying similes, the hardiness and speed of the mounts, the intricate variations in their pace and so on. Much of this, even down to the finer details, corresponds to the camel sections of the early classical odes.

Although a skilled bedouin poet will add his own original touches, the representatives of the Najdi tradition sing the praises of their mounts very much in unison. One has only to run quickly through the work of the Šammari Abu Zwayyid, a poet famous for his camel descriptions in the north of Saudi Arabia, to find a striking resemblance to Dindān's verses on the subject.[85] Their camels' passion (*min mnāha*) is to traverse the deserts at a steady, strong pace. They are spirited thoroughbreds, so nervous that they shy at their own shadow. Their legs move rapidly like the wooden rollers (*maḥālah*) over a well and yet so loose and effortless is their gait as to deceive the onlooker's estimate of their speed. As they run their necks sway above the layer of quivering hot air close to the ground, like dancing and merry-making girls or like little boats driven by the wind and the current on a vast expanse of water. Their vehemence almost breaks the wooden crosspieces of the saddle. If the country slopes

---

[85] Poetry of Khalaf Abu Zwayyid has been published by as-Suwaydāʾ, ᶜAbd ar-Raḥmān, in *Min shuᶜarāʾ al-Jabal al-ᶜāmmīyīn*, Riyadh 1988, ii.

upwards the incline only challenges them to pick up their pace. And they will outstrip the other mounts when these begin to languish in the simmering heat of summer and the water-skins have become dry, safely delivering their experienced riders to their destination.

*Love Lyrics*

Dindān never married and, although it is not clear whether this was by preference or against his will, he stayed a bachelor all his life. Yet Dindān is far from insusceptible to the charm and physical attractiveness of the female sex, as his poetry shows; and I have personally witnessed how bedouin women enjoyed chatting with him and appreciated his company.

Dindān's work reflects his life as a nomad, with a particular emphasis on his camels and the conditions of their and his existence in the desert. Unlike poets living a settled life, as the famous bard of Nifi, ᶜAbdallah ibn Sbayyil, he did not have the leisure nor the frame of mind to concentrate on love lyrics (*ġazal*) as a preponderant theme. His *ġazal* therefore does not reach the level of sophistication achieved by ᶜAbdallah ibn Sbayyil and others.

In his work Dindān could not always escape the fact that *ġazal* is among the more highly conventionalized and stereotyped genres or themes of Najdi poetry. Just as there is an idealized camel mount, composed of as many ideal constituent parts, each of its traits and physical attributes individually portrayed and embellished with appropriate similes, so has Najdi poetry its idealized female. And as in the case of the camel, this ideal is very similar to the one presented by the poets of Arab antiquity. In his adoration of this effigy the poet pays homage to the female principle, which in his private mind may be connected with the real woman he fancies. But it is certainly not the purpose of *ġazal* to present a woman as an individually recognizable being.

If Najdi love lyrics as a rule remain within these confines, infringements on its conventions are quite common. For instance, the beauty who has caught the amorous attention of the poet is referred to in Najdi poetry not by name, but by the male pronoun and suffix (even though the enumeration of the attributes makes it crystal clear that the reference must be to a woman). In contravention of this principle Dindān in two poems (nos. 11 and 15) reveals the name of the object of his *ġazal*: Rasmah and a girl that listens to the letters *sīn*, *rāʾ* and *hāʾ*, i.e. Sārah.[86]

Poem no. 29 is somewhat exceptional in that it describes in plain language and without the usual veil of stereotype Dindān's chance encounter with a female acquaintance at the gates of the Meccan mosque. This poem therefore has the refreshing taste of an event not out of the wooden puppet theatre, but one that is firmly grounded in common human reality. As might be expected, this poem has not been included in Ḥmēr's edition. One may safely assume, therefore, that in Arabia a much greater amount of vivid love poetry is in circulation than one would believe by judging from what has appeared in print.

In the main it is impossible to reach any conclusions as to Dindān's personal experience in life based on the *ġazal* sections. The only glimpse I caught was a vague suggestion that he had not been able to marry a woman he loved. The reference in poem no. 11 to the adamant, hostile folk in charge of the girl he adored from afar may reflect this failure. But since it is also a conventional motif one will never know for sure—and this measure of ambiguity created by the conventionalized expression in *ġazal* poetry is a necessary precaution in a traditional society in which the exposure of a woman's identity, especially if she is a young woman waiting to be married, is considered a grave violation of the family's honour.

In the world of Dindān's poetry, one may add, female beauty and charm are part and parcel of the dream of *ribīʿ*, the fecundity of nature as it becomes manifest in the wake of life-bringing rains. The well-rounded hips and firm breasts of Rasmah remind him of nothing so much as the bulging hump of a calf sucking to his heart's content the milk of two she-camels that have adopted it as their fosterchild (poem no. 15).

Within the overall structure of the poems the *ġazal* section either comes after the description of the messenger's camel (*naṣṣah* 'steer your mount to so and so'); immediately after or within the *nasīb* and marked by the formula of transition *min ʿana*, *ʿalēk ya-* '(my suffering is) because of you, (O beauty of such and such traits)'; as part of a

---

[86] The latter way of hinting at the name of the beloved is not uncommon in Najdi poetry, but the straightforward mentioning of the name is against the rules. It is probably for that reason that the name of Rasmah has been purged from the Ḥmēr edition, see next chapter.

rain poem, *yissi* 'may (the clouds) water (the well where my love is encamped)'; or as part of the message delivered by the camel riders to the poem's destinee.

The latter arrangement is found in poem no. 24. Here the poet's complaints about his suffering on account of his sweetheart are part of *al-murāsalāt ash-shiʿrīyah*, the genre of poetic correspondence brought to greater perfection in the exchanges of poems between Ibn Sbayyil and the poet Fēḥān ibn Zirībān.[87] One minor independent piece (no. 28) consists exclusively of *ġazal*. Finally, poem no. 23 features the *aṭlāl* motif, the sorrow a poet feels when he chances upon the traces of an abandoned encampment and is reminded of the happy days spent with friends or loved ones who have departed long since. Though no explicit mention is made of an erotic motif, it occurs within the context of the *nasīb* in a manner reminiscent of the *aṭlāl* scene in classical poetry. Even the *ṭayf*, the ghost of the beloved who makes its apparition at night, is there in the form of *ḥilm al-lēl*, the nightly dream!

### *Panegyrics*

Besides the more personal store Dindān sets on his reputation as an artist, pride in his own tribe is an integral part of his self-esteem and sense of honour. *Mufākharah*, boastful panegyrics on his own tribe, the Duwāsir, is a main theme in three poems. In two of these the *mufākharah* theme flows naturally from the rain section. Following the transitional formula *yafraḥ bh* 'to the joy of' (the camels and owners of date palms), the poet continues to describe the might and courage the Duwāsir are capable of mustering in the defence of their possessions. For the Duwāsir, being both *ḥaḏar* and *baduw*, settled village-folk and nomads, believe that the palm gardens of the Wādi and their desert plains and mountains, the Haḏb ad-Duwāsir, are the envy of all surrounding tribes.

In poem no. 2 the theme is introduced by the association of the camels with the fiery horses pacing side by side with the herds, and of the horses with a scene of battle featuring a charge by the tribe's cavalrymen in order to recapture the camels taken by the enemy. Like *wa-rubba* and *wa-qad* in the classical *qaṣīdah*, the formula *ćam* (CA *kam*) 'how many' (places we conquered, enemy chiefs we

---

[87] See Sowayan (1985), 25 and 180-182.

defeated) marks the opening of this section in poems nos. 2 and 18.[88] In the latter poem Dindān recounts the legendary feats of his tribesmen as they beat off attacks by potentates like the ar-Ras͟hīd rulers of Hail and the S͟harīfs of Mecca in defence of their date palms. In a third piece of *mufāk͟harah* more specifically about the Haḍb ad-Duwāsir (poem no. 22) Dindān proudly affirms that his tribe will never allow even one rock of this desert to fall into any rival's hands. If 'wolf cries to wolf', i.e. when the tribes call together their forces in preparation for war, the Duwāsir dress in the 'cloak of purity', their honour and integrity, free from any infamy or stain that would 'blacken their face'.[89] They loosen the knots the enemy has tied in his rope, i.e. they undo and wreck the decisions and campaign plans carefully drawn up by their adversaries.

Having been taught a sharp lesson, the other tribe does not dare to come close to the Wādi and encamps at a respectful distance. What counts, however, are one's intentions—a point also made in poem no. 21 in which Dindān sets out his personal code of conduct—and when these are friendly and sincere the other tribes are welcome to be the Duwāsir's guests. For theirs are the land and noble traditions of Badrān, the ancestor of the Sudayrī family that is affiliated with the house of Saud through marriage, and of Āl Zāyid, the division of the Duwāsir that includes the population of the Wādi. These are all *ṣulb jadd*, the children sprung from the marrow of their forefathers, for it is an ancient belief that a man's offspring is stored in the marrow of his spine. As proof of their *zōd*, the feeling of superiority a tribe demonstrates in its arrogant and blustering attitude towards the other tribes, the Duwāsir did not content themselves with the mere conquest of a tribal homeland in the desert, but also took the settled lands of the Wādi. These are the feats in which the Duwāsir glorify, 'whereas others fancy themselves great warlords after capturing someone's young male camel' (18/22). 'No matter how tall one stands, we stand even taller' (2/26), is Dindān's boast.

In some poems Dindān dispatches his messenger to unspecified *bini* ᶜ*amm*, close kinsmen, or Duwāsir poets with whom he exchanges troups of gaily caparisoned riding camels—a metaphor for the poetic correspondence between Najdi poets—or friends who have run into

---

[88] Cf. the entries *ćam* and *yāma* of the glossary.
[89] See glossary under *ngy*.

trouble (poem no. 26). In the poet's laudatory address of the destinee, the *madīḥ*, the boastful panegyrics emphasize the pride in their common ancestry and the ties of kinship from which the participants in these exchanges derive their strength.

In general Dindān's words of praise are reserved first for God, then for his fellow-tribesmen and then for his own powers as a poet. Perhaps it is because of Dindān's participation in the "battle" of al-Ǵīᶜah, both in his capacity as a fighting man and as a poet, that in the two war songs he composed on that occasion (nos. 30 and 31) all these panegyrical elements have found joint expression.

## Moral Censorship and Oral Bedouin Poetry: The Ḥmēr Edition

### *The Cultural Context of Literate Intervention*

A comparison between the oral poetry of Dindān, as I recorded it, and the only existing edition of his work in Saudi Arabia throws an interesting light on the gulf that separates the world of a bedouin who has remained relatively untouched by modern developments from the religious, moral and political consciousness of his educated compatriots. It also demonstrates, if proof were needed, the helplessness of an oral artist, who economically and politically belongs to the class of the disinherited, in the face of manipulation by the powers of literacy. Dindān can make his voice heard in a literal sense, but he can only gain access to the media of large-scale reproduction and circulation at the price of a considerable loss of identity. One might draw an even more fundamental conclusion: Dindān represents the traditional bedouin, tribal outlook that has come increasingly under pressure from the official Islamic and political ethos. The edition of Dindān's work in the second volume of the anthology of Duwāsir poetry *Wāḥat a<u>sh</u>-<u>sh</u>iᶜr a<u>sh</u>-<u>sh</u>aᶜbī* (*The Valley of Popular Poetry*) by ᶜAbdallah Ḥmēr Sāyir ad-Dōsiri clearly bears the mark of this struggle to impose the orthodox view on the utterances of somewhat unreconstructed members of society like Dindān.

From a modern Western point of view such editorial interference would be judged as reprehensible. When faced with a case like this, however, one should not forget that it has taken Western enlightenment and liberalism centuries to free its literary expression from the dictates of political, religious and moral authorities. As one of the results of this successful struggle for the individual's right to freedom of expression and because of the prestige literature enjoys as the standard-bearer of this right, the need to respect the integrity of an author's work has now become enshrined as a moral imperative. But even in present times Western intellectuals are aware that these hard-fought gains are precarious and need to be guarded by constant vigilance against the ever-present danger that the old authoritarianism will reassert itself.

In Saudi Arabia, as in most other countries outside the Western experience, the situation is fundamentally different. Therefore one should pause to take into account the particularities and complexities of any given cultural environment before rushing to pass value judgments on editorial policies from a purely Western perspective. First, in spite of the mutilation Dindān's work has undergone in Ḥmēr's edition, there is no such thing as a case Dindān vs. Ḥmēr. Dindān was not even aware of the discrepancies between his oral poetry and the published edition before I arrived in the Wādi and began to question him on this point. His reaction to the discovery seemed to indicate that he did not care too much about the fate of his work in published form. Dindān told Ḥmēr that the latter's exercise of editorial discretion had been brought to his attention through me. But he certainly did not bear Ḥmēr a grudge for it and the relations between the two men, who both belong to the tribe of ar-Rijbān, seemed unaffected.

Yet Dindān has an high esteem of his own talents and takes his art with the greatest seriousness. Though unable to keep a written record of his work, each single poem was entrusted to his memory as it reached its definite form through the process of composition and was kept there as if it had been engraved in print. Poems I recorded more than once do not show any variations and Dindān made it very clear to me that he did not entertain the slightest doubts as to the exact wording and fixedness of his work in his mind. With other oral poets variations in the memorized poem may occur over time, but nevertheless it is generally accepted among the connoisseurs and the wider public that each orally composed poem does have an original version which is the authentic one.[90] In the course of my fieldwork I never met anyone who entertained any doubts as to the fact that a poem's parenthood and the responsibility for its authorship are

90 See also S. A. Sowayan (1985), 190.

attributable on a purely individual basis—even if the process of composition, committing the poem to memory, its delivery before the audience and circulation takes place entirely in oral fashion.

On the other hand one should be aware that a Najdi oral poet, unlike his literate Western and Arab colleagues, cannot develop his artistic identity by choosing *à la carte* from an almost infinite menu the cultural influences that are most suited to his individual taste and constitution. In literary culture as in other domains the Saudi oral poet is still firmly embedded in the collectivity. In his social attitudes and behaviour the individual is expected to conform to the models of tradition and the norms of convention. Therefore it is only natural that his literary expression should faithfully reflect this pattern. Indeed, an uneducated poet in the Saudi province, like Dindān, is hardly conscious that any alternatives for this pattern exist. In this sense, Najdi popular poetry always partakes of the collective experience and, once brought into circulation through the poet's audience, becomes to some extent public property. This explains Dindān's comment when it appeared in the course of our association that Ḥmēr had added a verse of his own making to the end of poem no. 2:

*hāḏa wla ngiṣ ḥadin min ṭāyil ḥgūgih* \\
*kull al-gibāyil lha ṭōlāt w-amjādi*

I say this without detracting from anyone's merits: \\
All tribes possess similar pride and glory.

The final section of this poem by Dindān is a classical piece of *mufākharah*, tribal boasting, on the historical exploits and present standing of the Duwāsir. But Dindān's claim that the Duwāsir 'stand taller' than any other tribe, though it is part of the exaggeration proper to this genre, apparently nettled his editor so that he felt compelled to add a moderating gloss. Dindān said the last verse was not his, but he did not reprove Ḥmēr for the addition. *Hu ṣādiǵ*, 'there is truth in what he said,' Dindān admitted generously.

As his poetry demonstrates, Dindān is always quick to rise to a challenge from one of his competitors in the local circuit of oral poetry. But the world of literacy is, so to speak, outside his purview. That his work is published in Riyadh and might even appear abroad leaves him indifferent. Dindān seemed to accept that the entry of his work into print was an event completely outside his reach or control which would probably be best left to men with knowledge and experience in that field. If Ḥmēr decided to cut this or add that, then so be it.

Ḥmēr, on his part, was probably motivated in his editorial interventions by the desire that no one should be able to take exception to anything that appeared in his anthology. As a promoter of the local cultural heritage and someone who keenly cultivated his relations with members of the cultural elite in the capital, Ḥmēr was mainly interested in highlighting the virtues of the Duwāsir. By leaving out or pasting over elements that in his opinion fell below the level of officially sanctioned discourse, he merely sought to forestall any criticism that would reflect negatively on him personally and stand in the way of his ambition.

But the gulf that separates Dindān's oral text from Ḥmēr's scriptural edition runs deeper than these mundane concerns. It also marks the difference between a bedouin *fiṭri*—a 'natural man' who remains faithful to his art and nomadic life as dictated by the rhythm of his inspiration and the cycle of the seasons, regardless of the consequences of his stubbornness—and a provincial intellectual who pursues an ideological agenda, if need be at the expense of truth and beauty. This explains why in his 'tidying-up' of Dindān's poetry Ḥmēr even went beyond what official censorship would have demanded.

Ḥmēr is an employee in the Department of Education in al-Khamāsīn, the administrative capital of the Wādi, who takes an active interest in Islamic missionary activities and maintains close links with the religious and political establishment of the Wādi. Ḥmēr's outlook might be called neo-Islamic rather than conservative, for he acts from the conviction that a heightened religious consciousness is a requisite for the nation's advancement. In the view of Ḥmēr, and other Dōsiris driven by this brand of idealism, negative features of life in the Wādi—such as tribal chauvinism, the incessant bickering and discord among its villages, families and tribes, the cultural backwardness of the area and new dangers like drugs and moral laxity—can only be overcome through more Islamic education.

It was probably in this spirit that Ḥmēr looked at Dindān's work. Five poems (nos. 27-31) were not included in the anthology. The two poems on the armed confrontation with Ghaṭān at the well of al-Ǵīʿah were put aside for self-evident political reasons and one piece of love lyrics (no. 29) certainly on moral grounds. What remained were twenty-six poems with a total of 519 verses. From this body of verse Ḥmēr excised about one hundred verses, whereas he added almost twenty verses of his own making (both entire lines and hemistichs of single verses) in order to achieve the right balance or to restore propriety in lieu of language he judged offensive to educated sensibility. Furthermore, he made in excess of one hundred minor changes by replacing one or more words in individual verses. The result, though in many ways different from the uncorrected oral "original", has nevertheless considerably facilitated the task of transcribing the text of the tapes I recorded.

### *Major Changes in the Oral Text*

Ḥmēr's most drastic editorial decision was the excision of sixty-five verses from a group of five poems (nos. 9, 15, 19, 21, 25). In each case the character of the poem was thereby completely altered. The passages in poem no. 9 (verses 10-17) and no. 25 (verses 11-17) in which the poet deploys his ultimate poetic deterrence against his rivals by claiming for his own art the entire universe (see pages 11-12, 22 and 60-62) must have been deleted on religious grounds. In poem no. 21 the key section on Dindān's personal bedouin code of honour (verses 20-32) is lacking in the Ḥmēr edition, whereas the preceding more conventional part concerning the whimsicality of the 'world' (*ad-dinya*) and the hope offered by faith in God and the hereafter has been maintained.

Rather more difficult to understand is the cruel deformation inflicted on two charming pieces of love lyrics. In poem no. 19 the three wonderful extended similes that are the core of this freestanding prelude (*nasīb*) have been cast aside completely (verses 4-14 and 18-24, see pages 50-51, 53-54). What remains are eight verses, including two of the three verses in which the poet addresses himself directly to his heartthrob. Moreover, the last three verses of this reduced fragment have been added by the editor, obviously with the intent to round it off with a measure of prudish morality:

1. *maḏnūn ʿēni ḥibbih axla l-muwālīf* \\
   *bēn al-bniyy ćannih shēl al-yimāni*
2. *kāmil wṣūfih ma baʿadha tuwāṣīf* \\
   *mnaffilin bēn al-ʿaḏāra z-zyāni*
3. *ʿirfi w-ʿirfih šarraf al-ḥibb tašrīf* \\
   *ḥibbin ʿala ṭūl ad-dahar ma yhāni*

1. The apple of my eye I love so dearly that others hardly count; \\
   In the flock of girls she stands out like Canopus among the stars.

2. Her beauty has attained all that perfection can attain; \\
   Lovely are the other maidens, but she has the winning touch.
3. Our acquaintance confers honour on love, \\
   A love that will remain without stain for all eternity.

Indeed, it is unthinkable that these wooden verses could have been composed by Dindān and their sole merit is that the difference between a true poet and a fabricator could not have been demonstrated more clearly.

A similar fate has befallen poem no. 15. In the Ḥmēr edition this charming and spontaneous lyrical piece of twelve verses has been pruned to a mere five lines, the last of which is Ḥmēr's personal contribution. The three introductory verses on the classical theme of the contrast between the poet's old age and his passionate, amorous heart have been omitted. Instead the Ḥmēr edition opens with the transition marked by a comparison between the playful, sprightly running of the poet's young she-camel and the singing and dancing of a group of young ladies. There three dots have come in the place of Rasmah, the name of Dindān's sweetheart. After that only the verse on the black eyes of the beauty to whom the three dots refer has been maintained—the rest of the description presumably being too carnal to the editor's taste, although Dindān's love lyrics nowhere exceed the bounds of convention. As usual Ḥmēr's own concluding verse substitutes abstract concepts for the graphic concreteness of Dindān's imagery:

*kāmlin w-mkammilin ḏ̣abiy az-zibārah* \\
*bi-l-jamāl w-bi-d-dalāl w-bi-ṯ-ṯibāti*

Complete in its perfection, the gazelle of the sands, \\
In beauty and coquetry and good sense.

Similarly, the impression left by the magnificent poem no. 12 (see pages 27 and 63) is spoilt by the deletion of verses 3-7 and 17 and the dull note added to the *ġazal*, which in the original celebrates the triumph of imagination over the hardships of bedouin life:

*ḥibbi w-ḥibbih gāṣrin dūnih al-ᶜēb* \\
*ḥibb aš-šaraf minnāk ᶜizzin w-taᶜḏ̣īm*

My love and hers stayed far from anything shameful, \\
An honourable love from a distance in pride and glory.

And the last verse added by the editor to poem no. 17 (in lieu of verses 11 and 12) is in a similar vein:

*fa-š-šaraf min bēnna ᶜihdin ᶜalayyah* \\
*wla yiᶜīb in ḥibbina fīh l-mzāḥi*

Honour between us is a covenant binding upon me, \\
But our love cannot be blamed if occasionally we speak in jest.

In poem no. 24, verses 15 and 16 were deleted and again the editor completed the poem with a verse assuring the reader that honour and pride were fully safeguarded.

*Minor changes*

Besides the major changes, some of which I have mentioned specifically, the countless minor changes introduced in the oral *dīwān* by the editor can be traced to some of the following motivations:

– A desire to correct Dindān's use of language in matters with religious connotations or having to do with the supernatural, e.g.:
*jinni* > *ṭāyir* ('jinnee' > 'bird') 4/3;
*ᶜifrīt majnūnin* > *lo kān fi l-ġadra* ('a crazy demon' > 'even in the darkest night') 8/10;
*min bidd min ṣalla w-ṣāmi* > *min al-bīḏ maxmūṣ al-ḥzāmi* ('among all those who pray and fast' > 'among the narrow-waisted beauties') 11/19;[91]
*ḥall fi ṣadri gyāmah* > *ṭār min jafni manāmih* ('all hell', lit. resurrection, 'breaks loose in my breast' > 'sweet sleep fled from my eyelid') 11/20;
*illa yirudd illi yifukk al-xawāṣīm* > *wla hu ᶜal allah kāydin ḏa at-taḥākīm* ('only He who separates sworn enemies can turn the tide' > 'for God who dispenses judgment nothing is difficult') 12/13;
*la ja n-nuwāyib nᶜāh allah m axallīha* > *la ja n-nuwāyib xaḏ allah min ᶜagab fīha* ('God's curse be upon him! I won't shrink from my grave task' > 'grave tasks must be performed, may God take him who fails to do so!'), apparently in order to avoid the strong *nᶜāh allah*, 21/4.

– Apart from the major excisions of poems and passages dealing with tribal feuding, some minor changes have been introduced for political reasons:
in poem no. 18, verse 13, *ḥākim* 'ruler' has been replaced by *ṭāmiᶜ* 'attacker greedy for booty' in order to indicate that no legitimate authority is meant, but a trespassing raider;

---

[91] Cf. Musil (1928), 135, *ana aṣūm w-aṣalli l-nāgḏāt al-ᶜaćārīš* 'I wish to fast and pray, but only in honour of beauties with loosened hair.'

in the same poem ar-Rišīdi, i.e. ar-Rashīd (the rulers of Hail), has been replaced by *al-mᶜādi* 'the aggressor', and *wi-š-širīf ibn Hāšim* 'the (Meccan) Sharīfs of the Ibn Hāshim family' by dots, 18/14 and 18/16;
as in poem no. 2, the tribal boasting of Dindān in poem no. 18 is mitigated by an additional verse which makes it clear that in reality no tribe is better than the other and that all are equals and brothers: *la mdaḥt amdaḥ rjālin tiḥūz an-nifālah miṯil ma fi l-gibāyil min ᶜzāz al-migāmi* 'if I bestow praise I intend all men who attain excellence, as men held in great esteem are to be found in any tribe.'

– To replace bedouin rudeness or plain speech with more civilized, decent expressions, e.g.:
*li-l-ᶜajāyiz* 'to old hags' has been replaced by three dots, 6/10;
*walla warāh ibn al-ḥarāmi* > *walla warāh az-zēn gāmi* ('or that scoundrel took her away' > 'or lofty motives protected her') 11/18;
the pejorative mention of *ḥaḏar* 'the settled population', in contrast to the *baduw* 'the bedouins', in verses 13/19 and 17/11 has been removed;
the vindictive connotations of the words *jōr* ('oppression, malicious rubbing in of one's superiority') and *jāyir* probably prompted their replacement by *zēnha yifrig* 'her beauty makes her different from', 15/6, and *middna jāyirin fōg al-mikāyīl dāmi* > *w-majdna kāsbīnih bi-l-fᶜūl aṭ-ṭuwāmi* ('for our measure always spites the measure of power others can muster' > 'our glory we conquer with superior deeds') 18/19;
the replacement of the hemistich describing the foreign, i.e. Christian, exporters of cars as *ćlāb*, 'dogs', by *kull šinin fōg al-jidīd mjahhzīnih* ('a new car equipped with all desirable accessories') 16/7;
*gult ana l-mōt jāni* > *kāmil al-ḥuzn jāni* ('then it was as if I would die', i.e. from lovesickness > 'I was completely overcome by sadness') 19/3;
*daġalha al-ḥurr min tāli* > *lha sabḥin w-sirbāli* ('thereupon covered forcibly by a thoroughbred stud' > 'she moves with the movements of a swimmer and at a steady pace') 20/5;
*la kān yimnāh min bōlih mwaḏḏīha* > *la kān lāšin banat lih fi ᶜalāwīha* ('even though his right hand performs his ablutions with his own piss' > 'even though he is a good-for-nothing enjoying a high position in the world') 21/16;
in verse 13 of poem no. 26 the editor has obscured the fact that the friends to whom Dindān addresses his words are in jail.

– The editor introduced many changes meant to improve on style, imagery and metre, mostly with unfortunate results.

The deletions that destroyed poem no. 19 are an example of wanton editorial interference, or perhaps the extended simile is a stylistic device that does not find favour with the editor. A similar misjudgment led the editor to move the last verse of poem no. 10 to a position between verses 3 and 4, so that the poet's prayers to God constitute one block. The effect of this intervention is that the rain and prayer sections have become less intertwined than probably was intended by the poet.

Other changes may have been prompted by the desire to correct slight irregularities in the metre, as in the second hemistich of the first verse of poem no. 8, which reads in the Ḥmēr edition: *hayyaḏ̣ ᶜalayy rijm al-ᶜana nāšiyy al-ǵīl* 'on the mountain of sorrow I felt the verses beginning to stir inside me.'

The wish to avoid repetition may be the reason that in verse 8 of poem 22 *la ᶜawa ḏībin l-ḏīb* ('when wolves howl in response to one another') was replaced by *la rtifaᶜ ṣōt an-nidīb* ('when the messenger raises his voice').

Most stylistic changes, however, seem rather arbitrary, like the replacement of *bannat ᶜḏābih* ('the scent wafting from her lips') by *bannat jidīlih* ('the scent of her tresses'). In some cases the idea may have been to approach the style closer to that of literary expression, e.g. *yiǵᶜid an-nīm* ('awakens, makes sit up the sleeping at night') > *yūgiḏ̣ an-nīm* in 12/25 and 16/3; and *tinbit al-ḥēl fi l-ḥāli* > *ḏōg ma baᶜad-ha ḥāli* ('that makes strength shoot up at once' > 'the best taste of all') 26/18.

– The Ḥmēr edition shows a general tendency to translate Dindān's bedouin "patois" into the more literary language current among the educated, e.g.:
*w-ixbar* > *w-iᶜlam*, 4/13; *le hi* > *gāmat*, 2/14.

Some lexical items used by Dindān have their roots in ancient, classical Arabic, but my questioning learnt that they are no longer understood by townsfolk like Ḥmēr, hence: *fiᶜmih* > *wablih*, 1/6; *mabnūgah* > *madlūgah* ('poured') 2/11; *haṯāyir* > *ġazāyir*, 14/9. A telling detail in this respect is the frequent change of Dindān's *fi* into the more literary *bi-*[92], e.g. *fi atlāh* > *b-atlāh* 14/16, and in 24/1,

---

[92] See also Ingham, Bruce, *North East Arabian Dialects*, London 1982, 89-91.

together with other adaptations away from the bedouin expression, as in *yġayyir ʿalayy fi nāyfāt al-mišārīfi* ('feeling out of sorts on these lofty crests') > *yigūd an-nišīd bi-ʿālyāt al-mišārīfi*.

A more humouristic instance of the misunderstandings to which interpretations of the bedouin language by townsfolk can lead is the replacement of *ḏinīn* by *dinīn* in 13/12. Ḥmēr's explanation was that *dinīn al-ʿabas* 'the tinkling of the urine' referred to the cracking sound produced by the crystallized drops of urine on the hair of the camel's tail. Dindān, however, told me that the word he used was *ḏinīn al-ʿabas* with the meaning of 'fragrance, smell of the urine-spattered tail'.

## Prosody and Language

### *Language*

The language of the poems and the short narrative sections is in essence that of the Najdi dialects as described in the existing scholarly studies on this subject.[93] Rather than repeat the available information on the linguistic characteristics of these dialects, I may refer readers who are interested in these aspects to the works concerned and limit myself to the following few remarks.

*Vowels*

Whereas in the northern dialects the short vowel *u* has been assimilated to the front vowel *i*,[94] the *u* is a regular feature of the dialect of the Duwāsir. In this respect the Dōsiri dialect resembles those of the southwest (the southern Ḥijāz) and Najrān as described by Prochazka.[95] For *gilt* in northern and central Najd, the Duwāsir say *gult*, for *gimt* they say *gumt*, and so on.

The vowel *u* occurs frequently in the imperfect of geminate verbs, as Johnstone already concluded from the Dōsiri speech in Kuwait,[96] but also in in other verbs that have a medial vowel *u* in the imperfect in Classical Arabic (CA). The following examples are found in the

---

[93] See the 'Sources of Reference' for some titles in this field.

[94] See S.A. Sowayan (1985), 149 and Prochazka, *Saudi Arabian Dialects*, London 1988, 17.

[95] 'In Najrān, and possibly in Bīshah, *u* as a phoneme occurs more extensively: *gult* "I said",' Prochazka (1988), 17.

[96] Johnstone, T.M. 'Further Studies on the Dōsiri Dialect of Arabic as Spoken in Kuwait', *BSOAS*, 27 (1964), 92.

text: *yiṣubb, yišukk, yifukk, yirudd, yiṭurr, yixuff, yiḥuṭṭ*; and *yaḏkur, yargud, yarfuḏ, yadxul, tarkuḏ, yaḏbuṭ*; and even in a verb that has medial vowel *i* in CA, *yašbuk*, and in the perfect, *kufar*.

Many geminate nouns also have the vowel *u*: *ġull, ḥurr, gunn, kull, gubb, gullihum*. Other nouns are: *gurb, surbah, xusrān, ḥugrān, šuṭrah, buṣrik, guḥguḥ, jurrah*. The reflex of the CA preposition *ᶜaqiba* is *ᶜugib* instead of *ᶜigib* in central and northern Najd. Also, the first vowel of some plurals is *u*: *ḥukkām, kurrāᶜ, šurrid, ᶜuggab*. And the plurals of the CA *fuᶜl* type: *xuḏr, šugr, ḥumr, šugḥ, zurg, ṣugᶜ, ġurr, ṣumm, guṭm, xubl*.

The 3 m. s. suffix personal pronoun is *-ih*, not *-uh*. I have rendered the feminine ending of nouns as *-ah* rather than *-ih*, though the latter is also quite common. The vowel of the prepositions *bi-* and *li-* is not *a* when linked with the definite article, as for instance in the dialect of Šammar, but is generally pronounced as *i*: *bi-l-*, *li-l-* (and not *ba-l-*, *la-l-*). Similarly, the combination of the inseparable conjunction *wāw* and the definite article does not result in *wa-l-*, but in *wi-l-*.

*Reflexes of Diphthongs*

As one might expect, the text also shows some features which enable us to identify the speech of the Duwāsir as being closely related to the dialects of central Najd. For instance, the speech of Dindān and the other Duwāsir shares one immediately recognizable characteristic with the dialect of ᶜTēbah (ᶜUtaybah): the reflex of the classical diphthong *ay* is sometimes realized as *ā*, and not *ē* as in the northern dialects, e.g. *ᶜalāha, ᶜalāna* <9/33,13/19,32d> instead of *ᶜalēha*—or as a sharp *èy*, as in *ᶜèynha* <2/9>, *ᶜèylāt* <2/25> and *šèyb al-gara* <10/13>. Also the diphthong *ay* occurs side by side with the long vowel *ē*, e.g. *ᶜayrāt* and *ᶜērāt*, *aymān* and *ēmān*.

Furthermore there is a tendency for reflexes of the CA diphthong *aw* to become the long vowel *ā* if it occurs in non-final position, though the long vowel *ō* found in other Najdi dialects and the diphthong *aw* also occur, e.g.:

*ḥāḏ* <2/11> instead of *ḥōḏ*
*ālād* <2/15> instead of *awlād*
*ārād* <2/11,13/17> < *awrād*
*jāᶜān* <9/13> instead of *jōᶜān* (CA *jawᶜān*)
*āfa* imperf. *yāfi* <11/6,16> instead of *ōfa* (CA *awfā*)
*mṣālbāt* <8/5> instead of *mṣōlbāt* < *mṣawlibāt*
*ḏālāk* <32d> instead of *ḏōlāk*

*lāla* <4/4> instead of *lōla* < *law la*
*māzūn* <22/3> < *mawzūn*

In the Duwāsir dialect the 3 m. pl. ending of the perfect verb also tends to change into *ā* when it is followed by the female suffix pronoun, e.g.:
*sāġāha* <33b> instead of *sāġōha*
*iḥtimāha* <33/18> instead of *iḥtimōha*
*farraġāha* <17/6> instead of *farraġōha*
*ḥarrikāha* <17/7> instead of *ḥarrikōha*
*ṭridāha* <32b> instead of *ṭridōha*

Besides the verb *ōḥa* (CA *awḥā*), one also finds *āḥa* <4/21>. More difficult to explain is *māxḏīn* <2/23,26> instead of *mūxḏīn*.

*Affrication*

Affrication of the reflexes of CA *qāf* and *kāf* > *g* and *k* > *ǵ* and *ć* is perhaps even more widespread in the Dōsiri dialect than in the dialects of the north. And it is certainly much more pervasive than one would conclude from the Dōsiri texts collected by T.M. Johnstone in Kuwait. Frequency of affrication is not related to any difference between the speech of bedouins and that of the settled population, but applies to all Duwāsir who live in the Wādi.[97] Of course it also goes for the area of the Duwāsir that the frequency of affrication decreases in proportion to the formality of the social context and the level of education of the speaker.

*The definite article*

Before a word beginning with a vowel and after a word ending in a vowel the definite article is *l-*, e.g.: *l-ajwād, l-arkān, l-anḏa l-buwāṭīᶜ, ᶜūj al-ḥanāya l-yābsāt*. Where the definite article precedes nouns beginning with a consonant, or comes between consonants, it is realized with a vocalic onset, *il-*, but transcribed as *al-*; occasionally the definite article is realized as *li-*, as in *ḥakāyim li-ᶜinnah* <2/15>, but is transcribed as *l-*. If the definite article occurs in combination with the conjunction *w-* it has been transcribed as *wi-l-*, as explained in the paragraph on vowels.[98]

---

[97] Johnstone (1964), 85-87. There are other differences between the dialect of the Duwāsir in the Wādi and the texts recorded by Johnstone in the Gulf, like the more frequent use of the passive verb among the former, but these will not all be discussed here in detail.

[98] Cf. Johnstone, T.M., 'Some Characteristics of the Dōsiri Dialect of Arabic as Spoken in Kuwait', *BSOAS*, 24 (1961), 272-273.

*Tanwīn*

*Tanwīn* is a common feature in Dindān's poetry and in the speech of the Dōsiri dialect.[99] The *tanwīn* is also added to nouns which correspond to CA diptotes ending in an *alif mamdūdah* and a glottal *hamzah*, like *malḥan* (CA *malḥāʾ*), *sōdan* (CA *sawdāʾ*), *xaṭlan* (CA *k͟haṭlāʾ*). Both kinds of *tanwīn* occur in *xaṭwāt sōdan snādin* <2/8>.

During performance the *tanwīn* ending *-in* is frequently assimilated to the following word, e.g.: *ḥammāytil-l-illi* < *ḥammāytin l-illi* <8/13>,[100] *Sinḥillya* < *Sinḥin lya* <2/5>, *raḥmitil-li-ḏ̣-ḏ̣uwāmi* < *raḥmitin li-ḏ̣-ḏ̣uwāmi* <18/8>. Or the *nūn* is omitted, as in *milḥil-sabrāt an-niḏar* < *milḥin l-sabrāt an-niḏar* <2/24>, *miṯil ḏību* < *miṯil ḏībin* <5/10>, *migsiyy rāʿīh* < *migsiyin rāʿīh* <5/11>, *bu ṯimāni* < *bu ṯimānin* <11/14>.

*The passive verb*

In contrast to the Dōsiri material collected by T.M. Johnstone in Kuwait, the passive forms of the verb occur quite frequently in the text.[101] The use of the 3 m. s. passive of the hollow verb in poem no. 12 is clearly related to the rhymes *-īm* and *-īb*, hence *līm, ṣīb, jīb, sīm, ḏīb*. But these forms also occur in other positions: *šīf* <24/2>, *zīd* <25/17>, *sīm* <28/1>, *xfiy* <21/8> (cf. *šriy*, Prochazka, 119), *ḥuṭṭ* <25/14> (cf. *midd*, Prochazka, 117); and the derived forms *ḥirrik* <16/4>, and *iḏḏin* <26/12> (cf. *kissir*, Prochazka, 116), *miššī* <26/22> (cf. *simmi*, Prochazka, 120); and with the suffix pronoun, *ćifīna* <26/21>, *wiṣṣīna* <30/9>.

The imperfect passive often occurs with a negation: *ma tmāḥ* <17/7> (cf. *yšāf*, Prochazka, 123), *ma yḥaṭṭ* <25/10> (cf. *ymadd*, Prochazka, 121), *wala tihda* <28/1>, *wala tiṭra* <27/14>, *la yihga bha* <30/8> (cf. *yišra*, Prochazka, 123), *la b-la tijlab* <27/14> (cf. *yiḏrab*, Prochazka, 120). And the derived forms: *ma tṭarra* <26/6> (cf. *ysamma*, Prochazka, 123), *ma yġallag* <30/1> (cf. *ykassar*, Prochazka, 121), *ma yrawwaʿ* <11/5>, *ma twāṭa* <26/5>. But it also occurs without negation: *yiḥma* <3/3>, *yiftaḥ* <30/10>, *yidna lih* <32/1>, *b-īgāl* ('it is said', where the prefix *bi-* adds a future or durative sense) <21/16>, *īḥāl* ('it is transferred') <26/24>, *yṯanna* <26/16,28/3>, *yidra bha, yiṯna bha* <30/25,27>, *tiṭwa* <33/28>,

---

99 Cf. Johnstone (1961), 264-266.

100 Cf. *ʿizwit illi* < *ʿizwitin li*, Musil (1928), 263.

101 Johnstone (1964), 90-91.

*yūxd̲o* <32a> (cf. *yūxad̲ūn, yūxad̲ōn*, Prochazka, 122), *riddan* <7/16> (cf. *zimman, sibban*, Prochazka, 117), *yinhaš* <33/4>.

*Nouns*

In the poetry the form *tifiʿʿāl*, and for the quadrilateral root *tifiʿlāl*, is found: *tiʿizzāl* <1/5>, *tinizzāl* <1/6,26/10>, *tišʿimāl* <1/11>, *tigiṣṣār* <10/2>, *tid̲ibbār* <10/10>. This form of the noun clearly functions as an energetic, but it occurs only in the position of the rhyme at the end of a line of verse. This use may therefore be confined to poetry. The reflex of the CA plural form *afʿāl* is often *faʿāl*: *xafāf* < *akhfāf*, *ʿamār* < *aʿmār*, *faʿāl* < *afʿāl*, *ʿayān* < *aʿyān*, *ʿaḏa* < *aʿḏa*, *ʿalām* < *aʿlām*, *ḥazām* < *aḥzām*, *ḥarār* < *aḥrār*.

*Adjectives*

The text shows a remarkable frequency of the *fʿāl* (CA *fiʿāl*) form for the plural adjectives, e.g. *kbār, xfāf, glāl, wt̲ān, ṭwāl, jdād, ṣḥāḥ, t̲gāl, ḥt̲āl, hbāl, rzān, ḥzān, zyān, mtān, dgāg, wsāʿ, hzāl, jlāl, nhāl, ḏʿāf*. This may be for metrical reasons. For instance, in poem no. 9 many of these plurals occur in the camel section at the beginning of a hemistich. Together with the following definite article they produce the syllabic sequence v-- that must be repeated at the beginning of each hemistich of this metre (which corresponds to the CA *aṭ-ṭawīl*).

*Particles*

The particles *la* and *lya* have a subordinating function equivalent to CA *id̲hā*, 'if, when'.[102] In this function these particles are followed by a verb in the perfect. In many cases the particle *min*, or *min* with attached suffix pronoun, is interposed, e.g. *la min jalāha* <3/16>, *la min tiṣāfag* <3/18>, *la minh aḥma* <4/11>, *lya minnih kifax* <6/21>.

In combination with the particle of negation *la*, the subordinators may also function as a conditional conjunction, e.g. *lya la ṣ-ṣarāyim* <6/21>; and, more frequently, *lāla* (a reflex of CA *law lā* which became *lōla* in the northern dialects), e.g. *lāla ḥablih* <4/4>, *lāla guww ḥlāgih* <4/13>.

The particles *la* and *lya* function not only as a reflex of *id̲hā*, but

---

[102] Cf. T.M. Johnstone (1964), 93, 'It (this particle) is the equivalent, in the dialects in which it is found, to the CA particle *id̲hā*, both as a temporal and conditional, and as a demonstrative particle.' See also Sowayan (1992), 65-72.

also of the CA preposition *ilā*, 'to, towards, as far as, till, until' (*la l-* in combination with the definite article): *min Ḏida la jiba l-Murrah* <18/9>, *min ᶜaṣir Badrān la l-jadd al-girīb* <22/3>, *min ribīᶜin la ribīᶜ* <7/13>, *min xašim Sinḥin lya l-Inčīr* <2/5>.

The negative particle *la*, often linked with *w-* to become *wla, wala*, can be repeated for emphasis: *la b-la tijlab* 'she is absolutely not on sale.'

The emphatic *b-* inserted between the first and second *la* of the last example may also be written *lāb la*. This form is probably a reflex of the CA construction *laysa bi-* or *mā bi-*. Thus *la b-ġāwīha* <7/1> may derive from the classical *lastu bi-ġāwin*. However, this compound form is now regarded as a single unit, like the construction *ma hu bi-* > *ma hūb*.[103] The same observation applies to the negation of other pronouns: *m(a) hīb* <32e>, *mānīb* <29/2>, *falānīb* <14/5>, *mānāb* <21/29>. The fact that *bi-* is no longer regarded as a separate element in the complex becomes especially clear in the context of the last example: *mānāb min hu ᶜala l-adnēn daygāni* 'we are not the kind of men to assert ourselves at the expense of our close relatives' <21/29>.

The particle *min* is commonly inserted before the personal pronoun *hu* to form a complex with the meaning of CA *man* 'one who, those who, whoever': *ᶜādāt min hu gaddam al-jūd* 'it is customary for those who practice generosity' <26/22>. *Min* also functions as a reflex of CA *man* without the addition of the pronoun, in conjunction with the vocative particle *ya-*: *w-ismaᶜu ya-min ḥaḏar* 'listen, you who were present!' <30/3>.

The temporal particle *lēn* is a reflex of CA *ilā an* 'until, till', and is followed by the perfect of the verb: *lēn riddan* <7/16>.

A typical feature of the Dōsiri dialect is the use of the assertive or syndetic particle *lē*, often in conjunction with a personal pronoun: *lē hi tšeᶜib* <2/14>, *lē hi wṣalathum* <32c>, *wlē ḏīk al-bill māxūḏtin* <32d>, *wlēh jāyyhum yamši* <33e>, *wlē hi ᶜind ḏōdha* <33g>, *wlē-hum yišūfūnah* <33i>.[104] In some cases *lē* may have the meaning of 'lo and behold', like *ya* and *lya* in the northern dialects, but generally it is less strong and functions as a syndetic particle introducing the nominal main clause following a subordinate clause introduced by

---

[103] Cf. Johnstone (1961), 281, note 1, and Prochazka (1988), 127.
[104] Cf. Johnstone (1964), 94.

the conjunction *yōm* 'when'. In the latter function it only occurs in the narrative sections.

Another characteristic particle is *alinn*, in this text always in complex with the 2 m. s. suffix pronoun, *alinnik*, and followed by the imperfect verb expressing a wish or desire, 'may you' (perhaps a reflex of CA *alā inna*, 'surely, verily'); *alinnik tᶜāwinni* <9/5>, *alinnik tǵaddīna* <14/8>.

Besides *illa*, *kūn* or *ya-kūn* is used as the equivalent of CA *illā*, 'unless, except': *kūn bi-l-ḥisna* <22/9>, *wla ᶜād minhum wāḥid ya-kūn ana* <;23>.

*Assimilation and elision*

Assimilation or elision of one of the contiguous vowels at the end of a word and the beginning of the following word is both common in rapid speech and as a stylistic feature in poetry. This tendency can be observed especially for the long vowels of *la* and *ma*, the initial short vowel of *illi* and the final *nūn* of the *tanwīn*, the conditional particle *in* and the 3 f. pl. imperfect ending of the verb. For instance, *yaṭribin la ōḥan al-ǵirmāl* ('they', i.e. the female riding camels, 'are cheered when they hear the rider's chanting') is realized as *yaṭribillōḥan*, in which the *nūn* ending of the first verb is assimilated to the *l* of *la*, while the long vowel of *la* is elided.

Examples with *illi* are (besides the complex *yalli*): *ja lli* <6/4>, *barāḥ al-fiḏa lli* <3/14>, *rakkābha lli* <8/10>.

And with the subordinator *la*: *l agbalat l-ārād* <3/17>, *l adlijat* <6/23>, *l ōḥat* <22/1>. For metrical reasons the short vowel *i* and the long vowel *ā* are elided at the beginning and end of the verb *ingiḏa* in: *la ngiḏ amrih* <16/1>.

The long vowel of the negation *ma* (which is also realized with a short vowel as *mi* or *mu*, as in *mihīb* <2/14>) is frequently elided: *mazyan* (< *ma azyan*) <10/12>, *m ansa* <21/20>, *m hīb* <32e>.

The *nūn* of the conditional particle *in* is often assimilated to the following verb if that verb begins with the consonant *r*: *ir-rfaᶜt* <11/8>, *w-ir-rikad* <23/8>.

## *Metre*

The regularity and variety of metres are further proof of Dindān's versatility and mastery of his art. His poems fully bear out the system of scansion worked out by S.A. Sowayan in the chapter on prosody and language in his *Nabaṭi Poetry*, which is a breakthrough in the search for solutions to the problems of scansion in Najdi poetry. As it would exceed the scope of this edition to repeat all the points made by Sowayan, I will refer the reader to the relevant pages of his work.

For brevity's sake a syllabic matrix has been added (pp. 92-95), showing the scansion of the first line of each poem (because of a slight irregularity in the first verse of poem no. 4 the second verse of this poem has been included), as well as the number of the metre in the 51 metrical patterns and its metre class according to the syllabic breakdown on p. 159 of *Nabaṭi Poetry*. From this it appears that Dindān's 31 poems can be divided into groups corresponding to the following classical metres (though the nomenclature of the classical Arabic prosody is not used by the Najdi *nabaṭi* poets), with the number of poems composed in the metre concerned indicated between brackets: *aṭ-ṭawīl* (10), *ar-ramal* (8), *al-basīṭ* (7), *al-madīd* (3), *al-mumtadd* (1), *ar-rajaz* (1) and one poem exclusively in long syllables.

Although only the first lines are included in the syllabic matrix, I have scanned every single line of this edition. The conclusion was that these metres are sustained throughout the poems, although minor irregularities are not uncommon.

– In essence the technique of scansion is to break down each hemistich into a sequence of long and short syllables, while dissolving the consonant clusters of the dialect and restoring the elided or metathesized vowel back to its original position to form an independent short syllable with the preceding consonant: *yᶜāwin lsāni* > *yi ᶜā win li sā nī*, *ḥimiltin* > *ḥim li tin*, *gašiltin* > *gaš li tin*, *mijizyāt* > *mij zi yāt*, *yiḥisb innih* > *yiḥ si bin nih*, *yiḥirzūn afᶜāl* > *yiḥ ri zū naf ᶜāl*. The resulting syllabic sequence will correspond to its realization when this poetry is chanted.

– In scansion the anaptyctic vowel introduced to break up a final consonant cluster, if the last consononant is a sonorant (*l, m, n, r, w, y*), is elided: *ḥašuw* is scanned as *ḥaš wi*, *rijim* as *rij mi*, *mizin* as *miz ni*, *daluw* as *dal wi*, *ᶜaṣir* as *ᶜaṣ ri*, *ḥabil* as *ḥab li*, *b-isim* as *bis mi*, *gabil* as *gab li*, *kuḥil* as *kuḥ li*, *samin* as *sam ni*.

– If a word in a non-initial position begins with an initial vowel, this vowel and the following consonant are linked to the final consonant of the preceding word to form a long syllable: *kiṯīr al-ḥaṯāyim* > *ki ṯī ral ḥa ṯā yim*; or only the vowel is linked to the final consonant to form a short syllable: *šuft ana* > *šuf ta nā*. In case the preceding word ends in a long vowel, this long vowel is reduced to a short one, as in *yamla l-maḥānīb* > *yam lal ma ḥā nīb, ʿala l-maʿna* > *ʿa lal maʿ nā, riga fi ḏ-ḏaḥa n-naššād* > *ri gā fiḏ ḏa ḥan naš šā d, lifāna l-kalām* > *li fā nal ka lām, w-šuft ana l-ḥāl* > *w šuf ta nal ḥā l*; or the final long vowel is dropped and its consonant is linked to the initial short vowel and consonant of the following word to form a closed syllable, *ma adri* > *mad rī*. As mentioned, the definite article in the dialect of the Duwāsir in many cases is *l-*, and therefore the elided initial vowel will not appear.

– An important difference with the classical metres is that in Najdi poetry a short syllable cannot be followed by another short syllable: between two short syllables there must always be no less than two but no more than three long syllables. If the restoration of the elided vowels in breaking up the consonant clusters would result in a sequence of two short vowels, the vowel of the second syllable is dropped and its consonant is linked to the preceding syllable to make it a long one: *wala bi-mxōjilāt* > *wa lā bim xō ji lāt*.

– The unit of scansion in the metrical matrix is the hemistich which is treated as one succession of long and short syllables. Therefore the boundaries of the words do not play a role in scansion and should be disregarded, as demonstrated in the following examples (if a short syllable is indicated only by a consonant the reader has to add a short vowel *i*):

<2/4> *ṭālibk lēlin saḥābih xāyiṭ ftūgih* > *ṭā lib k lē lin sa ḥā bih xā yi ṭif tū gih*

<3/19> *la ja l-ṭarš al-wrūd mn aḏ-ḏma ṣarrah* > *lā jā l ṭar šal w rū dim naḏ ḏ mā ṣar rah*

<6/9> *yalli balēt bh r-rxūm al-buwālīʿi* > *yal lī ba lē tib har r xū mal bu wā lī ʿī*

<6/34> *tarāh ar-risīn lya gṭaʿann an-nibābīʿi* > *ta rā har ri sī nil yag ṭa ʿan nan ni bā bī ʿī*

<7/7> *wi-l-xafāf mn ar-rṯūm mdarramāt* > *wil xa fā fim nar r ṯū mim dar ra māt*

<8/5> *fajj an-nḥūr mṣālbāt aš-šilīli* > *faj jan n ḥū rim ṣā l bā taš ši lī lī*

<9/26> *tigūl al-wrūk mn aḥmar az-zall maćsiyyah* > *ti gū lal w rū kim naḥ ma raz zal l mać siy yah*

<9/28> *tšādi s-sbāʿ wjīh l-anḏa wi-hinn azyān* > *ti šā dis s bā ʿū jī h lan ḏa wi hin naz yān*

<9/33> *tifukk al-ʿṣiyy mn aḏ-ḏlāf aš-šimāmiyyah* > *ti fuk kal ʿi ṣiy yim naḏ ḏ lā faš ši mā miy yah*

<26/9> *tšīl al-ḥmūl fḥūlha min rćāb ʿmān* > *t šī lal ḥ mū lif ḥū l hā min r ćā biʿ mān*

The following additional points can be made with regard to scansion:

– When they close a syllable the long vowels *ī* and *ū*, being equivalent to *iy* and *uw*, may be dissolved into two short vowels, the first of which forms a short syllable with the preceding consonant, while the second semi-vowel functions as a consonant to open the next long syllable CVC: *ḥasbi allah* is scanned as *ḥas bi yal lah* <6/5>, *ʿindi dʿiyyah* as *ʿin di yid ʿiy yah* <9/17>, *walad xāli illi* as *wa lad xā li yil lī* <9/35>, *widdi afḏīha* as *wid di yaf ḏī hā* <21/3>. The reverse, *yi* becoming *ī*, is also possible: *labadd yišīn tālīha* > *la bad dī šī n tā lī hā* <21/14>. Or in the case of the long vowel *ū*: *hu aṣ-ṣādig al-gīli* > *hu waṣ ṣā di gal gī lī* <13/22>.

– The vowel of the first syllable of the verbs corresponding to the CA derived forms *tafaʿʿala* and *tafāʿala* is frequently treated as a long vowel if the verb occurs at the beginning of a hemistich: in *tarāyaʿat* <1/12,2/19>, *talāfitat* <2/19>, *tahajjifat* <19/5>, *taxāzarat* <19/13>, *taxāṭifōhum* <19/23> the first syllable *ta* is therefore scanned as *tā*.

– In general the poet has a certain latitude in the treatment of the vowel of the first syllable of a hemistich. For instance, in *ʿarīdt* <2/11>, *wala* <3/21>, *ašūf* <12/5>, *ubūy* <21/20>, *ʿala* <31/13,14> this vowel is long according to the metrical scheme.

– On the other hand the long vowel of the subordinator *la* is sometimes treated as short, e.g. in *la jarr aṣ-ṣōt* <2/8>, *la kān ḥwārha ġādi* <2/13>. At the beginning of a hemistich the second syllable of *ya-llah* or *wallah* is sometimes short according to the poem's pattern of scansion (17/1,23/13,30/1,18).

– In metres beginning with a short syllable, followed by two long ones (corresponding to the classical *aṭ-ṭawīl*), the short syllable is sometimes omitted and the line begins with two long syllables, e.g. *ya-lajj*, *ya-tall*, *ya-llāh* <6/7,8,9>.

– Normally every syllable in the scansion matrix begins with a consonant. At the beginning of a hemistich, however, a syllable may open with a vowel (for instance, the definite article *al-*) and be counted as long: *anḥēt ʿugbih* <3/2>, *illi yǵaddi* <3/5>, *al-mjāmiʿ* <5/4>, *asḥamin* <5/7>, *in dabbarat* <8/3>, *as-sāg* <8/6>, *illi ġadat* <12/8>, *ilʿabi* <15/5>, *al-bārḥah* <21/1>, *al-baḥar* <25/3>, *anšdik* <25/7> and so on.

– If the poet has added the conjunction *w-* to the beginning of a hemistich and this *w-* does not fit the metre, I have nevertheless included it in the transcription. In these cases the *w-* is no more than the vocal acccompaniment of a pause, affording the poet a moment of respite from the strain of recitation, and it should be omitted in scansion.

– Often a long vowel *ā* is added to the preposition *maʿ* (CA *maʿa*) in order to fulfil the requirements of the metrical scheme: *maʿa wajhih sirīʿ* <5/9>, *maʿa milḥāz rīʿ* <5/10>, *maʿa jahhāl* <6/8>, *maʿa bīḏ al-ḥzūm* <6/27>.

– At the beginning of a hemistich the geminated consonant of *ćann* (< CA *ka-anna*) is often treated as a single *nūn* for the sake of scansion: *ćan rāsha* <3/19>, *ćan sana ʿēnih* <5/8>, *ćan miḏāriʿha* <7/6>, *ćan ḥamar ʿyūnha* <7/10>, *ćan ġawāribha* <7/11>.

– The *nūn* of the ending of the 3 f. pl. of the perfect (*-an*), the imperfect (*-in*), the suffix pronoun (*-hin*), and the subordinator *la min* are frequently geminated for the purpose of scansion: *la minn arham* <4/3>, *lya gṭaʿann* <6/34>, *yšādinn al-buwāćīr* <9/18>, *ʿaṯānīn-hinn mtān* <9/19>. The same remark applies to the *s̲h̲īn* ending of *wiš* ('what') > *wišš* <21/12,23/6>.

### *Rhyme and Tone-Colour*

Unlike classical Arabic poetry, which has only one rhyme at the end of the second hemistich, Najdi poetry has a double monorhyme: one for the first hemistich and another for the second. The only exceptions in Dindān's poetry are the strophic *mrawbaʿ* poem (no. 4, see pp. 65-66 and Sowayan, *Nabaṭi Poetry*, 174) and the *ramal* poems nos. 7 and 27, which have one rhyme only for the end of each verse and an irregular rhyme for the first hemistichs. Like classical poetry, the two poems recited by Dindān in his capacity as a transmitter have only one single rhyme, which is an indication that they may have been composed more than a century or even centuries ago.

The rhyming consonants (*ar-rawiyy*) of greatest occurrence are the *nūn* and *lām* (more than a third of the total number), followed by *mīm, rāʾ* and then *ḥāʾ*. In five poems the *rawiyy* is the same in the first and second hemistichs, while the *ridf*, the preceding vowel, and/or the prolongation of the *rawiyy*, are different. The first two rain poems not only have the same metre, but also nearly identical rhymes (see pp. 24-25).

In the introduction to two poems (nos. 8 and 11) Dindān states that they were composed as an elaboration on or in response to (*banēt ᶜalāha, raddēt bih*) verses said by another poet and illustrates this with a brief quote from their verses. In both cases Dindān has followed the rules of poetic correspondence by using the same metre and rhyme as those adopted by the poet whose verses inspired his own.[105] The element of artistic contest inherent in poetic correspondence is further demonstrated by Dindān's mimicking the wordplay of the other poet's first verse in the second verse of poem no. 8: *ya-rāćbin ḥīlin ḥalāḥīl ḥīli, wi-lya mišan yašdin ṣifīf al-maḥāḥīl* is echoed by *ya-rāćbin jillin jahājīl jīli, miṯl an-naᶜām ar-rubd jillin jahājīl* of Dindān's second verse.

Like other *nabaṭi* poets, Dindān delights in the euphonic effects of such florid alliterative sequences, together with the repetition of consonant-vowel combinations in medial and final positions, to which Arabic phonology so eminently lends itself. The verses 2-6 of one poem, no. 26, are especially remarkable for the tone-colour achieved by the density of the poet's employment of rhetorical devices (alliteration, assonance, consonance, internal rhyme) in order to create an impression of modulated sound harmony. Though this passage is exceptional for its exuberant sound-manipulation, there is no dearth of similar auditory effects in the rest of this and other poems: *aš-šifa wi-š-šifag* <26/8>; *ṣifīfin ṣirīf* <26/9>; the concentration of pharyngeal and uvular sounds in verses 23 and 24 of the same poem; the soothing, swaying tone-colour of *tizaᶜzaᶜ tizūzāᶜ* <24/5>[106]; the energetic, bounding impression conveyed by *xazz w-fazz w-nazz w-rāḥi* <4/24>; *harrābtin-ḥarrābtin* <3/17>; the hissing and sliding sounds *s, z, š* in the first hemistich of <27/13>; the repetition of the voiceless dental emphatic *ṭ* and *r* in <30/12>—these are but a few examples of sound effects reinforcing the expressiveness of these verses. One's appreciation of such virtuosic displays is, of course, a matter of taste. There

---

105 See Sowayan (1985), 180.

106 Cf. Musil (1928), 151: *ća-zīᶜzāᶜ mzawwaᶜin yōm yinzāᶜ*.

is no doubt, however, that in the judgment of Dindān and his local audience these euphonic effects, in addition to the metre and rhyme, provide further proof of the poet's technical mastery and skill as an artist.

### *Matrix of Scansion*

This matrix is based on a metrical analysis of the opening lines of Dindān's poems. Only in the case of poem no. 4, which consists of long syllables with the exception of nine short syllables, the second verse has been substituted. The same metre is maintained throughout the poem. Where a short syllable is indicated only by a consonant, a short vowel *i* (either the elided vowel or an additional short vowel *i*) should be inserted after the consonant. The syllabic arrangement of each opening verse is followed by a number referring to the syllabic breakdown of metres on p. 159 of S.A. Sowayan's *Nabaṭi Poetry* and the corresponding classical metre.

1. *d̲abbēt rijmin bana r-riḥmān šihgūgih:*
   *d̲ab bē t rij min ba nar riḥ mā n ših gū gih*
   *rijmin xala l-asmar al-jinḥān midhāli:*
   *rij min xa lā las ma ral jin ḥā n mid hā lī*
   36, *al-basīṭ*.
2. *d̲abbēt rijmin d̲aḥan f aˁla ḥaja tōgih:*
   *d̲ab bē t rij min d̲a ḥan faˁ lā ḥa jā ṭō gih*
   *taṣfiġ ˁalāwi ġrūgih bard l-anwādi:*
   *taṣ fiġ ˁa lā wī ġ rū gih bar d lan wā dī*
   36, *al-basīṭ*.
3. *d̲abbēt fi nāyfin ˁizzīl min ġarrih:*
   *d̲ab bē t fī nā yi fin ˁiz zī l min ġar rih*
   *midhāl sumr al-wḥūš ummāt jinḥāni:*
   *mid hā l sum ral w ḥū šum mā t jin ḥā nī*
   36, *al-basīṭ*.
4. *yāṭa bi-fjūj al-ḥizmāni:*
   *yā ṭā bif jū jal ḥiz mā nī*
   *ma yind̲ād illa bi-l-lāḥi:*
   *mā yin d̲ā dil lā bil lā ḥī*
   51.
5. *bādyin rijmin l-ṣalf al-hawa fōgih wušīm:*
   *bā di yin rij min l ṣal fal ha wā fō gih wu šīm*
   *jiˁl yissinnih ruwāyiḥ maxāyīl ar-ribīˁ:*
   *jiˁ l yis sin nih ru wā yiḥ ma xā yī lar ri bīˁ*
   32, *al-madīd*.
6. *riga fi d̲-d̲aḥa n-naššād fi ˁāliy al-mihlāl:*
   *ri gā fid̲ d̲a ḥan naš šā d fī ˁā li yal mih lāl*

*lya ḏāg ṣadrih sanna*ᶜ *al-gāf tasnī*ᶜ*i:*
*l yā ḏā g ṣad rih san na* ᶜ*al gā f tas nī* ᶜ*ī*
27, *aṭ-ṭawīl.*
7. *al-galam hātih tara* ᶜ*indi kalām:*
*al ga lam hā tih ta rā* ᶜ*in dī ka lām*
*la b-ġāwīha wala bi-mxōjilāt:*
*lā b ġā wī hā wa lā bim xō ji lāt*
13, *ar-ramal.*
8. *ḏabbēt rijmin zād ġulli ġalīli:*
*ḏab bē t rij min zā d ġul lī ġa lī lī*
*lēn hu ḏā*ᶜ *ar-rāy wi-*ᶜ*mōmas al-ģīl:*
*lē nih w ḏā* ᶜ*ar rā y wi*ᶜ *mō ma sal ģīl*
48, *aṭ-ṭawīl.*
9. *ana hāḏ ma bi* ᶜ*ūḏ bi-llah min aš-šayṭān:*
*a nā hā ḏ mā bī* ᶜ*ū ḏ bil lah mi naš šay ṭān*
*afaṣṣil* ᶜ*ala šaffi b-kēfi wala fiyyah:*
*a faṣ ṣil* ᶜ*a lā šaf fī b kē fī wa lā fiy yah*
27, *aṭ-ṭawīl.*
10. *ḏabb aḏ-ḏaḥa n-naššād* ᶜ*āli l-amāṯīl:*
*ḏab baḏ ḏa ḥan naš šā d* ᶜ*ā lī la mā ṯīl*
*rijmin yhayyiḏni* ᶜ*ala li*ᶜ*b l-afkār:*
*rij min y hay yiḏ nī* ᶜ*a lā li*ᶜ *b laf kār*
48, *aṭ-ṭawīl.*
11. *bādyin rijmin ṯimānīn alf gāmah:*
*bā di yin rij min ṯi mā nī nal f gā mah*
*w-afṭar illi min jimī*ᶜ *al-gāf ṣāmi:*
*waf ṭa ril lī min ji mī* ᶜ*al gā f ṣā mī*
14, *ar-ramal.*
12. *dann al galam w-iktib kalām at-ta*ᶜ*ājīb:*
*dan nal ga lam wik tib ka lā mat ta* ᶜ*ā jīb*
*gāfin nḥalli bih* ᶜ*ala gōlt al-mīm:*
*gā fin n ḥal lī bih* ᶜ*a lā gō l tal mīm*
48, *aṭ-ṭawīl.*
13. *riga fi ḏ-ḏaḥa n-naššād fi margibih la* ᶜ*ād:*
*ri gā fiḏ ḏa ḥan naš šā d fī mar gi bih lā* ᶜ*ād*
*riga fi ṭiwīl mgawwarāt al-ma*ᶜ*āzīli:*
*ri gā fī ṭi wī lim gaw wa rā tal ma* ᶜ*ā zī lī*
27, *aṭ-ṭawīl.*
14. *ana bādiyin fi rās rijmin m abi margāh:*
*a nā bā di yin fī rā s rij min ma bī mar gāh*
*ḥadāni* ᶜ*ala* ᶜ*āli marāģībih al-gīli:*
*ḥa dā nī* ᶜ*a lā* ᶜ*ā lī ma rā ģī bi hal gī lī*
27, *aṭ-ṭawīl.*
15. *šāybin wi-l-galb yarji fi l-biḏārah:*
*šā yi bin wil gal b yar jī fil bi ḏā rah*
*widdih innih yirji*ᶜ *illi kān fāti:*
*wid di hin nih yir ji* ᶜ*il lī kā n fā tī*
14, *ar-ramal.*

16. *ya-wijūdi gāᶜidin wi-s-sadd bāḥi:*
*yā wi jū dī gā ᶜi din wis sad d bā ḥī*
*la ngiḏ amrih wi-ṣ-ṣalāḥ mᶜaṭṭilīnih:*
*lan gi ḏam rih wiṣ ṣa lā ḥim ᶜaṭ ṭi lī nih*
14, *ar-ramal.*
17. *ya-llah la tajzāć bi-l-xēr inkiriyyah:*
*yal la lā taj zā ć bil xē rin ki riy yah*
*ġaṭrifat m adri tinīḥ aw hi tnāḥi:*
*gaṭ ri fat mad rī ti nī ḥaw hī t nā ḥī*
14, *ar-ramal.*
18. *šarraf aš-šāᶜir ad-Dindān rijmin l-ḥālih:*
*šar ra faš šā ᶜi rad din dā n rij min l ḥā lih*
*gāl šaffih b-kēfih min ḥasīn al-kalāmi:*
*gā l šaf fih b kē fih min ḥa sī nal ka lā mī*
43, *al-mumtadd.*
19. *ᶜAbdallah ad-Dindān ḏabb al-mišārīf:*
*ᶜab dal la had din dā n ḏab bal mi šā rīf*
*rijmin taġašwāh al-xyāl ar-rzāni:*
*rij min ta ġaš wā hal x yā lar r zā nī*
48, *aṭ-ṭawīl.*
20. *ya-rāćib illi tibūj al-xāwiy al-xāli:*
*yā rā ći bil lī ti bū jal xā wi yal xā lī*
*min ᶜāširin jaddha taḏrib bh an-nāsi:*
*min ᶜā ši rin jad d hā taḏ rib b han nā sī*
36, *al-basīṭ.*
21. *al-bārḥah sāhrin wi-n-nōm ma jāni:*
*al bā r ḥah sā h rin win nō m mā jā nī*
*ma targud al-ᶜēn la ḥall al-ģida fīha:*
*mā tar gu dal ᶜē n lā ḥal lal ģi dā fī hā*
36, *al-basīṭ.*
22. *rāćib illi ma baᶜad dawwaraw fīha l-ḥalīb:*
*rā ći bil lī mā ba ᶜad daw wa raw fī hal ḥa līb*
*l ōḥat al-laᶜᶜāb tarmaḥ simārat ḏillha:*
*lō ḥa tal laᶜ ᶜā b tar maḥ si mā rat ḏil l hā*
32, *al-madīd.*
23. *šarraf ad-Dindān fi rijmin biyāni:*
*šar ra fad din dā n fī rij min bi yā nī*
*hayyaḏ illi ḥālf innih ma yġanni:*
*hay ya ḏil lī ḥā l fin nih mā y ġan nī*
14, *ar-ramal.*
24. *ana bādiyin fi margibin w-alᶜan aš-šayṭān:*
*a nā bā di yin fī mar gi bin wal ᶜa naš šay ṭān*
*yġayyir ᶜalayy fi nāyfāt al-mišārīfi:*
*y ġay yir ᶜa lay fī nā yi fā tal mi šā rī fī*
27, *aṭ-ṭawīl.*
25. *ya-nidībi w-irtiḥil bint an-naᶜāmah:*
*yā ni dī bī wir ti ḥil bin tan na ᶜā mah*
*ma ywaṭṭi rāsha tall al-xṭāmi:*

*mā y waṭ ṭī rā s hā tal lal x ṭā mī*
14, *ar-ramal.*
26. *ana hāḏ ma bi ʿūḏ bi-llah min aš-šayṭān:*
*a nā hā ḏ mā bī ʿū ḏ bil lah mi naš šay ṭān*
*kalāmin yšālīni w-ana ḏāyiġin bāli:*
*ka lā min y šā lī nī wa nā ḏā yi ġin bā lī*
27, *aṭ-ṭawīl.*
27. *šarraf ad-Dindān rijmin fi Sdēr:*
*šar ra fad din dā n rij min fī s dēr*
*hayyiḏih ma gīl fi ʿirḏih w-gāl:*
*hay yi ḏih mā gī l fī ʿir ḏih w gāl*
13, *ar-ramal.*
28. *ya-dāntin min liḏīḏ al-milḥ madhūnah:*
*yā dā n tin min li ḏī ḏal mil ḥ mad hū nah*
*la sīm fīha wala tihda bi-l-aṯmāni:*
*lā sī m fī hā wa lā tih dā bi laṯ mā nī*
36, *al-basīṭ.*
29. *ḥasbi ʿal illi daʿāni lēn nābētih:*
*ḥas bī ʿa lil lī da ʿā nī lē n nā bē tih*
*bēn al-ʿamad wi-l-migām w-bēn l-arkāni:*
*bē nal ʿa mad wil mi gā mū bē n lar kā nī*
36, *al-basīṭ.*
30. *ya-llah yalli tiksir al-ʿaḏm w-innih ša jibar:*
*yal la yal lī tik si ral ʿaḏ m win nih šā ji bar*
*ṭālbīnik ṭalbitin ma yġallag bābha:*
*ṭā l bī nik ṭal bi tin mā y ġal lag bā b hā*
32, *al-madīd.*
31. *aš-šāʿir ad-Dindān ġanna w-iftikar:*
*aš šā ʿi rad din dā n ġan nā wif ti kar*
*bētin ʿala l-maʿna yruddih bi-l-fiṣāḥ:*
*bē tin ʿa lal maʿ nā y rud dih bil fi ṣāḥ*
22, *ar-rajaz.*

# TEXT AND TRANSLATION

## POEM 1[1]

Metre:--v--v---v---(*al-basīṭ*)

*jāna wagt w-gumna naṭlib allah bi-r-rajiᶜ, agūl:*

1. *ḏabbēt rijmin bana r-riḥmān šihgūgih*
*rijmin xala l-asmar al-jinḥān midhāli*
2. *rijmin jinūbin mn aṣ-Ṣuwwān min fōgih*
*ᶜugb al-ᶜarab ma wiṭa fi d-dār nazzāli*
3. *ya-mall galbin tniff an-nūd ṭārūgih*
*niff aḏ-ḏaᶜaf min ġadīrin taww ma sāli*
4. *ya-llah b-lēlin ḥagūgin taṣifǵ brūgih*
*yardim ᶜagābih rizīnin fīh zilzāli*
5. *yimṭir min al-Ḥazim la l-Mīᶜāl w-wsūgih*
*ᶜala n-Nuwāṣif ribābih lih tiᶜizzāli*
6. *fiᶜmih ᶜala l-irǵ šaggag rās ṣiᶜfūgih*
*yanṯir ᶜala š-Šagg wablih lih tinizzāli*
7. *yafraḥ bh illi ᶜyādih ma wifa sōgih*[2]
*w-tirjiᶜ bh illi min al-migrāb hizzāli*
8. *šōlin ḥalāya rǵāb aṣ-ṣēd bi-ᶜnūgih*
*ḥimm aḏ-ḏra lli ṯimanha dāyman ġāli*
9. *sūd al-wubar ka-l-faḥam nayyah bana fōgih*
*šīb al-ᶜaṯānīn w-allah ma lha mṯāli*
10. *ya-zīnha jiᶜlha bi-l-xēr marzūgah*
*šīb al-gara jiᶜlha llah ṭūl l-amhāli*

---

[1] In this poem and the following one the rhyme of the first hemistich is *-ūgih*, or *-ōgih* (because 'as a result of the monophthongization of diphthongs, *ū* and *ō* can serve interchangeably as *ridf*, as can *ī* and *ē*,' S.A. Sowayan (1985), 162). When the end of the rhyme is not the 3 m. s. pronominal suffix, but the feminine ending of the noun, I have brought out the distinction by transcribing it as *-ah*, not *-ih*. The distinction corresponds to a similar, albeit very slight, difference in Dindān's pronunciation.

[2] *ma wifa sōgih*: it was explained to me that the date palms must be irrigated during the first hundred nights after the date harvest, *aṣ-ṣarām*, in the season of *aṣ-ṣfiri*, autumn, and not during the rest of the winter. If a good amount of rain fell in those hundred days the man in charge of the irrigation who draws the water from the well with the help of a camel especially trained for that purpose, *as-sānyah*, could relax for a while because the palms had already been watered by the rain.

## POEM 1

We were visited by drought and we began imploring God to send us the life-bringing rain. This is what I said:

1. I climbed a rock, a high pinnacle modelled by the Merciful, //
   A lonely rock which dark-winged falcons made their abode,
2. A rock beyond aṣ-Ṣuwwān towards the south; //
   Since the bedouins broke up camp no newcomers have tread its soil.
3. O my heart, that is swept by the howling winds, //
   As foam and dust are blown from the surface of a desert pool left by a torrent.
4. O God, grant us a night with the promise of flashing lightning //
   And heavy clouds, their backs piling up into a rumbling cumulus.
5. They bring rains from al-Ḥazim to the ridges of al-Mīʿāl mountains; //
   Over an-Nuwāṣif one shower after another trails its shrouds;
6. Its violent gushes tear into the fine crests of the sand-dunes //
   And on aš-Šagg the downpour splashes with thundering force,
7. To the joy of cultivators who were toiling to irrigate their majestic palms from wells, //
   And refreshing camels, weakened by pasturing far from water in the hot season;
8. Camels with necks as graceful as those of gazelles //
   And dark backs, animals always commanding high prices,
9. Well covered with fat and their woolly hair coal-black
   With some silvery ones behind their ears; by God, they are matchless!
10. These fine animals, may they be blessed with happiness; //
    Those greyish backs, may God grant them a long life!

11. *ćan ṣōtha l agbalat li-l-ḥašuw masyūgah*
*ṣōt ar-raᶜad fi ǵinīfin lih tišᶜimāli*
12. *la ᶜawwiṭat bi-l-ḥanīn w-gult maḏyūgah*
*tarāyaᶜat l-awwalāt l-jillha t-tāli*
13. *hajjat ᶜalāha xfāf al-ḥašuw maṣfūgah*
*ćanha širīfin yisīr b-jamᶜ jihhāli*
*w-salāmatkum.*

## POEM 2[3]

Metre:--v--v---v---(*al-basīṭ*)

*naṭlib allah bi-r-rajiᶜ*

1. *ḏabbēt rijmin ḏaḥan f aᶜla ḥaja ṭōgih*
*taṣfiǵ ᶜalāwi ġrūgih bard l-anwādi*
2. *rijmin širīfin ᶜala l-amṯāl ṣāᶜūgih*
*hayyaḏ jidīd al-ᶜana margāh la ᶜādi*[4]
3. *ya-llāh yalli giṭīb ᶜrāh māṯūgah*
*ya-ġāfir aḏ-ḏanb ya-xallāg ya-hādi*
4. *ṭālibk lēlin saḥābih xāyiṭ ftūgih*[5]
*ćann at-thāmi ḥamārih fīh mingādi*
5. *ćann al-mišāᶜīl bēn al-mizin wi-sḥūgih*
*min xāsim Sinḥin lya l-Inćīr min ġādi*
6. *tiṣbiḥ mzūnih ᶜala l-Jazlāt madfūgah*

---

[3] Nineteen verses of this poem have been included in *Min as̲h̲ᶜār ad-Dawāsir*, a collection of Dōsiri poetry published by al-Fiṣām, Maḥbūb ibn Saᶜd ibn Mudawwis ad-Dōsirī, with notes and commentary by Abū ᶜAbd ar-Raḥmān ibn ᶜAqīl aẓ-Ẓāhirī, Riyadh 1989-1990, i, 301-304. Besides the omission of a number of verses, this version differs in details from my recorded text and that of the Ḥmēr edition.

[4] In the *nasīb* of Najdi poetry the verb *hāḏ* 'to be stirred' and its derived forms *hayyaḏ* and *tahayyaḏ* commonly link the emotional state of the poet to the process of artistic creation (cf. CA *hāḍa* 'to renew the pain' as in *hāḍa al-ḥuzn qalbah* 'his heart was afflicted by grief time and again').

[5] Cf. *tarfi mrīḏāt an-nisāyim ftūgih* 'balmy winds mended the openings between the clouds', i.e. made them into a seamless deck, K̲h̲amīs, ᶜAbdallah ibn Muḥammad ibn, *al-Adab as̲h̲-s̲h̲aᶜbī fī Jazīrat al-ᶜArab*, Riyadh 1982, 246.

11. When one of them rushes to the calves, driving them in front of her, //
Her grumbling is like the thunder in a cloud throbbing with flashes;
12. And when she utters a plaintive, murmuring sound as if in distress,//
The camels pacing in front pause and look around to the big animals behind,
13. While the young ones rejoin her in a startled canter as if slapped by her voice. //
So she strides in the herd, like a prince amidst a throng of doughty warriors.

## POEM 2

We asked God for the life-bringing rain:

1. In the morning hours I climbed a rock, to its very pinnacle, //
Where a cool breeze blows through the crevices,
2. A rock from where one has an unbounded view over the other landmarks; //
There sorrow welled up in me with renewed force: Wish I hadn't climbed that peak!
3. O God, He whose strong knots are well secured, //
O Forgiver of sin, Creator and man's Guide!
4. From You I ask for a night decked with seamless clouds, //
Like swarms of red Tihāmah locusts, coming in wave upon wave;
5. Thunderclouds, as if lit up by torches, striking down with force //
From the edge of Sinḥ's headland and beyond it to al-Inćīr;
6. Clouds that are pushed along to al-Jazlāt, //

*gāmat ta<sup>c</sup>āgab <sup>c</sup>alēh al-mizin l-arkādi*[6]

7. *lēlih <sup>c</sup>arūḏin yigūd an-nās bi-brūgih*
*w-illi yi<sup>c</sup>iddih miḏannih ma ga<sup>c</sup>ad wādi*
8. *tafraḥ bh illi l jarr aṣ-ṣōt maṭfūgah*[7]
*xaṭwāt sōdan snādin ḥajzaha bādi*
9. *aṯfānha ma tḥiss al-baṭin mafhūgah*
*miṯil al-faḥal <sup>c</sup>ēnha fi kull mingādi*
10. *xaṭlan mn ar-rijil sōd al-lōn ma<sup>c</sup>nūgah*
*ćan rāsha bādyin fi r-rijim bi-ynādi*
11. *<sup>c</sup>arīḏt al-matin tašrab kull mabnūgah*
*tarka l-hal ḥāḏha fi yōm l-ārādi*
12. *tirzim ly ōḥat ṣibīb ad-daluw maslūgah*[8]
*w-tafra<sup>c</sup> w-taḏra<sup>c</sup> wala li-ḏ-ḏarb tinḏādi*
13. *<sup>c</sup>aššāgtin ti<sup>c</sup>šig al-gallāṭ ma<sup>c</sup>šūgih*
*tamlah w-tazlah la kān ḥwārha ġādi*
14. *la warridat hārbin ma hīb malḥūgah*
*lē hi tsē<sup>c</sup>ib <sup>c</sup>ala min kān warrādi*

---

[6] *ta<sup>c</sup>āgab* for *tita<sup>c</sup>āgab*, cf. Prochazka (1988), 48, *taxānag*, 3 f. s. imperf. of the VI form of the verb. In the Najdi dialects the 3 f. s., 2 f. s. and 2 pl. personal prefixes of the V and VI forms of the imperf. verb are elided, Prochazka (1988), 45.

[7] *l* for the subordinating particle *la*. The long vowel is pronounced as a short one for the sake of metre.

[8] *ly*, the long vowel of *lya* has merged with the initial long vowel of *ōḥat*.

One heavy cloud rolling in the wake of the other,

7. A vast darkness, its flashes of lightning pointing the way to the inhabitants of the land.[9] //
Those who pass on the message report that not a wadi missed out,
8. To the joy of a she-camel that comes at full trot when called, //
One of those big, black animals with a bulging hump;
9. The callous spots on the knees of her hind legs are spaced outward, never touching her belly;//
Like a stud camel her imperious gaze ranges in all directions.[10]
10. Her legs are long, her colour is black and her neck slender, //
Crowned by a head like a man who shouts warning cries on top of a knoll; [11]
11. A broad-backed animal that gulps down water by buckets full, //
And when the camels are being watered, she leans against the men who are filling the trough.
12. When she hears the sound of water being splashed into it from the bucket she roars; //
By pushing and shoving she muscles her way to it, indifferent to the blows she gets.
13. She loves the man who is sent to draw the water and he is fond of her; //
At a fast trot she comes, undisturbed, though her young is elsewhere;[12]
14. When she rushes to the watering place no other camel keeps up with her; //
With a festive, swinging gait she heads straight for the man at the well.[13]

---

[9] The distant lightning tells the bedouins where rain is likely to have fallen and where as a consequence edible plants and grasses will shoot up in the wake of the rains, see glossary under *xyl*.

[10] If the callous spots are too close to the body they will chafe the belly with every step. A stud camel's bossy gaze constantly ranges over the herd as he jealously guards his females.

[11] The shouts of the sentry warning the tribe that raiders are about to seize the pasturing camels.

[12] The she-camel is so fond of the herdsman that she momentarily forgets to watch her calf.

[13] In verses 8-14 Dindān describes the behaviour of one of his favourite big-bodied she-camels on the day of watering. She is so attached to the herdsman that she is momentarily distracted from her calf and rushes to the well. There she tries to get at the water even before he has finished drawing the water from the well and

15. *tabra l-gubbin twarrid kull maftūgah*
*tagḏ̣am ḥakāyim l-ᶜinnah taḥt l-ālādi*
16. *la laḥǵaw al-bill ᶜala d-duxxān masyūgah*
*miṯil al-ḥadāya b-mirkāḏ̣in w-misnādi*
17. *tarkuḏ̣ ᶜala l-mōt l-aḥmar la ḥtama sūgih*
*la ja l-ᶜajj ar-rumak fi l-jaww ᶜimmādi*
18. *al-jēš dīsat w-guḥṣ al-xēl mamḥūgah*
*wi-l-minhazim migṭibin f atlāh ṭarrādi*
19. *talāfitat li-l-ᶜazāwi kull mašfūgah*
*tarāyaᶜat yōm tūḥi ṣōt l-ajwādi*
20. *hāḏa ṭirīḥin w-ḏa ṭ-ṭēr intikas fōgih*
*w-hāḏi ǵilīᶜin b-ṭalᶜ al-ḥabil tingādi*
21. *f-in ja nahārin yišīb al-ᶜēn bi-ḥgūgih*
*yōmin zḥāmin yfattir dafr l-aznādi*
22. *sićć al-jimal bi-l-ḥadīd w-ᶜajjalaw sōgih*
*yanṭaḥ jmūᶜin tsīr b-ġēr ᶜaddādi*
23. *ćam bandarin māxḏīnin bi-l-ǵana sūgih*
*miṯil as-Slayyil maᶜa l-Aflāj wi-l-Wādi*

---

filling the trough. But in spite of the trouble she gives him, he is fond of her because of her spirited behaviour and attachment to him.

15. She is escorted by broad-chested horses who like to drench sharp weapons in the enemy's blood, //
Champing the bit impatiently under their youthful riders.
16. When they overtake the captured camels that are driven on amidst the smoke of gunfire, //
They are like kites: pouncing, flying up and pouncing again.[14]
17. In the heat of battle they gallop into the face of red death without flinching, //
When columns of dust are thrown up into the air by the horses' hoofs.
18. The camel troops were overwhelmed and the cream of their cavalry was crushed,[15] //
While others scuttled away, feeling the pursuers' breathing down their necks.
19. The anxious camels of the captured herd pricked up their ears when they heard the battle-cries, //
Pausing to listen as they recognized the voices of the brave.
20. Here lies one struck down and there the vultures are stooped over a corpse, //
And yet another one is flung from his horse the full length of his reins;
21. On such a day, when even eyelashes turn grey with horror, //
A violent clash in which forearms grow weary from the constant stabbing, //
22. The camels are hobbled with iron chains and driven steadily //
As the tribe confronts head on the swarming troops of the enemy.[16]
23. Many places we conquered by the force of our spears, //
Like as-Slayyil, al-Aflāj and the Wādi,

---

[14] When the camels have been captured and are driven away by raiders, the owners go in pursuit of their property on horseback. The battle is described from the point of view of the pursuers.

[15] This reference is to the camel troops and cavalry of the raiders who took the tribe's herds.

[16] It was explained to me that in war the Duwāsir used to chain their camels with a *gēd* (the iron chain with which horses are normally fettered, but here it probably means that both forelegs were tied together) so that they could not escape in the turmoil of battle and could not easily be driven away by the enemy as booty. It also indicates the commitment of the Duwāsir not to yield and to defend their herds at all cost. Thus, driving their fettered camels slowly but steadily, they would confront the enemy.

24. *bi-syūf hindin tgiṣṣ ar-rūs maflūgah*
*wi-ćyāl milḥin l-sabrāt an-niḏ̣ar zādi*
25. *Duwāsirin kull fiʿlin fiʿlhum šōgih*
*ālād Zāyid hal al-ʿaylāt wi-l-ǵādi*
26. *min ṭāl ṭōlin taʿadda ṭōlna fōgih*
*min ḥillna māxḏīnin ḥaggna l-ʿādi*
27. *ḥaggin lna l-jūd f-inn al-jūd ṭārūgih*
*yahdi ʿala mašribih wi-ydillh al-ġādi*
*w-salāmatkum.*

## POEM 3

Metre:--v--v---v---(*al-basīṭ*)

*jāna wagt w-yōm jāna wagt rigēt fi ḏāk al-mabda, jāna n-naww wi-l-amṭār w-rigēt fi ḏāk al-mabda, agūl:*

1. *ḏabbēt fi nāyfin ʿizzīl min ġarrih*
*midhāl sumr al-wḥūš ummāt jinḥāni*
2. *anḥēt ʿugbih ġṣūn al-galb minfarrah*
*farrat jarādin tarakkaz fīh ʿimdāni*
3. *ya-wanniti wannat illi yašrab al-murrah*
*yiḥma ʿala l-ʿišbat as-sōda wala zāni*
4. *ya-llāh ya-ʿālim an-niyyāt wi-s-sirrah*
*yalli jimīʿ al-jimāyil lih w-l-iḥsāni*
5. *illi yǵaddi niṣīb al-ʿabd min barrih*
*wi-lya nawa yanfiʿih maddih b-ġufrāni*
6. *yamḥa grūnin yijūn aḏ̣ʿaf mn aḏ-ḏarrah*
*w-yabʿaṯ bi-nafrin ynašši minh ʿirbāni*
7. *ṭālibk lēlin min al-mašrig lya l-ḥarrah*
*bargih ʿagūgin ḥagūgin fīh rannāni*
8. *mitgannʿih ka-l-xyām al-bīḏ̣ minšarrah*

24. With sabres made of black steel that cleave and cut off the enemy's head //
And stocks of powder that feed our straight-barreled rifles.
25. Duwāsir whose valiant deeds are a delight to behold, //
The offspring of Zāyid, known for their temerity and good sense;
26. No matter how tall one stands, we stand even taller. //
From time immemorial we seize our due rights,
27. One of them being a reputation for generosity and its ways, //
Recognized by the lost traveller, lead to its source.

## POEM 3

We went through a period of drought. Then I climbed that mountain and the rain-carrying clouds came at the appointed time. When I had climbed that mountain I said:

1. I ascended a steep mountain—pity him who is tricked into climbing its peak!—//
The abode of dark, long-winged birds of prey.
2. Later, when I made my descent, the branches of my heart were rent, //
Like a swarm of locusts that turned into a whirling vortex.
3. My cries of woe are like those of a sick man drinking a bitter potion, //
But is not cured by the brew of black herbs.
4. O God, He who knows the soul's intentions and secrets, //
Who is the source of all beneficent and good acts;
5. He who in His kindness bestows guidance on the believer //
And, if He wishes, grants him prosperity and forgiveness;
6. He who brushes away ages as if they were but specks //
And breathes life into a man from whose loins then spring entire tribes.
7. From You I ask a night stretching from the east towards al-Ḥarrah, //
Heralded by flashes of lightning and rolling thunder as unmistakable signs; //
8. A night covered as if with an encampment of white tents //

*liᶜb aṭ-ṭifal fīh liᶜb ummāt ḥīrāni*
9. *min kān liḥġih ḏiᶜīfin mihzilin sarrih*
*yiḏhir nibāt al-ḥamād al-xāmd al-fāni*
10. *ćann al-ḥabaṣ fi nuwāṣi māh minjarrah*
*ćann al-laᶜāᶜīb taḏrib fīh ṭīrāni*
11. *yimṭir jiṯīlih min al-Kōkab lya s-Sirrah*
*l agfa maxālin tigaffa jurritih ṯāni*
12. *sēlih lya ja raġābin misniyin ṭarrih*
*tiṣbiḥ wjīh al-ᶜadām al-bīḏ jirfāni*
13. *ma kān ja min ᶜataš wādin nahab jarrih*
*yansif šarāyid hašīmih fōg l-arkāni*
14. *yinši bih al-mizin yabrid l-arḏ min ḥarrih*
*yazraᶜ barāḥ al-fiḏa lli ṭāl ᶜaryāni*
15. *yissi midāhīl malḥan waṭfit al-jurrah*
*fajḥan min al-xuff la min fōg l-aṯfāni*
16. *sōdan ćima n-nīl ćanha Ḥammat al-Murrah*
*la min jalāha nahār al-ġēm waddāni*
17. *harrābtin l agbalat l-ārād minṯarrah*
*w-ḥarrābtin tirtići li-kbār l-amtāni*
18. *ćanha širīfin yġaddi mugdim al-jarrah*
*la min tiṣāfag ᶜala l-mārūd bidwāni*
19. *la ja l-ṭarš al-wrūd mn aḏ-ḏma ṣarrah*
*ćan rāsha r-rāćib illi yadfaᶜ as-sāni*
20. *ḏa tansfih bi-n-naḥar wi-ṭ-ṭārif tṭurrih*

And crisscrossed by cloud racks chasing one another like playful she-camels with young.

9. The raincloud's arrival cheers the worn-out, skinny animals // And brings forth the plant life from the empty, barren gravel plains,
10. As if flocks of black-and-white headed Najdi sheep are coasting on its forelocks, // And as if merrymakers are beating drums inside it.
11. Its load of rain falls from al-Kōkab to as-Sirrah; // As soon as one cloud drifts away the next one follows in its traces.
12. Its torrent rips open the thirsty ground parched by a relentless drought, // While its impact causes the flanks of the sand-dunes to crumble and cave in.
13. Where the torrent bed makes a turn its sides and bottom are torn away // And what remains of the debris is swept onto the banks of the watercourse.
14. The arrival of the clouds cools off the scorched land // And brings to blossom the wide, empty wastes that lay bare for so long.
15. They irrigate the places frequented by a bluish-black she-camel that leaves large footprints; // Its legs curve slightly outwards between the pads and the calluses on the knees.
16. She appears dark like indigo or like the Ḥammat al-Murrah mountain // When its slopes are washed by the pouring rain on an overcast day.
17. She dashes to the fore from among the scattered herd as it heads towards the watering place; // Pugnacious she shoves the large backs of her comrades,
18. Like a prince who rides at the head of his army. // When a host of bedouins vie for the water at the well, //
19. And the herds of animals arriving thirsty from a stay in the desert pastures make a din, // Her head towers above the mass like a rider spurring on a mount that draws water for irrigation.
20. The ones close by she jostles by pushing with her breast, and

*w-min ḏaddatih rāḥ min masgāh ḏamyāni*
21. *tarsax ᶜala ᶜābir al-miṣlāb bi-l-garrah*
*wala tġāyib yikūn al-ḥōḏ malyāni*
22. *ya-zīnha jiᶜlha bi-l-xēr mistarrah*
*la rawwaḥat min mićānin fīh mićnāni*
*w-salāmatk.*

## POEM 4[17]

Metre:--------

1. *ya-nidībi fōg ᶜmāni*
*niḏwin yarᶜa bh ad-dindāni*
2. *yāṭa bi-fjūj al-ḥizmāni*
*ma yindād illa bi-l-lāḥi*
3. *niḏwin ᶜajlin la min darham*
*miṯil al-jinni la minn arham*[18]
4. *lāla ḥablih yōm istabram*
*kān illi fōgih ǵid ṭāḥi*
5. *hayyaḏ ᶜēni fi fazzātih*
*ǵid ᶜaḏḏabni bi-mlāwātih*
6. *ᶜajlin zōlih fi hajjātih*
*la min daflij fi l-mirwāḥi*
7. *jawwid massik fi miṣlābih*
*w-iḥḏar ᶜumrik ya-rakkābih*
8. *w-ilzam ḥablih ya-gaḏḏābih*
*la min hāwaz li-l-jimmāḥi*
9. *amma ćannih hīǵin ġāyir*
*walla ćannih ṭērin ṭāyir*

[17] The metre, sound structure and vocabulary of this poem, composed of long syllables (except for nine short ones), convey an impression of sheer delight in the movements of a spirited camel mount. While listening to Dindān's performance, it occurred to me that the rhythmical patterning of this poem is an exciting imitation of the camel's hoofs clattering down on the hard desert soil like hailstones, as described in verse 22.

[18] Cf. Musil (1928), 151, *ćann aš-šiḏa ᶜala janābēh fāᶜi* '(the she-camel) runs as if a spook were crawling along both her flanks'.

those at a little remove she kicks; //
Any beast that incurred her wrath departs thirsty from the watering place.
21. Rock-solid she stands over the wooden rim of the watering trough; //
As long as it remains filled with water nothing can make her go.
22. Ah, how beautiful she is, may God gladden her with His bounty, //
When she returns at the end of day from pastures where *mićnān*-plants grow.

## POEM 4

1. O messenger riding a camel from Oman, //
A lean, hardened mount, spurred on by the rider's chanting.
2. He winds his way through the rolling, stony hills, //
Slowing down only when the reins are pulled.
3. A sinewy camel that travels at a fast trot, //
Like a jinnee scampering away with neighs of fear.
4. Were it not for his firm grip on the cords, //
The mount's rider would be thrown off.
5. His bursts of speed put me in raptures //
As I struggled to control his capers.
6. Seen from a distance his silhouette is a fast moving object //
When he hurries home in the late afternoon.
7. Clutch a wooden crosspiece of the saddle and hold on to it //
And beware of tumbling off, you rider!
8. Be careful not to let go of the reins, clasp them tightly //
When he challenges you with his feints at cavorting!
9. Like a male ostrich he rushes on, //
Or like a falcon that lifts into the air,

10. *yihwi min rūs al-jidāyir*
*la minnih šāf al-milwāḥi*
11. *yasraḥ min lammat firīǵih*
*la minh aḥma fi ṭirīǵih*
12. *yixlif rāyik min zirīǵih*
*ćannih xaṭwa najmin ṭāḥi*
13. *ćann al-fand an-nāᶜim sāgih*
*w-ixbar lāla guww ḥlāgih*
14. *ma yabga ᶜalēh ᶜlāgih*
*yaṭwi diyyān al-barāḥi*
15. *ma yinġaṭṭ lya ġaṭṭētih*
*yiᶜjib ᶜēnik la tallētih*
16. *ha ṯumm tallik ṯumm arxētih*
*ćann īdēh īdayy sabbāḥi*
17. *aḥmar lōnih mašyih bāriᶜ*
*ćannih xaṭwa hīǵin xāriᶜ*
18. *ma yindād l-garᶜ al-ǵāriᶜ*
*ᶜajjih ćannih zarg rmāḥi*
19. *šibrin zōrih min kirsūᶜih*
*gēsat xuffih yōm yzūᶜih*
20. *miṯl ryālin taww ṣnūᶜih*
*yajmaᶜ haḏīlin w-idbāḥi*
21. *m āḥa r-rāćib damṯ rdūfih*
*ᶜindih ᶜilmin yixlif ḥōfih*
22. *ćann al-barda ḏarb ćfūfih*
*la adlaj fi l-ḥazim aṣ-ṣiḥṣāḥi*
23. *yidwi miṯil idwāy aḏ-ḏībi*
*la b-yṭīr wla yamši bi*
24. *f-in ja mihjāj al-ḥaḏībi*
*xazz w-fazz w-nazz w-rāḥi*
*w-salāmatk.*

## POEM 5

Metre:-v---v--v---v-(*al-madīd*)

*ruḥna ḥinna ṣōb al-xabt illi dūn Makkah, w-yōm jēna al-xabt f-jēna min dīratna biᶜīd w-ištaḥanna w-hīᶜ, agūl:*

10. And swoops down from the high pinnacles //
When he sees the falconeer waving some pieces of cloth.
11. In the morning he sets out from his tribal camp //
And once he has settled to a spirited pace,
12. His speed leaves you breathless with amazement
As he streaks along like a falling star.
13. His shanks are smooth and straight like a bough, //
And surely, were it not for the strength of his nose-ring,
14. He'd have flung off the trappings on his back. //
He burns up the miles in the wide, empty plains;
15. Your efforts to slow him down are in vain: //
It is a delight to see how he responds to the reins, //
16. When you pull and then ease off again, //
His legs paddling like a swimmer's arms.
17. His colour is reddish, his ride magnificent; //
Running like an ostrich frightened to death,
18. Heedless of the rider's efforts to temper him,
He stirs up clouds of dust that skim through the air like a spear.
19. His elbows are a full span of the hand from the horny sole under his breast,
And when he lifts his pads you see //
20. How round they are, and smooth like newly minted coins. //
Even at a fast, steady trot, he presses on with his neck stretched low. //
21. The softness of his haunches make for a painless ride, //
And he moves at a gait so smooth as to be deceptive.
22. His pads thrum the ground like hailstones //
When he speeds over the hard patches in a soft plain rimmed by sharp bluffs,
23. Trotting along like a scurrying wolf. //
Though he is not flying, neither is he running,
24. And when he plunges into a gorge, treading the soft ground at the foot of its slopes, //
He accelerates, bolts, bounds away and vanishes.

## POEM 5

We went to a plain some distance short of Mecca. When we arrived at the plain we were far from our homeland and our hearts became very heavy. Then I said:

1. *bādyin rijmin l-ṣalf al-hawa fōgih wušīm*
   *jiᶜl yissinnih ruwāyiḥ maxāyīl ar-ribīᶜ*
2. *fi Ṭifīlin wi-l-hawa min miġībih mistigīm*
   *talġafih šihb al-maᶜāṣīr wi-l-mabda rifīᶜ*
3. *fāḥ damᶜ al-ᶜēn la ṭarraw al-ᶜaṣir al-gidīm*
   *fōḥ figrin bīḥ saddih wu-hu bīrih rijīᶜ*
4. *al-mjāmiᶜ wi-l-mfārig jaᶜal galbi hašīm*
   *hašim zarb al-bān fōg aṣ-ṣifa ǵid hu xalīᶜ*
5. *rāćib illi la nahamtih lya ᶜindih zijīm*
   *miṯil ṣōt an-nimr ḥill aṣ-ṣifāri mistisīᶜ*
6. *la rifaᶜt al-ḥabil f-ilwih lya mass al-ḥakīm*
   *li-l-ḥalag l-aṣfar ᶜala birṯᶜat xašmih giḏ̣īᶜ*
7. *asḥamin ᶜaḏ̣mih min al-ᶜeff min ḥillih silīm*
   *gurṣ xuffih ma yiji lih min al-ᶜibla nidīᶜ*
8. *ćan sana ᶜēnih sana jamr ᶜirnin lih jiḥīm*
   *yōm habba nūrha tiṣṭili jamrin wilīᶜ*
9. *la ᶜaṭa maᶜ mijrihidd al-ḥadab miṯl aḏ̣-ḏ̣ilīm*
   *la sibag fayyih w-fayyih maᶜa wajhih sirīᶜ*
10. *kull m ōḥa l-liᶜib gām ytiḏ̣arras lih giḏ̣īm*
    *miṯil ḏībin yōm yihḏil maᶜa milḥāz rīᶜ*
11. *migsiyin rāᶜīh ćannih l-rakkābih xaṣīm*
    *ćann yalġaf marzig al-gōm min xilfih niǵīᶜ*
12. *la hazaf w-inzaff w-inxaff min lēlih msīm*
    *yixlif hwiyt al-habāyib w-girbāᶜ al-girīᶜ*

*w-salāmatk.*

## POEM 6

Metre: (v)--v---v--v---(*aṭ-ṭawīl*)

1. *riga fi ḏ̣-ḏ̣aḥa n-naššād fi ᶜāliy al-mihlāl*
   *lya ḏ̣āg ṣadrih sannaᶜ al-gāf tasnīᶜi*
2. *tahayyaḏ̣ w-wann w-ḏ̣āmrih ćann fīh išᶜāl*
   *w-ćann aš-šbūb mwallaᶜin fīh tōlīᶜi*
3. *baġēt al-ćinīn w-yōm barragt la m aḥtāl*

1. I climbed a peak lashed by howling winds—//
   May the clouds of spring in passing soak it with rain—
2. On Ṭifīl, where the wind blows straight from the west, //
   Its high summit whipped by violent dust storms.
3. When I hear mention of the days of yore tears well up, //
   Like water in an abandoned well that is dug up again.
4. The many meetings and partings rent my heart, //
   Like withered twigs of *bān*-trees that fell down onto the boulders.
5. O rider of a camel that makes a stammering sound when exhorted, //
   Like the snarls of wild leopards in autumn,
6. When you put on the ropes, pull them hard and tighten the knot //
   At the copper ring fastened on the bridge of his nose.
7. A fresh black camel with a sound bone structure //
   And the round disks of his pads never hurt by sharp stones;
8. In his eyes shines a light like that of the red-hot coals of *ʿirn*-wood //
   After the fire has died down and the embers continue to glow.
9. When he traverses the bare, rugged wastes like a running ostrich, //
   He does not tire of racing against the shade gliding swiftly at his side;
10. And when he hears the rider's chanting he gnashes his teeth. //
    He resembles a wolf cantering through a cleft in a mountain,
11. Wrestling to escape from the control of his rider as if he were his sworn enemy, //
    Like camels that are pricked from behind with a sharp thorn,
12. Thin and wasted after enduring a march all night long, //
    Buffeted by the winds and startled by its own clattering noise.

## POEM 6

1. After sunrise the bard climbed the high crest of a mountain, //
   Downhearted he vented his spleen in verse after verse.
2. Grief welled up and he moaned as if roasted //
   By a fire that had been lit in his breast.
3. I wanted to bear my suffering in silence, but found I could not, //

*lya ćann galbi yantiginh al-miǵālīˁi*
4. *aġanni b-gāfin lēn ja lli warāh nhāl*
*w-ṣakkat ˁalayy jill al-ǵuwāriˁ mahānīˁi*
5. *ana damˁ ˁēni ḥasbi allah ˁala l-anḏāl*
*ġawārīb sēlih ḏ̣ayyigann al-mahāyīˁi*
6. *wu-hu yittimal bi yōm aġanni wu-hu ma sāl*
*w-asanniˁ kalāmi yōm axīf inni aḏ̣īˁi*
7. *ya-lajj galbi miṯil ma lajlij al-maḥḥāl*
*tnazziḥ ǵilībih dārbāt al-marājīˁi*
8. *ya-tall galbi tall dalwin maˁa jahhāl*
*ˁala ġēr tasnīˁin fiḏ̣atha n-nuwāćīˁi*
9. *ya-llāh ya-jazil al-ˁaṭa miġniyin bi-l-māl*
*yalli balēt bh r-rxūm al-buwālīˁi*
10. *bini mitribīn ar-rāy ma yiḥirzūn afˁāl*
*ḏ̣ˁāf ar-ruwābiˁ li-l-ˁajāyiz miṭāwīˁi*
11. *alinnik tfarrij li-l-manāˁīr ḏ̣add al-ḥāl*
*tiḥibb al-marājil miṯil ḥibb al-aṭāmīˁi*
12. *xassārtin li-mgannid al-binn fi l-finjāl*
*w-ḏabbāḥtin li-l-ḥīl ḥill al-mijāwīˁi*
13. *nawwāstin li-l-ḥiff laṭṭāmt al-ˁiyyāl*
*faˁāyilhum illi bayynātin lha šīˁi*
14. *ya-rāćib illi ćannhin malḥiy as-siyyāl*
*lya rawwaḥan miṯil an-naˁām al-maxārīˁi*
15. *ḥamalha n-niṣīb w-jābha w-allah al-ḥammāl*
*sidas sitt ḥīlin min mnāha z-zalāwīˁi*

For I felt as if pincers began plucking out my heart.
4. No sooner did I chant one verse, than others came like camels rushing to a well, //
Pressing around me and lowering their big heads to the water.
5. My tears flowed—may God protect me against the wretches—//
Until its copious stream filled every confluence of the valleys.
6. So it seemed to me, though there was no flow, as I chanted //
And straightened my verses, fearful of getting utterly lost.
7. My heart whined like the squeaking of the wooden wheels suspended above a well //
While well-trained camels briskly draw its water.
8. Or is it torment like that of a leather bucket hoisted by a clumsy youngster, //
And ripped open by sharp stones protruding from the sides of the well?
9. O God, Bountiful Giver, Bestower of livestock, //
O Scourge of good-for-nothings and greedy-guts,
10. Despicable patsies, incapable of noble deeds, //
Feeble-minded weaklings ordered around by old hags;
11. I pray You to remove ill-fortune from the stalwart men, //
Since they have a liking for manly virtues as one is greedy for booty;
12. Men who pour cup after cup of well-spiced coffee, regardless of the cost, //
And reckless slaughterers of fat sheep in times of famine;
13. Men who track down the adversary, no matter how far off, and strike at wrongdoers; //
Their feats are manifest and famous everywhere.
14. O rider of a camel slender like a scraped off acacia-tree,[19]
Returning in late afternoon as frightened ostriches run with their necks held low;
15. Fortune carried them to us, a precious load from God, //
Six camels, six years old, their wombs barren, fond of fast travelling;[20]

---

[19] Camels like to rub themselves against the stem of certain trees, scraping off the bark.

[20] On important missions the camels of the messengers should be of the same colour and alike in age and type, cf. Musil (1928), 319, and Ingham, Bruce, 'Camel Terminology among the Āl Murrah Bedouins', *ZAL* 22 (1990), 77, who also observes that these delegations are often composed of six camels. The same point is

16\. *ḥarāyir šimālin yaṭribin l ōḥan al-ġirmāl*
*w-ya-zīnha min $^{c}$ugb l-igfa marāyī$^{c}$i*
17\. *tšādi sigāyif ḏ̣ubbisin min šbūb al-lāl*
*timaḥmaḥ šaḥamha ma biga lha za$^{c}$āzī$^{c}$i*
18\. *ṯalāṯ sniwātin zāydin birrhinn ḥyāl*
*w-kabbab ḥaṣāyirha nibāt al-marābī$^{c}$i*
19\. *lya gaḏ̣ḏ̣ibaw l-arsān hajjat lha juwwāl*
*tijiwwāl ṣēdin ḏāyrin ma$^{c}$ niba rī$^{c}$i*
20\. *baġaw ṭabxatēnin w-azlibathum min al-migyāl*
*wi-hi ḏ̣āryātin fi l-baha bi-l-mizāwī$^{c}$i*
21\. *tiṣalfag lya minnih kifax ṭārif ad-dismāl*
*lya la ṣ-ṣarāyim kassarann al-miṣārī$^{c}$i*
22\. *ya-zīn ṭarg ēmānha la zimat l-amṯāl*
*lya daflij aṭ-ṭārif nahār al-migāṭī$^{c}$i*
23\. *tšād al-fḥūl al-hāyjah l adlijat giffāl*
*tmāris bi-halha yōm šāfat l-asānī$^{c}$i*
24\. *ṭwāl al-$^{c}$awātig min mnāha biṭa s-sirbāl*
*wsā$^{c}$ az-zġūn mnaffijāt al-karāsī$^{c}$i*
25\. *jsām al-miḏāri$^{c}$ wi-l-muwāṭi tigūl ryāl*
*tšād al-maha jird al-ma$^{c}$ānig mahāḏ̣ī$^{c}$i*
26\. *ma$^{c}$a sajjihinn al-gāylah lēlihin $^{c}$ammāl*

---

made in verses 7/16, 9/21 and 27/3. In its seventh year a riding camel reaches its greatest strength, see glossary under *sds*.

16. They are a noble breed from the north, happy to be urged on by song; //
A beautiful sight they are when they return from a journey,
17. Looking like dried out planks from the blistering heat, //
Their reserves of fat molten away till hardly anything was left.
18. They were granted a period of three years without young //
Till their flanks bulged from grazing the spring pastures.[21]
19. When their riders grip the halter they take off at speed, //
Zigzagging like gazelles surprised in a sloping defile,
20. Startled from the shade of a tree by riders pausing at noon for two brews of coffee; //
Camels accustomed to crossing featureless plains at a hurried gait,
21. Swinging to and fro when frightened by the fluttering tip of the rider's headgear; //
Were it not for the thongs of the halter they would break the saddle apart.
22. It is wonderful to behold their legs moving rapidly towards distant ridges,[22] //
While the one in front sets the pace on their traverse of the desert.
23. They journey at night, their bellies slim like those of rutting males,[23] //
Exerting themselves even more when they reach the well-marked tracks.
24. Their cheeks are elongated; what they like is an easy, steady gait; //
Their axillae are wide and their elbows spaced from the belly;
25. Their legs are big and strong, their soles round like coins; //
Their necks are stretched low and covered with short hair, resembling those of wild cows;
26. Hardy runners in the noon heat and all night without pause, //

---

[21] The best riding camels are thoroughbreds that have been exempted from carrying young or hard work in their early years and are not saddled until they have reached full strength.

[22] When camels crossing a featureless plain perceive the outline of a landmark in the distance ahead, they pick up their pace as if encouraged to reach it as quickly as possible.

[23] Rutting stud camels eat very little during the mating season and in consequence lose a good deal of weight.

*tšādi duwānīǵ al-bḥūr al-midānīᶜi*
27. *lha fi r-ryād al-mistuwi fi l-ᶜašiyy zilzāl*
*taxāfag maᶜa bīḏ al-ḥzūm al-garādīᶜi*
28. *kbār at-tarāyib yōm tiǵfi tigūl jmāl*
*tnāfiḥ tinīfāḥ al-ᶜaḏāra l-mibārīᶜi*
29. *xfāf al-muwāṭi ruṣṣixin wi-l-ᶜamār ṯgāl*
*ṣḥāḥ as-simāri ma hamazha marāǵīᶜi*
30. *ᶜalāha l-ᶜnēni wi-l-muwārik bha miyyāl*
*maᶜ al-ᶜāj l-aswad ḥannišōh aṣ-ṣanānīᶜi*
31. *w-sūd as-sifāyif yōm ṣaffat lhinn ḏlāl*
*tuwāma ᶜala ᶜayrāt l-anḏa l-buwātīᶜi*
32. *ᶜalāha ᶜyālin min bini ṭayybīn al-fāl*
*ydillūn fi ḏ-ḏalma ġabiyy al-mitābīᶜi*
33. *lya jann bēt ᶜBēd ᶜīd an-niḏa l-hizzāl*
*siᶜd ar-rikāyib ḏārbāt al-maxāwīᶜi*
34. *tixuṣṣih b-ᶜilmi lēn taški ᶜalēh al-ḥāl*
*tarāh ar-risīn lya gṭaᶜann an-nibābīᶜi*
*w-salāmatk.*

POEM 7

Metre:-v---v---v-(*ar-ramal*)

*mnāsibatha aṭ-ṭarab.*

1. *al-galam hātih tara ᶜindi kalām*
*la b-ġāwīha wala bi-mxōjilāt*
2. *rāćbin miṯl al-maḥāḥīl aṣ-ṣifīf*
*ćannha siḥm as-sbāᶜ al-ᶜādyāt*
3. *ćannha ṣēdin tijāwal min šiᶜīb*

Like ships at sea lurching on the waves.
27. In the evening the ground of the flat expanses trembles under their feet, //
Clattering on the rolling, flint-strewn hills.
28. The big-bellied beasts look like stallions seen from behind, //
Their legs rocking like girls dancing unveiled.
29. Their swift feet are firmly planted under the heavy bodies, //
And their sound pads were never wounded and patched up.
30. From their backs hang colourful woollen bags and leather cushions //
Ornamented by craftsmen, together with the dark saddle,
31. And the black tassels throw rows of long shadows on the earth //
While dangling from the back of the swift and persevering animals.
32. They are mounted by young men born under a lucky star //
Who do not go astray when following the hidden, winding tracks at night.
33. The wasted animals rejoice once they arrive at the house of ᶜBēd,
Bliss of mounts travelling the wide plains;
34. Give him my special regards before passing on my complaint, //
For he (ᶜBēd) is a plentiful well at a time when the hollows with rain-water have dried up.[24]

## POEM 7

This poem I composed for mere pleasure:

1. Bring the pen, for I have verses to say;[25] //
I am not one to mangle them, nor do they turn out flawed.
2. O rider of camels spinning like a row of pulley-wheels above a well; //
Like dark jackals running their fastest,
3. Or a drove of gazelles leaping zigzag from a ravine,

---

[24] 'He is a plentiful well' etc. means that ᶜBēd is generous and hospitable even in times of hardship when other men keep for themselves whatever supplies they have.
[25] See note 32, p. 40.

*yanḥaz al-bēda misīr al-mūjfāt*
4. *zēnha la rawwaḥat ḥazzat ᶜṣēr*
*ćannha ᶜūj al-ḥanāya l-yābsāt*
5. *ma ḥala ṣifr aṣ-ṣarāyim bi-l-xšūm*
*yōm tidlij bi-l-hadīl mṣālbāt*
6. *ćan midāriᶜha nuwāᶜīr al-ǵilīb*
*wi-l-ᶜḏūd jsām fijjin wāfyāt*
7. *wi-r-rǵāb tgūl mašdūb al-jirīd*
*wi-l-xafāf mn ar-rṯūm mdarramāt*
8. *wi-ḏ-ḏyūl aš-šitr fi nasl an-nijīb*
*ćannha fōg al-fxūḏ mjabbaᶜāt*
9. *wi-l-wrūk mn al-fxūḏ ila l-figār*
*miṯl bībān al-gṣūr mṣakkikāt*
10. *ćan ḥamār ᶜyūnha mišhāb ćīr*
*wi-l-lḥiyy mn al-xdūd msaḥḥamāt*
11. *ćan ġawāribha marāǵīb al-xšūm*
*ḥizzibin miṯl al-fḥūl al-hāyjāt*
12. *ćannha la samᶜan aṣ-ṣōt aṣ-ṣilīb*
*jōl rubdin min miḥīrin ḏāyirāt*
13. *hāmlātin min ribīᶜin la ribīᶜ*
*fi xaḏārin nabt ṣēfin mijizyāt*
14. *barg ᶜāmin kull ubūhin min biᶜīr*
*nasil ḥurrin bi-l-uṣūl mnaᶜᶜatāt*
15. *liᶜibha bi-ᶜnūgha fōg as-sarāb*
*fīh min liᶜb al-ᶜaḏāra l-mitrifāt*
16. *ḥāylātin wagm sitt snīn nīb*
*lēn riddan bi-l-xadāyim wālmāt*

*w-salāmatk.*

Their feet drum the ground of the barren waste at a rapid pace.
4. A fine spectacle they are as they return toward the evening,[26]
Looking like curved and dried-out litter poles,
5. And how nice the copper ring of the halter fastened to their noses! //
When they journey indefatigably without slowing down,
6. Their legs resemble wooden rollers turning above a well; //
The upper parts of their forelegs are muscular and set wide apart;
7. Their necks are like pared off branches of a palm-tree, //
And their pads were never pierced by sharp stones.[27]
8. The tails of these thoroughbreds are short //
As if they were clipped above the posteriors;
9. The haunches, from the thighs to the lower end of the hump, //
Are like palace gates shut tight,
10. The red glow in their eyes like the end of a stick kindled in the fireplace. //
The hairs on the throat under their cheeks are between red and black;
11. Their shoulders rise up like bluffs where watchmen stand guard.
Bulky animals and aggressive like rutting males;
12. When they hear a harsh voice yelling, //
They run like a flock of ostriches startled from a meadow in a valley.
13. From spring to spring they roamed the pastures at will, //
Grazing the green annuals without need for water.
14. They were all born in the same year, sired by one stallion, //
The offspring of thoroughbreds with impeccable pedigrees;
15. Rising above the layer of quivering hot air hugging the ground, their necks are dancing //
Not unlike the playful movements of delicate maidens;
16. About six years old, having grown eye-teeth, and not impregnated, //
Until they were ready and made to obey the reins.

---

[26] 'A good female riding camel is at her best speed before and after sunset,' Musil (1928), 148.

[27] See glossary under *ḫfy*. The soft pads of the camels were not scarred by the sharp pieces of lava and stones of volcanic areas, because they have only been used for travelling in desert areas with softer ground.

## POEM 8

Metre:--v---v--v--(*aṭ-ṭawīl*)

*mnāsibatha wāḥid yigūl:*

a. *ya-rāćbin ḥīlin ḥalāḥīl ḥīli*
*wi-lya mišan yašdin ṣifīf al-maḥāḥīl*
b. *rakkābha ma gāl ᶜallig ṣimīli*
*yašrab hawa wi-ḏhūrhinnah migāyīl*[28]

*w-banēt ᶜalāha. aš-šāᶜir ᶜabdin Dōsiri māt, ismih ᶜĀyiḏ. ar-rijim, ḏilᶜin ṭiwīl, ćam min wāḥid, ma hūb wāḥid, fi l-jinūb, jibal Sanāmah, ᶜala ṭūl al-mabda ḏāk, gwārin ḥumr.*

1. *ḏabbēt rijmin zād ġulli ġalīli*
*lēn hu ḏāᶜ ar-rāy wi-ᶜmōmas al-ġīl*
2. *ya-rāćibin jillin jahājīl jīli*
*miṯl an-naᶜām ar-rubd jillin jahājīl*
3. *in dabbarat ćanha l-ᶜnūz al-jifīli*
*w-in agbalat ćanha l-idāmi migābīl*
4. *sūd al-midāmiᶜ ćannha xaṭṭ nīli*
*nūṭ ar-rgāb mṭalwaḥātin bi-tafṣīl*
5. *fajj an-nḥūr mṣālbāt aš-šilīli*
*la rawwaḥat miṯl al-bitāt al-mahālīl*
6. *as-sāg min ḥadd al-maᶜāġil jilīli*
*w-aḏyālha tašdi mrāṭ aš-šimālīl*
7. *guṭm al-xafāf mwaddiyāt aṯ-ṯigīli*
*tašdi maḥājirha suwād al-maġāyīl*
8. *talḥag ᶜala s-sāgah ḏarāyib l-aṣīli*
*la sarribaw sūd aš-šnūn al-mibālīl*

---

[28] *ḏhūrhinnah*, the 3 f. pl. suffix pronoun *-hinnah* is used here instead of the common *-hin* for the sake of metre, cf. Prochazka (1988), 126.

## POEM 8

It was inspired by someone who said:

a. O rider of splendid camels, barren of womb, //
Pacing like a row of waterwheels above a well.
b. Their rider did not say, 'Attach my milk skin!' //
He drinks the air and spends the siesta hours on their backs.

I answered in verses of the same rhyme and metre. The poet is a black Dōsiri who died. His name was ʿĀyiḏ. The peak I climbed was a high mountain, or rather one of many mountains I climbed. This one is in the south, Sanāmah mountain, about as high as that elevation, a group of red-hued knolls.

1. I climbed a mountain in a state of mounting fury, //
Till my mind clouded over and I groped for words.
2. O rider of a squadron of big-bodied riding camels, //
A sizeable squadron resembling speckled, ash-coloured ostriches.
3. They make off like panicky does leading a herd of gazelles, //
And in approaching they are like small whitish gazelles.
4. The inner angles of their eyes are black as if streaked with indigo; //
Their necks are long and slenderly shaped;
5. They are broad in the breast and maintain a sprightly pace; //
On the home stretch their feet are spinning like axes on which pulley-wheels turn.
6. Their legs are massive from the knee joints upwards, //
And their tails resemble stalks of date bunches that lost most of their fruits.
7. They deliver heavy loads on hoofs clipped round, //
And the blackness under their brows is like that of water running among dense vegetation.
8. Surging from the rear they overtake the thoroughbreds up in front, //
Even though the last drops in their riders' old water-skins have been spent.

9. *ćanha lya min sarbalat li-l-haḏīli*
*ṣēdin maᶜa ṣugᶜ al-ḥzūm al-jahāwīl*
10. *rakkābha lli ᶜādtih ma yiᶜīli*
*ᶜifrīt majnūnin yᶜarf at-timāṯīl*
11. *aṣgar min al-ᶜuggab mḥīlin mzīli*
*fi lēlt aḏ-ḏalma yidill ad-duwālīl*
12. *yanṣa bini ᶜammin tnajji ḏ-ḏilīli*
*sallim ᶜalēhum kullihum bi-t-tibātīl*
13. *ḥammāytin l-illi jidāha ǵilīli*
*w-ahl at-tiṯanni ᶜind jillin miṯāǵīl*

## POEM 9

Metre: (v)--v---v--v---(*aṭ-ṭawīl*)

1. *ana hāḏ ma bi ᶜūḏ bi-llah min aš-šayṭān*
*afaṣṣil ᶜala šaffi b-kēfi wala fiyyah*
2. *lifāna l-kalām w-šuft ana l-ḥāl minni šān*
*giḏa ma xaḏa ḥāli mn aṭ-ṭīb maṯniyyah*
3. *ᶜizzīl min hu kull yōmin wu-hu fi šān*
*kiṯīr al-ḥaṯāyim la bida lih šifa niyyah*
4. *fa-ya mill galbin ḥall fīh ad-diba l-ḥannān*
*jiṯīlih ᶜala galbi taᶜāgab maᶜāšiyyah*
5. *ya-llāh yalli kull ma rād b-amrin kān*
*alinnik tᶜāwinni lya jāz li niyyah*
6. *ana wēn adawwir li maᶜa ḏa l-lsān lsān*
*yᶜāwin lsāni la yibīn al-xalal fiyyah*
7. *ana b-aḥmid allah yōm ja li ᶜala ma zān*

9. Picking up their speed from an easy canter to a fast trot, //
Like a drove of gazelles they skitter over the ridges of the hills. //
10. Their rider is not in the habit of losing his way; //
A daring wizard, who knows the desert like the back of his hand,
11. Smarter than eagles, wily and cunning, //
In starless nights he puts other guides on the right course.
12. Upon arrival at my kin, rescuers of frightened refugees, //
Greet them respectfully, all of them, one by one, //
13. For they are protectors of those who have but little strength, //
And defenders of heavily-laden camel trains.

## POEM 9

1. Deeply stirred I took my refuge with God against Satan; //
My verses I string exactly as pleases me, come what may.
2. The poem that came to my ears profoundly unsettled me: //
It took away double whatever strength I had gathered.
3. Pity him whose every day is spent in misery //
And whose heaviness of heart spoils his appetite for life.
4. Woe unto a heart swarmed over by creeping young locusts, //
Wave after wave alighting on the heart's branches at dusk.[29]
5. O God, He whose acts of will are transformed into fact at once, //
May You help me in carrying out my intentions!
6. Where can I turn for a tongue, other than the one I already have, //
To help me express what this one is incapable of saying?
7. God I praised the day I recovered my poetic bearings //

---

[29] 'The large green varieties (of the locusts) often cover shrubs by the myriad and do not move till the dew has evaporated,' Musil (1928), 93. 'These sunk thickets were full of locusts, which we saw sitting thick as rain-drops upon all the thorny branches,' Doughty, Charles M., *Travels in Arabia Deserta*, London 1936, i, 442. In *nabaṭi* poetry worries and anxieties besetting the heart are often compared to swarms of locusts alighting on trees and shrubs in the desert, as in Ibn Sbayyil's verse:
*galbi ćima wādyin min al-jind mamrūḥ*
*liyāl ma bih gišʿatin ma raʿāha*
'My heart resembles a valley chosen by locusts as their resting place
During nights when no shrub escaped being their pasture,' al-Faraj (1952), i, 209.

*thīḏ al-ᶜibār illi min al-ᶜām maćniyyah*
8. *tifahhamt fi gāfin wmarni bih r-riḥmān*
*talāḥat mizāmīrih w-ġārat marāćiyyah*
9. *ṭara li jimīᶜ illi yṭarra wu-hu ma kān*
*lya fāḥ ṣadri miṯl fōḥ al-ḥasāwiyyah*[30]
10. *kalēt as-sima w-arḏih wala waggat al-liḥyān*
*maᶜ al-ᶜarš kullih ma yiji lugmitin liyyah*
11. *širibt al-bḥūr w-jīt mitġānimin ḏamyān*
*jimīᶜ al-mišārib ma tiji rišfitin liyyah*
12. *saḥant al-jbāl dwan wala takḥil al-burmān*
*w-jimīᶜ aš-šijar ma mayyal al-ᶜēn hāḏiyyah*
13. *kalēt al-gumar wi-š-šams w-amsēt ana jāᶜān*
*wala ᶜād bih šinn āklih ᶜizzita liyyah*
14. *kalēt as-snīn w-kāsirin bērag aš-šayṭān*
*w-širibt al-habāyib wi-l-jnūn sjidat liyyah*
15. *libist an-nahār ṯwēb xāmin ᶜala l-amtān*
*w-suwād al-liyāli li bšūtin šimāliyyah*
16. *w-jimaᶜt an-njūm w-niyyat al-xubṯ li-l-ᶜidwān*
*ᶜala šān abīhum yaskinūn al-ḥarāmiyyah*
17. *w-tarāni dixīl allah wiliyyi ᶜaḏīm aš-šān*
*w-bāġ al-xalāyiġ ma lhum ᶜindi dᶜiyyah*
18. *ya-rāćib illi ġaffalōha min al-migṭān*
*fiṭīrin yšādinn al-buwāćīr maḥniyyah*
19. *tibāyaḏ luwāḥīhin ᶜaṯānīnhinn mtān*
*yšādin nḥūrihn ad-darāwīz mabniyyah*
20. *ᶜarībāt jaddin miḏhirin ṣīthin l-ēmān*
*ṯimānīn jaddin ᶜaddha fi l-ᶜmāniyyah*
21. *tšādi manāćibha l-byādi suwan asnān*

---

[30] Cf. Ibn K̲h̲amīs (1982), 419, *fi l-xala fāḥ galbi fōḥ dallah*, 'In the empty wastes my heart seethed like boiling coffee in a pot.'

And my heart broke out in sobs after suffering in silence for a year.

8. The verses dictated to me by the Merciful I understood, //
As they responded to one another's melody and marched on me in battle array.
9. Everything imaginable occurred to me at once, strange as it seems, //
While my breast boiled over like coffee in a pot made in al-Aḥsāʾ.
10. Earth and sky I gobbled up, but for me it wasn't even chicken feed, //
With the throne of heaven thrown in, it's but a poor chunk;
11. Gulping down the seas didn't quench my thirst, //
But then I'd drain the oceans in one sip;
12. If all mountains were ground into kohl, it would not even cover the corners of my eyes, //
Nor would all trees provide enough sticks to smear it with.
13. After supping on sun and moon my stomach still rumbled with hunger, //
And now there is nothing else left to eat, poor me.
14. I swallowed the years and smashed Satan's banner; //
I imbibed the winds and the jinn prostrated themselves for me;
15. As a cloak of coarse wool I threw the day around my shoulders, //
And I wrapped myself in the dark of night as in a furred mantle;
16. I gathered the stars, as well as all the spite I could muster, //
With the intention of silencing them for good, that rabble!
17. To God, the mighty Lord I entrust myself, //
And as for the rest of mankind, I don't give a damn.
18. O rider of mounts left unimpregnated since this summer's camp, //
Fully grown she-camels, so lean as to resemble the curved grip of a cane;
19. Their cheeks are streaked with grey and the bristles behind their ears are firmly planted, //
And their breasts are vaulting like palace gates.
20. A pure race with a renowned ancestor, famous for its speed, //
Their eighty forefathers all hailing from Oman,
21. Born in the same year, their shoulders ample like winter mantles, //

*w-d̲irᶜānha mit̲l an-nuwāᶜīr malḥiyyah*
22. *ᶜalāha l-muwāriċ māylātin ᶜala l-amtān*
*w-xirj al-ᶜnēni wi-s-sifāyif laha fayyah*
23. *taxāzar tixīzār al-giṭa l-wārid al-ᶜaṭšān*
*yibi ġaltitin min rāyiḥ al-wabl mamliyyah*
24. *kbār at-tarāyib taww ma šaggat an-nībān*
*ᶜala gaṭᶜah an-nāziḥ rċābi naḥāwiyyah*
25. *banāt al-ᶜmāni tajmaᶜ as-sēr wi-l-ġūrān*
*tšādi l-maha bi-mfallij al-milḥ marmiyyah*
26. *tšādi d̲yūlihn aš-šimālīl fi l-ᶜaydān*
*tigūl al-wrūk mn aḥmar az-zall maċsiyyah*
27. *tšādi maḥāḥīlin bitātih ᶜala ᶜūdān*
*taxāfag naᶜāmih yōm tassi suwāniyyah*
28. *tšādi s-sbāᶜ wjīh l-and̲a wi-hinn azyān*
*ṣifār aṣ-ṣarāyim fi l-ᶜarānīn māriyyah*
29. *taᶜāzīl waṣf azwārha katbat at-tījān*
*wsāᶜ az-zġūn mn al-ᶜawārīċ māgiyyah*
30. *kbār at̲-t̲imāyil wi-l-muwāṭi ċima d-dīwān*
*tġarrib raxārīx al-wiṭa l-mintiziḥ liyyah*
31. *tixīdām waṣf rġābha wi-l-ᶜamār rzān*
*giṣab xayzarānin fi yidēn al-ᶜrēd̲iyyah*
32. *kbār al-laḥam min ḥadd ma raffaᶜat l-at̲fān*
*glāl al-laḥam min ḥadd ma ṭamminat hiyyah*
33. *ᶜalāha ḥalāyan min ḥalāya l-jmāl wt̲ān*
*tfukk al-ᶜṣiyy mn ad̲-d̲lāf aš-šimāmiyyah*
34. *tanṣa D̲yābin jiᶜl yafdōnih ar-ridyān*
*min illi faᶜāyilhum jidīdin w-gudmiyyah*
35. *ana hād̲ ma bi zīn gāfih ᶜasāh mᶜān*
*walad xāli illi ṭōltih ṭōltin liyyah*

Their slender legs turning as rapid as waterwheels.

22. The leather cushions hang from the small of their backs, // And the saddle-bags and tassels cast long shadows on the ground.
23. They watch one another as they swerve in close formation, like thirsty sand grouse // Flying to a hole in the rocks filled with water by a recent downpour.
24. Big-bellied animals whose eye-teeth just broke through, // My mounts are eager to traverse the immense desert;
25. Thoroughbreds from Oman, their gate both swift and smooth, // Like wild cows fired upon with muzzle-loaders.
26. Their tails resemble date bunches hanging from the palms, // Their haunches as if draped with light-brown carpets;
27. Mounts that move furiously like rollers turning on wooden spindles, // Their poles shaking as the camels harnessed to the rope hoist the bucket from the well.
28. The snouts of the hardy camels are like those of jackals, // The copper of their nose-rings sparkles in the sun;
29. The callous stays under their breasts resemble insignia on a uniform. // Legs set well apart from the body thanks to spacious axillae,
30. Broad around the flanks, their pads round like coins, // They whisk me through otherwise endless wastes,
31. Swaggering with their necks, their bodies firmly planted, // Swaying rhythmically like sticks in the hands of war dancers.
32. Muscular from the calluses on the knee joints and up, // Their legs are almost bare of flesh lower down;
33. In appearance they are similar to good-tempered stallions, // Yet so spirited as to wrench off the crosspieces from the saddle's supports.
34. Thus you'll arrive at Ḏyāb—may the wretches of this world be his ransom!—// Known for his noble feats, both recent and old.
35. His splendid verses moved me—may God comfort him: // My cousin whose pride is my pride as well.

36. *lifatna n-niḍa w-aṣbaḥt min šānkum mištān*
*w-lifatk an-niḍa hi maᶜ rikāyibk ᶜāniyyah*

## POEM 10

Metre:--v---v--v--(*aṭ-ṭawīl*)

1. *ḏabb aḏ-ḏaḥa n-naššād ᶜāli l-amāṯīl*
*rijmin yhayyiḏni ᶜala liᶜb l-afkār*
2. *w-agbal ᶜalayy min kull fajjin timāṯīl*
*w-ḥabb al-wiliyy min kull šinn at-tigiṣṣār*
3. *ya-llāh ya-ᶜallām ma xfi w-ma gīl*
*ya-xālig al-jannah dixīlik min an-nār*
4. *adxul ᶜalēk mn al-miḥan wi-l-ġarābīl*
*la ja nahārin yašxaṣin fīh l-abṣār*
5. *ᶜasa rizīn mġaltimāt al-maxāyīl*
*yimṭir ᶜala m anḥa min al-Ḥumr w-īsār*
6. *wablih yṯawwir jilliha fi l-migāyīl*
*w-ġibb al-maḥal min ḥaḏḏiha tirjiᶜ ad-dār*
7. *yinḥi ᶜala l-Faršah saḥābin hamālīl*
*yaṣfiġ b-sēlin miṯl māyāt l-abḥār*
8. *jiᶜlih ᶜala min Ḏāᶜnin la l-Maḥābīl*
*w-arxa garāḥ al-ma ᶜala Ġīᶜat al-Ġār*
9. *yarfuḏ ᶜala xašim al-Ḥala wi-l-Ḥaṯāmīl*
*wi-tgannaᶜat l-Abrag mahādīb l-amṭār*
10. *yanṯir ḥaṯāyil māh fōg al-ġarāmīl*
*w-anḥa ᶜala bīḏ an-nidaf lih tiḏibbār*

36. Your hardy camels came to us and kept me astir till morning light,[31] //
So we sent our lean animals, together with your mounts, as a brotherly gift.[32]

## POEM 10

1. After sunrise the poet climbed to a high ridge, //
A mountain that brought me into a pensive mood.
2. From every nook and cranny the verses advanced on me, //
Though the Lord loves moderation in everything.
3. O God, He who knows all that man keeps hidden and says, //
O Creator of paradise, Your protection I seek from the fire of hell,
4. Your protection from tribulations and disasters //
On the day when people stare vacantly into space.[33]
5. I hope You send us pitch-black clouds, heavy with moist, //
That rain on the land sloping down from al-Ḥumr and to its left.
6. A downpour that brings to their feet the big-bodied camels resting in the shade around noon, //
Happy that after the drought their pastures will recover;
7. Rain that beats down on al-Faršah in scattered showers //
And unleashes a torrent like a hundred seas.
8. May it extend from Ḏ̣āᶜin to al-Maḥābīl //
And release its sweet water on Ǵīᶜat al-Ġār,
9. Drumming the earth on the edge of al-Ḥala's steep spur and al-Ḥaṯāmīl, //
Enveloping al-Abrag in shrouds of rain;
10. A deluge that is sprayed over the sand-dunes, //
Thrumming the sand-covered tops of the eroded rocks with its downpour.

---

31 When the poet heard the verses brought by the messengers he was moved to compose a response at once and this work kept him awake all night.

32 The exchange of camel mounts, supposedly carrying the messenger who is to deliver the poem to its addressee, is a common image in the genre of poetic correspondence and a metaphor for the exchange of verses between its participants.

33 The reference is to the resurrection when people watch in terror as the awesome spectacle of the Day of Judgment unfolds before their eyes.

11\. *yissi midāhīl al-xalāya l-mišāmīl*
*illi mišat fi nīrtin $^{c}$ugib nawwār*
12\. *yāma ḥala mirbā$^{c}$ha fi d-dahāćīl*
*w-mazyan $^{c}$ala mirwāḥha mal$^{c}$ab al-fār*
13\. *tar$^{c}$a nibātin fi ġṣūnha $^{c}$aṯākīl*
*tistarr bih šāb al-gara kull mi$^{c}$ṭār*
14\. *ya-$^{c}$ālmin ḥāl al-ḥalāl al-mahāzīl*
*yalli mġann al-xēr $^{c}$indik lya ġār*

## POEM 11

Metre:-v---v---v--(*ar-ramal*)

*mnāsibatha nišīdtin gultha w-gāl šā$^{c}$irn āxarin:*

a. *ji$^{c}$l rijmik sahhal al-wāli $^{c}$adāmah*
*mixṭiyyn ma gult māzūn al-kalāmi*

*w-raddēt bih:*

1\. *bādyin rijmin ṯimānīn alf gāmah*
*w-afṭar illi min jimī$^{c}$ al-gāf ṣāmi*
2\. *mall galbin hayyiḏih ṣōt al-ḥamāmah*
*ġaṭrifat bi-ṣ-ṣōt fi sūd al-$^{c}$jāmi*
3\. *hāḏt al-galb al-m$^{c}$anna fi kalāmih*
*w-in bića ġanna b-ma ġanna l-ḥamāmi*
4\. *wanniti wannat yitīmin min $^{c}$amāmih*
*wannitin taṣ$^{c}$ag bha ṣumm al-$^{c}$ḏāmi*
5\. *rāćib illi ma yrawwa$^{c}$ bi-l-misāmah*
*fīh ćann al-miḥgibah xaṭṭ al-wšāmi*
6\. *mirḏi$^{c}$ih rā$^{c}$īh lēn āfa fṭāmih*
*zāydin lih hu wara $^{c}$āmin bi-$^{c}$āmi*
7\. *abyaḏin ka-l-$^{c}$aḏim ma fīh al-$^{c}$alāmah*

11. May it irrigate the favourite haunts of camels with udders trussed in bras //
Wandering in a land that blossomed, then became drought-stricken.
12. How wonderful to see them graze on the sandy slopes //
And the jumping mouses dance on their traces in the evening.
13. They nibble from shrubs adorned with clusters of leaves, //
The delight of the grey-backed camels with resilient humps.
14. O God, He who knows the plight of our wasted livestock, //
Who showers His providence when fortune is at its lowest ebb.

## POEM 11

This poem was said in response to the verses of another poet who said:

a. May the Lord flatten your mountain's top! //
What you said is wrong, certainly not fine poetry.

And this was my reply:

1. I climbed a mountain soaring up four hundred and eighty thousand feet high; //
There he who vowed to abstain from all rhyming broke his fast.
2. Ah, heart aroused by the sound of a dove, //
Cooing with a will somewhere in the steep black chasms;
3. She stirred a heart deprived of speech by sorrow, //
And, crying, it broke into a song not unlike the dove's tune.
4. My lament is like that of an orphan beaten by his uncles, //
A lament that pierces the marrow of one's bones.
5. O rider of a camel not subjected to the pack-saddle, //
With a girth resembling tattoo lines around its breast;
6. Postponing its weaning the owner had allowed it to suckle, //
Adding one more year to its year of grace;[34]
7. Whitish like a bone, without any speckles, //

[34] Normally the calf of a camel is suckled one whole year. In this case two more years have been added before the young was completely weaned. Therefore it grew into an exceptionally strong riding camel.

*dāxilih lōn aš-šigār bla timāmi*
8. *in rfaᶜt aṣ-ṣōt yāxiḏ min jlāmih*
*miṯil xaṭwa gāydin yafraᶜ l-idāmi*
9. *la nahamtih fīh min waṣf an-naᶜāmah*
*tiṣṭifiǵ b-ašnāgha wi-l-jariy ḥāmi*
10. *fi zima rijmin yḥalli fi ṭumāmih*
*ḏaff b-ašnāgin tǵarrib kull zāmi*
11. *kāsirin ᶜungih w-ćaffih fi xṭāmih*
*miṯil hīǵin šāf zōlin fi l-marāmi*
12. *ćan suwād al-ᶜēn min gāfi rṯāmih*
*mistiḏillin kaṯṯarat māh al-ġyāmi*
13. *naṣṣh illi mubṭiyin minni salāmih*
*ᶜugib gurbih nawwisat minh al-ᶜalāmi*
14. *bu ṯimānin yōm yashi min lṯāmih*
*miṯil barrāgin taḥit naww al-wsāmi*
15. *šibh ᶜafran fi migādīm al-jahāmah*
*šūftin li-n-nās fi rūs al-miḏāmi*
16. *dawwrih bi-s-sīn wi-r-ra min timāmih*
*w-iᶜrifih bi-l-ha w-tāfi bih l-isāmi*
17. *nāysin minh al-xabar m adri ᶜalāmah*
*min wara Gaḥṭān walla ṣōb Yāmi*
18. *min jinūb aš-Šām walla fi Thāmah*
*bi-r-Rmah walla warāh ibn al-ḥarāmi*
19. *hu hamāmi yōm kullin fi hamāmih*
*šarᶜati min bidd min ṣalla w-ṣāmi*
20. *la ltahamtih ḥall fi ṣadri gyāmah*
*šān ḥilw az-zād ᶜindi wi-l-manāmi*
21. *widdna bih mēr ma bīᶜ istilāmih*

But with something of a reddish hue as an admixture.
8. Just by raising your voice when singing you make him pick up the pace, //
Like the leading female rushing to the front of the herd of white gazelles;
9. And if you shout to him he dashes off like an ostrich //
That flaps its wings while running at the top of its speed,
10. And, on reaching the end of a slope overlooking a plain, //
Folds the feathered stumps, bringing distant heights close in a wink.
11. Holding his neck low, the halter firmly in the rider's grip, //
The mount runs like a male ostrich scared by a silhouette at shooting range;
12. The black of his eyes behind the ropes of the halter's noseband //
Reminds one of a hollow in the rocks brimful with rain-water.
13. Ride this camel to her whose greetings I have not had for a long time; //
At first she lived close by, now we hear but little from her.
14. When she slightly lowers her veil her front teeth show, //
Like lightning f̱lashing under the clouds of late autumn;
15. Her gait is like that of a fair she-camel followed by the mass of the mixed herds, //
Truly, a sight to behold in the distant desert pastures.
16. Search for her under the letter *sīn* and add the *rāʾ*, //
Then the *hāʾ* and you know her name in full.[35]
17. Since she moved to lands far away I have had no tidings from her: //
Perhaps she lives beyond the Gḥaṭān tribe, or towards the Yām,
18. South of Syria or in the Tihāmah plain, //
In Wādi ar-Rmah or that rascal took her away.
19. On her I dote, just as everybody cherishes his romantic dreams; //
Among all who pray and fast, she is the one to whom I am devoted.
20. When I think of her, I am thrown into convulsions, //
The best food loses its taste and of sweet sleep I am robbed.
21. How I wish to call her mine, yet this price has eluded me, //

[35] The girl's name is Sārah.

*ᶜind aladd an-nās w-amḥaghum xṣāmi*
22. *lēt jasm al-ᶜūd la yadni ṣarāmih*
*ᶜugib biᶜd al-ᶜafin xaṭrin bi l-hyāmi*

POEM 12

Metre:--v---v--v--(*aṭ-ṭawīl*)

*balla mūgtīn w-naṭlub allah bi-l-ḥaya, mūgtīn miṯil ha-l-ḥīn, agūl:*

1. *dann al-galam w-iktib kalām at-taᶜājīb*
*gāfin nḥalli bih ᶜala gōlt al-mīm*
2. *ya-šēx galbi gālibath ad-duwālīb*
*w-ġanna b-gāfin haššam al-ḥāl tahšīm*
3. *w-ḏāg aḏ-ḏimīr w-ja li-ṣadri tiḏārīb*
*w-ćannih yjurr ġṣūn galbi maḥājīm*
4. *fi l-barr ćanni fi miḏīġ al-lahābīb*
*lēn ixtalaft w-habb fi l-galb tansīm*
5. *ašūf fi ṣadri ćima sāyiḥ as-sīb*
*yašrab ᶜala māh al-jahām ar-ruwādīm*
6. *al-galb zarᶜih waddaᶜath al-habāhīb*
*ḥatt al-warag w-aṣbaḥ ġṣūnih miṣārīm*
7. *lāᶜih simūmin talhab al-galb talhīb*
*w-ahjar xaḏārih ᶜugib ma hum manāᶜīm*
8. *ya-llāh ya-rabb al-fiṭīr al-marāġīb*
*illi ġadat min ṭūl mass ad-dahar hīm*
9. *illi wizat bi-glūbhinn al-luwāhīb*
*w-ma tākil illa miḥrigāt al-ᶜarāġīm*
10. *wi-šᶜūfha lli kān sūdin ġadat šīb*
*wi-wjīhha ṭ-ṭiyyār ġid hi mahādīm*
11. *šuft al-xalāya l-xilf ġid hi miḏāhīb*
*w-aslāb ahalha miṯil waṣf al-faḥāḥīm*
12. *w-aḥrag baxaṣ l-aġdām ḥarr al-mišāhīb*

For the most obstinate of men, and the most vengeful, have her in custody.

22. Ah, may that juicy twig not be lopped any time soon! //
Now that resentment has gone, I am almost in the throes of despair.

## POEM 12

We suffered from the drought and asked God to send us rain. It was a period of drought like the one we are going through nowadays. I said:

1. Bring a pen and write my cleverly crafted words, //
Verses made to rhyme on the letter *mīm*.
2. Dear friend, my heart has been tossed around by fate //
And, grief-stricken, it wailed in a melody that left me a shattered man.
3. Distress clouded my mind and palpitated in my breast, //
As if cupping glasses were tapping my heart's arteries.
4. In the open desert I felt as if hemmed in by walls, //
While the winds of moodiness tugged at my heart.
5. You'd say inside my breast a little stream welled forth, //
Its water gulped down by large, mixed herds of camels.
6. Gusty winds carried away my heart's young crop //
Till its twigs stood out bare, stripped even of their leaves;
7. Singed by the flames of a hot breeze from the south, //
The luscious green of old was gone.
8. O God, O Lord of the well-guarded she-camels, //
Emaciated animals in a drought-stricken land;
9. The flames of the blistering heat are licking their hearts; //
They have nothing to eat, except charred branches of the *wahaṭ*-tree.
10. The hair on their spines, once black, turned grey //
And their heads, once upright and alert, are hanging down.
11. I watched how she-camels, after giving birth, wandered around like zombies, //
And their owners, dressed in sooty rags, looked like charcoal burners;
12. Their bare soles were scorched by the ground as if by red-

*w-min kadd min ḥibb al-ᶜanāzīm ma līm*
13. *w-ḏibna w-ḏāb al-ḥāl wi-l-māl taḏyīb*
*illa yirudd illi yifukk al-xawāṣīm*
14. *wi-ᶜmōmisat l-arya w-ḏ̣āᶜat l-aṭābīb*
*w-narḏ̣a ᶜala dibrat wiliyy al-ḥawākīm*
15. *l-insān laww yšukk ma jāb ma jīb*
*yaḏkur wliyyih fi l-liyāl al-migādīm*
16. *w-yiṣbir ᶜala ma ja mn allah lya ṣīb*
*w-yagnaᶜ bi-ḥukm allah w-yarḏ̣a l-migāsīm*
17. *w-allah wimar fi kull šayyin tisābīb*
*wa-n-nagṣ fi māl al-maxālīġ taᶜlīm*
18. *w-ma jāt bi-d-dinya min al-xubṯ wi-ṭ-ṭīb*
*tālīh yadᶜi fi nifādih b-taᶜdīm*
19. *ya-llah bi-lēlin māh yamla l-maḥānīb*
*yiṣbiḥ ġaṯīrih min ġabābih mijāṯīm*
20. *jiᶜlih ᶜala Gamra ḥadatha l-Mijālīb*[36]
*w-amṭar ᶜala l-Jazla saḥābin maġāyīm*
21. *nawwih ᶜagābih miṯil ṣugᶜ al-mahāḏīb*
*w-anḥa migādīmih ćima šurrid ar-rīm*
22. *yarfuḏ̣ ribābih fi trābih mićāhīb*
*ćannih miġāhīr al-jahām al-mijāhīm*
23. *yissi frūᶜ al-ġars ṣifr al-karānīb*
*hidb al-jirīd illi ḥaṯarha mikāmīm*
24. *yissi marād mxaḏ̣ḏ̣b al-ġarn bi-ṭ-ṭīb*
*illi nibātih nāᶜmin ma baᶜad sīm*
25. *illi ḥadīṯih yaslib al-ᶜagil taslīb*
*w-bannat ᶜḏābih fi d-dija yiġᶜid an-nīm*
26. *ḥilwin kalām al-ᶜaḏb zēn at-taᶜājīb*
*ya-zīn fi ᶜašrih ṣifīf al-xawātīm*
27. *ayy al-ᶜasal w-ayya ḥadīṯih lya ḏīb*
*b-aḥla ḥadīṯih min ḥalīb al-mišāḥīm*

*w-salām.*

---

[36] *ḥadatha*, in the poet's imagination one mountain or landmark drives the clouds to the next one, cf. verse 14/11.

glowing kindling; //
But whosoever toils to provide for his camels is not to blame.
13. Our reserves of health and livestock just melted away; //
Only He who separates sworn enemies can turn the tide.
14. People were at their wits' end and no remedy in sight, //
But we resign ourselves to the dispensations of Providence.
15. If man starts to doubt because of what was allotted to him, he will not gain anything, //
And he will remember his Lord in the hard nights to come.
16. When struck by misfortune he endures, //
Accepting God's decree and submitting himself to his fate,
17. For nothing happens unless it was ordained by God; //
There are certainly lessons in the losses His children sustain;
18. Whatever this world brings, both good and bad, //
In the end all perish and are wiped from existence.
19. O God, send us a cloudy night that makes the dry watercourses stream, //
A night that leaves puddles on the ground in the morning;
20. Let it spread to Gamra from al-Mijālīb, //
And may heavy clouds release their rain on al-Jazla,
21. A huge cumulus, its back raised like the rounded tops of steep, rocky mountains, //
Its front parts curving down as gazelles on the run,
22. Slanting curtains of rain pouring down on the earth, //
As if they were the calves of herds of black camels;
23. Rains that irrigate the branches of palms and their yellow stalks, //
Heavy with bunches of young dates that are enveloped for protection,
24. And irrigate the watering place of her whose curls are sprinkled with perfume, //
Whose juicy fruits were not yet put up for sale;
25. She whose conversation is pure delight; //
The scent wafting from her lips awakens the sleeping at night;
26. One never ceases to marvel at her delicious, amusing chatter, //
And the charming arrangement of the rings on her fingers;
27. Liquid honey cannot bear comparison to the words from her lips, //
Even the milk of fattened camels is not as sweet as her speech.

## POEM 13

Metre: v--v---v--v---(*aṭ-ṭawīl*)

1. *riga fi ḏ-ḏaḥa n-naššād fi margibih la ᶜād*
*riga fi ṭiwīl mgawwarāt al-maᶜāzīli*
2. *bida b-isim rabbih gabil mabdāh fi l-anšād*
*w-ḏikir ṭalbit allah gabil badᶜ at-timāṯīli*
3. *ṣḥīḥin w-aliḥḥih kiṯir ma yiḥṣy al-ᶜaddād*[37]
*ᶜala ḥājtin w-arji ᶜaṭāyāh tajri li*
4. *ya-llah b-lēlin ma yxuffih nisam l-anwād*
*ḥagūgin yšaǵǵiǵ māh ġōr al-ġamālīli*
5. *bikir lēlt al-jimᶜah bi-rāy al-kirīm w-ṣād*
*w-taᶜāgab ᶜalēh mrawwḥāt aš-šimāšīli*
6. *tigaṣṣaf rᶜūdih lēn zall ar-rbūᶜ w-ᶜād*
*ġada l-ma biyāḏih fi mzūnih hawāšīli*
7. *tahaššam ᶜala l-Faršah maᶜa ḥazzat al-mihjād*
*xaḏa radd ᶜašrin fi Ġḏayyin mahājīli*
8. *ᶜarūḏin saḥābih yiltiᶜij bārǵih mingād*
*yxalli maᶜa bīḏ al-maḥāni maġāyīli*
9. *min al-ᶜirg li-l-Hajlah ǵinīfin min r-raᶜᶜād*
*w-ᶜala ᶜibilt al-Jazla baradha ḥazāwīli*
10. *taḥaddar ᶜala rūs al-ġarāmīl māh gṣād*
*yidukk al-hamal min bārdāt al-migāyīli*
11. *jiṯīlih ᶜala l-Ǵimra yṭurrih ṯimad Muġmād*
*ribābih ćima zurg al-jmāl al-maḥāmīli*
12. *siga dār šiyyāb al-ᶜaṯānīn w-kull snād*
*ḏinīn al-ᶜabas fīha ćima bannat al-hēli*
13. *ṭwāl al-ġawārib tilḥiǵ al-gunn kull mrād*

---

[37] Cf. al-Faraj (1952), 183, *tliḥḥini laḥḥat xalūjin niḏīrih*, 'she harasses, urges me as one is bothered by a she-camel whose calf was killed.'

## POEM 13

1. After sunrise the bard climbed a height and wished he hadn't //
Climbed to the top of those soaring, conical peaks.
2. He pronounced 'in the name of the Lord' before striking up his song, //
And prayed to God before he began composing his verses.
3. Truly, countless were the entreaties I sent up; //
My need was great and so was the hope I placed in His munificence.
4. O God, send us a night whose clouds are not dispersed by the winds, //
Making good on their promise with floods that rip up the bottoms of the narrow valleys;
5. Clouds brought by the night, early on Friday, surely by decree of the Noble; //
And in their wake drove after drove came drifting along,
6. With thunder crashing till Wednesday had passed, and yet another week, //
As the pure water came bucketing down from the heavy overcast,
7. And thrummed on al-Faršah around midnight, //
While in Ġḏayy ten times as much collected in puddles.
8. A broad front of clouds, flashing with lightning, //
Left little ponds in the sand-coloured bends of the watercourses.
9. From the spurs of sand to al-Hajlah the sky rumbled with thunder, //
And on ʿIblat al-Jazla the hailstones lay in heaps.
10. On the crests of the dunes the rain fell in sheets, //
And roused the free-roaming camels from their noon rest.
11. The land between al-Ǵimra to the depression of al-Muġmād got the best soaker //
From clouds like a train of whitish, heavily-laden camels.
12. It irrigated the home of sturdy camels with tufts of grey hair on their necks, //
The urine that frosted on their tails scenting not unlike cardamom.
13. Even a milksop has no trouble attaining his goal on those steep shoulders; //

*kbār al-figār mḥajjalāt al-ᶜasābīli*
14. *baᶜad nayyiha ḥaṭṭat ćiṯīr al-misīr wnād*
*tiṭāwa hašīmin min ᶜaḏāha mahāzīli*[38]
15. *siga ᶜiddha al-wasmi lih as-sēl ya-Fahhād*
*ya-llah sigath mzalzilāt al-maxāyīli*
16. *yāma ḥala šōf al-muwāri ᶜalēh jdād*
*taxālaf mšawmīsin wi-l-uxra miḏālīli*
17. *tigūd aṣ-ṣidīr w-ḏi tiji ka-l-mḥūṣ ārād*
*tibi ᶜirfitin fīha l-maha lih migāyīli*
18. *ya-rāzig illi ma yibi ṭāriy al-misnād*
*ribībin l-dārin šarᶜati fi midāhīli*
19. *šawāna d-dahar w-aġla ᶜalēna l-ḥaḏīr az-zād*
*ṣakk ᶜalāna mṣarrift al-grūš ad-dalālīli*
20. *ᶜasa llah yiḥīl al-ᶜisr minna w-min l-ajwād*
*jizīl al-mdūd w-yinzil al-xēr tanzīli*
21. *w-taftaḥ lha bābin mn al-ᶜarš ya-jawwād*
*b-rizgin tilīn bh al-ćbūd al-maġālīli*
22. *lih al-xēr b-amr llah lih l-mulk wi-l-mīᶜād*
*w-minna bi-ᶜilm allah hu aṣ-ṣādig al-gīli*
*sibḥānih.*

## POEM 14

Metre: v--v---v--v---(*aṭ-ṭawīl*)

1. *ana bādiyin fi rās rijmin m abi margāh*
*ḥadāni ᶜala ᶜāli marāġībih al-gīli*
2. *talāḥēt ana wi-mġanniy al-warg fi mabdāh*
*nġaṭrif b-ṣōtin lēn hāḏ al-jahāhīli*

---

[38] *tiṭāwa* for the 3 f. s. imperf. of the VI form of the verb *ttiṭāwa*, see note 6, p. 102.

They have towering backs and the teats of their udders are speckled with white;
14. Constant travelling burnt up their fat and exhausted them //
And now they trudge along, all skin and bone.
15. May the autumn rains replenish their well with a torrent, O Fahhād; //
O Lord, may the rumbling clouds water its land.
16. What a delight to see the signs of trails freshly trodden //
By camels, a single file walking sunward moving past the shaded faces of the opposite train:
17. As the watered camels return, others hasten to the well in lines stretched as ropes, //
All of them craving to graze the meadows where oryxes rest in the shade.
18. O Provider of her who resents talk of far journeys in search of pasture, //
One whose attachment to her home is only matched by mine to her haunts;
19. Scorched by drought and villagers who raised the price of our staples, //
We suffered at the hands of money-lenders and their cunning.
20. May God free us and all noble souls from hardship; //
He bestows His bounty lavishly and sends down to us His blessings.
21. O Beneficent One, open one of the gates of Your throne for the flow //
Of sustenance that softens the hard, shrivelled livers.
22. He decrees the good, His is the reign and the last day. //
God's commands we must obey, He who speaks the true words.

God be praised.

## POEM 14

1. I climbed the peak of a lofty mountain against my wish, //
Driven to that high vantage point by the poetic urge.
2. On its summit I joined in a duet with a turtledove, //
Singing lustily until even the obtuse were roused.

3. *lya ćann galbi fi ćilīl al-faḥam yaṣlāh*
*lya jīt ana fi ᶜāliyāt al-mahālīli*
4. *wara l-galb ma lih ᶜārfin ᶜāǵlin yanhāh*
*yiruddih mn az-zallah li-darb ad-duwālīli*
5. *lya ṣār minni nāṣiḥ al-ᶜilm ma yagrāh*
*falānīb rabbin li-l-glūb al-mahābīli*[39]
6. *ya-llāh yalli kull ḥayyin ᶜala marjāh*
*jizīl al-ᶜaṭa lli ma wara ḥīltih ḥīli*
7. *ya-ᶜālmin al-ġēb ma ġābiyin yixfāh*
*an adxul ᶜalēk mn al-miḥan wi-z-zalāzīli*
8. *alinnik tǵaddīna ᶜala ṭāᶜtih wi-rḏ̣āh*
*ᶜasāna njannib min ṭirīǵ al-miḏ̣ālīli*
9. *ana ṭālbik lēlin ynaṯṯir ḥaṯāyir māh*
*ᶜala ḥašrij al-Bēḏa ġada lih hamālīli*
10. *talāḥam min al-Faršah lya Jabjibin mamšāh*
*w-sara lēl dahhāšin tigaffa l-maxāyīli*
11. *ḥagūgin maxāyīlih ᶜala Ḏ̣āᶜinin manšāh*
*truddih lya l-Janbah xšūm al-Muwāᶜīli*[40]
12. *taᶜāgab šaxātīrih ᶜala l-Hajlat al-mismāh*
*siga dār zēnāt al-ᶜarāba l-mišāmīli*
13. *siga dār malḥan kāyfin dalliha miswāh*
*tigūl in wubarha ḏ̣āhrin b-aswad an-nīli*
14. *ya-zīnha bi-d-dīć fōg al-ḥajab tazhāh*
*w-ćanha tsaḥḥib fi l-muwāṭi zarābīli*
15. *ᶜala labbat al-Manjūr w-anḥa ᶜala Ġaḏ̣yāh*
*saḥābih ᶜala xašm al-Gṭayyiᶜ juwādīli*
16. *yihill ašhab al-ma wi-r-raᶜad rāćdin f atlāh*
*thaššim gnūfih fi frūᶜ al-ġarāmīli*
17. *ᶜarūḏin ᶜala l-wādi tidāyag ᶜala maḏmāh*
*w-tiganna ᶜ Ṭwēǵin fīh miṯil al-mišāᶜīli*

---

[39] Verses 3-5 are variations on the repertory of Najdi love poetry. Compare for instance the first hemistichs of verses 3, 4, and 5 with the following ones in the *dīwān* of Ibn Sbayyil: *wa-l-galb šibbat bih saᶜāyir wgūdih* 'the heart was set ablaze and burst out in flames'; *gilt āh lo galbi ġarīrin nahētih* 'I said, "Ah, if my heart were young and inexperienced, I would have called it to order"', and *nahēt galbi ᶜan hawāh w-ᶜaṣāni* 'I ordered my heart to stay away from its passion, but it disobeyed me'; *wa-l-harj ma yanfaᶜ wla hu b-ġāri* 'mere words are of no avail and useless', al-Faraj (1952), 167, 182, 201 and 212.

[40] See note 36.

3. I felt as if my heart was being roasted on a slow fire, //
Once I sat by myself on that high ridge.
4. Why is there no experienced, wise person to restrain my heart //
And turn it away from wrong to the path of prudence
5. If it doesn't wish to heed my well-intentioned advice; //
After all, I have no business minding foolish hearts.
6. O God, You who are every living being's source of hope; //
Liberal with His bounty, His is the final disposition;
7. He knows what is veiled, nothing remains hidden for Him; //
Against life's troubles and disasters I seek Your protection;
8. May You lead us into obeisance and acceptance, //
And may we steer clear from the path of sin.
9. My request is for a night of gushing rain, //
Pouring down in the deep torrent bed of al-Bēḏa,
10. A seamless overcast from al-Faršah to Jabjib, //
A stupendous night, its clouds drifting along the sky,
11. True harbingers of rain that keep piling up over Ḏāᶜin, //
Pushed to al-Janbah's well by the bluffs of al-Muwāᶜīl.
12. Its water streams down in torrents on al-Hajlah, //
Drenching the land of fine thoroughbred camels with nets around their udders,
13. And the land of one well-shaped blue-black she-camel, //
Her curly hair shining with an indigo lustre,
14. Marvelously adorned with tussocks of black wool on the hips,[41] //
Dragging her feet as if shod in clumsy leather boots;
15. And also the sand drifts at the feet of al-Manjūr's dunes and Ġaḏya, //
While the clouds float densely packed over the spur of al-Gṭayyiᶜ.
16. The grey sheets of rain keep falling, the thunder rumbling in their train, //
And the sky's water splashes in the gullies of the sand-hills;
17. A broad cloudfront that soaks the thirsty ground of the Wādi, //
And envelops the Ṭwēġ escarpment in a display of flashing lights.

---

[41] These tussocks are attached to the place where the slings upholding the nets around the udders that prevent calves from drinking their mother's milk are tied across the hip and under the tail.

18. *tigūl aṭ-ṭarāġi ma gaᶜad wādiyin ma jāh*
*midat raddat allah li-l-ḥalāl al-mahāzīli*
19. *lya jaff sēlih gām jazil al-ᶜaṭa yālāh*
*tanazzal saḥābih fi manābit l-atāwīli*
20. *ᶜala šān ḏa midhālna lli lina mašhāh*
*lina fīh fi ḥill aṣ-ṣifāri maḥālīli*

## POEM 15[42]

Metre:-v---v---v--(*ar-ramal*)

1. *šāybin wi-l-galb yarji fi l-biḏārah*
*widdih innih yirjiᶜ illi kān fāti*
2. *wall ya-galbin tizāyad fi ᶜibārih*
*w-in nahētih ma ḥaṣal ᶜindih ṯibāti*
3. *ġāṣbih bi-l-ᶜagil wall innih xabārah*
*nāṣḥih dūn al-xaṭa bi-l-miġdiyāti*
4. *bakriti xubbi ᶜasāć allah mjārah*
*jāric allah ma yiji rijlić ḥafāti*
5. *ilᶜabi li-l-jariy fi ḥāmi garārih*
*liᶜb ġirṯān al-bniyy al-mitrifāti*
6. *liᶜib Rasmah yōmha fi l-bīḏ šārah*
*fargha jōrin ᶜala šugḥ al-banāti*
7. *ᶜēnha ᶜēn asmarin ḥaggag miṭārih*
*fi ṭiwīlāt ar-rjūm an-nāyfāti*
8. *dāmlin ṣāfi ᶜafārih bi-ṣ-ṣifārah*
*wi-l-jidāyil la r-rdūf mnaggaḏāti*
9. *wi-l-manāćib miṯil mamṭūr az-zibārah*
*wi-n-nhūd mn al-jibīn mzabbarāti*
10. *wi-r-ridāyif miṯil šaṭṭin fi ḥwārah*

---

[42] It so happened that this poem was recorded at the time of sunset and that Dindān had almost reached the end of his recitation when the call for the evening prayer was sounded in the camp. The transcribed text cannot convey the wonderful impression made by the orchestral mixture of sounds into which the poem's last verses were blended: the reproving tone in the voice of Dindān's host—who had not failed to notice the frivolous content of Dindān's verses while busy feeding his camels and now reminded the poet of the hour—, the chorus of groaning camels, and Dindān's final *la ilāh ill allāh* 'There is no God but Allah', spoken an octave lower than the poem and uttered in a long sigh as if his consciousness suddenly filled with deep religious feeling.

18. Wayfarers bring the news: no valley on the clouds' path missed out, //
For God wanted the worn-out livestock to recover its strength.
19. As soon as the torrent subsided the Bountiful made it flow again //
And ordered His clouds to unload over the salty *atāwīl*-plants.
20. No wonder we always long for this haunt //
And there you'll find our camp in the autumn days.

## POEM 15

1. I am old but my heart pines for its youth //
And wishes for the return of days bygone.
2. Get lost, heart given to sobbing and wailing, //
Unable to steady itself when admonished!
3. My attempts to coerce by reason fall flat, //
When I counsel it to stay away from sin and be sensible.
4. My young lady camel, trot and may God protect you, //
Protect your pads from being hurt by sharp stones.
5. Play and frolic as you keep running your fastest, //
As girls of soft and tender age gambol about!
6. Among the fair, skittish Rasmah stands out, //
Cruelly outshining her cream-coloured friends:
7. Her eyes are fierce like those of a falcon in full flight, //
Swooping down from soaring mountain peaks;
8. The white of her skin shades into olive, //
And her profuse curls tumble down on her bottom;
9. Her haunches are smooth like sand-hills sprayed by rain, //
And her round breasts protrude firmly from her chest,
10. Whereas her hips bulge like the hump of a camel calf //

*bēn ḏīrēnin ᶜalāha mihmilāti*
11. *ḥaggha jahhālik inn al-ᶜilm šārah*
*tirtiḥil li-z-zēn sēxāt al-banāti*
12. *ᶜind manᶜūrin ṣibūrin bi-l-xasārah*
*wi-ḏ-ḏarib minh al-ᶜlūm aṭ-ṭayyibāti*

## POEM 16

Metre:-v---v---v--(*ar-ramal*)

*aᶜālij fi Makkah wi-l-bill hamal, ḏīᶜ*

1. *ya-wijūdi gāᶜidin wi-s-sadd bāḥi*
*la ngiḏ amrih wi-ṣ-ṣalāḥ mᶜaṭṭilīnih*
2. *ᶜizziti l-illi fwādih ma starāḥi*
*bāyḥin saddih w-mabḥūṯin ćinīnih*
3. *wall ya-galbin dana minh an-nijāḥi*
*w-in nahētih yiǵᶜid an-nāyim winīnih*
4. *ᶜēn yalli damᶜaha fi l-ḥajir fāḥi*
*fōḥ figr al-bīr la ḥirrik difīnih*
5. *rāćib illi ćan winīnih fi l-barāḥi*
*wannat illi fīh jinnin ḥāćrīnih*
6. *rakkibaw fīh al-ᶜajal tawwih ṣḥāḥi*
*b-arbiᶜīnin min grāših mintiǵīnih*
7. *min wiṭan l-ixwān yasraḥ min ṣibāḥi*
*ᶜāmrin taww al-ćlāb mwarrdīnih*
8. *fōgh aḏ-ḏafrān ṣibyān al-falāḥi*
*kull ġimrin ṣulb jaddih miḥtiwīnih*
9. *minwit illi nāhimin yabġa l-marāḥi*
*ma yiḏūg an-nōm min fargih xadīnih*

Pampered with the milk of two devoted foster-mothers.
11. Listen, hairbrained youth, her reputation is well deserved
And becoming to a beauty ruling over the female tribe,
12. In the custody of a stalwart who patiently bears his losses, //
A gentleman whose renown has spread far and wide.[43]

## POEM 16

I was receiving medical treatment in Mecca and my camels were roaming the pastures without supervision; they were left to themselves.

1. There I sit, suffering and unable to restrain myself; //
I have come to grief, my life has been ruined.
2. Woe unto him whose heart refuses to be comforted: //
Its pent-up feelings are given free rein and its secrets are open to scrutiny.
3. Off with you! O heart that has almost stewed to readiness //
And whose moaning awakens the sleeping when I try to bridle it!
4. My tears kept welling up and filled my eyes, //
Like a well whose sand-filled bottom is scraped up.
5. O rider of a vehicle roaring in the featureless waste, //
Like one who is possessed by a demon,
6. A car fitted with brand-new tyres,
Selected from the dealer's showroom for forty thousand riyāls.
7. In the early morning he sets out from the land of our brothers //
Driving his spanking new car, a recent import from the dogs.[44]
8. The crew on board are all brash and jaunty youngsters, //
Bold men who store in their marrow the seed of equally brave ancestors.
9. A vehicle that suits the dreams of a man hankering to depart, //
One deprived of sleep by the separation from his love.

---

[43] Her father patiently bears the self-inflicted losses caused by his boundless hospitality, for the chivalry of the desert requires from a man that he entertain unsparingly any visitor who calls on him or happens to pass by. The poet wishes to convey that his beloved combines beauty with an excellent pedigree as the daughter of a member of the moral nobility of the desert.

[44] 'The dogs', a slur denoting infidels, people of a different faith, Christians.

10. *ḥālfin la gīl li ma hūb ṣāḥi*
*m atrikih wi-l-miᶜtimir yanṣa l-Midīnah*
11. *naṭṭaḥ aṣ-ṣaddām nisnās ar-ryāḥi*
*wi-l-ḥabīb illi biᶜīdin wāṣlīnih*
12. *bu jibīnin miṯl maṣgūl as-slāḥi*
*wi-l-ᶜasal fi ma ḥaća bih kātbīnih*
13. *ya-hal al-mangūd ᶜirḏ̣i mistibāḥi*
*min kala ᶜirḏ̣ al-ġyāb msāmḥīnih*

## POEM 17

Metre:-v---v---v--(*ar-ramal*)

*ḥamāmah tġanni w-ana jāyyin sjērtin mgayyilin fīha, xābrin inni jīt fīh ana wiyya snāfiyytin gabil, gāmat al-ḥamāmah tġarrid ᶜala rāsi ma xallatni anūm, w-agūl*

1. *ya-llah la tajzāć bi-l-xēr inkiriyyah*
*ġaṭrifat m adri tinīḥ aw hi tnāḥi*
2. *zaᶜzaᶜat Rīmah wi-hi ma bih miṭiyyah*
*liᶜbha balla ᶜala gadd al-manāḥi*
3. *liᶜbha ġayyin w-ana jāli dᶜiyyah*
*la baġat ṭārat w-ana ma li janāḥi*
4. *ḥaṭṭat al-galb al-ḥazīn yiji šuwiyyah*
*lēn ǵirǵiᶜ bih gišīmin li-n-nijāḥi*
5. *lēn fāḏat ᶜabrat al-ᶜēn aš-šigiyyah*
*w-infara ṯōb al-ᶜaza wi-s-sadd bāḥi*
6. *miṯil bīrin farraġāha ᶜēlimiyyah*
*figirha ma yardiᶜih nēs al-bṭāḥi*
7. *ḥarrikāha wirdha ǵid hi siriyyah*

10. If it is said of me, 'He is not in his right mind,' I swear //
Not to give up on her, for in the end the pilgrim will reach Medina.
11. Steering his car head-on in the wind he lets the bumper cleave the air //
And does not pause until they have arrived at the loved one living far away,
12. She whose brow shines like a polished sword //
And whose conversation is sugared with honey.
13. You, fault-finders, my honour has become public property, //
But they who smirch one's honour in his absence will be forgiven.

## POEM 17

This one was inspired by a turtledove I found cooing in a tree when I wanted to rest in its shade. You should know that I had sat there long ago in the company of a charming young lady. So lustily was this turtledove cooing above my head that I was unable to sleep. So I said:

1. O God, may no good befall this nasty bird //
That pumps its lungs to bemoan or in vainglory, who can tell?
2. 'Rīmah' I heard her coo, though she owns no camel. //
For her song there is no apparent reason other than whim,[45]
3. And fancy, whereas I have a task to perform; //
She takes to the air when she likes, but I have no wings.
4. Through her fault my sad heart was roasted by fire //
Till it was braised to readiness over the red embers.
5. Tears began to flow from my miserable eyes, //
And I gave in to despair, the gown of solace torn to shreds,
6. Like a rich-flowing well that is being emptied, //
Its mouth not clogged by the sands of the valley bottom;
7. A well dug out by a watering party so that it began to flow; //

---

[45] Rīmah, a name given to a she-camel.

*fawwa$^{c}$at bi-l-jamm l-azrag ma tmāḥi*
8. *min $^{c}$ana ġaḏ̣ḏ̣ an-nahad jaṯl az-zuwiyyah*
*mixmiṣ al-maṯnāt ubu xaddin simāḥi*
9. *bu nhūdin miṯil lōn al-magfiziyyah*
*fi jibīnin miṯil maṣgūl as-slāḥi*
10. *la šibaḥni ćann fi $^{c}$ēnih hawiyyah*
*ćan hadab $^{c}$ēnih yihūzik bi-r-rmāḥi*
11. *min banāt al-baduw ma hīb ḥḏ̣iriyyah*
*ma ligāna miṯlih aḥdin fi n-nuwāḥi*
12. *bu ṯimānin la ḏ̣aḥak bīḏ̣in $^{c}$aḏiyyah*
*ka-l-barad walla ćima lōn al-malāḥi*

## POEM 18

Metre:-v--v---v--v--(*al-mumtadd*)

*naby l-miṭar*

1. *šarraf aš-šā$^{c}$ir ad-Dindān rijmin l-ḥālih*
*gāl šaffih b-kēfih min ḥasīn al-kalāmi*
2. *ya-llah inni ṭalabtik min ruwāyiḥ xyālih*
*mirjifin mirdifin yaḏbuṭ nḥūr al-ġyāmi*
3. *ćann ḏ̣arb al-midāfi$^{c}$ fi tuwāli ṯgālih*
*ćan migādīm rubbānih hajīj al-jahāmi*
4. *sayyal al-haḏb wablih yōm rabbi nuwa lih*
*yirji$^{c}$ al-galb l-asna min ḥanīn al-$^{c}$jāmi*
5. *ji$^{c}$l yissi jiba l-Manjūr xaddih w-jālih*
*rāfḏ̣in bārġih yafra suwād aḏ̣-ḏ̣alāmi*
6. *ćan mṣaggal syūf al-hind ṣīfat ša$^{c}$ālih*
*yōm ćahhab saḥābih fi ḏ̣hūr al-$^{c}$adāmi*

No need to scoop up its limpid water, for it came gushing to the surface.[46]
8. All this because of one with luscious breasts and flowing hair, //
Narrow in the waist and with cheeks silky and smooth;
9. Her bust, white as the dates of the *magfizi*-palm, //
Protrudes from a chest that shines like polished arms;
10. When her gaze fixes on me it is like a dagger's thrust, //
And it's as if her eyelashes jab at you with sharp spears.
11. She's a true bedouin girl, not one of those village folk. //
You may travel far and wide, but her equal you won't find:
12. When she laughs with her fine, white teeth //
They glitter at you like hailstones or grains of ice.

## POEM 18

We were longing for the rain:

1. The poet ad-Dindān ascended a mountain all alone //
And burst into exquisite verses made to suit his own taste.
2. O God, from You I asked for a share of the fast-travelling clouds, //
One rumbling with thunder, its posterior raised toward the overcast behind;
3. In the rear of its heavy train one hears what sounds like gunfire, //
And preceding it, wefts of cloudlets race like panicky camels.
4. On the ordained day my Lord unleashed a cloudburst on al-Haḏb, //
And torrents came roaring down to restore life to the parched hearts.
5. May He water the basin around al-Manjūr's well, its earth and shaft, //
With pouring rain and lightning ripping through the dark,
6. And flashes like the glittering steel of Indian swords, //
While the clouds dip towards the crests of the sand-hills;

---

[46] If a well is plentiful there is no need for a man to climb down into it and scoop up the water, see glossary under *myḥ*.

7. *sāmrin ṭūl lēlih lēn naṯṯar zlālih*
*fōg galfaʿ Sanāmah ʿugib ma ḥall gāmi*
8. *ćan suwād al-ġadāri fi nuwāṣi ǵbālih*
*mijhimin yašxal al-ma raḥmitin li-ḏ̣-ḏ̣uwāmi*
9. *min Ḏ̣ida la jiba l-Murrah zibīrin ḥṯālih*
*ġibb sēlih yġanni fīh warg al-ḥamāmi*
10. *yafraḥ illi mahāzīlin šarāyid ḥalālih*
*yōm naššа ʿala dārih ḥagūg al-wsāmi*
11. *intaḥa ṣōb ġarsin mistićinnin ḏ̣lālih*
*yabhaj illi juwayʿin fi liyāl aṣ-ṣarāmi*
12. *miḥtimīnih lya min kull ḏībin ʿawa lih*
*b-amlaḥ as-sēf wi-dwāl al-ʿyāl at-timāmi*
13. *wādiyin dūnih al-ḥākim fiḏ̣ēna dwālih*
*yōm ḥinna ʿala dāsāt l-arya ʿzāmi*
14. *ja r-Rišīdi yibīh b-jarritin fi ḉfālih*
*maʿ gara l-ḥazim l-aswad min jinūb al-Ldāmi*
15. *f-iġtiša l-milḥ jamʿih lēn jannab hbālih*
*w-istigād aṣ-ṣaʿab w-aṣbaḥ yiṭīʿ al-xṭāmi*
16. *wi-š-širīf ibin Hāšim zārǵih b-iḥtmālih*
*fātnin fi l-midar w-allah nuwa lih ʿadāmi*
17. *jāh jamʿin yišūg al-ʿēn māḏ̣i faʿālih*
*fōg gubbin tṯawwir bi-l-ḥawāfir ʿasāmi*
18. *la ʿamadna xaṭan min ʿāylin bi-l-ʿamālah*
*yagmiʿūnih b-maftūg as-syūf aš-šuwāmi*

7. All night long their pure water splashes down, //
And lies in puddles among the flat layers of rock of Sanāmah.
8. The pitch-black colour in the brow of its thunderheads //
Is like a figure sieving the water in compassion for the thirsty.
9. From Ḏida to the cirque of al-Murrah's well the streams assemble, //
To the tune of the turtledove once the torrent has subsided.
10. Whoever saw his livestock dwindle rejoices //
When the clouds bringing the winter rains amass over his land,
11. And roll towards the dense foliage of the palm plantations, //
To the mirth of those who went hungry in the season of the date-harvest.[47]
12. Their palms they protected against hordes of howling wolves[48] //
With the grey steel of their swords and hosts of fiery warriors.
13. We cordoned off the Wādi and put the ruler's armies to flight, //
Determined to carry out the battle plan we threshed out in our tribal counsels.
14. Ar-Ras͟hīd, leading his loyal troops in a war of conquest,[49] //
Came marching over the black plateau to the south of al-Ldām.
15. A barrage of fire wrapped them in powder-smoke, forcing the fools to retreat; //
We tamed the refractory and taught them to obey our nosering.
16. Likewise the S͟harīf Ibn Hās͟him deluded himself into believing[50] //
Our land could be snatched; but God handed him a rout:
17. In his way he found dazzling troops in pursuit of victory, //
On broad-chested horses that throw up clouds of dust with their hoofs.
18. If some scoundrel gets it into his head to work his evil on us, //
Our men subdue him by wielding their sharp Syrian swords.

---

47 Normally even the very poor did not have to go hungry in the season of the date-harvest, since they would be allowed to collect any dates that fell to the ground. In a period of extreme drought, however, the harvest might partly fail. Also, it might refer to drought-stricken bedouins who are unable to barter butter for dates in the markets of the Wādi as they used to do in autumn.

48 'Howling wolves', i.e. enemy tribes hungry to seize the riches and land of the Duwāsir.

49 Ar-Ras͟hīd, the ruling family of Hail (Ḥāʾil) before the Saudi conquest.

50 Ibn Hās͟him, the S͟harīfs of Mecca, the ruling family of that town before the Saudi conquest.

19. *ḥiffna miḏ̣ᶜifīnih min ᶜṣūr al-jahālah*
*middna jāyirin fōg al-mikāyīl dāmi*
20. *ćam ᶜaǵīdin kisarna ᶜizz rabᶜih b-fālih*
*yibrimūn ar-rya w-inna nfukk al-ḥzāmi*
21. *la mišēna b-jamᶜin ćann ṣāli šaᶜālih*
*ćīr nārin yifukk mn al-ḥadīd al-lḥāmi*
22. *nāxḏ al-midin fōg an-nās zōdin nfālih*
*yōm min fād ḥiggin yiḥisb innih yimāmi*
23. *ᶜānt illi jimīᶜ al-xēr lih wi-ṯ-ṯana lih*
*w-fiᶜl mirwīn ᶜaṭšān ar-rṣāṣ al-ḥyāmi*
24. *Āl Zāyid hal ar-rāyāt w-ahl al-jalālah*
*ya-salāmi ᶜalēhum ᶜidd rīš at-thāmi*
25. *ya-salāmi ᶜala ahl al-jūd w-ahl aš-šikālah*
*ᶜidd min kān ṣalla w-iᶜtana bi-ṣ-ṣyāmi*
*w-salāmatk.*

## POEM 19

Metre:--v---v--v--(*aṭ-ṭawīl*)

1. *ᶜAbdallah ad-Dindān ḏabb al-mišārīf*
*rijmin taġašwāh al-xyāl ar-rzāni*
2. *afḏ̣ēt ma ćannēt bēn as-sarājīf*
*w-gāmat thišš al-ma l-ᶜyūn al-ḥzāni*
3. *yāma b-ṣadri xāfyin ma baᶜad šīf*
*w-in jīt b-aćna gult ana l-mōt jāni*
4. *ya-lajjiti lajjat giṭīᶜ al-miḏ̣ālīf*
*sabᶜ ijbitin fōg al-misāǵi ḥawāni*

19. Since the times of ignorance we are in the habit of humbling our enemies,[51] //
For the power we bring to bear is always more than what they can muster.
20. Many a raid leader we deprived of his men's pride in his good fortune: //
They weave their plots and we unravel them.
21. When our men march, resplendent in their armour, //
They are like fiery flames that melt iron's solder.
22. We sweep up entire towns, together with their people, for good measure, //
Whereas others fancy themselves great warlords after robbing a young camel;
23. But only with the help of Him to whom all good and praise belong, //
And the valour of those whose guns have an insatiable appetite for bullets.
24. They are the offspring of Zāyid, men of poise and might; //
Greetings to them as many as the wings of Tihāmah locusts,
25. Greetings to these noble worthies //
In numbers great as those who pray to God and observe the fasting.

## POEM 19

1. ᶜAbdallah ad-Dindān climbed the high cliffs //
Of a mountain soaked with rain by heavy clouds.
2. There I gave free rein to the feelings pent up between my ribs, //
And, disconsolate, I burst out in tears.
3. If only people knew what secrets I kept hidden: //
My attempts at restraint put me through the pains of death.
4. I moan and groan like a herd of camels standing with bent necks, //
Looking over the brink of the well for more than three days,

---

[51] 'The times of ignorance', the *jāhilīyah*, the period before Islam. It may also refer to the 'second *jāhilīyah*', the period before the Wahhābī reform movement became dominant among the tribes and towns of what is now Saudi Arabia.

5. *tahajjifat min ᶜugib riᶜiy l-xazārīf*
*samᶜat ṣyāḥ al-wird lēlat ṯimāni*
6. *ᶜugb aš-šaḥam ǵid hi ǵidīd al-manāšīf*
*mann aḏ̣-ḏ̣ma miṣyāfha yōm zāni*
7. *ćanha hašīm aṭ-ṭalḥ tamši gifāgīf*
*ḥazzat miġīb shēl wi-l-gēḏ̣ dāni*
8. *ṣabbaw lha min mašrabin xallaha tᶜīf*
*jarrat ḥanīnin šayyab al-miṭribāni*
9. *māha ġamīrih ṯawwarath al-maġārīf*
*w-mayyāḥha hajrih ṭuwāh al-wsāni*
10. *aw lajjiti lajjat ṯimān al-mahāyīf*
*ᶜala bitāt al-ᶜēlam ar-rēhajāni*
11. *tiǵfi bha sūd al-bkār al-mišāᶜīf*
*šīb aḏ̣-ḏ̣yūl mrabbaᶜāt al-miṯāni*
12. *nūṭ ar-rǵāb illi šaḥamha marādīf*
*hizz al-figār umm al-wṣūf az-zyāni*
13. *tigalliban ṣōb al-maᶜādil maḥārīf*
*w-taxāzarat fi ᶜabdha bi-l-ᶜayāni*
14. *tissi l-ġrūs illi ṯimarha manāṣīf*
*hidb al-jirīd illi frūᶜih mtāni*
15. *ᶜalēk yalli lih ṯimānin marāhīf*
*fi ḏibbilin miṯl al-ḥarīr al-ᶜmāni*
16. *min minwit illi yanšif ar-rīǵ tanšīf*
*tabrid luwāhīb al-mġill aḏ̣-ḏ̣imāni*
17. *li ṣāḥbin xaddih ćima sallat as-sēf*
*bēn al-ᶜarab ćannih shēl al-yimāni*

5. Their humps sagging, gone whatever remained from grazing on the *khazārīf*-plants, //
And then, on the fourth day, heard the shouts of the herdsmen.
6. Once covered with fat, they now look like shrivelled thongs: //
Cruel thirst robbed them of the strength they gained from spring's pastures.
7. Like a bundle of dead acacia-wood they trudge along //
At the time of Canopus' eclipse when the great heat sets in.
8. Disgusted by the foul smell of the water poured into the trough, //
The animals groaned so pitifully as to make a happy fellow turn grey.
9. When he stirred the filth on the water with a ladle, //
The man scooping up the water inside the well fainted, overcome by the stench.
10. Or is it like the screeching of eight pulley-wheels //
Turning on their axles over a plenteous, never-ceasing well,
11. Pulled with vehemence by black, young she-camels;
Hairy on the spine, tails greyish and flanks bulging, //
12. Animals with slender necks, bodies covered with layers of fat //
And quivering humps: they are perfection incarnate.
13. When they have walked down the sloping path and turn around, //
They give a furtive look to the black slave that drives them on.[52]
14. The palm-trees irrigated by them carry fruits that are half-ripe, //
And firm branches supported by supple, curved stems.
15. My suffering is because of you and your sharp front teeth, //
Set in lips soft as silk from Oman;
16. How fortunate is he who sucks her saliva //
That cools the flames of hearts burning with desire;
17. Yes, because of her whose cheeks are burnished as a sword's blade, //
She glitters among the bedouins like Canopus at the southern horizon.

---

[52] Only a cruel driver will beat his animals when they make their way back up the tow path towards the *mʿaddal*, the turning point at the well, and begin pulling the rope of the bucket again, see pp. 46-47.

18. *ya-tall galbi tall rakb al-manākīf*
    *rawwaḥ maᶜa girdūb ḥazmin biyāni*
19. *samᶜ aṣ-ṣyāḥ w-ṭayyarōh aṭ-ṭuwāḥīf*
    *wakkad ᶜajāj mlāwyāt al-ᶜnāni*
20. *laḥġat b-ahalha yalᶜabūn al-ġaṭārīf*
    *kullin yigūl al-ḥagg ᶜindi naḥāni*
21. *waṭṭaw ᶜala nūṭ ar-rġāb al-muwājīf*
    *w-haffaw maᶜa girdūb ḥazmin ṭimāni*
22. *lāla simār al-lēl ġabba l-maxālīf*
    *ma rāḥ minhum min yimiss al-bṭāni*[53]
23. *taxāṭifōhum fi nḥūr al-mizāġīf*
    *waṭṭaw ᶜalābīhum bi-ḥadd as-snāni*
24. *lēn istiṭāᶜ aš-šarh minhum ᶜala kēf*
    *w-rāḥ aṣ-ṣaᶜab minhum ćima l-mirjaᶜāni*

*w-salāmatkum.*

## POEM 20

Metre:--v--v---v---(*al-basīṭ*)

*d̲ilūln aᶜasifha*

1. *ya-rāćib illi tibūj al-xāwiy al-xāli*
   *min ᶜāširin jaddha tad̲rib bh an-nāsi*
2. *samran twarrid lya minnih ġada l-lāli*
   *ġaṭṭin sarābih yšayyib mafriġ ar-rāsi*
3. *samra simārih šaᶜālih lih tišᶜimāli*
   *ćan lōnha mišxaṣin zādōh bi-nḥāsi*
4. *la dayyam al-lāl ġamrin dūn l-amt̲āli*

[53] *min yimiss al-bṭān* 'those who pull the belly girth', i.e. all the raiders would have been killed.

18. Ah, the pull at my heart is like that felt by mounted men returning from a raid, //
As they plunge over the ridge of a low hill.
19. They heard the alarm cries and the sound of shots fired at them, //
And, no mistake, they saw clouds of dust thrown up by snorting steeds.[54]
20. The horsemen overtook them, singing war songs, //
While vying for their kill, everyone saying 'My quarry!'
21. The raiders kicked the necks of their fleet camels, //
And helter-skelter rushed down from the crest of the stony hill.
22. Were it not for the dark of night that covered the winding trails, //
None of them ever would have touched his camel's belly girths again.
23. The pursuers outflanked the raiders, then took them in their horses' breasts, //
And stabbed them with the points of their spears in the neck,
24. Until the fiery among them became as meek as lambs, //
And the intractable as tame as camels trained to draw water.

## POEM 20

This is about a riding-camel I was training.

1. O rider of a camel that traverses the empty wilderness; //
To the tenth degree its ancestors were famous breeding stallions.
2. A dark camel that carries its rider to his destination through the mirage //
And dust devils in the quivering air that cover one's head with grey.
3. A camel of a deep brownish hue, its hair glowing //
With the sparkle of coins overlaid with copper.
4. When the landmarks are hidden from view by dust whirling in the blistering heat, //

[54] I.e. the horsemen of the plundered tribe in pursuit of their captured animals.

*tūridk fi l-gēḏ wi-ṣ-ṣimlān yibbāsi*
5. *bint al-$^{c}$māni daġalha al-ḥurr min tāli*
*rīḥ an-nijāyib yijīha minh nisnāsi*
6. *šaffi $^{c}$ala kārha f-inn kārha ašla li*
*la min ġadat $^{c}$ūṣ l-anḏa miṯl l-agwāsi*
*w-salāmatk.*
*al-$^{c}$sāfah, tarbuṭha lēn tgāwid wi-tdarribha wi-t$^{c}$addilha lēn trūḥ bik maḥall ma tibi, hāḏi l-$^{c}$sāfah.*

## POEM 21

Metre:--v--v---v---(*al-basīṭ*)

1. *al-bārḥah sāhrin wi-n-nōm ma jāni*
*ma targud al-$^{c}$ēn la ḥall al-ġida fīha*
2. *min harjitin jābha l-maflūl Gabbāni*
*jāni xabarha wu-hu ma xāf gāfīha*
3. *bayyantha lēn yadri kull faṭṭāni*
*w-afḏēt ana ha w-ana ma widdi afḏīha*
4. *al$^{c}$ab w-ana ḏāyġin mānīb ṭarbāni*
*la ja n-nuwāyib n$^{c}$āh allah m axallīha*
5. *afaṣṣil al-gāf tafṣīlin b-fuṣḥāni*
*w-rā$^{c}$ al-ġuwāri$^{c}$ lzūmin ma yxallīha*
6. *in dandanaw gumt an al$^{c}$ab li$^{c}$b dindāni*
*w-in ġaṭrifaw bi-l-ġuwāri$^{c}$ gumt aġaddīha*
7. *ma yargi$^{c}$ al-mintuwi la ṣār mištāni*
*kiṯr al-hawājīs miġbilha w-miġfīha*
8. *ya-llāh ya-$^{c}$ālmin ma xfi w-ma bāni*
*ya-rāzig an-nafs ḥillin dām bāgīha*
9. *ya-xayyirin la naxētih ma ma$^{c}$ah ṯāni*
*waḥdih lih al-mulk wi-l-$^{c}$izzāt bānīha*
10. *agūl ji$^{c}$lik $^{c}$ala dīnik twaffāni*

She delivers you safely in midsummer, though your milk-skins be dry.

5. She was born from an Omani she-camel covered forcibly by a first-class stud; //
The auspicious scent of a thoroughbred race came wafting to her.
6. That's the kind of prestigious mount I desire; she suits me //
To ride on distant journeys with her hardened, bow-shaped sisters.

You break in a riding camel by tying her [to a pole or another object] and leading her round. So you train her and let her go back and forth until she willingly goes wherever you want her to go. That's breaking in a camel.

## POEM 21

1. Last night I stayed awake, unable to sleep; //
Unwisely, my eyes refused to close,
2. Because of talk spread by that fool, Gabḅāni. //
I was told what he said without fearing what might follow.
3. Just by looking at me a smart fellow could tell what was wrong; //
Against my wish I gave away the secret I'd kept to myself;
4. Dismayed, I broke into a plaintive song; //
Faced with a grave task—God's curse be upon him—I won't shrink.
5. My verses I carefully mould in eloquent language: //
One given to poetry cannot possibly abandon his art;
6. When others hum the tune, I strike up the merry melody, //
When they ululate the song, I keep the rhyme going.
7. Despondency doesn't bring one nearer to the object of his quest, //
Nor does anguishing when one is plagued by worries.
8. O God, He who is aware of things hidden and manifest, //
Provider of the soul for the period of its life span,
9. When in dire straits I call on His grace; there is no other God, //
To Him alone belongs the Kingdom and all glory.
10. I say: when I die, let it be in Your faith, //

ᶜiḏni min aš-širk wi-drūbih w-ahālīha
11. dinyāk ma hīb taswa rubᶜ dīwāni
w-inna niḥibb aṭ-ṭumāyiᶜ wi-r-rija fīha
12. gāmat tigallab ᶜala min kān daygāni[55]
ma gṭabt mamša sanaᶜha wišš ṭārīha
13. ašfig ᶜala l-māl walla kull šin fāni
wi-n-nafs min ᶜugib ḏa tajzaᶜ l-wālīha
14. f-la tīǵin in min ṣaḥat lih murritin zāni
min zayyanat lih labadd yišīn tālīha
15. amma luwat lih b-mālih layy xusrāni
walla dana minh yōmin ma ltifat fīha
16. f-in ćaṯir māl al-fita b-īgāl daygāni
la kān yimnāh min bōlih mwaḏ̣ḏ̣īha
17. law inn sāsih rumādin taḥit jidrāni
walla ridiyyin fᶜūlih ᶜāǵbin fīha
18. la kān gunnin yiji lih gōl wi-lsāni
ᶜindih ḥaćāya wu-hu ma yibtiṣir fīha
19. ya-rabb ᶜinna ᶜala t-tagwa wi-l-īgāni
iṣrif drūb ar-rida minna w-ṭārīha
20. ubūy gabli b-rāy al-ᶜizz waṣṣāni
ḥalaft m ansa wiṣātin ǵid hadānīha
21. illi yḥiss ar-rifīǵ w-yūjiᶜ al-ᶜāni
yiṣbir ᶜala wajᶜatih la kān yūḥīha
22. illa yišūfih ᶜaduwwin fīh duxxāni
yajmaᶜ l-isābīb lih wi-mḥarǵilin fīha
23. walla yirīdih b-xuḏlānin w-ḥugrāni
f-inn al-ḥaǵāri tǵayyib ḏihn rāᶜīha
24. f-law in txallīh ṭībin gīl ᶜajzāni
ma tindimiḥ zallitih la ṣār bāǵīha

55 *tigallab*, 3 f. s. imperf. of the V form of the verb, cf. Prochazka (1988), 48, *tikallam*, and note 6.

And save me from heresy, its ways and people.
11. Your nether world is not worth even a quarter, //
Though we much covet and hope for its spoils.
12. The world played its tricks on the brave and noble; //
Watching its spectacle I can't make head or tail of it.
13. I am anxious about my livestock, but then everything will perish; //
That's why after all the soul turns to its Lord with fear.
14. If the world does you a favour once, don't trust all will be fine: //
The kindness it pretends is but a prelude to trouble ahead;
15. Either its tricks with man's livestock tie him up in knots, //
Or one day it steals upon him when he's engrossed in other things.
16. If some fellow happens to be well-to-do, people think the world of him, //
Even though his right hand performs his ablutions with his own urine[56]
17. And he springs from ashes discarded against a wall in an alley, //
Or if he is a wretch who bungles whatever he undertakes,
18. Be he a bum endowed with speech and a tongue, //
Whose prattle shows no sign of true understanding.
19. O Lord, help us to be devout and steadfast in faith, //
And to avoid the ways of evil and the thought thereof.
20. Earlier my father's counsel was always to be beyond reproach, //
And I swore not to forget his moral bequest to me.
21. If a man hurts a friend and is rude to a kinsman in need, //
These indignities must be suffered in patience, though one's feelings are wounded;
22. Unless one faces an enemy seething with spite, //
Bent on his destruction and plotting to trip him,
23. Or to leave him in the lurch and expose him to scorn, //
For contempt brings one out of his senses.
24. If you shrug it off magnanimously you are considered a weakling; //
Don't pardon his slight if he acted deliberately!

---

[56] The right hand should be used for noble purposes, like fighting in war, dispensing generosity and hospitality to visitors, eating and sharing food with others etc. The left hand is reserved for cleaning oneself. The reversal of the hands' roles in this verse underlines the ignoble, despicable character of the person described.

25. *f-in gām min guwwitih raddōh ᶜāyzāni*
*bayyan xaza fašlitih w-aḏhar maᶜārīha*
26. *yiṣbir lya ṣār bih jālin ᶜala ṯ-ṯāni*
*yafᶜal b-yimnan tbayyiḏ wajh rāᶜīha*
27. *f-ᶜizz allah inna ᶜala r-ridyān ṣibrāni*
*našhar b-ṭībih w-zallātih nġabbīha*
28. *w-ćam wāḥdin ma ᶜaraf li-l-ᶜilm miḥyāni*
*widdih bha mēr rāyih gāṣirin fīha*
29. *mānāb min hu ᶜala l-adnēn daygāni*
*w-in ja l-bala min biᶜīdin ma ydānīha*
30. *jālih rifīᶜin ᶜala mabnan w-sīsāni*
*w-mibāni al-ᶜizz tamnaᶜ min ḥawāmīha*
31. *w-iṣbir swāt al-jmāl ummāt ćitbāni*
*taćna lya kān yalḥag baddha fīha*
32. *f-in lazmna l-ᶜilm nird al-mōt ᶜizrāni*
*ᶜawāyidih warṯ jaddin ma nxallīha*

*w-salāmatkum.*

## POEM 22

Metre:-v---v--v---v-(*al-madīd*)

1. *rāćib illi ma baᶜad dawwaraw fīha l-ḥalīb*
*l ōḥat al-laᶜᶜāb tarmaḥ simārat ḏillha*
2. *naṣṣha lli yafrigūn al-ḥabīb mn al-ḥabīb*
*lābtin laṭm al-mᶜādīn ᶜādātin lha*

25. If he resorts to force, then reduce him to impotence, //
So as to put his empty boasts to shame and to expose his defects.
26. A man who is a rampart to his fellows forbears, //
Trusting his right hand's bravery to whiten his face.[57]
27. Great God, we are slow to anger in dealing with cads, //
Preferring to vaunt their virtues and to conceal their faults.
28. Many people don't have the faintest idea what dignity is about: //
They sincerely wish for it, but to attain it is beyond their power.
29. We don't belong to those who excel at striking fear in their own kin //
And who stay aloof when other tribes make their onslaught.
30. A real man is a high rampart on unshakable foundations, //
For the walls of pride's edifice are unscalable.
31. One must endure like camels suffering from the pack-saddle,[58] //
Bearing the pain when the weight presses through the saddle's stuffed lining.
32. When war is proclaimed we lead the vanguard, mocking at death, //
For to the customs inherited from our forefathers we remain true.

## POEM 22

1. O rider of a mount not yet used as a milch camel, //
A spirited animal that kicks at her own shadow when the rider sings his ditties.
2. Ride her to men who plunge their enemy's folk into mourning, //
A clan that routinely plays havoc with its foes,

---

[57] It is the right hand's job to perform acts of bravery that 'whiten the face', i.e. protect and safeguard one's honour from any blemish or slight.

[58] *ćitab* pl. *ćitbān*, the pack-saddle to which the ropes of the *ġarb*, the large, elongated bucket, are attached when the camels trained to draw water for irrigation purposes are brought to the tow path that slopes down from the well and begin their labour.

3. *dārkum min ᶜaṣir Badrān la l-jadd al-girīb*
*xirjha ḥīl amlaḥ ad-darj māzūnin lha*
4. *miššat al-Haḏb al-msamma ᶜawa lih kull ḏīb*
*m axbilik yalli tibi minh ḥēdin xallha*
5. *la ᶜawa ḏībin min al-Haḏb lajj alfēn ḏīb*
*kull ubūha Haḏbha warṯ jiddānin lha*
6. *kuḥilha l-bārūd wi-d-damm wi-r-rāy aṣ-ṣilīb*
*wi-s-slāl al-xuḏr ya-na fda min šallha*
7. *nōm ᶜēni fiᶜilkum ya-mṭawwiᶜt al-ḥarīb*[59]
*ya-šbūb al-ḥarb y-ahl al-marājil kulliha*
8. *ilbisu ṯōb an-niga la ᶜawa dībin l-ḏīb*
*wi-l-ḥbāl illi ᶜagad rūsha b-yiḥilliha*
9. *lēn yissiᶜ bi-l-maḥaṭṭ aš-širīb mn aš-širīb*
*kūn bi-l-ḥisna fla llah b-gaṭṭāᶜin lha*
*w-salāmatkum.*

POEM 23

Metre:-v---v---v--(*ar-ramal*)

*jīt mrāḥ ᶜirbin xābrin inna firīǵ, wala ᶜād minhum wāḥid, mingiḏi ya-kūn ana fa-talaᶜwaz xāṭri, f-agūl:*

---

59 *nōm ᶜēni*, lit. ‘the sleep of my eye’, i.e. the peace of mind that allows one to enjoy a sound sleep at night, as opposed to one who stays awake fretting about a slight or acts insulting to his own or his kinsmen’s sense of honour. A group’s bravery and warlike reputation safeguard the collective honour and keep its individual members in the relaxed, healthy condition that results from undisturbed rest at night.

3. Undisputed masters of their land from Badrān's time until today.[60] //
   Their decorated saddle-bags are kept well stocked with ammunition;
4. They are the marrow of al-Haḏb's spine, facing down packs of wolves: //
   Don't be so foolish as to touch even one of its rocks, leave them alone!
5. For every wolf that howls, two thousand wolves from al-Haḏb howl back; //
   All of them inherited al-Haḏb by right from their ancestors;
6. Its kohl is made of gunpowder, blood and unflinching determination, //
   As well as swords made of bluish steel, may I be the ransom of those carrying them!
7. Your feats of arms fill me with pride, O subduers of enemy bands; //
   You are war's kindling and all manly virtues you rightly claim.
8. Wrap yourselves in chivalry's mantle when the wolves begin to howl! //
   The ropes' knotty ends will be unravelled by our men,[61]
9. Until the tribes pitch their camp at a respectful distance; //
   But a friendly approach is not something God would repudiate.[62]

## POEM 23

It was composed when I visited the site of an abandoned encampment and was reminded that not one bedouin of that group was still alive. They all died except me. Then I felt very sick at heart and said:

---

[60] Badrān, the ancestor of the Bidārīn tribe of the Duwāsir to which the influential as-Sudayrī family belongs.

[61] The knotty, twisted ends of the ropes are a metaphor for the strategy and tactics agreed upon in the enemy's counsels. These knots are unravelled, i.e. the plans are undone by the defending tribe, the Duwāsir.

[62] If the enemy repents, reconciliation is always possible and friendly relations can be resumed.

1. *šarraf ad-Dindān fi rijmin biyāni*
*hayyaḏ̣ illi ḥālf innih ma yġanni*
2. *zōᶜ galbin zōᶜ farxin fi ćnāni*
*ṭār yōm ma ḥall janāḥēn istiwanni*
3. *ḏi rsūm ahl al-wiṭan ǵid hi fuwāni*
*wi-r-ruwābi fōg manzilhum bananni*
4. *rāḥt ad-dinya ᶜala ćam min zimāni*
*kull garnin ḏi ᶜalāmātih giḏ̣anni*
5. *ya-wijūdi ma wiṭa xalgih wiṭāni*
*wi-l-glūb al-ġāflah ma yafhaminni*
6. *in ṭalabt al-galb ᶜihdin ma ᶜaṭāni*
*wišš ᶜiḏrih li-r-raḥāyil la dananni*
7. *mall galbin ṭāyilin ġullih w-ćāni*
*miṯl nijrin kull ma ḥassōh danni*
8. *in ṣigaᶜ l-aṣbār yašhar bi-ᶜwiyāni*
*w-in rikad daggih ḍlūᶜih lajlijanni*
9. *in jaġar bi-ṣ-ṣōt ṣakkih miṭribāni*
*w-in ᶜawa bi-l-hōl min samᶜih ywinni*
10. *iḥḏar ink tmurr l-aḥbābik mićāni*
*miṯil ḥilm al-lēl ćanha ma jaranni*
11. *tiltihim ma fāt wi-l-midhāl fāni*
*mixṭirin tiṣbiḥ ᶜyūnik yiḥzananni*
12. *ya-mᶜallimni tara ma bi kifāni*
*ᶜālmin jāhil tara galbi miḏ̣inni*
13. *wallah ma yabrid luwāhīb aḏ̣-ḏ̣imāni*
*kūn rićb al-fīḥ yōm yrawwḥinni*
14. *zīnhin tāl an-nahār hrēćlāni*
*bēn ḏifḏāfin w-bēn ysarbilinni*
15. *šaff bāli dām yōmi ma daᶜāni*
*ma ḥala bard al-hawa bi-ḏ̣hūrhinni*

1. Ad-Dindān made his ascent to the top of a prominent mountain, //
And, though he had sworn never to sing anymore, he could not resist the inner urge.
2. In my breast my heart fluttered like a falcon chick flapping its wings, //
Once it feels strong enough to fly from its nest.
3. Behold the traces of fellow-tribesmen who passed away, //
And the drifting sands that covered their abandoned camp!
4. How many epochs were turned over by Time's wheel //
That obliterates the vestiges of every century!
5. I suffered all the pains visited on God's creation, //
An experience the lighthearted are unable to fathom.
6. All my requests for a truce my heart rejected;
How will he exculpate himself when death's cortège draws near?
7. Woe unto a heart that struggled to conceal its bitterness! //
Like a mortar made of copper, it rings out when beaten.
8. When its rim is struck with force it screams and whines, //
And when its bottom is pounded its ribs raise a clamour.
9. If it begins to purr, then knock it merrily, //
But if it howls in terror, the company groans in sympathy.
10. Beware of places once inhabited by your beloved ones: //
Like dreams at night, they seem to have never existed at all.
11. On those deserted haunts I was assailed by memories of days past, //
Absorbed in mournful thoughts and almost crying.
12. Don't upbraid me: I have enough trouble as it is; //
At that kind of naive advice I could have guessed myself.
13. By God, there is only one way to dampen the flames of a thirsting heart: //
To roam the desert on swift camels running their best.
14. Nothing throws me in raptures like their calm, swaggering gait, //
Now moving at an easy pace, then trotting steadily, in the late afternoon.
15. Until the end of my days this will be my heart's deepest desire: //
To feel the cool air stream over my face as I ride on their backs.

## POEM 24

Metre: v--v---v--v---(*aṭ-ṭawīl*)

1. *ana bādiyin fi margibin w-alᶜan aš-šayṭān*
*yġayyir ᶜalayy fi nāyfāt al-mišārīfi*
2. *ya-mall galbin mistixillin ᶜala lli kān*
*kalatha l-ᶜabāyir ġēr m ōḥēt ma šīfi*
3. *ya-rāćib illi ćannhin malḥiy al-ᶜūdān*
*dgāgin ṭwālin midinfātin mahādīfi*
4. *banāt al-ᶜmāni kulliha min ḏ̣ana ḏ̣abyān*
*timarwaj timirwāj al-ḥamām al-muwālīfi*
5. *lya rawwaḥat ḏirᶜānha ćannha l-ǵinyān*
*tizaᶜzaᶜ tizūzāᶜ al-ᶜyād al-marādīfi*
6. *wsāᶜ an-nḥūr mnaffijātin min az-zīrān*
*ṭwāl ar-rǵāb mgaṭṭᶜāt ar-rahārīfi*
7. *ṭwāl al-ġawārib dillijin dillihin wi-smān*
*tšādi maḥāḥīl al-bitāt al-mahāyīfi*
8. *ya-zīn fōg ḏ̣hūrha lammat al-jiḏᶜān*
*ᶜala ᶜūṣ l-anḏ̣a yalᶜabūn al-ġaṭārīfi*
9. *tnāhib wiṭa l-ḥadba lya gaḏ̣ḏ̣ibaw l-arsān*
*tšād al-ġarānīǵ al-wgūf al-miḏ̣ālīfi*
10. *lya min lifann aš-šāᶜir ᶜBēd ibin Ḥamdān*
*txuṣṣih ᶜala šānh yᶜarf al-maᶜārīfi*
11. *nihōni yigūlūn al-hawa xallih al-ćiḏbān*
*w-ana xābrin darb al-hawa ma baᶜad ᶜīfi*
12. *lya jīt b-adlah marrni gāyid al-ġizlān*
*w-la šuft zōlih gult ḥiyyēt ya-rīfi*
13. *ala ya-haniyy an-nāyim ad-dālih aṭ-ṭarbān*
*w-ana ćann galbi fōg ḥām al-maraḏ̣īfi*

# POEM 24

1. From the look-out post I climbed I curse Satan, //
   Feeling out of sorts on these lofty crests.
2. Woe unto a heart that frets about the past, //
   In the throes of its sobbing; greater misery was never seen.
3. O rider of camels chiselled like tapered sticks, //
   Gracious and robust, their bellies taut, the slender necks stretched low;
4. Daughters of Omani thoroughbreds, the offspring of gazelles, //
   They strut with a swagger like amorous pigeons.
5. At full stride their legs resemble the branches of a *ǵana*-tree, //
   Swaying gently like tall palms heavy with date bunches.
6. Their chests are broad, their axillae widely spaced, //
   Their necks are long: they are the cruisers of the vast gravel plains;
7. Stout animals with muscular shoulders, travelling smoothly without roars of protest //
   At a rapid pace like pulley-wheels turning on their axles above a well.
8. The gang of youngsters present a marvelous sight, //
   As they sing boastful songs on their lean and hardy mounts,
9. Holding the reins in a firm grip while the camels burn up the miles on the rugged highlands, //
   Elegantly curved as cranes standing in a pensive pose.
10. When your riding animals arrive at the poet ᶜBēd ibn Ḥamdān, //
    Greet him respectfully, for he is a man of culture.
11. People censored me, 'Forget about romance,' the liars said, //
    Whereas I attest that for me romancing lost none of its lure.
12. When I sought forgetfulness the doe première walked by;[63] //
    And as I descried her figure I mumbled, 'Salute, my darling!'
13. How I envy the oblivious who sleep contentedly, //
    While my heart is getting burnt on baking stones.

---

[63] The poet compares his beloved's elegant poise with that exhibited by the leading female of a gazelle herd.

14. *ᶜasa lli nihōni min gidīm al-hawa ᶜidwān*
*ya-xubl ᶜaḏḏāl al-glūb al-muwālīfi*
15. *yāma ḥala širb aš-šifāya min al-ᶜaṭšān*
*w-mazz aṯ-ṯimān al-bīḏ ḥibbin b-tarhīfi*
16. *ġarīrin wiṭāni ġarrni miṭrig ar-rayḥān*
*ṣaram zarᶜ galbi w-aṭligih fi l-mizālīfi*
17. *yibiy ḏabḥati lēn allah ahdāh ᶜala l-īgān*
*luwa l-galb layy al-ġidd fōg al-ᶜaṣārīfi*

## POEM 25

Metre:-v---v---v--(*ar-ramal*)

1. *ya-nidībi w-irtiḥil bint an-naᶜāmah*
*ma ywaṭṭi rāsha tall al-xṭāmi*
2. *naṣṣha lli ᶜindihum talga l-karāmah*
*xuṣṣ ubu Ḏ̣āfir b-mardūd as-salāmi*
3. *al-baḥar la fāḏ̣ ma šayyin yiḏ̣āmih*
*ṭamm ḥatta l-naww min fōg az-zuwāmi*
4. *at-thāmi jāk lih fi l-jaww ḥāmah*[64]
*wi-š-šta gaṭᶜat slūmih min šmāmi*
5. *ar-rḥiyy mn al-Kwēt ila Thāmah*
*wi-l-ᶜadad ᶜindik tara hāḏa kalāmi*
6. *ᶜidd raml al-ᶜirġ w-iḥḏar fi timāmih*
*w-iḥṣ ᶜaddih fi xadārīs aḏ̣-ḏ̣alāmi*
7. *anšdik yōm ant ma ᶜindik bahāmah*
*ᶜārfin tadri b-maḏ̣mūn al-kalāmi*
8. *wēš ġimrin ma miša li-n-nūr gāmah*

---

64 Sowayan calls this *-k* the *-k* of courtesy, since it refers to an idealized, abstract listener. The attachment of the masculine singular second person pronominal suffix *-k* is a feature of the Najdi oral narrative style: 'The verb *ja* is the only verb to which the *-k* of courtesy can be suffixed directly. With other verbs *lak* is used instead,' Sowayan (1992), 53.

14. May those who censored me for my amorous habits be punished by enemy raiders: //
Only a fool would rebuke loving hearts.
15. To a thirsting lover nothing tastes sweeter than moist lips, //
And sucking the white front teeth in a voluptuous kiss.[65]
16. A young lady, shaped like the twig of sweet basil, trod me down and made a fool of me; //
She cut my heart's sprouts and toppled it over the precipice.
17. Until God leads her to the path of true faith, she'll plot my death, //
Twisting my heart as thongs are twisted that tie the bucket's rope to the saddle of a camel drawing water.

## POEM 25

1. O messenger mounted on the ostrich's twin sister, //
Much as you pull her nose-rope, she won't lower her head.
2. Ride her to men who will prepare you a hospitable welcome; //
Give my special and repeated greetings to Abu Ḏāfir!
3. When the sea surges, nothing has the power to contain it: //
Even the clouds above the hilltops are swept up by its waters.
4. Or swarms of Tihāmah locusts that darken the sky; //
No sooner than winter has turned its back,
5. Their whirling columns are seen from Kuwait to Tihāmah. //
Count those numbers and you'll know how much I have to say.[66]
6. Also, count the grains of sand in a dune, not skipping one of them, //
But make sure you do your counting right during a dark, moonless night.
7. I'll ask you this riddle, since your wit is not bovine, //
But sharp, and easily penetrates the meaning of words.
8. What fellow stands at a man's height when facing the light, //

---

[65] Dindān gave an apologetic giggle as he recited this verse.

[66] Halfway through this verse new visitors entered the room where the recording session took place. Greetings were exchanged and then Dindān continued his recitation exactly at the point where he had been interrupted.

*w-in giḟāh an-nūr dabbar w-istigāmi*
9. *fi ḏahar wajnan tġīr bla guwāmah*
*baṭinha yadᶜi ḏaharha li-l-ᶜadāmi*
10. *dāyman bi-šdādha ṯamha hamāmah*
*ma yḥaṭṭ al-kūr minha li-l-migāmi*
11. *bānyin li gašiltin ᶜajmin dimāmih*
*ṭīnha māṣin yṣubbih ṣabb šāmi*
12. *sāsha fi sābᶜ arḏin fi ḏalāmih*
*rāsha fi l-ᶜarš yašbuk al-ḥawāmi*
13. *mitinha tisᶜīn ᶜāmin ḏi gyāmih*
*kasirha ᶜasrin ᶜala kull al-ḥarāmi*
14. *xazrifaw bi-n-najim gaṣrih fi ḥamāmih*
*lēn ṣaḥḥ w-ḥuṭṭ milkih b-istilāmi*
15. *wi-l-gumar wi-š-šams fi l-maᶜmūr šāmah*
*yiġtidi bih kull min ṣalla w-ṣāmi*
16. *wi-l-fana fōgih tara hāḏa migāmih*
*hu ᶜizrānin ᶜala l-mōt as-salāmi*
17. *f-in ḥaḏaftih ḥaḏfitin gaḏḏat ᶜḏāmih*
*ḥālfin ya-min ḥaḏaftih zīd gāmi*
18. *wi-l-kalām aḏ-ḏarb ya-māl as-salāmah*
*miṯilha walla fala lāzim kalāmi*
19. *la tigūl inni tara ᶜindi fahāmah*
*kull naššādin lzūm innih fahāmi*
20. *wi-l-kalām iᶜrif ḥalālih min ḥarāmih*
*ᶜarrbih xallih kalāmin min ġlāmi*
21. *ya-ᶜašīr illi zaha xaddih wšāmih*
*bint ḏarbīn ar-rjāl ahl at-timāmi*
22. *f-in kalām al-ᶜagil xutmānih wdāmih*
*miṯil ḏōb as-samin fi ḥilw aṭ-ṭaᶜāmi*

But runs straight ahead when the light is in his back?[67]
9. He rides a hardy she-camel that goes on the attack though she has no legs, //
And her inside reduces her outside to nothingness?
10. Always on the ride, cramming her mouth with food, //
She is never unsaddled or given a pause.[68]
11. I am building a villa with blind, round walls, //
Cemented with electrified iron, poured by Syrian masons;[69]
12. The foundations are rooted in the darkness of the seventh earth, //
While its roof's ridge scrapes the supports of heaven's throne.
13. A journey of ninety years, that's my villa's size; //
No way a rascal could break its defences.
14. They embellished the battlements with small lamps //
As a finishing touch, and then the conveyance took place.
15. The moon and sun were added as jewels to the building's crown, //
Guiding by their glitter all who pray and fast;
16. And above it extinction in person holds sway, //
ʿIzrāʾīl, the angel of death, peace be upon him.
17. If I would pelt my foe with projectiles, I would shatter his bones, //
And in doing so, I swear, my stature would only increase.
18. Well-chosen words are the best guarantee for one's security, //
Keep that in mind or else be advised to stay silent.
19. Don't say, 'I do understand the meaning of things!' //
For indeed no poet can do without discernment.
20. Learn to distinguish good from wrong in speech, //
And then say it plainly and clearly in manly language.
21. This I say to you, companion of a wife with tattooed cheeks, //
The daughter of well-bred men, excellent people.
22. For the clever poet keeps his best for the last, //
Like clarified butter poured over a savoury dish.

---

67 The answer is: a man's shadow.

68 The answer is: *ad-dinya*, 'the world', pictured here as an insatiable, aggressive she-camel, for the world is a place of vain ambition and deception that devours all those who ride on her back.

69 The construction of an unassailable fortress is a metaphor for the poet's art, which likewise is impervious to attempts by rivals to outdo it or find shortcomings in it, see p. 22 and p. 36, note 22.

## POEM 26

Metre: v--v---v--v---(*aṭ-ṭawīl*)

1. *ana hāḏ̣ ma bi ʿūḏ bi-llah min aš-šayṭān*
   *kalāmin yšālīni w-ana ḏ̣āyiġin bāli*
2. *ya-rāćib illi nayyiha yanbih al-biddān*
   *ḥalāḥīl ḥīlin ḥālt al-ḥīl niḥḥāli*
3. *ḥalāḥīl ḥīlin ma baʿad jāt bi-l-ḥīrān*
   *ḥalāḥīl ḥīlin ćannha ṣēd l-ashāli*
4. *jahājīl jīlin tijtuwil ćannha l-ġizlān*
   *jahājīl jīlin tijtuwil yōm tinjāli*
5. *jahājīl jīlin ma twāṭa ʿala l-arsān*
   *jahājīl jēšin li-l-ḥalag fīh jiljāli*
6. *ṯimānin ṯimanha ma tṭarra ʿala l-aṯmān*
   *laha fi raxārīx at-taxātīx zilzāli*
7. *fiṭīrin tgaṭṭiʿ fi zaʿamha ḥalag l-arsān*
   *twājif lya min rawwaḥat maʿ xala l-xāli*
8. *tšādi naʿāmin ʿugib ma wakkidat l-aʿyān*
   *hajījin maʿa rās aš-šifa wi-š-šifag tāli*
9. *tšīl al-ḥmūl fḥūlha min rćāb ʿmān*
   *ṣifīfin ṣirīf akwārha ḥōf l-ihḏāli*
10. *drīmat simārīha maʿa guḥguḥ al-ḥizmān*
    *drīmat maxālin bi-l-barad lih tinizzāli*
11. *tasraḥ ṣalāt aṣ-ṣibḥ min fēḏ̣t al-ʿIlmān*
    *laha fi ḏ̣-ḏ̣aḥa fi sarḥat aṯ-Ṯōr migyāli*
12. *txall al-jibal b-īsārha wi-l-Biyāḏ̣ aymān*
    *miṣāfīrha fi l-ʿŌd yōm iḏḏin at-tāli*
13. *tnaššid w-talga min ydillik ʿala l-maydān*
    *ʿyālin tiji fi l-ḥabs ḏarbīn l-afʿāli*
14. *naṣṣ as-salām Mnāḥiyin xīrt al-jiḏʿān*
    *w-naṣṣ as-salām l-Xāldin ḥāmi at-tāli*
15. *w-naṣṣ as-salām Mfarrjin mikrim aḏ̣-ḏ̣īfān*

POEM 26

1. I was roused to speak my mind—with God I seek refuge from Satan—//
In words that give relief from the heaviness of my heart.
2. O rider of camels whose hump pushes up the saddle's cushion,
Splendid mounts with wiry limbs and wombs that never conceived;
3. Beautiful animals as yet unburdened with calves, //
A feast for the eye, like game bounding over a plain.
4. Their squadron moves nimbly, like a drove of gazelles, //
Swerving and zigzagging in tight formation.
5. They have been given free rein and run at full stride,
Accompanied by the jingling of their halters' copper rings.
6. Eight camels, so precious that their price can't be mentioned, //
Their hoofs thudding into the sand of the immense wastes.
7. Camels nine years old, so spirited as to wrench off their halters' rings, //
Their tassels swaying wildly as they hurry through the empty desert,
8. Like ostriches once they know the hunters have spied them, //
In panicky flight over the incline of the highland at dusk.
9. Carriers of heavy loads, sired by Omani studs, //
Side by side, the creaking saddles in one line, they trot.
10. Their feet strike the white pebbles of the rolling plain, //
Like a cloud bombarding the earth with hailstones.
11. After the morning prayer you set out from the wide depression of al-ᶜIlmān, //
And later that morning you'll rest in the shade of at̲-T̲ōr's tree.
12. Keep the broken land to your left and the flats of al-Biyāḏ̣ to your right; //
With the second call to the dawn prayer you'll be in al-ᶜŌd.
13. Ask the people there for the way to the square, //
Where some of our honourable youngsters have been put in jail.
14. Give greetings to Mnāḥi, that excellent lad, //
And to K̲h̲ālid, the defender of the camel train's rear,
15. And also to Mfarrij, the hospitable entertainer of guests, //

*w-sallim ᶜala Rāšid raᶜa l-mōgif al-ᶜāli*
16. *sallim ᶜalēhum ᶜidd ma nša min al-waddān*
*salāmin yṯanna min gidīmin lya t-tāli*
17. *salāmin ḥalātih tazraᶜ al-ḥibb fi l-abdān*
*tšādi ḥalāt ad-darr min ḥimm l-ajhāli*
18. *salāmin lifākum fīh riggin maᶜa ḥifwān*
*salāmin ḥalātih tinbit al-ḥēl fi l-ḥāli*
19. *gaᶜadna w-ḥinna miltihīnin ᶜala burhān*
*nibi jayyihum lākann w-allāh ma ja li*
20. *wićanna ᶜala min yagḏi an-nōb fi ma kān*
*wićanna ᶜalēhum jiᶜlhum ṭūl l-amhāli*
21. *ćifōna ćifīna fagd minhum lna ṣidgān*
*ṭwāl aš-šbūr mṭawwiᶜat kull ᶜayyāli*
22. *ćifōna ṭ-ṭalāyib yōm miššī lha miḥyān*
*w-ᶜādāt min hu gaddam al-jūd yićtāli*
23. *ṯumm inšdu Rāšid ᶜasāh ingiḏa lih šān*
*ᶜasa l-ḥōl min ṣōbih ᶜala ġērih inḥāli*
24. *ᶜasa l-ḥōl minh īḥāl ḏabbāḥ ḥīl aḏ-ḏān*
*yišīl al-mxalla yōm xallōh l-anḏāli*
25. *yūmi l-hal ᶜūṣ an-nijāyib maᶜa r-rīᶜān*
*manāxat byūtih li-l-marāmīl midhāli*
26. *min lābtin tirwi šiba marhaf al-ᶜūdān*

And to Rāshid, who pitches his camp on elevated grounds.[70]
16. Bring them greetings numerous as clouds amassing on the horizon, //
A greeting we kept repeating from the old times till today,
17. Greetings so warm and friendly as to make one's body glow, //
Sweet as the milk of black, young camels with calf.
18. These greetings we send you with kindness and respect, //
Greetings that reinvigorate one's health and state of mind.
19. We stayed behind, because we really are too busy with our camels; //
We wanted to come along, but God knows there was no way.
20. We relied on men who performed similar tasks in the past; //
Yes, in them we put our trust, may they be granted a long life.
21. May they act well on our behalf—may other kinsmen make up for the loss of our friends,[71] //
Men whose reach is long and who wrestle down every wrong-doer.
22. May they successfully accomplish their mission and everything be settled with skill, //
For usually those who practise generosity are richly rewarded.
23. Then ask Rāshid how he fares; I pray for his troubles to end, //
And that his problem may be shifted to someone else.
24. If only he got rid of it, the unstinting butcher of fat sheep! //
He is one who carries from the battlefield the wounded deserted by the cowards;
25. To men journeying on lean thoroughbreds and herdsmen he waves;[72] //
In front of his tents it is always bustling with starving travellers kneeling their mounts.
26. His clan is famous for dipping sharp spears in enemy blood; //

---

[70] Men who practise the virtue of hospitality do not pitch their tent in a dip in the terrain where it is hidden from the view of travellers, but on the top of an elevation in order to attract visitors.

[71] The messengers carrying the poem made up for the fact that the poet was unable to come in person. The hope is expressed that other worthy men will temporarily fill the gaps in the tribe's collective ranks left by the jailed friends.

[72] I.e. he tries to attract the attention of wayfarers in order to invite them to a meal and entertainment in his tent.

*tḥazm al-ganāziʿ ʿind ṭarʿāt l-ajhāli*
27. *f-in kān raćbih ḥimiltin ma liga maydān*
*fa-la ʿindina šayyin ʿala miṯilhum ġāli*
28. *salāmat nibākum w-islimu min xaṭar ma šān*
*salāmat niba min zayyan allah lih al-fāli*
29. *ṣalātin ʿala ḏićir an-nibiy bi-mrit ar-riḥmān*
*nṣalli ʿalēhum ma wmarna bih al-wāli*
30. *nṣalli ʿalēhum naṭlib ar-rabb bi-l-ġufrān*
*ṣalātin nisīr bha min al-jāl la l-jāli*

## POEM 27

Metre:-v---v---v-(*ar-ramal*)

1. *šarraf ad-Dindān rijmin fi Sdēr*
*hayyiḏih ma gīl fi ʿirḏih w-gāl*
2. *ya w-rabb al-bēt ya idna b-xēr*[73]
*min mdūd illi ʿaṭāyāh jzāl*
3. *ya-nidībi w-irtiḥil jēšin xafīf*
*siddisin sittin mzawwīha l-ḥyāl*
4. *ćannha jōl al-giṭa jillin jimīʿ*
*miṯil zurg al-warg ʿayrātin jlāl*
5. *ćannha la rawwaḥat ṣēdin snūd*
*aw naʿāmin jallaʿat ʿugb al-jfāl*
6. *ḥāylin tarʿa zimālīġ ar-rsūm*
*yiʿijbik dirhām samḥāt al-ġbāl*
7. *šāybātin yōm talġafha s-simūm*
*ćannha malḥi hašīmin min siyāl*

---

[73] *al-bēt*, 'the dwelling', here means the holy place at Mecca.

Wrapping their scarfs around their heads, they defend their herds tooth and nail.[74]

27. If he despairs of straightening the problem that burdens him, //
Truly, we are ready for any sacrifice to help men like him.
28. Blessed be your tidings, may you be spared from danger and evil! //
Your memory we treasure, may God grant you good fortune.
29. We end with prayers on the Prophet's name, as ordained by the Merciful, //
For them we pray according to the commandments of the Lord;
30. For them we pray and we ask God for forgiveness, //
A prayer we cherish wherever we go between the precipices at both ends of the earth.[75]

POEM 27

1. Ad-Dindān climbed to the top of a mountain in as-Sdēr, //
Deeply hurt by tales smirching his honour.
2. O Lord of the House, please bestow on us Your bounty //
From the supplies of He whose gifts are generous.
3. Messenger of mine, travel on lightly-laden mounts, //
Six of them, six years old, well covered with layers of fat,
4. Hefty animals that move like a covey of sand grouse, //
Or a flight of bluish pigeons; mighty and rugged camels.
5. At full stride they resemble a flock of gazelle darting uphill, //
Or startled ostriches when they have attained their highest speed.
6. Exempt from procreational duty, they graze the annuals sprouting in the wake of the rains. //
Nothing gladdens you more than seeing them hasten to meet you:
7. Grey from the dust lashed up by the hot winds from the south, //
Thin as dry, tapered sticks that fell from acacia-trees;

---

[74] Normally the tips of the headscarf hang down or are draped over the shoulder. Only in preparation for arduous work or a fight are the tips wrapped around the head and tied together.

[75] The traditional belief holds that the earth is a flat expanse ending at both sides in an abrupt precipice.

8. *ćann xabṭ nṣūmha fōg al-ḥzūm*
*xabṭ bardan min mahādīb al-xyāl*
9. *ćan manāćibha ṣifa ṣugᶜ al-hḏ̣āb*
*jāflātin min miḏ̣āyīǵ al-jbāl*
10. *ćan miḏ̣āriᶜha fnūdin nāᶜmāt*
*wi-l-ᶜḏ̣ūd mnaffijātin bi-l-ᶜadāl*
11. *wi-l-fxūḏ mn al-wrūk mᶜazzalāt*
*wi-l-muwāṭi miṯl maṣbūb ar-ryāl*
12. *wi-l-wjīh mn al-ᶜawātiǵ ṭāyirāt*
*wi-ḏ-ḏyūl gyās basṭ arbaᶜ ǵfāl*
13. *sibg zafg al-milḥ walla zarg šōf*
*yagṭaᶜinn al-bīd giṭṭāᶜ al-ḥbāl*
14. *la bla tijlab wala tiṭra b-sōm*
*min fiṭīrin miḏ̣hirathinn al-jmāl*

## POEM 28

Metre:--v--v---v---(*al-basīṭ*)

1. *ya-dāntin min liḏīḏ al-milḥ madhūnah*
*la sīm fīha wala tihda bi-l-aṯmāni*
2. *ma tinᶜaṭa bi-ṯ-ṯiman la kān māzūnah*
*ma ᶜād yalzam risanha wāḥdin ṯāni*
3. *nibnūbtin min xyār al-bīḏ mazyūnah*
*ridfin w-ǵarnin tiṯanna fōg l-amtāni*
4. *min šāfha misriᶜin yamši ᶜala hūnih*
*ḥār al-ǵidam bih yibi saḥḥāb l-ardāni*
5. *bu ḥijjitin miṯil xaṭṭ an-nīl magrūnah*
*suwādha fāṣlin fi lōnha ṯ-ṯāni*
6. *ubu nhūdin tšād al-bēḏ̣ maknūnah*
*fi manḥirin miṯil barg aṣ-ṣēf la bāni*
7. *wirᶜin ᶜadīm al-wiṣāyif lābti dūnih*
*šaḥḥaw bha min ǵalāha ṣulb jiddāni*

8. On the rolling stony hills their hoofs make a drumming sound, //
Like hailstones clattering down from slanting clouds;
9. Their shoulders are like slabs of rock on the round tops of the basalt peaks. //
As they rush forward from the opening of mountain gorges,
10. One admires their forelegs, smooth and straight as twigs of trees, //
And their powerful upper legs, the muscles spaced exactly right.
11. The thighs are profiled distinctly from the haunches, //
And their pads have been cast round like coins;
12. Above their cheeks their faces carry a lively expression; //
The measure of their tails is four hand-breadths.
13. They streak by like the flash of a bullet or the twinkling of an eye, //
Crossing the glistening plains as fast as one cuts a rope.
14. They are not for sale, nor would anyone think of bargaining away //
Animals born from mature she-camels covered by thoroughbred stallions.

## POEM 28

1. O pearl anointed with grace and beauty, //
That can't be bought, not even for princely sums;
2. No price, no matter how high, can be set for a thing so precious. //
No hand other than her master's will steady her bridle;
3. Her fresh charms outshine those of the choicest of maidens, //
Her swelling buttocks and the tresses cascading down her back.
4. If a man walking in a hurry beholds her, he slackens: //
Spellbound by the skirt-trailing enchantress, his gait grows unsteady.
5. The paired arches of her eyebrows look as if drawn with indigo, //
Their black even more striking for the contrast with her skin.
6. Her breasts, small and firm like eggs hidden in a nest, //
Protrude from the low line of a neck dazzling as lightning in summer.
7. She's a peerless beauty, jealously guarded by my clan, //
For with a rare gem like her my kinsmen are loath to part.

## POEM 29

Metre:--v--v---v---(*al-basīṭ*)

*jēna ḥajīj, nisti*ᶜ*i fi l-ḥaram [yiṭāf], wāḥidtin da*ᶜ*atni, nādatni, tibīni adḥam ma*ᶜ*hum, ma* ᶜ*indaha* ᶜ*lūm, f-agūl:*

1. *ḥasbi* ᶜ*al illi da*ᶜ*āni lēn nābētih*
   *bēn al-*ᶜ*amad wi-l-migām w-bēn l-arkāni*
2. *f-wallāh la ruḥt adawwir lih wala jītih*
   *w-agḏēt mānīb šōfih kān w-agwāni*
3. *midhālhum la sigāh al-wabil marrētih*
   *mitšāliyin lēn jītih wi-l-bala jāni*
4. *yāma b-galbi* ᶜ*alēhum mār ćannētih*
   *min ḏilliti yiftiri bih kull faṭṭāni*
5. *lāla l-miza kān ṣiml aṯ-ṯōb šaggētih*[76]
   *w-amši ma*ᶜ *illi yibūn as-sitir* ᶜ*aryāni*
6. *ma* ᶜ*ād fi l-*ᶜ*umir misyārin* ᶜ*ala bētih*
   *wi-mšāhidih dām mōt an-nās ma jāni*
7. *ya-lētni fi mrāḥ al-*ᶜ*īd nawwētih*
   *yōm ašmalaw w-aṣbaḥat l-aḏ̣*ᶜ*ān šattāni*

---

[76] A similar feeling of desperation is expressed in the following verse by an amorous Rwala poet in Musil (1928), 200:
*wallāh lōla l-ḥaya l-arkab* ᶜ*ala šībi*
*w-ašūf li dīrtin w-ajli l-ahālīha*
'By God, if it were not for modesty, I would mount my travel-hardened camel, Search another country, and flee to the people who encamp there' (i.e. the poet would elope with his sweetheart and seek protection with another tribe).

## POEM 29

We went on pilgrimage to Mecca and as we were circumambulating the Ka$^{c}$aba in the holy shrine, I heard a woman calling my name. She wanted me to join them in pushing our way through the crowd, but she did not have anything particular in mind. Then I said:

1. I trust in God to protect me from her who kept calling me till I said 'Yes', //
   Between the pillars, the *migām* and the colonnade.[77]
2. By God, I did not go looking for her, nor did I join her; //
   I cast my eyes down, not wishing to see her, though I felt tempted.
3. May the clouds pass over their tribal haunts without releasing their rain: //
   I was fine until she crossed my path; then my misery began.
4. Ah, how I suffered on their account, while hiding it in my heart, //
   For fear that some smart fellow would ferret out my secret.
5. If not for shame, I would have ripped off the old rags of my pilgrim's cloth //
   To walk naked among those who came seeking forgiveness' veil.[78]
6. There will be no more visits to her tent: //
   Until the day of my death I will not set my eyes on her again.
7. How I wish I had made for her at the assembly of the Bairam feast //
   Before they headed north and the camel trains scattered in all directions;

---

[77] The reference is to *maqām Ibrāhīm*. The pillars are the columns marking the entrances to the *ḥaram*, the Meccan holy sanctuary.

[78] Note this verse's wonderful expression of the poet's bewilderment at his conflicting religious and erotic emotions. Thus the pilgrim's garb and the veil, a metaphor for the Lord's forgiveness, also acquire the connotation of diffidence and concealment of one's true feelings, which is a standard motif in love poetry. The 'nakedness' that would result from the poet giving in to his impulse has therefore an additional meaning, besides the literal and religious ones, namely that the love he had kept hidden as a secret in his heart would be divulged and exposed (as expressed in the formula *bayyaḥ saddih* 'he unveiled, gave away the secret of his heart').

8. *ya-lētni yōm jītih kān ḥabbētih*
*ḥaṭṭēt šugr al-jidāyil fōg ḏirᶜāni*

## POEM 30

Metre:-v---v--v---v-(*al-madīd*)

1. *ya-llah yalli tiksir al-ᶜaḏm w-innih ša jibar*
*ṭālbīnik ṭalbitin ma yġallag bābha*
2. *ṭalbitin tirjiᶜ ġṣūn al-hašīm mn aš-šijar*
*ma tiji raḥmat min al-ma l-garāḥ illa bha*
3. *hāḏ ma bi harjitin w-ismiᶜu ya-min ḥaḏar*
*harjitin minha l-ᶜaḏāra ramat b-aslābha*
4. *gult an ixluṣ ya-ridiyy an-niṣīb wla ᶜtibar*
*ḥijjitin la riḥm ubūha w-ubu min jābha*
5. *tarsix al-Jazla ᶜala s-sēf wi-l-māw al-ḥamar*
*wi-l-mḥabbab wi-l-mṣabbab riġīġ ṯyābha*
6. *dām ḥinna ṣālḥīnin fīh migwat ṣifar*[79]
*w-in ḥarabna ᶜašān ḥatta xṣūṣ trābha*
7. *miṯil simmin kull ma zīd fi mān inkidar*
*min ḥnūšin yaṣfig as-simm bēn anyābha*
8. *dūnha bi-l-māw la garr fi l-ᶜēn al-biṣar*
*jālbīnin dūnha r-rūḥ la yihga bha*
9. *min taxallaf fi nahārin ćifāh alli ḥaḏar*
*ᶜādtin warṯin min al-jadd wiṣṣīna bha*
10. *ḥarb tisᶜīn as-sanat ᶜindina ćannah šahar*
*wi-l-ḥarāyib ᶜizzina yōm yiftaḥ bābha*
11. *ḏi ᶜawāyidna ᶜala ma tigaddam w-ittaxar*
*ka-l-isūd illi yguḏḏ al-laḥam miḏrābha*
12. *min ḥarabna gāsiyin lān ᶜaḏmih w-inkisar*

---

[79] The meaning of this hemistich is not entirely clear to me. The word *ṣifar* is used here as a synonym of *ṣfiri* (see glossary under *ṣfr*); *ṣālḥīnin*, like *miṣālīḥ*, sing. *miṣlāḥ*, means 'herdsmen who are expert at selecting good pastures and fattening their animals'. However, *migwat* could be derived either from *wagt* 'time', or from *gūt* 'food, nourishment'.

8. How I wish I had kissed her when we met, //
And had buried my arms in her chestnut-coloured luxurious locks.[80]

POEM 30

1. O God, He who breaks the bones and heals them, if He wishes, //
We ask You for a favour: may its door not be barred;
2. A request that restores life to dry stumps of dead trees; //
Only prayers as these bring down heaven's merciful water.
3. My ire was provoked by a tale—you who were present, listen!—//
Tales that caused our tribe's maidens to rend their clothes.
4. I said, 'Get away, you scoundrel! Don't you dare //
Make that claim! Cursed be those who invented and spread it!'
5. Al-Jazla stands firmly protected by our swords and bullets, //
Her diaphanous gown made of pointed iron and cast lead,
6. As long as we graze our camels on its pastures in the autumn season: //
For us every grain of its soil is worth a fight.
7. Like pure poison that turns limpid water into a deadly potion, //
Squirting from the fangs of snakes,
8. You'll find us in al-Jazla's way, while there remains sight in our eyes; //
In her defense we hold our lives cheap, and no mistake!
9. Those who were present made up for the laggards, //
Faithful to the customs our ancestors bequeathed to us.
10. A war lasting ninety years to us seems no more than a month: //
In war we glory once its gate is opened.
11. These are our habits, in the days of old as well as at present; //
We are like lions whose paws tear open the flesh of their kill;
12. Whoever wages ruthless war on us, his bones grow shaky and fall apart, //

[80] Initially Dindān stopped his recitation of this poem after verse no. 7. Only when faced with an uproar of the company assembled in the room where the recording took place, did Dindān no longer hide behind facetious protestations of ignorance and forgetfulness and did he consent to recite the last verse, which came out almost smothered in laughing.

*w-aṣbaḥat bagᶜa tṭurrih b-ṭārif nābha*
13. *ṣabbaḥōna ṭalᶜat an-nūr w-inbāj as-sifar*
*fi jmūᶜin ma ᶜarafna nᶜidd ḥsābha*
14. *ṯumm zahamna ṣulb jaddin ysawwūn al-ᶜibar*
*xubirtin ćanhum isūdin tᶜuḏḏ ašnābha*
15. *maššaᶜaw sūdin min an-nīl sabrāt an-niḏar*
*midbiḥātin ćann sūd al-ḥnūš rǵābha*
16. *w-ištibak šōb ašhab al-milḥ w-iblīsin ḥaḏar*
*kull madǵūšin yimīnih ᶜala migḏābha*
17. *ᶜind xašm aš-Šiḏuw wi-l-bīr w-hi al-mistigarr*
*wallaᶜaw ḏawwin ḏahar fi s-sama mišhābha*
18. *wallah ma fi š-Šiḏuw zōdin wara sabᶜat ᶜašar*
*w-agᶜadaw nāsin wrūdin tsinn ḥrābha*
19. *naṭṭaḥōhum maǵrib aš-šams wi-l-wārid ṣidar*
*ᶜāf Zēdin ᶜugib ma ḏāg suww asbābha*
20. *ḏa li-ᶜēna šimmax an-nīb ḥaskāt al-wubar*
*al-fiṭīr illi swāt al-jirīd rǵābha*
21. *wallah in tasnid maᶜ al-Jōb la zāf az-zahar*
*w-in tḥaddir Jabjibin w-ant ma tarḏa bha*
22. *bayyiḏ allah wajh min šāf bi-l-ᶜēn w-ḥaḏar*
*ḥaggh al-bēḏa tnaṯṯir ᶜalēh ṯyābha*
23. *ya-nidībi w-irtiḥil ḥāyilin fajj an-naḥar*
*ᶜērtin la rawwaḥat yiᶜijbik ṣillābha*
24. *ṣōb ṣibyān Āl Zāyid b-mardūd al-xabar*
*sirrhum bi-l-ᶜilm la alfēt ya-rakkābha*
25. *siᶜd minhum lābtih miḥzimih xazn aḏ-ḏifar*

As the sharp canines of doom set to mauling him.
13. At the first light of day, as dawn spread its wings, they raided us, //
In numbers so great that they could not be counted.
14. We called out our kinsmen, whose courage works marvels, //
Fellow-clansmen like lions with ferociously fanging jaws.
15. The guns they uncased were glossy as if dyed with indigo, //
The long barrels folded back like the necks of black snakes.
16. Bursts of fire erupted and, amidst clouds of gunpowder, all hell broke loose, //
With every dauntless warrior's right arm fastened on his gun's butt.
17. At the bluffs of aš-Šiḏuw and our basecamp at its well //
They lighted a fire that set the sky aglow.
18. By God, at aš-Šiḏuw our men numbered no more than seventeen, //
But they held at bay legions bristling with sharpened blades.
19. At sunset they confronted the enemy's advance and turned it into a rout: //
Having tasted of the evil he provoked, Zēd decided he had had enough.
20. We held out for the sake of the long eye-teeth and knotty wool //
Of fully grown she-camels with necks gracious as palm branches.
21. By God, what animals as they pick their way through the green of al-Jōb's sloping valley bottom, //
Or on their way down Jabjib, whether you agree to their presence or not.
22. May God whiten the faces of those who were there to fight; //
If our beauties throw off their garments for them, they deserve it.
23. Messenger of mine, ride off on a powerful, broad-chested mount, //
A wiry animal of admirable endurance and speed,
24. Towards our boys of Āl Zāyid with the reports. //
On your arrival give them the glad tidings at once, O rider!
25. Fortunate is he whose kin gird him like a belt of heroism![81]

---

[81] See glossary under *ḥzm*.

*hal fᶜūlin min ᶜṣūr al-jahal yidra bha*
26. *la ltahamnāhum rifaᶜna bi-ṣōtin mištahar*[82]
*yaṭraḥ illi ṭāyirin ṣōb wajh trābha*
27. *ᶜugibha minni ṣalātin ᶜala sīd al-bišar*
*wi-s-salām w-sunnat Mḥammadin yiṯna bha*
*w-salāmatk.*

## POEM 31

Metre:--v---v---v-(*ar-rajaz*)

1. *aš-šāᶜir ad-Dindān ġanna w-iftikar*
*bētin ᶜala l-maᶜna yruddih bi-l-fiṣāḥ*
2. *ya-ṣulb jaddi ballġūna bi-l-xabar*
*min ᶜindikum rāyin sidīdin w-igtirāḥ*
3. *la labst al-Jazla laha lōn al-ḥamar*
*migyālna fīha taḥat fayy al-malāḥ*
4. *darjin w-ṣubbin min gidīmin miᶜtibar*
*w-milḥin ndūfih fi šahālīl al-garāḥ*
5. *min ḏillitin la yaćmin al-māw al-ḥamar*
*naḏrib bih al-ᶜāti ᶜala wajh aṣ-ṣarāḥ*
6. *ma hammna min ṣīb walla min ᶜaṯar*
*min dūn warṯ al-jadd ma niṭri ṣ-ṣalāḥ*
7. *illi yibi šibrin min al-Jazla kufar*
*ḥaggih ḥdūd al-mirhifāt mn as-slāḥ*
8. *Jazlan xalagha llah ćima waṣf al-gumar*
*yūḏi lha nūrin ᶜala l-arḏ al-barāḥ*
9. *lha figārin nābiyin wi-lha naḥar*
*w-inna bha min dūn xalg allah šḥāḥ*
10. *wi-lha jalālin ᶜindina wi-lha faxar*
*kull abrigin minha lina ᶜindih mrāḥ*
11. *hi dārna ma dāmna minna bišar*
*minha w-fīha ma nhōjis bi-l-marāḥ*
12. *jiᶜl al-wiliyy yinši ᶜalāha bi-l-miṭar*
*ġurr al-mzūn illi lha fi l-lēl ḏāḥ*

---

[82] Dindān's tribal battle cry is *ya-ālād ibn Ḥarāršah, ya-ᶜyāl ubūy.*

As early as the days of ignorance their bravery was famed.
26. When we wish for their succour and shout their names for all to hear, //
The pouncing enemy crashes down and bites the dust.
27. Now it remains for me to invoke the Lord's blessings on the first among man, //
And greetings, for to Muḥammad's example praise belongs.

## POEM 31

1. The poet ad-Dindān set his thoughts to a tune, //
Moulding each verse so as to express its meaning with eloquence.
2. Flesh and blood of my forefathers, tell us the news //
About the firm decisions and proposals resulting from your counsels!
3. If al-Jazla becomes shrouded in a reddish glow, //
From the clouds of gunsmoke we'll take our shade at noon:
4. From our powder and shot of ancient repute, //
Pounded saltpetre, mixed with limpid spring water.
5. Fearful of opinion if we'd kept our powder dry, //
Without flinching we levelled a barrage of fire at the aggressor,
6. Indifferent to the fate of those we hit and brought down: //
When our patrimony is at stake we don't think of suing for peace.
7. Whoever makes a grab for al-Jazla, even one inch of it, is an infidel, //
And deserves to be cut down by our sharp-edged swords.
8. Jazla was created by God to the likeness of the moon, //
To illuminate the wide, empty plain with her lustre.
9. She has a towering hump and a sloping breast: //
More than anything else in God's creation we hold her dear.
10. She holds us in awe; she's our glory and pride. //
At her every knoll our animals have rested at night.
11. She's our home as long as we are reckoned among the living, //
And the idea that we might ever abandon it simply doesn't occur.
12. May the Lord bring her the wind-blown rains, //
From white-tipped clouds that brighten the night with lightning,

13\. *yinši bih ar-riḥmān fi wagt as-saḥar*
*ᶜala xšūm ar-Ruxim yaḏfi lih janāḥ*
14\. *ṣalāt rabbi ᶜidd waddān as-simar*
*ᶜala r-risūl ᶜdād nisnās ar-ryāḥ*
*w-salāmatkum.*

13. Amassed in thick layers at first dawn by the Merciful, //
And stretching out their wings to cover ar-Rukhim's cliffs.
14. My Lord's benedictions, profuse as rains falling all night long, //
On the Prophet as often as breezes come and go.

## DINDĀN AS A RĀWI

The following two poems, and their narrative introduction, were recited by Dindān in his capacity as a transmitter (see p. 19). The transcription of the narrative sections has been composed from two different recordings and one version written down at Dindān's dictation. Some of the alternative phrases Dindān used in the different versions of the narratives have been added in the text between brackets. Remarks by members of the audience and my own comments are between square brackets.

### POEM 32

*The Narrative and Poem of al-Xwēr*[83]

a. *ṭāḥ hinna rajiᶜ ᶜala jbāl al-haḏ̣b ḏi (ṭāḥ ᶜala Ġāyir w-ᶜala s-Skak rajiᶜ, guwiyy). w-ja fīha ᶜišbin mityāmnin mityāsir ma lha ᶜadād. w-ᶜillmo bih, fi l-xāfah, min awwilih, yōm al-ᶜarab yḏillūn mn al-ᶜarab, yūxḏo! w-yōm jiḏab-hum al-ᶜišb f-rāḥaw lih, ṣōbih. w-jaw ḏ̣āhrīn mn al-Wādi b-aḏwādhum w-xēlhum.*

b. *w-gāmat bintin Għaṭāniyyah ubūha nziliyyin fi l-Wādi w-ᶜāraḏ̣athum ḏōdha. ṭridāha w-hajjaw iblha w-gālaw: ma nibīć! fārǵīna ya-bint! w-ᶜayyat tfāriǵhum.*

c. *w-yōm wṣalaw al-ḥaya wi-ḏ̣ribaw al-Jufrah lē fīha min al-ᶜišb aṭ-ṭiwīl, mtaᶜaddi al-ᶜišb aš-šjar. w-yōm ǵidhum mgayyilīn fi ḏīk as-sarḥah lē hi wṣalathum yṯāliṯ bha giᶜūdha, yajmaḥ, wi-hi tiṣīḥ, rībah.*

*d. (yōm ǵidhum fi s-Skak la ćāyin ᶜalāha ḏālāk al-gōm w-xḏōha, ᶜala ṯal-āṯīn mardūfah ᶜalāha sittīn rajjāl). wlē ḏīk al-bill māxūḏtin, hiḏīk miṯil ḥarj an-naxil miǵfīnin bha al-gōm (yōm gāmaw lēhum yšūfūn ebāᶜirhum midābīr, mrāyḥīn bha al-gōm).*

---

[83] A version in eight verses of this poem has been published by al-Fiṣām, Maḥbūb ibn Saᶜd ibn Mudawwis ad-Dōsirī and Abū ᶜAbd ar-Raḥmān ibn ᶜAqīl aẓ-Ẓāhirī in *Min as̲h̲ᶜār ad-Dawāsir*, i, 212-213, who identify the poet as Zēd al-Xwēr as-Sabbāᶜi al-Misᶜari. Dindān added that Zēd belonged to Āl Xōrān of Āl bu Sabbāᶜ.

## POEM 32

a. A lot of rain fell on the mountains of the Hadb (the rain poured down in streams on Ġāyir and as-Skak). As a result the herbage shot up lush and plentiful in unheard-of amounts. They received the news of the rainfall—it was deep in the desert, in the days when the tribesmen were afraid of one another and men were plundered. The herbage attracted them and they set out in its direction. They left the Wādi together with their herds and horses.

b. Then they were accosted by a shepherdess from the Gḥaṭān tribe whose father had settled in the Wādi. They tried to chase her away and to stampede her camels, saying, 'We don't want your company, leave us alone, girl!' But she refused and kept following them, not wanting to go her own way.

c. When they arrived in the area irrigated by the rain and came to al-Jufrah, the herbage there had shot up so high that it stood taller than the trees. As they took their rest at noontime in the shade of an acacia-tree, suddenly there came the girl on her galloping young male camel—the animal bolted—shouting cries of alarm at the top of her voice.

d. (When they had come to as-Skak they were attacked and plundered by raiders, thirty riding camels carrying two men each, sixty in all.) What had happened was that their camels had been taken and were driven away like clumps of palm-trees by the attackers (the first thing they saw was that their camels were moving in the other direction, taken away by the enemy).

e. *raćbaw (talāwiḏaw, ḥawwizaw fi ḏhūrhin) w-laḥǵaw. yōm laḥǵōhum w-šāfaw gullihum (šāfaw al-xēl šwayy), xēl m hīb wājid, balla sab<sup>c</sup>ah, gāmaw y<sup>c</sup>ā<sup>c</sup>aw lha: āy āy āy (yad<sup>c</sup>ūn al-xēl, ytā<sup>c</sup>aw lha), ya<sup>c</sup>ni: ilḥagi, xallō-hum wiyyāhm.*

f. *w-tijīhum, jathum. w-yōm laḥǵōhum sawwaw fīhum sanādir ad-dinya, gall allah <sup>c</sup>alēhum bi-l-xēr. fakkaw al-bill (fi l-gāylah w-yōm ja bēn aṣ-ṣalātēn hum rāddīn al-bill) w-raddaw ma<sup>c</sup>ha xamsat <sup>c</sup>ašar ḏilūl wi-ḏbaḥaw minhum xamsah w-<sup>c</sup>išrīn liḥiytin fi l-Jufrah [hāḏa kullih <sup>c</sup>ala šān al-bint], ēh, allah, allah, giṣīrathum ma<sup>c</sup>hm. w-jāb sālfatha hāḏi. al-Xwēr šēx Āl Bū Sabbā<sup>c</sup>:*

Metre:--v---v----(*ar-rajaz*)

1. *gāl al-Xwēri w-illiḏi yidna lih*
   *ṣafra tṣāġi falkat al-miṣrā<sup>c</sup>i*
2. *ṣafra sinn <sup>c</sup>nānha bi-lḥiyyha*
   *yašdi l-mūsin fi yid aḏ-ḏarrā<sup>c</sup>i*
3. *ṣafra trīd mjarribin wi-yrīdha*
   *ma hīb min taṭmaḥ w-tabġi rā<sup>c</sup>i*
4. *ṣafra lya ngād al-<sup>c</sup>ajāj la ćanha*
   *šixtūr ṣēfin fi š-šifa ǵid ḏā<sup>c</sup>i*
5. *tā<sup>c</sup>aw l-surbatna f-jathum ḥaffah*
   *miṯil al-giṭa lli wārdin kurrā<sup>c</sup>i*
6. *la jāthum miṯil al-ḥadāya kaddah*
   *ṯumm ṭayyarat minhum t<sup>c</sup>ūd ryā<sup>c</sup>i*
7. *f-amma al-Jnēdi b-anaffil xaṭṭih*
   *yašdi l-ḥurrin la da<sup>c</sup>āh ad-dā<sup>c</sup>i*
8. *w-amma bin Filwat ma yġāyib ḥōlhum*
   *w-ćannih Klēfīx bēnna farrā<sup>c</sup>i*
9. *f-ašūf ana min hu yihūš b-šuṭrah*

e. They mounted their horses (they vaulted onto the backs of their horses) and caught up with the raiders. When they had come close and the others saw how few they were (saw that they were only a few horsemen), just a handful of horsemen, only seven, they began to yell to the horses, 'Eyh, eyh, eyh!' (they called the horses, made the kind of noises that encourages a horse to come). That means, 'Come on, catch up with us!' They let them come at them.

f. And there they came. When they reached them [the raiders], they [the Duwāsir] completely routed them. That day God did not want them [the raiders] to be lucky. The owners recaptured their camels (in the hours from noon until the time between the two prayers they retook their camels), in addition they took fifteen riding camels as booty, and they killed twenty-five men [lit. beards] of the other side in al-Jufrah [all this because of that girl]. Yes, that's right, she was their neighbour. So this is the story he told about her. Al-Khwēr is the sheikh of Āl Bū Sabbā$^c$.

1. Al-Khwēri said these verses as they brought up to him //
   A pure white mare obedient to the iron grip of the halter;
2. A white mare whose pin in the reins moves to and fro over her jaws, //
   Like a pair of scissors in the hand of a tailor;
3. A white mare longing for an experienced warrior, just as he longs to ride her: //
   It is not her ambition to be mounted by a shepherd who guards the herds.
4. A white mare whose tail amidst the clouds of battle //
   Is like a sprinkle of summer curling down somewhere in the steppe.
5. 'Eyh, eyh,' they called to our platoon, and it came charging //
   Like a covey of sand grouse whizzing through the air in close formation;
6. Or like kites swooping down, it's attack came in one plunge, //
   Then soaring to the sky, only to wheel back and make another dive.
7. As for al-Jnēdi, his bravery is worthy of my praise, //
   Like a noble falcon plummeting down when called by the falconeer;
8. And as for Ibn Filwah, he's not one to slink away in battle; //
   Like Klēfīkh he stands as a barrier between us and the enemy.
9. All around me I saw men wielding double-edged swords, //

*w-bān al-ḥadīd al-mixliṣ al-gaṭṭāʿi*
10. *inna ʿadānāhum bi-ḏarb rmāḥna*
*wi-syūfna fi rūshum širrāʿi*
11. *xamsah w-ʿišrīnin b-Jufrat Ġāyir*
*min kān hu min lābtih yirtāʿi*
12. *min al-hḏāb al-ḥumr minna rakḏah*
*tġanni bha al-ʿimmāl maʿ l-anwāʿi*
13. *ya-niʿm ya-Sibʿān ʿind rćābhum*
*f-inn an-nišīd ṭarāth al-jizzāʿi*
14. *ʿana l-Fnādah yōm šuft dmūʿha*
*lāni min jiddi w-lāni wāʿi*
15. *ʿanāć ya-najl al-ʿyūn nruddha*
*la kān fi ḏīġin w-maʿ mitbāʿi*
*w-salāmatkum.*

## POEM 33

*The Narrative and Poem of az-Ziʿbiyyah*[84]

a. *wāḥdin Ḥarbi gāṣar Ziʿb, jāwarhum (Ḥarbi, min Ḥarb, mjāwrin Ziʿb,*

---

[84] Another version of this poem has been published by Raddās, ʿAbdallah ibn Muḥammad ibn, *Shāʿirāt min al-bādiyah*, Riyadh 1984-85, i, 69-84. Ibn Raddās puts the age of the poem at about three centuries. He recorded it in Damām in A.H. 1384 (1964-65) from a very old female transmitter of the Murrah tribe, Baxūt al-Murriyyah. Ibn Raddās' version is the longer one: sixty-seven verses against the fifty-five recited by ad-Dindān. In comparing both versions one notes that the order of verses runs roughly in parallel. Moreover, the variations in the wording of the corresponding verses are relatively minor. Taking into account the difference in length one might therefore conclude that both versions overlap for about eighty percent. Given the fact that this long and complex poem was transmitted orally over a number of centuries and that both versions were recorded in two locations hundreds of miles apart, one can only marvel at the degree of similarity between both versions.

The order of verses in both versions corresponds as follows:
Dindān (D) 1-12 = Ibn Raddās (R) 1-12; D 13 = R 43; D 14-17 = R 15-18; D 18-20 = R 21-23; D 21-22 = R 28-29; D 23 = R 24; D 24-28 = R 30-34; D 29-31 = R 25-27; D 32 = R 37; D 33 = R 39; D 34 = R 38; D 35-37 = R 40-42; D 38-40 = R 44-46; D 41-42 = R 53-54; D 43 = R 56; D 44 = R 55; D 45 = R 61; D 46 = R 60; D 47 = R 58; D 48 = R 57; D 49 = R 59; D 50-55 = R 62-67.

The following are the numbers of the verses in Ibn Raddās that do not occur in Dindān's version: 13-14, 19-20 (both passages a mixture of *mufākharah* and admonishments to the poetess' own tribe), 35-36 (tribal *mufākharah*) and 47-52 (a passage which tells that the girl became lost, climbed into a tree and was found by a party of Duwāsir raiders).

The cutting blades of pure steel sparkling in the sunlight.
10. We attacked them and thrust at them our spears, //
And drenched our swords in the blood of their cleft skulls.
11. Twenty-five men were left dead at the depression of Ġāyir, //
A sight that left their fellow kinsmen aghast.
12. It happened at a gallop's distance from the reddish rocks, //
Now it is the theme of airs sung by the labourers irrigating the palms.
13. For sure, the Sbēʿ made a valiant stand in defence of their mounts, //
But the best songs are those that rouse the enemy's wrath.
14. We fought for al-Fnādah whose flowing tears //
Drove me into a fury and made me see red.[85]
15. For your sake, large-eyed beauty, I recaptured your camels; //
For you I would pursue them through ravines or over twisting trails.

## POEM 33

a. A Ḥarbi came to live with Ziʿb; he became their neighbour (a

---

A version of sixty-nine verses, together with a more elaborate narrative introduction, has been published by ath-Thumayrī, Muḥammad ibn Aḥmad, in *al-Funūn ash-shaʿbīyah fī al-Jazīrah al-ʿArabīyah*, Damascus 1972, 178-186. Ath-Thumayrī identifies the sheikh who married the woman of Ziʿb as Misʿar ibn Gwēd, the son of the sheikh of ad-Duwāsir. Thus the story and the poem might be considered as part of a myth of origin, tracing the lineage of the powerful Āl bu Sabbāʿ of the Misāʿrah to a common ancestry with the Ibn Gwēd sheikhs and, on the maternal side, to the ancient nobility of the Ziʿb tribe. In *al-Alf sanah al-ġāmiḍah min taʾrīkh Najd*, Riyadh 1988, 331-332, ʿAbd ar-Raḥmān as-Suwaydāʾ cites twenty-eight verses of the poem and discusses possible relationships with the Banū Hilāl cycle.

[85] Al-Fnādah (al-Funaydah) was the name of the Ghaṭāni shepherdess.

*giṣīr lhum nāzlin maᶜhm). w-yōm jāwarhum mjammiᶜ mn iblin wājdin, mijāhīm zyān (w-iblih tisᶜīn, sūd zyān, miṯl an-nāgah illi an awarrīk).*

b. *w-gāl aš-širīf (širīf Makkah): ᶜaṭūna, ya-Ziᶜb, ibil giṣīrkum walla aḏᶜaftkum (walla ḏibaḥnākum). w-gālaw: hāḏi tisᶜīn šagra, faras, dūn ibil giṣīrna w-xallih (w-gāmaw ᶜala tisᶜīn šagra w-sāgāha bidal ibil giṣīrhum; w-gāl az-Ziᶜbi ibn Ġāfil: aᶜṭīk tisᶜīn šagra filwitin dūnhum).*

c. *w-ᶜayya. aḥrimaw ᶜindih fi Makkah, bi-ṭaršhum w-ḏiᶜnānhum. w-yōm jaw yaṭlibūnih f-taġaḏḏab ᶜalēhum (w-gām aš-širīf mnāgid, mitᶜadwi, luhum). w-gām ᶜala xīrat šīxānhum wu-hu giṭaᶜ rāsih nikāl (w-giṭaᶜ rās wāḥdin min aš-šīxān).*

d. *w-hajjaw (w-ᶜaṭaw al-farār w-inḥāšaw) lēn jaw ᶜala māhum, ģilīb lhum fi Gāᶜat Wisaṭ (fi wajh Wiṣat min ģiblah). w-haṭṭaw alfēn bētin ᶜala jālha w-alfēn bētin fi l-maḏma, ḏi tḥammaha fi l-maḏma wi-ḏi tḥammaha ᶜala al-ma (w-yibūn illi fi l-maḏma tamnaᶜh la yijīh aḥad, la yijīh gōm, w-ill ᶜal al-ma yimnaᶜhum la yijīha gōm), [allibu gōm!] allibu gōm.*[86]

e. *w-yōm jaw ᶜala ģilībhum, nzalaw, wlēh jāyyhum yamši (jāhum aš-širīf b-ģīmānih). w-ṯār bēnhum gabūtin, aćān ᶜalēhum. w-ja bēnhum w-bēnih ḏabḥin guwiyy wi-ṭrād ḥillin ṭiwīl (w-gām al-ḥarb, bēnhum w-bēnih, ḥlūlin ṭiwīlah) ilēn ḥatt al-bint illi mnaššin bha ummha al-ḥāmil tijawwizat wuhum fi ḥarb. kull ma iḏbaḥaw gibāyiln jāb gibāyil.*

---

[86] *allibu gōm*, explained as *wallah illi bi-gōm* 'By God, they have a lot of men!' However, I was told by S. A. Sowayan that it may be a contracted form of *ya liᶜn ubu gōm* 'God damn, what an army!'

Ḥarbi, a man of the Ḥarb tribe, became a neighbour of Ziᶜb, a protected stranger living among them). As their neighbour he prospered and became the owner of many camels, nice black ones (he had ninety camels, beautiful black ones, like the she-camel I showed to you).

b. One day the Sharīf (the Sharīf of Mecca) said, 'O Ziᶜb, hand over to me the camels of your neighbour or you will be worsted (or we'll kill you)!' They [Ziᶜb] said, 'Here are ninety sorrel horses we are ready to offer instead of the camels owned by our neighbour on condition that you leave him alone' (and they set out from their tribal area driving ninety sorrel horses as ransom for the camels of their neighbour; and the Ziᶜbi Ibn Ġāfil said, 'I will give you ninety sorrel horses, fillies in their first year, besides the other ninety horses').

c. But he [the Sharīf] refused. They came to wait on him in Mecca with their herds and the camels carrying luggage and the litters in which the women travelled. When they petitioned him he became angry (the Sharīf became peevish, hostile to them). He took the pick of their sheikhs and had his head cut off as an exemplary punishment (and he cut off the head of one of their sheikhs).

d. Then they made off (they took to their heels, made a run for it) until they reached their watering-place, one of their wells in Gāᶜat Wisaṭ (facing Wisaṭ in the direction of Mecca). They pitched two thousand tents around the well and two thousand tents in the waterless desert: these protected [their herds and flocks] in the desert pasture and the others protected the wells (the idea was that those in the waterless desert would make sure that no one could get at what they had there, that the enemy would not touch it, and those at the well safeguarded what they owned there). [By God they had a lot of men!]. Yes, there were a lot of men.

e. As soon as they had arrived at their well and were encamped, the Sharīf marched on them (the Sharīf advanced on them with his warriors). Clouds of dust arose [thrown up by the galloping horses, i.e. war broke out]; he went on the attack. That was the beginning of a long period of murderous fighting and duelling on horseback (the war between them lasted a long time) until even the embryo-girl in her mother's belly had grown up and had married. Whenever they had cut to pieces the tribes the Sharīf marched on them, he would throw fresh tribal forces into the battle.

f. *w-yōm xaḏaw lhum ḥillin ṭiwīl w-ṭāl lhum as-sigim yiji ṯimān snīn aw tisʿah fḏāhum. w-hajjaw, tifaḏḏaw al-gōm, ahal az-Ziʿbiyyah, w-rāḥaw ṭiǵīǵ, inḥāšaw (yōm fḏāhum ṭaggaw an-nās).*

g. *w-yōm aćān aš-širīf wi-hi ʿind ḏōdha fi l-maḏma, ma darat ʿanhum (gʿadat bintin l-ibn Ġāfil ʿind ḏōdha, ma tadri ʿanhum). inksaraw al-ʿarab wi-hi gʿadat (w-lē hi ʿind ḏōdha, mṣaddrah).*

h. *w-xarrat bha ʿēnha wi-hi miʿtarḏitin ʿala l-biʿīr w-rāǵdah. w-sarat bha aḏ-ḏōd lēn m glaʿat bha. yōm aṣbaḥat al-biʿīr gāʿdin bha wi-ḏ-ḏōd sāri, rāyiḥ (sarat aḏ-ḏōd w-hammalatha w-gʿadat ʿala giʿīdha, w-yōm aṣbaḥat al-bill alla giʿīdha fi xala wi-n-nās ma baʿad).*

i. *w-yōm šāfat as-sēr ma ʿād bh aḥad w-ḥawwalat min rukbiyyaha w-rigat fi rās ḏīk aš-šjarat ḥaṭṭat lha fīh ʿšēš. gaddar allah ʿalāha rkēbin mn ad-Duwāsir, ġazuw, nawwaxaw fi š-šjarat mgayylīnin fīha (gayyalaw fi s-sarḥah) w-yōm šabbaw ḏawwhum wlēhum yišūfūnah. gāl: ḥawwili ya-bint, ḥawwili! wala ḥawwalat (ʿayyat tḥawwil) lēn ḥatta ʿaṭāha ʿahad allah, ma ybūgūn hum. gāl: ʿalēć allah w-imān allah ḥatta min ḥayyāt at-trāb.*

j. *ḥawwalaw bha, ġaḏḏāha w-sigāha, w-rāḥaw bha l-ahalhum. w-yōm jaw ahalhum la bintin hābbat rīḥin w-ʿajibathum. gāl wlid imīrhum, Misʿar: ya-būy ana b-āxiḏ ḏa l-bint, atizawwajha. gāl ubūh: buṣrik, tizawwajha.*

k. *w-ḥāmalat w-jat bi-walad, Sabbāʿ. Sabbāʿin jirmūd. yōm ǵid hu jayyid gām yaḏrib al-wirʿān wala ykāfūnih, ma ḥtālaw fīh (wala yiḥtālūnih). saw-wa fi l-wirʿān sanādir ad-dinya, ybaṭṭiṭhum, yxanniǵhum.*

f. Finally, when they been at war for a long time and their enmity had lasted about eight or nine years, the Sharīf overwhelmed them and they fled. The tribesmen, the kinsmen of the Ziᶜb girl, were overrun and they fled as fast as their feet would carry them; they ran for it (when he had defeated them the people fled).

g. When the Sharīf went on the attack the girl was with her herd in the desert pasture; she had no idea what was happening to her people (a daughter of Ibn Ġāfil was away with her herd, she did not know what was going on). The tribesmen were routed and she was somewhere else (and she was with the herd, moving away from the well into the desert pastures).

h. She could not keep her eyes open and while she was stretched out on the back of her male camel she fell asleep. Meanwhile the herd kept walking and carried her away. When she woke up in the morning her riding camel stood still and the herd had walked off, was gone (the herd had gone during the night and left her alone while she sat on her camel; when she woke up in the morning all camels, except the one on which she rode, had disappeared in the empty desert and her people were gone).

i. When she saw that she was all alone, she climbed from her mount and into the top of a tree and there she built a little nest for herself. It so happened [lit. God decreed] that a group of mounted Duwāsir, raiders, passed by and made their camels kneel down in order to take their noon rest in the shade of that tree (they rested at noon in the shade of that acacia-tree). When they lighted their fire they discovered her. He said, 'Climb down, girl, come down from the tree!' But she did not come down (she refused to come down) until he gave her a solemn promise; and those men did not cheat. He said, 'I swear by God that you will be safe even from the vipers in the sand.'

j. They helped her come down, he gave her something to eat and drink, and then they took her to their folk. When they came home the people saw that the girl had great promise and they were pleased with her. The son of their tribal chief, Misᶜar, said, 'Father, I want to take that girl as my wife, I want to marry her.' His father answered, 'Do as you see fit, you can marry her.'

k. She became pregnant and she gave birth to a son, Sabbāᶜ. Sabbāᶜ was a strong, tough boy. When he had grown up somewhat he beat the other boys; they were no match for him, they could not hold their own against him. He beat the hell out of those boys, he thrashed them, took them by the throat.

1. *gālaw: imnᶜūna min wlid al-hamiyyat illi gām yfarris wirᶜānna (illi yḏabbiḥ wirᶜānna). al-hamiyyah, yaᶜni, hi lāǵīnha fi l-xala. māćinat maᶜaha yōm gālaw hamiyyah (taġayyarat yōm samᶜat wlid al-hamiyyah). yōm ja l-lēl sara ᶜalāha ᶜaduww al-misilmīn:*

Metre: (v) (-)-v---v--v--(*aṭ-ṭawīl*)

1. *siga r-rabb ya-Sabbāᶜ dārin ḏikartha*
   *ma ᶜād minha lla muwāri ḥyūdha*
2. *Sabbāᶜ ummik tabći b-ᶜēnin ḥafiyyah*
   *dmūᶜha tixfi miḏāri xdūdha*
3. *laćan wgūd an-nār b-agṣa ḏimīri*
   *zād al-ġarām w-bayyaḥ allah sdūdha*
4. *laćann ḥajr al-ᶜēn fīha milīlah*
   *w-ćann yinhaš fōgha min brūdha*
5. *damᶜi yšādi šannat al-hōšiliyyah*
   *biᶜīdin mᶜaššāha ziᶜūjin giᶜūdha*
6. *Ziᶜbiyytin ya-ᶜamm māni hamiyyah*
   *wala min illi tāyhātin jdūdha*
7. *ana min Ziᶜb w-Ziᶜbin ly ōjahaw*
   *ᶜala l-xēl ᶜajlīnin sirīᶜin rdūdha*
8. *ṭirīḥhum la ṭāḥ šōfi tarāyaᶜaw*
   *tigūl fhūdin mixṭiyātin ṣyūdha*
9. *hal surbitin l agfat laćanha mhajjarah*
   *w-in agbalat ćann al-juwāzi wrūdha*
10. *laḥġaw ᶜala miṯil al-giṭa yōm warrad*
    *mitġānimin ᶜēnin garāḥin yirūdha*
11. *in ṣāḥ ṣāyiḥ min sibīb fzaᶜaw lih*
    *w-ᶜizzi l-ġimrin ṯabbarat bih bilūdha*

1. The people said, 'Spare us from the son of that stray woman who trounces our boys (who licks our boys)!' A stray woman, that is, they had found her by herself in the empty desert. When she heard them say 'stray woman' she was deeply offended (she was deeply upset when she heard the people say 'son of the stray woman'). When the night fell the enemy of the Muslims approached her [i.e. Satan as the demon of poetry]:

1. O Sabbā$^{c}$, may the Lord bring rain to a land I fondly remember, //
   And now only the crumbled stones that marked the wells remain.
2. Sabbā$^{c}$, your mother cries with wounded eyes, //
   And the tears keep rolling down her cheeks.
3. I feel as if a fire were lighted deep inside my breast; //
   So wistful I grew that God uncovered what I had suppressed.
4. The corners of my eyes are burnt by glowing embers //
   That deprive them of balmy coolness.
5. My tears stream down like water from an old, leaky water-skin, //
   Dangling from an agitated camel that has to go a long way before its evening stop.
6. Zi$^{c}$b is my tribe, dear fellow, I'm not a stray she-camel without owner, //
   Nor am I one of those whose ancestry is unknown.
7. To Zi$^{c}$b I belong, Zi$^{c}$b who confront their enemy //
   On horses that charge like a blue streak and make quick turnabouts.
8. If one of them is thrown from the saddle, they halt and counter, //
   Like lions playing havoc with game;
9. Cavalrymen whose retreat is like that of hobbled camels, //
   And whose attack is like that of gazelles rushing to the water.
10. They overtake the enemy on horses like sand grouse whizzing through the air, //
    To slake their thirst with water from their favourite spring.
11. When a guard on horseback sounds the alarm, they hasten to his rescue: //
    Woe unto a warrior whose nag then begins to limp and stumble.

12. *xēlin tġaḏḏa li-l-bala wi-l-maᶜāriḱ*
*tahrab ṣanādīd al-ᶜda fi ṭrūdha*
13. *namran ćima waṣf al-jarād at-thāmi*
*ma ṭāᶜaw al-ḥukkām min ᶜuḏm kūdha*
14. *jāna š-širīf b-dārin awwal ltigāna*
*kull al-gibāyil jāmᶜīnin jrūdha*
15. *ṭalab ᶜindina fi xūr hajmat giṣīrna*
*mṣammlin yabġi ḥanāzīb sūdha*
16. *yāma ᶜaṭāna jārna min sibiyyah*
*tisᶜīn šagran ḥasibha wi-mᶜadūdha*
17. *timāmha min aš-Šaybān xyālat Mhawwis*
*aṣāylin ṣanᶜ an-niṣāra gyūdha*
18. *ᶜayyaw ᶜalāha lābti w-iḥtimāha*
*bi-mṣaggalātin mirhifātin ḥdūdha*
19. *ḥarabna w-taww al-bint našwin bha ummha*
*lēn istaᶜaddat w-istawa zēn ᶜūdha*
20. *ᶜala l-ḥanāya naggiḏann al-jidāyil*
*šugr al-jidāyil ćāsyātin nhūdha*
21. *banāt ᶜammi kullihin šaggan al-xba*
*bīḏ at-tarāyib ḏāfyātin jᶜūdha*
22. *kullin nahār al-hōš tanxa rjālha*
*sitir al-ᶜaḏāra fi l-mlāga isūdha*
23. *wjīhhin ka-mizintin ᶜagribiyyah*
*hallat miṭarha yōm ḥannat rᶜūdha*
24. *labbāstin li-ṭ-ṭās wi-d-dirᶜ fi l-lga*
*ᶜala srūj al-xēl ᶜajlin wrūdha*
25. *min ṣanᶜ dāwūdin ᶜalēhum mišāriᶜ*

12. Our horses, fed on camel's milk, are ready for carnage and battle; //
Terrified, the brawny enemy warriors flee from their charges.
13. Their fighting men are numerous as locusts from Tihāmah, //
And too proud ever to make their submission to foreign rulers.
14. The Sharīf waged war on us in our former homeland, //
Meeting us with the armies he raised from all the tribes,
15. Wishing to seize the herd of milch camels of our neighbour, //
Implacably set to take possession of the black, burly animals.
16. Many a horse we gave our neighbour to ransom himself: //
We gave him ninety sorrel mares, no more, no less,
17. Crowning them with ash-Shaybān, the mount of Mhawwis, //
Thoroughbreds, their legs chained in iron made by the Christians.
18. Stubborn in their defense, my kinsmen waged battle //
With polished, double-edged cutting swords.
19. The mother was barely pregnant of the girl when the war began, //
And it did not end before she had grown into a shapely young lady.
20. Raising themselves in their litters, the maidens loosened their hair, //
And let the reddish-brown tresses fall over their breasts;[87]
21. Daughters of my close kin all, ripping open the curtains of their litter chairs,
They stepped out to show their fair-skinned chests and luxuriant locks,
22. And all day long cheered the fighters on to even greater bravery, //
Protectors of the chaste maidens who on the day of battle turn into lions,
23. Their faces wet and glistening like clouds in the time of Scorpio //
As they release torrents of rain and rumble with thunder.
24. Our warriors wear helmets and they are clad in coats of mail, //
Riding saddled horses that charge with lightning speed.
25. On their backs they drench their arms of pure steel, //

---

[87] Doughty (1936), i, 511, notes that among the tribes there 'are some brown-haired women and even yellowish,' who are considered beauties.

*tijībih rjālin min ġanāyim fhūdha*
26. *yāma ṭᶜanaw fi ḥarbitin ᶜōligiyyah*
*bi-šalfan talaḏ̣ḏ̣a yašrab ad-damm ᶜūdha*
27. *ill ētimaw fi yōm tisᶜīn muhrah*
*ma minhin illi ma tlāwi ᶜamūdha*
28. *w-tisᶜīn maᶜ tisᶜīn w-alfēn fāris*
*taḥit ṣilīb al-xadd tiṭwa lḥūdha*
29. *tisᶜīn lēlah wi-l-garāyiᶜ mᶜaggalah*
*ḥimm aḏ-ḏra mᶜaggalātin ᶜḏ̣ūdha*
30. *šugḥ al-bkār illi zahann al-janāyib*
*gāmat tḏ̣āliᶜ min miṯāni ᶜḏ̣ūdha*
31. *w-xēlin tnāḥi xēl l-ašrāf bi-l-ǵana*
*miṯil at-thāmi yōm aḥalli jrūdha*
32. *Ziᶜbin nahār al-majd wi-l-jūd wi-ṯ-ṯana*
*min ar-Ribᶜ al-Xāli la l-Ḥjāz ḥdūdha*
33. *in sannidaw fīh hajj minhum gibāyil*
*dārin yijūnha ḏ̣iddhum ma yiᶜūdha*
34. *w-in ajnibaw al-xēl minhum tḥawwiz*
*rudd al-juwāzi wi-l-wḏ̣ēḥi ᶜanūdha*
35. *wi-lya ntawaw fi dīrtin yāṣilūnha*
*tigāfat al-aḏ̣ᶜān ᶜajlin šdūdha*
36. *wi-rćābhum yamm al-ᶜda mitᶜibīnha*
*bīḏ̣ al-maḥāǵib migṭirātin lhūdha*
37. *yāma xaḏaw min ḏ̣iddihum min ġanīmah*
*w-min ḏāg minhum ḏ̣arbitin ma yiᶜūdha*
38. *ašūf min al-ḥarrah ḏ̣ᶜūnin tigallalat*

The booty of men who despoil lions of their gains,
26. Thrusting time and again with spearheads made in Hadramaut, //
Burning spears with shafts ever thirsting for blood.
27. Ninety fillies they turned into orphans in just one day: //
Not one of them escaped being tied to a pole.[88]
28. Ninety and ninety and two thousand horsemen //
Were laid in graves dug in the hard ground of the plain.
29. For ninety nights the herd of thoroughbreds remained hobbled, //
Dark-humped camels, their muscular upper legs tied together,[89]
30. And white young mothers with girths upholding the nets around their udders, //
That limp and stumble along with their folded, hobbled legs.
31. Javelin-throwing horsemen charged at the Sharīf's cavalry, //
Swarming over the enemy like locusts from Tihāmah.
32. Such was Ziᶜb in its heyday of glory, generosity and noblesse: //
Their tribal lands stretched from the Empty Quarter to al-Ḥijāz;
33. If they marched to the upland country, the tribes there fled in panic, //
And while they roamed a land, the adversaries dared not return;
34. And if they marched south the enemy's horsemen evaded them, //
Like gazelles and oryxes skittering behind their leading female.
35. If they decide to migrate to another area, nothing holds them back; //
Their camel trains follow one another in rapid succession,
36. While the men are wearing down the riding camels on their raids, //
Hair turned grey under the belly girths and ulcers dripping under the saddle.[90]
37. Stupendous was the booty they took from their opponents, //
And the blows they delivered could not be repaid.
38. I watch their heavily-laden camel trains setting out from al-Ḥarrah, //

---

88 The fillies are tied to a pole to prevent them from looking for their dead mothers and becoming lost.

89 The camels were hobbled for the duration of the battle to prevent them from escaping or being taken by the enemy.

90 On long marches the fur under the girths is chafed and turns white and the weight of the saddle causes painful ulcers.

*w-ubūy hadda bi-s-sarāya yigūdha*
39. *šaffi maʿah šagran tbārīh ʿandal*[91]
*murrin ybārīha w-murrin yigūdha*
40. *w-ana fitāt al-ḥayy bint ibin Ġāfil*
*ćam min fitātin ġarr fīha giʿūdha*
41. *ḏikart yōmin fāytin ǵid miḏ̣a lhum*
*lēlin ʿalēna min liyāli sʿūdha*
42. *ḏ̣awwin ǵdat li-l-māl min ġibb saryah*[92]
*ḏ̣awwin ǵdat ʿūdān l-urṭa wigūdha*
43. *tisʿīn garnin ṣēdna fi ʿašiyyah*
*wḏ̣ēḥiyytin najʿal dlāna jlūdha*
44. *laćan grūn aṣ-ṣēd min xilf bētna*
*hašīm al-ġaḏ̣a yijmaʿ li-ḥāmi wgūdha*
45. *inna nzalna al-Ḥazim tisʿīn lēlah*
*w-ġull l-aʿādi lājyin fi kbūdha*
46. *lina bēn Ḥibrin wi-l-Ġarābah manzil*
*nihidd bih zēn al-ʿarāba giʿūdha*
47. *rawwāyna yasri bi-lēlih w-yinṯini*
*yiji bi-r-ruwāya ḏ̣āymātin giʿūdha*
48. *gannāṣna yasraḥ bi-yōmih w-yinṯini*
*yiji bi-l-juwāzi dāmyātin xdūdha*
49. *ġazzāyna yasraḥ bi-lēlih w-yinṯini*
*yiji bi-l-ʿarāba ḏ̣āymatha dyūdha*
50. *gilībna ġazīrat al-jamm ʿēlam*
*ma yinšdūn ṣdūrha min wrūdha*
51. *ṭūlha ṯimānin maʿ ṯimānin maʿ arbaʿ*
*ǵibli Wāṣit fi malāwi nifūdha*
52. *wi-hi jinūb b-ḥadd al-ḥāḏ mn al-ġaḏ̣a*
*ma dārha z-zarrāʿ yabḏir blūdha*
53. *alfēn bētin nāzlīnin jibāha*

---

[91] Ibn Raddās (1984-85), i, 75, has *šaffa*, 'to move, be on higher ground, the highest point of the terrain', instead of *šaffi*.

[92] *ḏ̣awwin ǵdat*, probably a contraction of the *tanwīn* of *ḏ̣aww* and *awgidat* 'it (the fire) was lighted'. Ibn Raddās (1984-85), i, 76, has *ḏ̣awwin zimat* 'a fire flared up'.

With my father riding in the lead at the head of the horsemen.
39. I wish he had a sorrel mare flanked by a pure-white thoroughbred, //
A thoroughbred now running side by side, and then leading the other mare.
40. I am the tribe's first lady, the daughter of Ibn Ġāfil; //
More shepherd girls than me strayed off on camel back.
41. I remember the good times we spent together, long ago: //
A scene from one of those nights of perfect happiness.
42. A bonfire was lighted as a beacon for the returning herds, //
A fire fuelled with the wood of *urṭa*-shrubs.
43. Ninety pairs of horns, the game we killed in one week: //
Oryxes whose hides we made into leather buckets for drawing water.
44. The horns of the big antelopes were stacked up behind our tent, //
Like piles of dead *ġaḏa*-branches collected as firewood.
45. Once we camped in al-Ḥazim for ninety nights; //
The enemy had no choice but to swallow his pride.
46. And at our camping sites between Ḥibr and al-Ġarābah //
We let the stallions cover our she-camels.
47. Our watering party departed at night and returned //
With water-skins so heavy as to hurt the pack camels;
48. Our hunters used to set out in the morning and to return //
Carrying gazelles with bloodstained cheeks;
49. And our raiders journeyed at night to return //
With captured she-camels pained by the strain in their udders.
50. Our well is gushing water in abundance, like a fountain: //
Those making for it don't question those on their way back.[93]
51. Its depth is two times eight and four men's heights; //
Its location is from Wāsiṭ towards the *qiblah*, hidden among the winding dunes,
52. In the south, where the *ḥāḏ*-land borders on that of the *ġaḏa*-bushes; //
Not a land of which the soil is tilled and sown by farmers.
53. Two thousand tents were pitched in the well's cirque, //

---

[93] The well is known to be plentiful, hence there is no need for anxious questions about the state of its flow.

*w-alfēn bētin fi l-miḏāmi trūdha*
54. *taxālifaw fi yōm tisᶜīn liḥyah*
*ᶜala šān wagfat l-ajnibi fi nifūdha*
55. *dārin lna ma hīb dārin l-ġērna*
*yiḥiddha r-ramlah mišārib ᶜdūdha*

And another two thousand tents in the desert drew water from it.
54. One day ninety men from both sides were killed, //
When an enemy tribe took up position in its sand-hills.
55. For the land is ours, not that of anyone else, //
And the sands seal off the wells from which we draw our water.

# GLOSSARY

# NOTE ON THE GLOSSARY

In compiling the glossary I have followed by and large the procedure adopted by S.A. Sowayan in the glossary of his scholarly study on Šammar traditions, *The Arabian Oral Historical Narrative, an Ethnographic and Linguistic Analysis*. In addition, numerous lexical items in the text which are also listed in Sowayan's glossary have been explained by borrowing from that glossary and in each instance this is acknowledged by the addition of the abbreviation *Glos*. Whenever this seemed useful as a way of shedding more light on the linguistic and semantic context and range of the item, I have provided related material included in *Glos* under the same root (e.g. other derived forms or semantic connotations), even if these forms do not occur as such in the text.

Although this glossary's debt to Sowayan's outstanding contribution to our knowledge of the Najdi oral literature and dialects is by far the greatest, I have also benefited from the lexicographical information in other works, in particular A. Musil's *The Manners and Customs of the Rwala Bedouins*, J.J. Hess' *Von den Beduinen des Innern Arabiens* and publications by S.A. ibn Junaydil, A. as-Suwaydāʾ and other authorities in the field of Najdi poetry and popular culture. The information drawn from these other sources is also referred to by the abbreviated title of the work and the page number(s). Again, liberal use has been made of other data found in these works when in my opinion this might contribute to a better understanding of the lexical items in the text. The abbreviations used for references to these sources are listed at the end of this note.

The material from these sources has not always been incorporated exactly as it is found in the original, but has been made to conform to the system of transcription adopted in this work. Thus the citations of transliterated parts from sources using a divergent system of notation, especially Musil (1928) and, albeit to a lesser extent, Hess (1934), have undergone the greatest changes. Also, English quotations have sometimes been abridged and translations have been corrected or modified when necessary. The mentioning of a source in connection with a particular lexical item does not mean that the explanation given is always identical to the one found in that source. I have frequently added meanings, synonyms, explanations, and related Arabic forms of the word, whereas I have omitted others. If an item is followed by a string of different meanings, and if the given source refers to only one or some of these, I have tried to make this clear by including the reference to the source between the semicolons together with that particular part of the item's semantic range. References to sources are grouped together when there is only a difference in nuance between their explanations of an item's meaning.

For various reasons I have included Classical Arabic (CA) lexical material that in one way or another corresponds or is related to the vernacular item concerned. This information is added between brackets and is preceded by a marker CA. I have decided not to list the sources of this information separately; but as a rule the items under the heading CA and the description of their meaning have been drawn from two sources: E.W. Lane's *Arabic-English Lexicon* and Ibn Manẓūr's *Lisān al-ᶜArab*. Occasionally other sources have been consulted as well, e.g. Buṭrus al-Bustānī's *Muḥīṭ al-Muḥīṭ*, Manfred Ullmann's *Wörterbuch der klassischen arabischen Sprache* and Hans Wehr's *Dictionary of Modern Written Arabic*.

My reasons for pointing out parallels in the CA lexica are basically threefold. Firstly, students of Arabic who have not had an opportunity to get acquainted with the Peninsular dialects but are nevertheless interested in the subject of this edition, may find the interconnections made with CA convenient as a bridge to otherwise less readily identifiable dialect words, forms and expressions. Secondly, CA remains, so to speak, the archetype or mother-language from which these dialects have originated. An awareness of the etymological relationships that bind the language of the Najdi poetry and vernacular to CA can only enrich one's appreciation of the stage which these dialects represent in the evolution of the Arabic language and may evoke something of the cognitive and emotional associations the speakers of these dialects have inherited from history. Finally, I could not help being struck by the close resemblance between Dindān's poetic vocabulary and that of Arab antiquity: much of what Dindān says cannot be found in dictionaries of modern standard Arabic, but, as the linguistic face of a desert world that remained almost immutable over the centuries, many of the words used by Dindān can be traced in the pages of the great classical dictionaries. And in doing so one will discover that even items that were regarded as rare by the compilers of these dictionaries are alive and current among today's inhabitants of the desert.

The lexical items in the glossary have been grouped together under the radicals of the root so that each root constitutes a separate entry. The order of the entries, and to some extent the arrangement of the items within each entry, are those of the Arabic alphabet and dictionaries. CA *ḍ* and *ẓ* having merged into *ḏ̣* in the dialect of Najd, *ḏ̣* has been allotted the place of *ẓ* in the alphabetical order (see also the note on transcription).

Besides the obvious differences in vowelling and syllable structure, one may note from the juxtaposition of CA and dialect forms other features of linguistic change, such as the transposition of root consonants (*fajḥan* < CA *afḥaj*, *ṯaʿa* < CA *ʿaṯā*, *gaḏ̣ḏ̣ab* < CA *qabaḍa*) and in some cases the substitution of the emphatic *ṣ* for *s* (*miṣāxif, ṣiml, nṣūm*).

In the chapter on translation and the compilation of the glossary of the *The Arabian Oral Historical Narrative*, Sowayan discusses some of the methodological problems that present themselves when one attempts to systematize the Najdi dialectal lexicon and explains the decisions he took in order to resolve them. For instance, the *hamzah* has disappeared in the Najdi dialects, with the exception of some initial positions, as in *axaḏ* and *akal* (for the changes the glottal stop *hamzah* has undergone in the vernacular, see also the note on transcription). But the instability of the *hamzah*, even as the initial radical of the root, is demonstrated by the fact that in this position it often changes to *w*, as in *wimar* (CA *amara*); and it also happens that the initial *hamzah* is dropped and a final vowel is added to form the root of a defective verb: *xaḏa, kala*. When the initial glottal stop of a verbal form is preceded by a prefix, the *hamzah* disappears and the vowel of the prefix is lengthened (*tākil* < CA *taʾkul*); and when a suffix is added or the word is the first member of a construct phrase the initial glottal stop and its accompanying vowel are dropped, as in *hal an-nijāyib* (< *ahal* < CA *ahl*). This is also the case when the word with the initial *hamzah* is preceded by a word ending in a long vowel or when it takes a preposition, as in *bi-halha*. Nevertheless the *hamzah* has been retained as an initial radical in the arrangement of entries in this glossary when one or more derivatives of the root still have the original *hamzah*. Thus the verb *wimar* will be listed under the entry *ʾmr* (because the noun *amir* also occurs in the text), not under *wmr*. If not, the initial radical in the alphabetical arrangement is *w*: *wakkad* (CA *akkada*) will be found under the entry *wkd*.

The medial *hamzah* has been replaced by a lengthening of the preceding short vowel. Where the long vowel becomes an *ā* and it is not possible to determine on the basis of other derived forms whether the radical is *w* or *y*, the *hamzah* of the classical root is given as the medial radical of the entry. Thus *fāl* is found under the entry *fʾl*.

Not all problems in this respect can be solved to full satisfaction. For instance, the 3 m. s. imperf. form *yūḏi*, the participle *mūḏi*, and the noun *ḏaww* have in common that they correspond to forms derived from the CA stem *ḍwʾ*. Thus *ḏaww* corresponds to CA *ḍawʾ* (in accordance with the rule that in the Najdi dialect a glottal stop in final position after a diphthong or a long high vowel is dropped and the last element of the diphthong or vowel is geminated, see Sowayan, *Nabaṭi Poetry*, 151). The 3 m. s. imperf. and the participle suggest that these correspond to the IV form of the CA verb, *aḍāʾa*. In the dialect, verbs that have the *hamzah* as the third and final radical are transformed into defective verbs (e.g. *badaʾa* > *bida*). In the case of this doubly weak verb with medial *w* and final *hamzah*, the final long vowel—which remained after the *hamzah* had been dropped—became an inflected *y* (in accordance with the general tendency in the dialect for weak verbs with a final *wāw* to become weak verbs with a final *yāʾ*, e.g. *yarju* > *yarji*). This reduced the root to the two radicals *ḏ* and *y* (as in *ja* < CA *jāʾa*).

From the forms *yūḏi* and *mūḏi* it must be inferred that a new initial radical *w* has been added to the *ḏ* and *y*, leading to a realignment of the stem with the IV form of doubly weak verbs of the class *ōḥa, yūḥi* (CA *awḥā*) and *ōma, yūmi* (CA *awmaʾa*). One might hypothesize the following development of the stem: CA *aḍāʾa* > *aḏa* > *awḏa* > *ōḏa*. In that case the question arises whence the initial radical *wāw* has originated. Has it been introduced as compensation for the loss of the final *hamzah*, or to add a third root radical to the anomalous biconsonantal root and/or to align the root radicals with those of the verbs with an initial *w* and final *y* of the type *wḥy, wmy*? Or is it simply a matter of a shift in vowel emphasis towards the first syllable, CA *yuḍīʾ* > *yūḏi*, CA *muḍīʾ* > *mūḏi*? Given the lack of other inflected forms and the absence of the perfect of the IV form of this verb, at least in the material at my disposal, there is no way of knowing for certain whether the true identity of the first radical of the root is *ḏ* or *w*. In this glossary *mūḏi* and *yūḏi* can be found under the root entry *wḏy*, but there will always be an element of arbitrariness in such a choice.

Finally, particles are listed according to the order of their consonants, while initial and final *a* and medial *ā* are treated as *alif*.

For lexical items found in the poems, verses and narrative sections of the text the following system of references has been adopted. The number before the slash indicates the number of the poem and the number(s) (or letter of the alphabet) after the slash the number(s) of the verse(s) in the poem; the number immediately before the next slash is again the number of a poem and so on. The number after a semicolon refers to a short narrative section that introduces the poem of that number. A letter of the alphabet immediately after a number refers to the paragraph of a longer narrative section that introduces the poem of that number. E.g. <3/5,;5,8/a,9/2,3,4,33b> means that it can be found in verse 5 of poem no. 3 (3/5), in the short narrative introduction to poem 5 (;5), in the first verse of a poem to which Dindān's poem no. 8 was a reply (8/a), in verses 2, 3 and 4 of poem no.9 (9/2,3,4), and in the second paragraph of the narrative introduction to poem no. 33 (33b). The references to the text are illustrative and not inclusive of all instances where the word occurs.

In references to other sources the following abbreviations are used for the names of the authors and the year of publication (full titles are given in the Sources of Reference):

| | |
|---|---|
| Doughty | Doughty, Charles M. (1936) |
| Faraj | al-Faraj, Khālid ibn Muḥammad ad-Dōsirī (1952) |
| Fawzān | al-Fawzān, ʿAbdallah Nāṣir (1988) |
| Glos | Sowayan, Saad Abdullah (1992, Glossary) |
| Ḥa | Ḥaqīl, ʿAbd al-Karīm ibn Ḥamad ibn Ibrāhīm (1989) |
| Hess | Hess, J.J. (1938) |
| IngCa | Ingham, Bruce (1990) |
| JohnDoi | Johnstone, T.M. (1961) |
| JohnDoii | ,, ,, (1964) |
| JohnEa | ,, ,, (1967) |
| JuA | Junaydil, Saʿd ibn ʿAbdallah ibn (1980-81) |
| JuKha | ,, ,, ,, (1987) |
| JuMu | ,, ,, ,, (1978) |
| JuSa | ,, ,, ,, (1987-88) |
| KhaAd | Khamīs, ʿAbdallah ibn Muḥammad ibn (1982) |
| Lane | Lane, E.W., *Lexicon* |
| Lisān | Ibn Manẓūr, *Lisān al-ʿArab* |
| Maws | as-Saʿīd, Ṭalāl ʿUthmān (1987) |
| Musil | Musil, Alois (1928) |
| Palva | Palva, Heikki (1978) |
| PhilHe | Philby, H.St.J.B. (1922) |
| Proch | Prochazka, Th. (1988) |
| Raswan | Raswan, C.R. (1945) |

| | |
|---|---|
| Sow | Sowayan, S.A. (1992) |
| Sow (1981) | ,, ,, (1981) |
| Su i, ii | as-Suwaydāʾ, ʿAbd ar-Raḥmān ibn Zayd (*Min shuʿarāʾ al-Jabal*, 1988) |
| SuFa | ,, ,, ,, (1987) |
| ʿUbūdī | al-ʿUbūdī, Muḥammad ibn Nāṣir (*al-Amthāl*, 1979) |

Other abbreviations:

| | |
|---|---|
| CA | Classical Arabic |
| coll. | collective |
| contr. | contrary |
| dimin. | diminutive |
| f. | feminine |
| fem. | feminine |
| imp. | imperative |
| imperf. | imperfect |
| inf. n. | infinitive noun |
| lit. | literally |
| m. | masculine |
| masc. | masculine |
| n. un. | nomen unitatis |
| o.s. | oneself |
| part. | participial noun |
| pass. | passive |
| perf. | perfect |
| pl. | plural |
| pl. mult. | plural of multitude |
| pl. pauc. | plural of paucity |
| s. | singular |
| sing. | singular |
| s.o. | someone |
| s.th. | something |

# GLOSSARY

*ʾxḏ* — *axaḏ, xaḏa* 'to take; to seize, conquer; to rob, plunder, loot' <9/2,18/22,33/37>; 'to take as a wife, to marry a woman' <33j>. *yūxḏo* 'they are robbed' <32a>. *māxiḏ* pl. *māxḏīn* 'taking as spoil, seizing' <2/23,26> (CA *mūkhidh*). *māxūḏ* 'taken, seized, robbed' <32d>. *māxūḏah* 'a female who lost her virginity' *Musil*, 197. *ixīḏ* pl. *axāyiḏ* 'plunder, loot'; *axaḏhum ixīḏtin jayyidah* 'he looted them completely' *Musil*, 577.

*ʾdm* — *idmi* f. *idmiyyah* pl. *idāmi* 'gazelle, small whitish gazelle' *Hess*, 85; *Glos*; 'the gazelle of the *ḥarrah* country which is of greater bulk than the *ʿifri* of the *nifūd*' *Doughty* ii, 164 <8/3,11/8> (CA *admāʾ* pl. f. *udm* 'of a colour intermixed, or tinged, with whiteness', applied to a gazelle). *wdām, īdām* 'liquid sheep butter' <25/22> (CA *idām* 'condiment, fatty ingredient').

*ʾrṭ* — *urṭa* '*Calligonum comosum*' <33/42> (CA *arṭā* 'a kind of bush growing in the sands').

*ʾsd* — *isūd* 'lions' <30/11,14,33/22>.

*ʾss* — *sās* pl. *sīsān* 'basis, origin, breed' *Musil*, 292 <21/17,30, 25/12> (CA *asās*).

*ʾṣl* — *iṣīlah* pl. *iṣāyil* 'thoroughbred mare' <33/17>. *iṣīl* 'thoroughbred camel' <8/8>.

*ʾkl* — *akal* 'to eat'; *kalēt* 'I ate' <9/13>; *tākil* 'she eats' <12/9>.

*alinnik* — 'I hope, wish that you', similar in meaning to *ʿasāk* <6/11,9/5,14/8> (perhaps from CA *alā inna* as in *alā innahum* 'now surely they').

*ʾmr* — *wimar* 'to order, to decree' <9/8,12/17> (CA *amara*). *amir* 'business, affair, matter' *Glos* <9/5,16/1>; *b-amr allah* 'by God's decree' <13/22>.

*ʾml* — *yittimal bi* 'it seems to me, I felt as though' <6/6> (similar to the Egyptian *ithayya-li*).

*ʾmm* — *yimām* 'leader in prayer' *Hess*, 153; 'the formula used in addressing the Wahhābi prince Ibn Suʿūd' *Hess*, 89 <18/22> (CA *imām* 'imam, prayer leader; leader').

*ʾhl* — *ahal* pl. *ahāli* (with foll. genit.) 'inhabitants, people of; possessors of; worthy of', sing. *rā$^{c}$i*, *Glos*. *tmāris bi-halha* 'they (the she-camels) run at a strong pace with their riders' <6/23>; *hal an-nijāyib* 'the riders of thoroughbred camels' <26/25>.

*ʾwy* *awa, yāwi* 'to have mercy, consideration for' (CA *awā, yaʾwī l-* 'to be compassionate for, feel pity for').

*btt* *bitāt* (pl.) 'the axles of the wooden rollers suspended above a well that turn with a creaking sound when the camels used for drawing water begin to pull the ropes' <8/5, 9/27,19/10,24/7>.

*bt$^{c}$* *bita$^{c}$, yibta$^{c}$* 'to raid fearlessly at night' *Hess*, 98; the general meaning is 'to go about one's business resolutely, without wavering'. *bitū$^{c}$*, also *bāti$^{c}$*, *bātū$^{c}$* pl. *buwātī$^{c}$* 'daring, resolute, persevering, decisive' <6/31>; 'a resolute hero, a brave rider who does not shrink from the fight' *Musil*, 634; *Hess*, 98 (CA *bāti$^{c}$* 'strong').

*btl* *bi-t-tibātīl* 'one after the other, each one separately' <8/12> (CA *tabtīl* 'separation').

*bxṣ* *baxaṣ* 'sole of the foot' <12/12> (CA *bak̲h̲aṣah* pl. *bak̲h̲aṣ* 'flesh on the inside of the foot, under the hoof of a camel').

*bdd* *bidd* 'a tribal section, clan, a group of people; people' <11/19>. *badd* pl. *biddān, bdūd* 'a pillow, a stuffed lining that is put under the *ćitab* saddle so that the wooden props do not hurt the camel's back' *Musil* 68-69 <21/31,26/2> (CA *bidād, badīd*).

*bdl* *bidal* 'in lieu of, in compensation for' <33b> (CA *badal* 'a substitute; compensation').

*bdw* *baduw* (coll.), *bidwān* 'bedouins' <3/18,17/11> (CA *badw*).

*bdy* *bida* 'to climb, ascend; to start doing s.th.' *Glos*. *bādi* 'going to; climbing, ascending' <2/10,5/1,11/1,14/1,24/1>; 'high, visible' <2/8>; 'coming, approaching' *Musil*, 150; 'traveller by night, visitor (= *sāyir*)' *Musil*, 248. *mabda* 'a climb, ascent' <;3,5/2,14/2>; 'beginning, start' <13/2> (CA *badaʾa*). *bida lih* 'it occurred to him' <9/3> (CA *badā lah* 'it', i.e. an opinion or idea, 'presented itself to him'). *abda* 'to reveal, show; to disclose, recite a poem' *Musil*, 283.

*bd̲r* *bid̲ar, yabd̲ir* 'to sow' <33/52>; *bad̲rah* 'seed-corn; all that is sown' *Hess*, 114 (CA *badhara* 'to sow the seed'). *biḏr* pl. *bḏūr* 'child' (CA *badhr* 'seed; progeny'). *biḏārah* 'childhood' <15/1>.

*brṯ*$^{c}$ — *birṯ*$^{c}$*ah* 'bridge of the camel's nose' <5/6>.

*brḥ* — *barāḥ* 'wide, open space' <3/14,4/14,16/5,31/8> (CA *barāḥ* 'wide, spacious tract of land without trees, herbage or habitation'). *al-bārḥah* 'last night' *Musil*, 513-514, 575 <21/1> (CA *al-bāriḥah*).

*brd* — *barda* 'hail, hailstones' <4/22,27/8>; *barad* 'crystals of frozen dew' *Musil*, 144 (CA *barad*).

*brr* — *barr* 'goodness, kindness, gentleness, beneficence' <3/5> (CA *al-barr*, one of the names of God, 'the Merciful, Beneficent'); *birr* 'exemption (from being impregnated)' <6/18> (CA *birr* 'benevolent, kind treatment, conduct'). *barr* 'land, open desert' <12/4>.

*br*$^{c}$ — *bāri*$^{c}$ 'excellent, outstanding, superior' <4/17>. *mibārī*$^{c}$ (pl.) 'uncovered, without veils' <6/28>.

*brg* — *barrag* 'to think, ponder, investigate' <6/3>; *barrig bidārik gabil ma tittihim jārik* 'search your own house before accusing your neighbour (of theft)' $^{c}$*Ubūdī*, 260; *ma fi tabrīg* 'there is no doubt' *JuA*, 106 (CA *barraqa baṣarah* 'he looked hard, intently'). *barg* $^{c}$*āmin* 'born in the same year of she-camels covered by the same stallion' <7/14>. *abrag* 'a mountain whose slopes are partly covered by sand, dark rock partly covered with reddish sand' *Musil*, 676, 677 <31/10> (CA *abraq* 's.th. in which are two colours, black and white').

*brm* — *baram, yibrim* 'to twist, to fasten' <18/20>. *istabram* 'to keep firmly in one's hands, to hold tight' <4/4> (CA *barama* 'to twist, twine; to establish').

*brmn* — *burmān* explained as 'the angles of the eyes' <9/12>.

*brhz* — *ibrahazz* 'to pale (said of the darkness of night)'.

*bry* — *biri, yabri* 'to be restored to health, be cured, to recover' *Musil*, 513; 'to heal' *Musil*, 190. *bara* 'to walk alongside' <2/15>. *yibra lha* 'he stops and waits till joined (by the protecting troop)' *Musil*, 549. *bāra, ybāri* 'to accompany, walk alongside' (e.g. a mare being led alongside the camel on which its owner rides in order to keep her from becoming fatigued and save her energy for battle) <33/39> (CA *bārāh* 'he vied with him, imitated him; competed with him in running, tried to outstrip him'). *ṣidīg mbāri* 'accompanying friend' <u>*Kh*</u>*aAd*, 324.

*bsṭ* — *basṭ* 'breadth, width, length' <27/12> (CA *basṭah*).

*bšt* — *bišt* pl. *bšūt* 'a cloak; light-grey mantle shot with yellow' *Musil*, 120 <9/15>.

*bṣr* — *ibtiṣar* 'to be discerning; to understand, comprehend' <21/18>. *biṣar* 'eyesight' <30/8>. *buṣrik* 'as you see fit; as you like; whatever you think best; it is up to you' <33j>.

*bṭḥ* — *baṭḥa* pl. *bṭāḥ* 'a wide, sandy watercourse; a shallow river bed' *Musil*, 676 <17/6> (CA *baṭḥāʾ* pl. *biṭāḥ* 'a wide watercourse in which are coarse sand and fine pebbles').

*bṭṭ* — *ybaṭṭiṭ* 'he gives s.o. a thrashing, beats him' <33k> (CA *baṭṭa* 'to slit'; *ḍarabah fa-baṭbaṭah* 'he struck him and cut his skin or head').

*bṭn* — *bṭān* pl. *biṭin* 'girth' *Glos*. *bṭānah* 'a camel's hair rope forming a belly girth' *Musil*, 69, 353. *min yimiss al-bṭān* 'those who pull the belly girth', i.e. the raiders, bedouins <19/22> (CA *biṭān* pl. *buṭn* 'the belly girth of a camel').

*bṭy* — *biṭa as-sirbāl* 'a quiet, regular pace that the camel maintains with the help of the rider's monotonous singing' <6/24>. *mubṭiy* 'a long time ago', *mubṭiyin minni salāmih* 'it has been a long time since I last received his or her greetings' <11/13> (CA *baṭīʾ* 'tardy, slow, late').

*bᶜr* — *biᶜīr* pl. *ebāᶜir* 'camel' <7/14,33h>.

*bġy* — *baġa, yabġi* 'to want, desire, covet' <6/20>. *mabġi* 'what is desired' *Musil*, 217.

*bgᶜ* — *bagᶜa* 'evil fate, misfortune, disaster; violent death' *Musil*, 389 <30/12> (CA *sanah baqᶜāʾ* 'a barren year'; *baqaᶜathum ad-dāhiyah* 'the calamity befell them').

*bkr* — *bākūr* pl. *buwāčīr* 'a staff; a stick provided with a cord at one end, the other being bent in a semicircle' *Musil*, 127; *Hess*, 105 <9/18>. *bikir* 'early part of the day' <13/5> (CA *bakar* 'early morning, first part of the day'). *bakrah* pl. *bkār* 'a young she-camel of 2-4 years old that has not yet borne young' *Hess*, 76; 'a young she-camel between her first and eighth year of age' *Musil*, 334, 548 <15/4,19/11,33/30> (CA *bakrah* 'a young she-camel').

*bld* — *balad* 'to become tired, stop from exhaustion (a horse in battle, owing to oversweating or because it was so weakened by heat and thirst that it could not escape from the pursuing enemy)' *Musil*, 518. *bilūd, bilīd* 'a horse that lags behind a *sābiǵ*, a swift thoroughbred' <33/11> (CA *balīd*). *blūd* 'abode, country, place where one lives; land, ground' <33/52> (CA *bulūd* inf. n. of *balada*).

*blʿ* *bālūʿ* pl. *buwālīʿ* 'one who eats immoderately, voraciously; s.o. who lives off his fellows without contributing anything himself' <6/9> (CA *balaʿa* 'to swallow').

*bll* *ball* 'to moisten, wet'. *mablūl* pl. *mibālīl* 'moist, moistened' <8/8> (CA *balla* 'to moisten').

*balla* 'just, only' *JohnDoi*, 278; 'just like that, without any particular reason' <17/2>.

*bly* *bala, balēt bih* 'you pestered, afflicted him with' *Glos* <6/9>. *bala* 'affliction, calamity; disease' *Musil*, 513 <21/29,29/3>; 'terrors of war' <33/12>.

*bn* *bint* pl. *banāt, bniyy* 'daughter, girl' *Glos* <15/5>.

*bng* *mabnūg* synonym for *daluw* 'leather bucket' <2/11> (CA *mabnūq* 'something joined to something else'; *banīqah* 'any piece that is added in a garment or a leather bucket to widen it; loops into which buttons are inserted').

*bnn* *bannah*, 'sweet, pleasant fragrance' *Musil*, 141 <12/25, 13/12>. *binn* 'coffee-beans; coffee' <6/12>.

*bny* *bana* 'to build; to become built, put on' <1/9>; 'to be heaped up' <23/3>. *byūtin tbanna* lit. 'tents are being built; the pitching of tents' *Musil*, 250. *mabna* pl. *mibāni* 'building; foundation' <21/30>.

*bhj* *bahaj, yabhaj* 'to be glad, to rejoice' <18/11> (CA *bahija* 'to become happy, joyful, glad').

*bhm* *bahāmah* 'beast, (stupid) animal' <25/7> (CA *bahīmah* 'any animal that does not discriminate').

*bhy* *baha* 'empty, flat plain' <6/20> (CA *bahiya* 'to be empty').

*bwj* *bāj, yibūj* 'to traverse, cross a vast expanse of desert' *Musil*, 147 <20/1> (CA *al-bāʾijah* 'a vast expanse of sand'). *inbāj, yinbāj* 'to become resplendent, to appear in its lustre; to dawn' <30/13> (CA *bāja al-barq* 'the lightning appeared and flashed').

*bwg* *bāg, yibūg* 'to commit treachery against' *Musil*, 448; *Glos* <33i>. *bōg* 'treachery'; *bōgt al-bēt* 'disgracing of the tent' *Musil*, 442. *bāyiǵ* 'faithless' (e.g. said of one who attacks a friend). *bāgōhum bōgah* 'they attacked them treacherously' *Musil*, 449. *al-būgān sūdān al-wjīh* 'those faithless ones, those blackened faces'; *rāʿ al-bōg ma yarga fōg al-ćlāb* 'a faithless one will never rise above the dogs' *Musil*, 449 (CA *bāqa*, inf. n. *bawq*, 'to treat s.o. wrongfully; to come upon s.o. unawares; to rob s.o.').

*bwl* *bōl* 'urine' <21/16> (CA *bawl*).

*bwn* *bān* 'the ben-tree' <5/4> (CA *bān*).

*bww* *baww* 'stuffed skin of the slaughtered calf and given to its mother to smell and sniff at so that she continues to yield her milk' *Hess*, 78; see also *ḏīr* (CA *baww* 'a skin of a young unweaned camel stuffed with straw which is brought near to the mother of the young camel that has died in order that she may incline to it, and yield her milk').

*byḥ* *bāḥ*, *yibīḥ* 'to become manifest, to become public knowledge (said of s.th. that was previously hidden and secret)' <16/1,17/5>; pass. *bīḥ* 'it has become manifest, divulged, revealed' <5/3> (CA *bāḥa, yabūḥ* 'to become apparent, manifest; to reveal, disclose'; *bāḥa mā katamt* 'what I concealed became apparent'). *bayyaḥ* 'to expose, reveal, unveil' <33/3>. *bāyiḥ* 'exposed, disclosed' <16/2>. *mistibāḥ* 's.th. that is divulged and thus becomes a source of embarrassment to the person concerned' <16/13>.

*byd* *bēda* pl. *bīd* 'empty, waterless desert' <7/3,27/13> (CA *baydāʾ* pl. *bīd* 'waterless, level desert; plain tract without herbage'). *bīdi* pl. *byādi* ' a woollen cloak worn in winter' <9/21>.

*byr* *bīr* 'well' (CA *biʾr*).

*byḍ* *bayyaḍ* 'to whiten'; *yimnan tbayyiḍ wajh rāʿīha* 'a right hand that whitens the face of its owner', i.e. his honour is untainted thanks to his valour <21/26>; *bayyiḍ allah wajhik* 'may God whiten your face, honour' (said to s.o. who has rendered assistance or entertained the speaker hospitably) *Hess*, 169; *Glos* <30/22>, contr. of *sawwid allah wajhik* 'may God blacken your face', said to s.o. who has refused to render assistance, *Hess*, 169. *bēḍa* pl. *bīḍ* 'white' <6/27>; 'beautiful woman, both fair of skin and pure of character' *Glos* <28/3,30/22> (CA *bayḍāʾ*). *bīḍ al-maḥāġib, šīb al-ġawārib wa-l-maḥāġib* 'the camels' shoulder blades are grey and they have white spots below their belts because they are on the road all the time; the shoulder blades rub against the cushion on which the rider rests one foot while the other foot touches the *maḥāǧib*, the spot covered by the breast girth, which holds the saddle behind the forelegs on the breastbone' *Musil*, 298 <33/36>. *bēḏ̣* 'eggs' <28/6> (CA *bayḍ*). *biyāḏ̣* 'a country of a white colour' *Musil*, 641.

*tb*$^{c}$ — *tiba*$^{c}$ 'to follow, come after; to trail behind'. *tib*$^{c}$ 'a young calf' (because it follows its mother constantly). *mitbā*$^{c}$ pl. *mitābī*$^{c}$ 'winding trail (leading to an unknown destination)' <32/15>; *ġabiyy al-mitābī*$^{c}$ 'hidden roads or tracks' <6/32>.

*txtx* — *taxātīx* 'empty deserts' <26/6>.

*tara* — an intensifying particle functioning in almost the same manner as CA *inna*, see *Glos*; *tarāni* = *innanī* <9/17>.

*trb* — *trāb* 'earth, dust' <12/22,30/6,26> (CA *turāb*). *mitribīn ar-rāy* 'weaklings; despicable fellows' <6/10> (CA *mutrib* 'rich; without want'). *tarāyib* (pl.) 'front part of the flanks or belly of a camel' <6/28,9/24,33/21> (CA *tarībah* pl. *tarā*$^{\supset}$*ib* 'part of the breast, the ribs that are next to the collarbones').

*trf* — *mitrifāt* (pl. f.) 'delicate, tender' <15/5>; *tirf al-banāt* 'tender maidens' *Musil*, 562 <7/15> (CA *mutraf* 'one enjoying a soft, delicate life of ease and plenty').

*t*$^{c}$*b* — *mit*$^{c}$*ibīn* (pl.) 'wearing out, tiring out, exhausting' <33/36> (CA *mut*$^{c}$*ib*).

*t*$^{c}$*y* — *tā*$^{c}$*a* 'to call to a horse' *Faraj*, 179. *tā*$^{c}$*aw* 'they called 'eyh, eyh' (to a horse)' <32/5>; 'if I call a mare, I say of myself: *at*$^{c}$*i*' *Musil*, 379.

*tfg* — *taffāg* pl. *tiffāg, tifāfīǵ* 'gunman; sharpshooter, marksman'; *tfagah* pl. *tifag* 'rifle' *Musil*, 625, *Glos*.

*tll* — *tall* 'to pull hard'. *tall* 'a pull, tug, jerk' <4/16>; *ya-tall galbi* 'how my heart is pulling at its moorings', in poetry usually followed by one or more similes expressing the anxiety and suffering of the poet, <6/8> (CA *talla* 'to throw down; lower the rope into the well'; as with *wḥy* and *ḥss*, the meaning seems to have shifted to the receiving or incoming part of the action).

*tly* — *tāli* pl. *tuwāli* 'the following, what comes later, the last, the end' <18/3,26/8,16>; 'the rear (of a camel train or group of warriors, which is the most exposed and vulnerable to enemy attack)' <26/14>. *tālīh* 'what comes after, the last, the end' <12/18>; *tālīha* 'its end, outcome' <21/14>; *min tāli* 'thereafter; as of late' <20/5>; *fi atlāh* 'behind it; at its end' <2/18,14/16>; *tāl an-nahār* 'at the end of day' <23/14>. *mitli* pl. *mtāli* 'a she-camel that gives birth at the end of winter or in the early *ṣēf* season' *Hess*, 77 (CA *talā, yatlū* 'to follow, walk behind').

*thm* *thāmi* 'red locust from the Tihāmah litoral of the Red Sea', a recurrent image in poetry conveying the meaning of countless, unstoppable numbers of something (e.g. warriors, violent emotions etc.) <2/4,18/24,25/4,33/13>.

*twj* *tījān* 'stars, stripes or other insignia on a uniform, marks of distinction' <9/29> (CA *tāj* pl. *tījān* 'crown').

*twl* *atāwīl* 'a kind of plant, herbage, especially *ḥirbiṯ* (CA *ḥurbut̲h̲*), a dark plant with white flowers that grows in hard plains and is considered excellent grazing' <14/19> (CA *taʾwīl* 'a kind of herbaceous plant on which camels like to graze').

*taww* 'just, just now, recently, only a short time before' <1/3, 4/20,9/24,16/6,33/19> (CA *tawwah* 'a short period'; *tawwan* 'right away, at once, just now'); see also *Glos*.

*tyh* *tāh, yitīh* 'to lose one's way, to stray' *Musil*, 318, 399. *tāyhāt jdūdha* 'whose forefathers are lost' i.e. 'of unknown ancestry' <33/6>. *at-tyāha* 'those who are wandering' *Musil*, 520 (CA *tāha, yatīh* 'to deviate from, lose the way; to be confused, perplexed, confounded', part. *tāʾih* 'deviating from, losing the way').

*ṯbr* *ṯabbar* 'to (cause s.o. to) lag behind, to falter' <33/11>. *inṯibar* 'to stay behind, to be prevented from moving on with the others (e.g because one's horse falters)' (CA *t̲h̲abbara* 'to restrain; debar, prohibit s.o. from attaining his desire'). *ṯibārah* 'a second-rate horse, not a thoroughbred horse; a mare that limps and stumbles'.

*ṯrr* *minṯarr* 'dispersed; coming in droves, great numbers' <3/17> (CA *t̲h̲arra* 'flowing, releasing water in abundance').

*ṯʿy* *ṯaʿa, yaṯʿa* 'to make mischief, to rampage' (CA *ʿat̲h̲ā* by transposition of the root consonants).

*ṯfn* *ṯafnah* pl. *aṯfān* 'the callous protuberances on the camel's stifle-joints, i.e. between the thigh and the shank; the lower portion of the fore part of the knee on which the camel rests when lying down' *Musil*, 371 <2/9,3/15, 9/32> (CA *t͟hafinah* pl. *t͟hifān, t͟hafināt*). *ḥadd aṯ-ṯifān* 'up to the upper part of the hind leg'.

*ṯgl* *ṯiǧīl* 'heavy, unbearable' *Glos*. *miṯāǧīl* 'heavily-laden camels' <8/13>.

*ṯlṯ* *yṯāliṯ* = *yajmaḥ* 'he gallops, bolts' <32c>.

*ṯm* *ṯam* = *fam* 'mouth' <25/10>.

*ṯmd* *ṯimad* pl. *aṯmād* 'a small pool of water left by rain in hard and level ground; a cavity in which the rain-water collects; rain-water that remains beneath the sand'; it is also called *mšāš*, *Musil*, 681 <13/11> (CA *t͟hamad* 'a small, round hollow or cavity in which the rain-water collects and from which men drink during two months of the spring season, but which fails when the summer comes').

*ṯml* *ṯimāyil* 'bellies' <9/30> (CA *t͟hamīlah* pl. *t͟hamāʾil* 'remains of water, food etc. in the belly of the camel'). *ṯimīlah* pl. *ṯimāyil* 'a small depression in a rocky riverbed into which the rain-water runs under the gravel' *Musil*, 684; 'water-hole hidden under the ground, often in the soft loam under the gravel of a dry torrent channel' *Doughty* ii, 322.

*ṯmn* *ṯimān* 'the four lower and the four upper incisors' *Musil*, 561; *bu ṯimānin* 'a woman with glittering front teeth' <11/14>.

*ṯny* *ṯana, yaṯni* 'to fold; to double; to bend' *Glos*; 'to defend, ward off'; *min yaṯni* 'he who remains cool in danger and checks the advance of the enemy' *Musil*, 173, 264; *iṯni ʿala* (imp.) 'pour out (the coffee) once more for' *Musil*, 103 (CA *t͟hanāh* 'he turned him back'). *yṯanna* (pass.) 'it is doubled, repeated' <26/16,28/3>. *yinṯini* 'he returns, turns back from' <33/47>. *tiṯanni* '(the act of) defending, warding off' <8/13>. *maṯniy* 'double' <9/2> (CA *mat͟hnīy* 'double, folded'). *maṯnāh* 'waist, middle' <17/8> (CA *mit͟hnāh* 'folded middle part'); *miṯāni* 'middle parts; folds; joints' *Musil*, 131 <19/11,33/30>; *ma bih miṯāni* 'there is no return to it' *Musil*, 183. *ṯanāya* 'the four lower and four upper incisors' *Musil*, 175. *aṯna* 'to praise, eulogize' <30/27>; *ṯana* 'praise, eulogy, commendation' <33/32> (CA *at̲h̲nā* 'to praise, speak well of'; *t̲h̲anāʾ*).

*ṯwb* — *ṯōb* pl. *ṯyāb* 'gown, garb, clothes' <29/5,30/5>. *ṯwēb* dimin. of *ṯōb* 'garment, piece of cloth; a man's white shirt reaching to the heels' *Musil*, 118-119 <9/15> (CA *t̲h̲awb*).

*ṯwr* — *ṯawwar, yṯawwir* 'to raise; to rouse, to make s.o. or an animal rise up from his resting position, to get s.o. moving' <10/6,18/17,19/9>. *tiṯūr* 'she stands up on both fore and hind legs' *Musil*, 355. *mṯawwir* 'one who departs, sets out'; *al-ġazuw ṯawwaraw* 'the raiders started out for' *Hess*, 99.

*jbr* — *jibar, yajbir* 'to heal, restore to health; to set (broken bones), to splint, put in splints' <30/1> (CA *jabara* 'to set a bone; to restore s.o. from a state of poverty to wealth or sufficiency'). *jabbār* 'bonesetter' *Doughty* i, 252. *ya-llāh ya-jābir ᶜaḏm kill maksūr* 'O God, You who heals each broken bone' *Musil*, 304-305. *mjabbir* 'one who puts a fractured bone in splints'. *jbārah* pl. *jibāyir* 'splints for fractured bones' *Hess*, 148.

*jbᶜ* — *mjabbaᶜ* 'curtailed, shortened' (the bedouins shorten a horse's tail one year after its birth) <7/8> (CA *imraʾah jubbāᶜ* 'a woman of small stature').

*jbn* — *jibīn* 'forehead, brow; low line of the neck, chest, upper part of the breast' = *manḥir* (cf. <28/6>) <15/9,17/9> (CA *jabīn*).

*jby* — *jiba* 'the sides of a well; the earth around the well; an open cistern' *Musil*, 678 <18/5,9,33/53>. *jābiyyah* 'a shallow pit in the earth in which water for camels is poured' *Musil*, 678 (CA *jabā* 'place where a well is dug; the brink of a well; the ground around a well').

*jṯl* — *jiṯīl, jaṯil* 'great quantity; copious, abundant' <3/11,9/4, 13/11,17/8>; *jaṯlin tkassar ᶜanh rūs al-mifārīġ* 'hair so thick that it breaks the teeth of combs' *JuA*, 166 (CA *jat̲h̲l, jat̲h̲īl* 'much, abundant, thick, dense').

*jṯm* — *mijāṯīm* (pl.) 'lying (in puddles) on the ground' <12/19> (CA *jat̲h̲ama*, 'to cleave to the ground').

*jḥm* — *jiḥīm* 'hellfire; fiery fire' <5/8> (CA *jaḥīm*).

*jdd* — *lāni min jiddi* explained as 'I am besides myself (with rage, grief etc.)' <32/14>.

*jdr* *jidīrah* pl. *jidāyir* 'mountain' <4/10>; *jidrān* 'walls' <21/17> (CA *jadīrah* 'wall made of stones').

*jdl* *jādūl* pl. *juwādīl* 'the winding traces marking the paths of the camels on the pasture grounds' *Hess*, 61, similar in meaning to *jāddah* pl. *juwādd* 'the traces marking the caravan roads, path trodden out by camels in the flat desert' *Musil*, 678; 'going into various directions', as in *wa-l-galb min mamšāh ġādin juwādīl* 'because of her departure my heart was torn apart, ran off into all directions' *JuA*, 48; *mjōdilāt* '(she-camels) keeping on the path trodden by camels for centuries past' *Musil*, 337. *juwādīl* also means 'incessant, streaming, pouring (rain)' <14/15>.

*jidīlah* pl. *jidāyil* 'plaited tresses of women's hair' <15/8, 29/8,33/20>; *jādil* 'a shapely woman' *Su* ii, 90 (CA *jadīl* 'firmly twisted'; *majdūlah* 'a woman small in the belly and compact in flesh').

*jdy* *jida* 'power, means, resources' <8/13> (CA *jadāʾ* 'profit, utility, avail').

*jḏb* *jiḏab, yijḏib* 'to pull; to attract s.o. to, (to make s.o.) migrate to' <32a> (CA *jadhaba* 'to draw, pull').

*jḏᶜ* *jiḏaᶜ* pl. *jiḏᶜān* 'youth; brave, fearless youth' <24/8, 26/14> (CA *jadhaᶜ* 'youth, young man; one who is light-witted like a youth').

*jrb* *mjarrib* 'an experienced warrior' <32/3> (CA *mujarrib* 'one whose qualities have been tried, one who has proved himself').

*jrd* *jirīd* (coll.) 'palm branches (stripped of their leaves)' <7/7,12/23,19/14,30/20> (CA *jarīd*). *jird* (pl.) 'short-haired' <6/25> (CA *ajrad* pl. *jurd* 'having short and fine hair', a sign of excellent origin in a horse and any similar beast). *jarād* 'swarms of locusts' <3/2,33/13> (CA *jarād* coll. 'locusts'). *jardah* pl. *jrūd* 'troops, armies'; *jardah* 'armed men who advance against the enemy force as soon as they have received news of its approach' *Hess*, 99 <33/14,31>. *jarrad jrūd* 'he sent troop after troop of warriors' *Musil*, 602.

*jrr* *jarr* 'to draw; to drain' <12/3>. *jarr aṣ-ṣōt* 'to bellow, howl, roar' <2/8>. *jarr* 'the side and channel of a watercourse' <3/13>. *jurrah* pl. *jrar* 'footsteps, tracks, traces' *Hess*, 61; *Glos* <3/11,15>. *jirīr* 'rein' *Musil*, 563. *minjarrah* 'dragged, trailed along' <3/10> (CA *injarra*). *jarrah* 'a large army' <3/18,18/14> (cf. CA *jay<u>sh</u> jarrār* 'a large army that leaves a continuous track while marching').

*jrf* *jurf* pl. *jirfān* 'a crevice, steep river bank' *Musil*, 571, 678 <3/12> (CA *jurf*).

*jrmd* *jirmūd* 'a strong, muscular fellow' <33k> (CA *jirmiḍ* 'a hardy, strong one').

*jrhd* *mijrihidd* 'empty, barren' <5/9> (CA *ajrahaddat al-arḍ* 'the land was wide and barren, a land in which no plant or herbage grows').

*jzʿ* *jizaʿ, yajzaʿ* 'to fear, to be apprehensive' <21/13> (CA *jazaʿa* 'to pass across; to become impatient; to lack the strength to endure'). *jizzāʿ* 'what hurts, renders s.o. angry; what upsets, spites' <32/13>.

*jzl* *jizīl* 'generous, munificent; plentiful, in large measure' <13/20> (CA *jazīl*).

*jzy* *jiza* 'to reward' <17/1>. *jiza ʿan* 'to do without, have no need for' *Musil*, 83. *jiza* 'reward' *Musil*, 359-360. *ajza, yijzi* 'not to drink'; *al-jmāl jāzīn* 'the camels do not drink' (in winter when there is sufficient moisture on the herbage on which they pasture) *Hess*, 80; '(camels) not drinking, feeding of the sappy spring herbage' *Doughty* i, 260 (CA *jazaʾat al-ibl bi-r-ruṭb ʿan al-māʾ* 'the camels were satisfied with green pasture so as to be in no need of water'). *mijzi* '(gazelle or other desert animal) able to do without drinking water' <7/13>; also *jāzi* pl. *juwāzi* 'animals like gazelles and jumping mouses that are able to live through the summer without tasting water' *Hess*, 85; *Musil*, 538 <33/9,33/48>.

*jʿd* *jaʿad* pl. *jʿūd* 'plaited and combed hair' *Musil*, 560 <33/21>. *naggāḍ al-jaʿad* 'a man passionate in sexual intercourse, thus dishevelling the woman's hair' *Musil*, 560; this must be a misinterpretation, for this common epithet refers to the woman 'loosening her long tresses' (CA *jaʿd* 'curly, twisted hair').

*jʿl* *jiʿl* lit. 'may it be made to happen by God', followed by a clause describing the wished-for event <9/34,10/8,18/5, 21/10,26/20>.

*jġr* *jaġar* explained as 'to purr, hum' <23/9>.

*jfr* *jufrah* pl. *jfār, jfar* 'low ground in a plain, where rain-water gathers' *Musil*, 678 <32/11> (CA *jufrah* pl. *jifār, jufar* 'a round and wide cavity in the ground').

*jfl* — *jifal* 'to run in fright, flee in panic' (CA *jafala* 'to take fright and flee, run away at random; fleeing with its wings spread', said of an ostrich). *jāfil* pl. *jfāl, jāflāt, jifīl, jfūl* 'fleeing in a panicky gallop, fright' <8/3,27/5,9>.

*jlb* — *jilab* 'to offer for sale'; *la tijlab* 'she is not on sale' <27/14>. *jālib* pl. *jālbīn* 'offering for sale; *jālbīn dūnha r-rūḥ* 'they are ready to sacrifice their lives for her sake' <30/8>. *jalab* pl. *ajlāb* 'camels, goats and sheep brought to the market for sale' *Hess*, 147; *Doughty* i, 633. *jilūbah* 'a camel offered for sale' *Musil*, 549. *jallāb* 'a hawker' *Musil*, 141 (CA *jalaba* 'to drive, bring camels, merchandise, *jalūbah*, from one place to another for the purpose of trade').

*jljl* — *jiljāl* 'tinkling, jingling, ringing sound' <26/5> (CA *jaljāl* 'the sound of rain'; *juljul* 'a little bell, a hollow bell of copper, that is hung to the neck of a horse or a similar beast').

*jld* — *jild* pl. *jlūd* 'hide, leather' <33/43> (CA *jild* pl. *julūd*).

*jl*$^{c}$ — *jalla*$^{c}$ = *hajj* 'to run away at great speed' <27/5>; *jlā*$^{c}$ 'a bout of madness' *JuKha*, 120.

*jll* — *jill* 'great, big, bulky' <6/4>. *jilīl* 'strong, big; a big-bodied camel' *Hess*, 76 <8/6>. *jill, jlāl* 'big-bodied camels; strong, big she-camels; a she-camel older than three years, i.e. no longer a *ḥāši*' *Musil*, 12, 333, 542 <1/12,8/2,13,10/6,27/4> (CA *jill, jall* 'bulky, large in body' as opposed to *diqq*).

*jlm* — *jlām* i.e. *sabg* 'running, a rapid pace' <11/8>; *jilīm* 'cutting; resolute' (CA *jalama* 'to cut').

*jly* — *jala* 'to rinse, cleanse; to clear of dirt and dust etc.' *Musil*, 535 <3/16>; 'to clean teeth with tooth brushes made of *rāk*-sticks' *Hess*, 132; *Musil*, 224 (CA *jalāh* 'he rendered it clear, exposed it'). *jalla* 'to make s.o. flee' *Musil*, 262. *jallāy al-hmūm* '(God) who clears away one's troubles' *Musil*, 563.

*jmḥ* — *jimaḥ, yajmaḥ* 'to bolt, break away, become refractory, recalcitrant' <4/8,32c> (CA *jamaḥa*). *jimūḥ* 'a mare able to jump over any obstacle, that does not slip on soft, salt-covered ground, nor fall from a sunken bank, *jurf*, nor stick her feet into the holes made by the various field mice, hence never throws her rider' *Musil*, 514-515, 554.

*jmr* *jamr* ‘red-hot burning coals’ <5/8> (CA *jamrah*, coll. *jamr* ‘live coals’).

*jml* *jimīl* pl. *jimāyil* ‘good deed, charity, beneficence’ *Glos* <3/4>. *jimal* pl. *jmāl* ‘stud camel; a camel between its sixth and twentieth year’ *Musil*, 330-331 <2/22,6/28, 9/33,13/11,27/14>. *majmūl* ‘a beauty’ *Musil*, 186.

*jmm* *jamm* ‘the collecting of water in a well, the water of a well that has collected after it has been drawn from’; *ġazīrat al-jamm* ‘(a well) abundant in water’ <17/7,33/50> (CA *jamma*, inf. n. *jamm*, ‘it became much, abundant’, said of water in the well).

*jnb* *ajnab* ‘to travel in a southerly direction’ <33/34>. *jinūb* ‘south’ <33/52> (CA *janūb*). *ajnibi* pl. *ajnāb* ‘stranger, s.o. belonging to a different tribe; enemy’ <33/54>. *jin-ībah* pl. *janāyib* ‘caparison of a horse or camel’ <33/30>.

*jhl* *jāhil, jahhāl, majhūl* pl. *jihhāl, jhāl, jhālah* ‘ignorant, inexperienced one; young, reckless men; a lively, cheerful youth between his fourteenth and eighteenth years, who is imprudent and will be neither advised nor remonstrated with; hairbrained, hasty, inconsiderate lads, who think that all things can be accomplished by violence’ *Musil*, 116, 208, 343, 536, 549, 653; *Hess*, 139; *Doughty* i, 355 <1/13,6/8,14/2> (CA *jāhil* pl. *juhhāl*). *jihil* pl. *ajhāl* ‘young she-camels, *bkār*, when they have conceived for the first time and produce their first milk’ <26/17,26>. *jahā-jīl* ‘the fast travelling troop of camel riders’ i.e. *al-jēš*; ‘swift riding camels’ <8/2,26/4,5> (CA *mijhāl* ‘a she-camel brisk in her pace’).

*jhm* *jaham* ‘to rise early in the morning’ *Glos*; ‘to set out, start at midnight’ *Musil*, 464; ‘to set out betwixt the dog and the wolf’, i.e. ‘at dawn’ *Doughty* ii, 267 (CA *juhmah* ‘part of the night extending from midnight to the period a little before daybreak’). *jahām*, ‘indistinguishable object; mixed camel herds on the move’ *Musil*, 225; *Glos*; ‘the *ṭarš*, the herds of an entire camp’ *Hess*, 62; *Musil*, 80 <12/5,18/3>. *jah-āmah* ‘a camel herd seen from a distance; shapes that are not individually distinguishable’ *KhaAd*, 363; *Su* ii, 81 <11/15>. *mijāhīm* ‘herd of black camels’ *Musil*, 335 <12/22,33a> (as contrasted with *maġātīr* ‘herds of fair, white camels’). *mijhim* ‘black (rain cloud)’ <18/8>.

*jhwl* *jahāwīl* explained to me as 'many, a great number' <8/9>.

*jwb* *jūb, jūbah* 'any vast expanse of featureless desert' is called *jūbah* in Najd; *mjawwib* 'one who travels without halting until he has crossed such a desert' *JuMu*, 333 <30/21> (CA *jawb* pl. *juwab*).

*jwd* *jawwad* 'to hold tight; make tight' <4/7>. *mjawwid* 'tying, fastening firmly' (CA *jawwada* 'to do s.th. well'). *jūd* 'generosity, munificence, providence', see also *kyl*, <2/27,18/25,26/22,33/32> (CA *jūd*); *ahl jūd* 'magnanimous, noble-minded people' *Hess*, 170. *ajwād* 'good, noble men; good, friendly spirits' *Hess*, 160 <2/19>; also *ajāwīd Musil*, 102; *ibn ajwād* 'an honest, generous person' *Hess*, 170.

*jwr* *jār* 'to protect s.o. (as a neighbour)' <15/4>. *jāwar* 'to take up a dwelling in s.o.'s neighbourhood, thus becoming entitled to his protection' <33a>. *jār* 'neighbour' <33/16>. *mjāwir* 's.o. who becomes a neighbour of s.o. else' <33a> (CA *jāwara* 'to become one's neighbour; to bind oneself by a covenant to protect s.o.'). *mjār* 'protected' <15/4>.

*jōr* 'inequity, injustice, oppression', related in meaning to *zōd*, 'arrogance, superiority'. *fargha jōr* 'she is so superior to the others that the latter do not stand a fair chance in the contest' <15/6>. *jāyir* 'one acting wrongfully, unjustly' <18/19> (CA *jawr*).

*jwz* *jāz l.* 'to appeal to; to strike one's fancy' *Glos* <9/5>; *jāz min* 'to renounce; to abstain from, not indulge in' *Musil*, 138, 208 (CA *jāza* 'to pass by, beyond; to be allowable, right'). *jāyiz* 'pleasant, becoming' *Musil*, 461.

*jwḏ* *jāḏ, yijūḏ* 'to toss about (e.g. someone ill with fever), to move in an agitated manner' (CA *juwāẓ* 'lack of patience, annoyance, vexation').

*jw*$^{c}$ *jū*$^{c}$ 'hunger, want' *Musil* 360; also *mijāwī*$^{c}$ <6/12>. *jā*$^{c}$*ān* 'hungry' <9/13>; *juway*$^{c}$ <18/11>.

*jwl* *jāl* 'to fly, go away' *Musil*, 309; 'to migrate; to circle in flight; to roam, wander about' *Glos*. *injāl* = *jāl* <26/4> (CA *tajwāl* = *taṭwāf* 'the act of going repeatedly in circles'). *ijtuwil* 'to circle in flight or while running; to go to and fro' <26/4> (CA *ajtāla*). *tijāwal* 'to flee in a drove'

<7/3>. *tijiwwāl, juwwāl* 'wheeling about, running in zigzags' <6/19>. *jōl* 'a flock of birds or a herd of gazelles in flight' *Glos* <7/12,27/4>.

*jīl* 'many, in great numbers; a large number of one sort', i.e. many she-camels, all of them sterile <8/2, 26/4,5>. *jāl* 'steep side of a mountain; a long, steep escarpment by which a plateau falls off to a lower level; the bank of a river channel; the slope of a gully or valley; rocky wall of a well covered on the inside with stones' *Musil* 148, 343, 678 <18/5,33d>; 'protection; rampart' <21/26, 30> (CA *rajul laysa lah jāl* 'a man without determination that protects him like a well is protected by its stone walls'); *min al-jāl la l-jāl* 'from one side of the earth to the other', because the earth is thought of as a flat surface ending at both sides in a precipice <26/30>.

*jyš* — *jēš* 'group of riding camels', both *jēš al-ġazuw*, the camels of a raiding party, and the three or four camels in the possession of a bedouin, *Hess*, 75; 'camels used for riding and raiding, mounted camels' *Glos*; 'a plural for *d̲ilūl*, riding camel, if the number is larger than ten (if it is less than ten the word *rćāb* is used), but *jēš* may refer both to the riding camels and their riders' *Musil*, 332 <2/18,26/5,27/3>.

*ḥbb* — *aḥabb* 'to kiss' *Glos* <29/8>. *ḥibb, ḥabbah* 'a kiss' *Musil*, 342 <24/15>.

*ḥbṣ* — *ḥabaṣ* similar in meaning to *aḏ̣-ḏ̣ān* 'sheep'; the simile with thunderclouds stems from the fact that Najdi sheep are black while their heads are largely white <3/10>.

*ḥbl* — *ḥabil* pl. *ḥbāl* 'rope made of camel's hair' *Musil*, 64 <4/4> (CA *ḥabl*).

*ḥtt* — *ḥatt* 'to fall down' <12/6> (CA *ḥatta al-waraq* 'the leaves fell').

*ḥt̲r* — *ḥat̲ar* 'seeds, fruit of the palm-tree in the first stage of its appearance inside the spathe' <12/23> (CA *aḥt̲hara an-nak̲hl*, 'the spathe burst open longitudinally and the flowers became visible'). *ḥat̲āyir ma* 'raindrops' <14/9> (CA *ḥat̲hir* 'what becomes shattered and dispersed in grains etc.').

*ḥt̲l* — *ḥat̲īl* pl. *ḥat̲āyil, ḥt̲āl* 'dregs, remains'; here it simply means 'rain-water', perhaps because Dindān imagines that the rain is being "sieved" from the clouds <10/10,18/9> (cf. CA *ḥut̲h̲ālah*).

*ḥṯm* *ḥaṯāyim* explained as 's.th. that sticks in one's throat, s.th. that weighs heavily on one' <9/3>. *ḥaṯmah* 'heap, pile' (CA *ḥat̲h̲mah* 'a small pile of stones').

*ḥjb* *ḥajab* pl. *ḥijbān* 'the haunches, the higher parts of the *wrūk*, hips' *JuA*, 161 <14/14> (CA *ḥajab* coll. 'the parts of the hips that project above the flanks').

*ḥjj* *ḥijjah* pl. *ḥjāj* 'brow, eyebrow' *Musil*, 103, 115 <28/5>. *ḥijjah* 'argument; claim' <30/4> (CA *ḥujjah*).

*ḥjr* *maḥjar* pl. *maḥājir* 'part which is next around the eye' <8/7>; *ḥijr al-ᶜēn* 'the eye socket' *Glos* <16/4,33/4>.

*ḥjz* *ḥajiz* 'side of the hump; hump' <2/8> (CA *ḥajz*).

*ḥjl* *mḥajjalah* 'having white spots' <13/13>; '(a mare) with short white spots on the legs' *Musil*, 372; *ḥamra ḥajla* 'a light-brown she-camel with forelegs coloured a shade lighter' *Musil*, 335 (CA *taḥjīl* 'whiteness in the legs of a horse; whiteness in a she-camel's teats, occasioned by the *ṣirār*, the string which is tied over the she-camel's udders and over the piece of wood called *tawdiyah* [cf. *Musil*, 292, 298] in order that her young one may not suck her').

*ḥjm* *ḥajam, yḥajim* 'to bleed s.o., especially as a remedy for headaches, so that the *damm fāsid*, corrupt blood, is let out' *Hess*, 150. *maḥājīm* 'cupping glasses' <12/3> (CA *miḥjamah* pl. *maḥājim* 'utensil in which the cupper collects the blood').

*ḥjy* *ḥaja* 'refuge; the wall protecting the roofs of mud houses from view; corner in the women's compartment (of the tent) where women in childbirth or with abnormal menstruation rest' *Musil*, 300 <2/1> (CA *ḥajā* 'extremity, place of refuge').

*ḥdb* *ḥadab, ḥadbah* 'rugged and high ground' <5/9,24/9> (CA *ḥadab, ḥadabah*). *maḥādīb* '(cowardly men who ride) with bent backs (as they flee on their galloping horses)' *Musil*, 585. *al-bṭūṭ al-maḥādīb* 'fat-backed geese' *Musil*, 105, 107.

*ḥdr* *taḥaddar* 'to descend, to come down' <13/10> (CA *taḥaddara*). *ḥadar, ḥaddar, yḥaddir* 'to go, travel in a downward direction; to travel in a northeasterly direction (because the Arabian plateau slopes down in that direction) <30/21> (CA *ḥaddara* 'to descend, go downwards').

*ḥdy* *ḥada* ‘to urge, drive; to compel’ *Glos* <12/20,14/1>. *ḥādi* ‘driving, urging’ *Musil*, 219. *miḥda* = *miswigah* ‘stick used to prod the animal’. *ḥadāya* ‘kites’ <2/16,32/6> (CA *ḥidāʾah*).

*ḥḏr* *iḥḏar* ‘beware!’ <4/7,23/10,25/6> (CA *ḥadhira* ‘to be cautious’).

*ḥḏf* *ḥaḏaf* ‘to throw, cast, pelt’ *Glos*. *ḥaḏfah* ‘a throw, pelting’ <25/17>.

*ḥrb* *ḥirbah* pl. *ḥrāb* ‘narrow blade of a spear (a broad blade is called *šalfa*)’ *Musil*, 133 <30/18,33/26> (CA *ḥarbah* ‘javelin, spear’).

*ḥrǰ* *ḥarǰ* (coll.) ‘groves of palm-trees’ <32d> (CA *ḥarajah* ‘a wood, collection of trees, thicket’).

*ḥrr* *ḥurr* pl. *ḥarāyir* ‘camel of a noble breed, thoroughbred camel’ <6/16,7/14,20/5>; ‘the best type of hunting falcon’ *Musil*, 31, 292, 613 <32/7>. *ḥarār* ‘well-born men, warriors’ *Musil*, 474 (CA *ḥurr*). *ḥarrah* ‘a lava field; a rugged tract of land strewn with black and crumbling stones’ <33/38> (CA *ḥarrah*).

*ḥrz* *ḥaraz, yiḥirzūn* ‘they attain, are capable of, able to’ *JuA*, 152 <6/10>; *ḥrāzih* ‘all he can hold’ *Musil*, 166 (CA *aḥraza* ‘to gain, take possession of’).

*ḥrf* *miḥrāf* pl. *maḥārīf* ‘camels turning around, going back and forth’, said because the *sānyah*, the camel used to draw water from the well, is driven back and forth in the *masna*, a downward sloping path leading away from the well, while pulling the ropes of the bucket, and turns around at both ends of the slope, see under *ʿdl* <19/13>; hence *maḥarīf* ‘asking back and forth, inquiries’ *Musil*, 168.

*ḥrg* *aḥrag* ‘to burn, to scorch <12/12>. *miḥrigāt* (pl. f.) ‘burnt’ (CA *muḥraqāt*).

*ḥrgl* *mḥargil* explained as ‘scheming, seeking to deceive, to ruin s.o.’ <21/22>.

*ḥrk* *ḥarrak* i.e. *ḥaffar* ‘to remove; to dig out (a well)’; *ḥirrik* pass. ‘to be dug out, removed (sand that clogs a well due to either frequent use or its being neglected)’ <16/4,17/7>.

*ḥrm* *aḥram* ‘to enter the *ḥaram* of Mecca’ <33c> (CA *aḥrama*).

*ḥzb* *ḥizzib* (pl.) explained as ‘big; full of water and food’ <7/11> (CA *ḥazāb* ‘thick, coarse, bulky’).

*ḥzz* *ḥazzat* ‘about the time of’ <7/4,13/7,19/7>; *ḥazzat aš-šōf* 'with the first daybreak' *Musil*, 314 (CA *ḥazzah* 'a time; a particular time').

*ḥzm* *ḥazam, yḥazim* 'to tie; to bind, tie together' *Musil*, 87; *Glos* <26/26> (CA *ḥazama*). *ḥzām, miḥzim* 'girdle, girth; leather or woollen belt, broad leather belt with pockets for cartridges' *Musil*, 119, 167; 'gunner's belt, upon the baldric are little metal pipes, with their powder charges, and upon the girdle leather pouches for shot, flint and steel, and a hook whereupon a man will hang his sandals; the belt is adorned with copper studs and beset with little rattling chains'; *mḥazzamīn* 'men girded with these belts; it is commonly said of tribes well provided with firearms "they have many *mḥazzamīn*"' *Doughty* ii, 96 <18/20, 30/25> (CA *ḥizām, miḥzam*).

*ḥazim* pl. *ḥzūm, ḥizmān, ḥazām* 'an elevation, rather low, but long, and dotted with many small hillocks; these *ḥzūm* usually run parallel' *Musil*, 592, 679, and *Glos* <4/2, 22,6/27,8/9,19/18,26/10,27/8>. *Ḥazm ad-Duwāsir* is the name of the rugged, mountainous desert north of the sand dunes fencing off Wādi ad-Duwāsir <33/45>.

*ḥzwl* *ḥazāwīl* 'in heaps, piles' <13/9>. *ytaḥazwal* 'it lies collected in heaps' (CA *iḥzaʾalla* 'to be high and collected, heaped up, elevated'; *muḥzaʾill* 'high').

*ḥsb* *ḥasab, yaḥasb* 'to think; to reckon' <18/22>. *ḥasbi allah, ḥasbi ʿala* 'I count on God to protect me from' <6/5, 29/1> (CA *ḥasbuk allāh* 'God will be sufficient for you').

*ḥss* *ḥass, yiḥiss* 'to touch; to hurt, cause pain' <21/21,23/7>; *ḥassikum nafsikum* 'beware!' *Musil*, 490. *ma tḥiss al-baṭin* 'it does not touch the belly' <2/9>. *ḥiss* 'sound; the human voice' *Doughty* i, 307 (the intransitive meaning of the CA verb *ḥassa* has become transitive in the Najdi dialect).

*ḥsk* *ḥaskāt al-wubar* '(she-camels) with curly, prickly, knotty (*mitʿakriš*) hair' <30/20> (CA *ḥasak* 'thistle, prickly plants which cling to the fur of camels in their places').

*ḥsn* *ḥisna* 'good deed; amicable manner; fair means' *Glos*; 'what is done with a good, friendly intention' <22/9>; 'a protective relationship which lasts one year and two months, *allah ʿaṭāk ḥisna sanah wi-šharēn* "God has given you protection for one year and two months," said by a respected man who offers a murderer his protection' *Hess*,

95. *ta*ʿ*āl* ʿ*ala ḥisnāy w-sayyiti* 'surrender yourself unconditionally (lit. to my mercy or my displeasure)', said to an enemy who cannot escape, *Hess*, 97 (CA *ḥusnā*).

*ḥsy* *ḥasāwiyyah* 'a coffee-pot made in al-Aḥsāʾ oasis in eastern Arabia' <9/9>.

*ḥšrj* *ḥašrij* explained as 'a narrow spot among stones in a *ši*ʿ*īb*, a valley or watercourse dug out by the torrent' <14/9> (CA *ḥas͟hraj* 'water that lies under the ground of pebble-strewn watercourses; cavity in mountain in which water collects').

*ḥšw* *ḥāši* pl. *ḥašuw* 'young camel, a camel in its third year = *ḥiǵǵ*' *Musil*, 12, 333 <1/11,13> (CA *ḥas͟hw*).

*ḥṣr* *ḥaṣīrah* pl. *ḥaṣāyir* 'sides; haunches, hips' <6/18> (CA *ḥaṣīrah* 'part between the vein that appears in the side of a camel or horse and what is above it; sides').

*ḥṣn* *ḥṣān* pl. *ḥiṣin* 'stud horse; a stallion between its fifth and twentieth years, after that it is called ʿ*ōd*' *Musil*, 376 (CA *ḥiṣān* pl. *ḥuṣun*).

*ḥṣy* *aḥṣa, yiḥṣi* 'to count, number' <13/3>; *iḥṣ* 'count!' <25/6>.

*ḥṭṭ* *maḥaṭṭ* 'place where the camels are unloaded and a camp is pitched' <22/9> (CA *maḥaṭṭ*).

*ḥḏ̣b* *ḥaḏ̣īb* 'soft ground at the foot of a mountain' <4/24> (CA *ḥiḍb* pl. *aḥḍāb* 'the sides, slopes of a mountain').

*ḥḏ̣r* *ḥaḏ̣īr* i.e. *ḥaḏ̣ar*, pl. mult. *ḥiḏ̣rān*, sing. *ḥḏ̣iri*, fem. *ḥḏ̣iriyyah* 'inhabitants of the settled land, village folk, those who dwell in permanent houses, contr. of *baduw*, the bedouins' *Hess*, 57 <13/19>. *ḥḏ̣iriyyah* 'a village girl' <17/11>.

*ḥḏ̣ḏ̣* *ḥaḏ̣ḏ̣* pl. *ḥḏ̣ūḏ̣* 'luck, fortune, fate; expressions of bliss or love' *Musil*, 180 <10/6>; *ḥaḏ̣ḏ̣in yiṯūr* lit. 'luck uplifts itself', i.e. 'fortune smiles on us' *Musil*, 512 (CA *ḥaẓẓ*).

*ḥff* *ḥiff* 'enemy, adversary' <6/13,18/19>. *ḥaffah* 'a rush, assault with all might; all at once' <32/5>.

*ḥfw* *ḥifwān* = *taqdīr* '(show of) respect, esteem' <26/18> (CA *ḥafāwah* 'welcoming, salutation, show of respect').

*ḥfy* *ḥafa* 'to abrade, scar, hurt'; *ḥafat* 'she has become caloused or scarred, she walks barefoot' *Musil*, 275. *ḥafa, ḥafāh* 'scars, bleeding wounds in the foot; when a camel used to walking only on sand or small gravel must walk for some time through a volcanic area, strewn with sharp pieces of lava, the skin under her hoofs becomes covered with callous spots or scars so that blood flows at every step' *Musil*, 370 <15/4> (CA *ḥafā*ʾ 'state of having the foot or hoof chafed, abraded, worn'). *ḥafi* 'worn, wounded and bleeding' <33/2> (CA *ḥafī*); *ḥafāya* 'she-camels with bruised soles which bleed at every step' *Musil*, 300. *ḥāfi* 'barefoot' *Musil*, 204 (CA *ḥāfī*).

*ḥgb* *ḥagab* 'camel's hair rope, breast girth' *Musil*, 69, 308, 353. *miḥgibah* pl. *maḥāǵib* 'the spot covered by the *ḥagab*, the breast girth which holds the saddle behind the forelegs on the breastbone' *Musil*, 298 <11/5,33/36>. *bīḏ al-ḥawāǵib* 'camels with white spots below their girths because they are on the road all the time and their fur is chafed by the girths' (CA *iḥtaqaba* 'to bind s.th. behind the camel saddle').

*ḥgr* *ḥugrān* pl. *ḥaǵāri* 'disrespect, utter humiliation' *Musil*, 315 <21/23> (CA *ḥaqārah* 'contemptibleness, ignominy').

*ḥgg* *ḥagūg* 'a violent downpour'; *ṣidūgin ḥgūgih* 'clouds that do not deceive by their appearance, but truly deliver their promise of rain' <u>*KhaAd*</u>, 246 <1/4,3/7,13/4,14/11, 18/10>. *ḥiǵǵ* pl. *ḥagāyiǵ, ḥgigah* 'a camel in its third year' *Musil*, 333 <18/22> (CA *ḥiqq* 'a camel three years old that has entered its fourth year', so called because fit to be made use of).

*ḥkr* *ḥāćir* 'locking up s.th.; keeping s.th. to oneself' <16/5> (CA *ḥakara*).

*ḥkm* *ḥakīmah* pl. *ḥakāyim* 'bridle' <2/15> (CA *ḥakamah* 'part of the bridle that surrounds the jaws of the horse; ring on nose or mouth of the horse'). *ḥakīm* 'knot fastening that part of the halter' <5/6>.

*ḥky* *ḥaća* 'to talk' <16/12>. *ḥaćiy* pl. *ḥaćāya* 'speech, talk' <21/18> (CA *ḥakā*).

*ḥlḥl* *ḥalāḥīl* 'fast riding camels; nice, beautiful camels' <8/a, 26/3> (CA *ḥalḥāl* 'the act of urging on a she-camel by the cry *ḥal*').

*ḥlg* *ḥalag* pl. *ḥlāg* 'the copper nose-ring to which a rope can be attached for the purpose of leading the camel' <4/13,5/6, 26/5,7> (CA *ḥalqah* 'ring, anything circular').

*ḥll* *ḥall, yḥill* 'to halt, unload the camels and put up the tents' *Hess*, 60; 'to alight at' <9/4,18/7,21/1>; 'to loosen, untie, unravel' <22/8>. *maḥall* pl. *maḥālīl* 'camp, tents; place where the bedouins *ḥallaw*' <14/20>. *ḥill* pl. *ḥlūl* 'time, time of settlement in a place; period' <5/7,6/12, 21/8,33e>; *min ḥillna* 'from the very beginning (of our settlement in that area, of our existence as a tribe)' <2/26>; *ḥillin ṭiwīl* 'a long time' <33f>. *ḥalāl* 'herds of camels and small cattle, i.e. the *māl*, possessions of the bedouins' *Hess*, 62, 169, see *gōm*.

*ḥly* *ḥalla, yḥalli; taḥalla* 'to watch, look, see' *Musil*, 365; *Glos* <11/10>; 'to describe'. *nḥalli* 'we shape, mold'; also 'we describe in words, similes, make comparisons' <12/1, 33/31> (cf. CA *ḥallayt ar-rajul* 'I described the *ḥilyah*, i.e. the qualities or attributes, of the man'). *ḥilyah* 'shape, features (= *awṣāf, rsūm*)' *Musil*, 222. *ḥalāya* 'characteristics, attributes' <1/8,9/33>; 'the manner of acting, behaviour, speech, and movements' *Musil*, 189. *ḥalāh* 'the best of s.th.' *Glos* <26/17,18>.

*ḥmd* *ḥamād* 'a barren, scorched-looking plain covered with small gravel and much flint' *Musil*, 15, 152, 679 <3/9>.

*ḥmr* *ḥamār* 'red glow' <7/10>; 'swarms, multitudes (e.g. of locusts)' <2/4>.

*ḥml* *maḥmūl* pl. *maḥāmīl* 'loaded, laden with goods' <13/11>. *iḥtmālih* 'the conclusion he reached after weighing his chances (of achieving s.th.)' <18/16>.

*ḥmm* see *ḏry*. *ḥammah* 'blackness' <3/16> (CA *ḥummah*). *ḥimm al-ajhāl* 'black young she-camels' <26/17>. *ḥamām* 'the battlements of a wall' <25/14>.

*ḥmy* *yiḥma* (pass.) 'he is treated with, undergoes a cure to the exclusion of all other food' <3/3> (CA *ḥamīy* 'a sick man prohibited from food and drink that would injure him'). *ḥama, ḥamma* 'to protect against attackers' <33d>; *iḥmu lha al-bīr* 'seize the well for the camels!' *Musil* 359. *ḥāmi* 'protector' <26/14>; *ḥammāyah* 'protectors' <8/13>. *miḥtimi* 'protecting, defending' <18/12> (CA *ḥāmī* 'protector, defender of one's companions'). *ḥawāmi* 'walls; great mass of stone; fortifications' <21/30,25/12> (CA *ḥāmiyah* pl. *ḥawāmī* 'the stones with which a well is cased; large masses of rock'). *aḥma* 'to run at a hot pace' <4/11>. *iḥtama sūgih* '(the war's) market became heated with warriors offering their lives for sale, *ysūmūn*, and inviting prospective buyers, i.e. the enemy' <2/17> (CA *iḥtamā ġaḍaban* 'he became hot with anger'). *ḥamuw* hotness, heat, fieriness; the scalding tempest of the sun's rays' *Doughty* i, 423. *ḥāmi* 'hot, burning, fiery, blazing; fierce, passionate' <11/9,15/5,24/13,33/44> (CA *ḥamiya* 'to be vehemently hot'; *ḥāmī*).

*ḥnb* *miḥnāb* pl. *maḥānīb* 'the winding course followed by the *sēl*, the torrent that fills the wadis' <12/19> (cf. CA *taḥnīb* 'crookedness, curving shape').

*ḥnzb* *ḥanāzīb* 'robust, sturdy camels' <33/15> (CA *ḥazāb, ḥinzāb* 'thick, coarse, bulky').

*ḥnš* *ḥannišōh* explained to me as 'they embellished, adorned it' <6/30>. *ḥnūš* 'snakes' <30/7,15> (CA *ḥana͟sh* pl. *aḥnā͟sh* 'serpent, viper').

*ḥnn* *ḥann, yiḥinn* 'to rumble, moan, groan' *Hess*, 79; *taḥinn* '(a thirsty she-camel) murmurs, moans piteously' *Musil* 338, 349; *ḥannat r*$^c$*ūd* 'the thunder rumbled' <33/23>. *ḥanīn* 'yearning; a yearning, longing sound; grumbling, gurgling' <1/12,18/4,19/8>. *ḥannah* 'pitiable murmuring of a thirsty camel' *Musil*, 338 (CA *ḥannah* 'grumbling noise').

*ḥny* *ḥaniyyah* pl. *ḥanāya, ḥiniy* 'the bent litter pole, signifying a litter of the *ćitab* variety, with long curved poles' *Musil*, 249-250 <7/4,33/20>; 'curved poles surrounding the leather bowl of a water trough, *ḥōḏ*' *Musil*, 72 (CA *ḥinw, ḥanw* pl. mult. *ḥinīy* 'anything in which is a bending, curving; any curved piece of wood, like those used for the *qatab* saddle'; *ḥanīyah* pl. *ḥanāyā* 'bow; bowed, curved structure'). *maḥāni* 'curves in a watercourse' <13/8> (CA *maḥniyah* pl. *maḥānī* 'bend of a valley'). *maḥniy* 'bent, curved' <9/18>. *ḥāni* pl. *ḥawāni* 'bent downwards, stooped'; i.e. *taḥannat rǵābha* 'they stood with lowered necks' <19/4> (CA *ḥānī* pl. *ḥawānī* 'bending, curving').

*ḥwḏ* *ḥāḏ* 'a kind of plant' <33/52> (CA *ḥā͟dh* 'one of the *ḥamḍ*-plants, saline plants on which camels like to pasture').

*ḥwr* *ḥwār* pl. *ḥīrān* 'a calf during the first ninety days after its birth when it is fed on milk only' *Musil*, 333 <2/13,3/8, 26/3> (CA *ḥuwār* 'a young camel until weaned').

*ḥwz* *ḥawwaz, taḥawwaz* 'to withdraw' <33/34> (CA *taḥawwaza* 'to withdraw, retire to a distant place').

*ḥwš* *inḥāš* 'to make off, to flee, hurry away' <33d>; *nḥašna, w-xadna wagt w-ḥinna minḥāšīn* 'we fled, and we kept on fleeing for a long time' *Musil*, 646 (CA *inḥāsha* ʿ*anh* 'he took fright and fled from him'). *minḥāš* 'having made his escape' *Musil*, 138. *ḥawwāš* 'man who does the driving during a hunt' *Musil*, 26.

*ḥwḏ̣* *ḥōḏ̣, ḥāḏ̣* pl. *ḥīḏ̣ān, ḥyāḏ̣* 'leather trough in which the water for the animals is poured after being drawn from the well' *Musil*, 71-72, 340; *Hess*, 120 <2/11,3/21> (CA *ḥawḍ* pl. *ḥiyāḍ, ḥīḍān*).

*ḥwf* *ḥōf* 'what is expected of, one's assessment of; what in one's estimation approximates to' <26/9>; *yixlif ḥōfih* 'contrary to his expectations, different from what he thought' <4/21> (CA *ḥawf* 'being on the side of s.th.').

*ḥwl* *ḥāl dūn* 'to come between, interfere'; *ḥāl* ʿ*ala* 'to surround, to capture' *Musil*, 534. *ḥāl, yiḥīl* 'to cheat, deceive' *Musil*, 346. *ḥawwal* 'to come down, dismount' *Glos* <33i>. *aḥāl, yiḥīl* 'to transfer; to remove from; to turn, pass over to' <13/20>; 'to wander from well to well (said of a tribe or sub-tribe)' *Hess*, 59. *īḥāl* (pass.) 'it is removed, transferred' <26/24> (CA *aḥāla* 'to transfer'). *inḥāl* 'to be transferred, turned over to' <26/23>. *iḥtāl* 'to be a match for s.o.; to be able to, to know how to; to be able to hold one's own against, to find the means to resist' <6/3,33k> (CA *iḥtāla* 'to achieve by artful means'). *mḥīl* 'cunning' <8/11> (CA *muḥtāl* 'cunning, artful'). *ma wara ḥīltih ḥīl* 'he after whose *ḥīlah*, artifice, there is no other *ḥīl*, (recourse to) clever tricks' *Musil*, 187 <14/6>; *wiš ḥīlti* 'what shall I do now?' *Musil*, 162. *ḥīl* 'adroitness' KhaAd, 201. *ḥēl* 'strength' <26/18> (CA *ḥayl* 'strength, power, might, force' = *qūwah, ḥawl*). *ḥōl* 'problem, difficulty' <26/23, 24> (CA *ḥāl, ḥālah* 'predicament, in respect of changing circumstances').

*al-ḥāl*, 'the condition, state' and, more specifically, 'good condition (said of an animal reinvigorated and fattened by grazing in abundant pastures), health' <9/2, 12/13>; *ḥāli naḥat* 'my healthy condition, content is gone' *Musil*, 181. *ḥāyil* pl. *ḥīl, ḥāylāt* 'sterile, not impregnated and hence fat and strong animals' <6/12,7/16,26/2,3,24, 27/6,30/23> (CA *ḥāʾil* 'not conceiving, not becoming pregnant during a year or some years'). *ḥyāl* 'barrenness' *Glos*; hence 'strength, reserves of fat covering the body' <6/18,27/3>. *ḥīl* also means 'beautiful; of nice, strong, healthy condition' <22/3,26/2>.

*maḥālah* pl. *maḥḥāl, maḥāḥīl* 'wooden roller of a water hoist over which runs the rope holding the bucket, pulley reels' *Musil*, 339; *Hess* 64; *Doughty* i, 324 <6/7,7/2,8/a, 9/27,24/7>. *isin walla sanat bik al-maḥālah* 'hoist the bucket or the wooden roller will draw you down' *ʿUbūdī*, 97 (CA *maḥālah* pl. *maḥāl* 'roller over which the rope passes whereby water is drawn, sheave of a pulley'). *maḥāl* pl. *maḥāwīl* 'great distance between two wells' *Musil*, 680; 'waste, waterless desert' *Glos*.

*ḥwm* *ḥām, yiḥūm* 'to circle, hover, glide' *Musil*, 542. *mḥīm*, '(a thirsty camel) circling around the water trough, waiting to be watered'; also *ḥāyim* pl. *ḥyām* <18/23>, often used metaphorically as in *miruwyat al-ḥyām* 'those who drench the thirsty (spears in blood)', cf. *Sow*, 180. *ḥāmah* 'eddying, whirling movement' <25/4> (CA *ḥāma* 'to circle'; *ḥāʾim* 'circling').

*ḥwy* *miḥtiwi* 's.o. who collects s.th., possesses it' <16/8>. *ḥawa, yḥawi* 'to take into possession one's share of the booty by touching it with one's spear' *Hess*, 101 (CA *ḥawā, iḥtawā* 'to collect, bring together; to take possession of').

*ḥyd* *ḥēd* pl. *ḥyūd* 'the foot of a hill; a slope shutting in a plain' *Musil*, 680; 'mountain' *JuMu*, 727; 'rock, stone' <22/4, 33/1> (CA *ḥayd* 'a protuberant, prominent part of a thing').

*ḥyr* *ḥār* 'to be confounded, perplexed; to hesitate' <28/4> (CA *ḥāra*). *ḥāyir* 'troubled, disturbed' *Musil*, 167. *miḥīr* 'place where the water of a torrent collects' <7/12>; *miḥīrah* 'a shallow basin fertilized by evaporating surface water' *Musil*, 323. *ḥēr* pl. *ḥyūr* 'fenced palm garden' *Su* i, 188; *Glos* (CA *ḥāʾir, ḥayr* 'a depressed place in which water collects; garden').

*ḥyn* *miḥyān* 'expert, proficient, knowledgeable' <21/28, 26/22>.

*ḥyy* *ḥayy* 'tribe, kin' *Musil*, 165, 359 <33/40> (CA *ḥayy*). *ḥayyāt at-trāb* 'snakes' <33i> (CA *ḥayyah*). *ḥaya* 'abundant rains which assure a luxurious growth of annuals; without it no affluence, *ribīʿ*, will follow' *Musil*, 542 <32c>.

*xbb* *xabb*, imp. f. *xubbi*, 'to run sprightly' <15/4>; *xubbi xabīb* '(run at) an easy gait combined with playful prancing, as is wont of young, spirited mares' *Musil*, 516 (CA *khabba* 'to run at a quick pace', the pace called *khabab*).

*xbt* *xabt* 'a low, flat, wide expanse of land; a basin covered with gravel and sand, where small ponds are sometimes formed by rain-water which cannot run off' *Musil*, 679; 'open waste country of gravel and sand (in the Ḥijāz)' *Doughty* ii, 572 <;5> (CA *khabt*).

*xbr* *xabar* 'to know' <4/13>. *xabbar* 'to tell, inform s.o.' *Musil*, 529. *xābir* 'knowing' <;17,;23,24/11>. *xubrah* = *rabi*$^{c}$ 'group, one's own group' <30/14>. *xabārah* 'mouse holes; area of danger, trap' *Musil*, 678; *KhaAd*, 381 <15/3> (CA *khabār* 'soft sand in which are burrows and hollows, in which beasts sink and are embarrassed; burrows of large field-rats'; *man tajannaba al-khabār amina al-*$^{c}$*ithār* 'he who avoids the soft ground in which the feet sink will be secure from stumbling'). *xabrah* pl. *xabāri* 'large rain pool into which a whole herd can move and drink; a large or small depression in a plain in which the rain-water gathers' *Musil*, 340, 584, 679; 'a naked clay bottom in the desert, where shallow water is ponded after heavy rain, also *gā*$^{c}$' *Doughty* ii, 260.

*xbṭ* *xabṭ* 'drumming, beating of the ground' <27/8> (CA *khabṭ* 'a camel's striking or beating a thing with his fore-foot').

*xbl* *axbal* pl. *xubl* 'stupid, foolish' <22/4,24/14> (CA *khabil, akhbal* 'corrupted, unsound of mind, insane').

*xby* *xba* 'the hiding in which the daughters of tribal grandees are kept, e.g. the curtained litter-chair on a camel' <33/21> (CA *mukhabbaʾah* 'a girl who is kept in the house or tent, concealed from view, who is kept behind the curtain, who is not yet married').

*xtm* *xātam* pl. *xawātim* 'ring (with a stone, *faṣṣ*)' *Hess*, 131 <12/26> (CA *khātam* pl. *khawātim*).

*xjl* *mxōjilāt, mxōlijāt* (pl. f.) 'flawed' <7/1> (CA *mukhjil* 'confounded; rent, worn out').

*xdd* *xadd* 'earth, firm ground, surface' <18/5>; *xadd* pl. *xdūd* 'cheek' <19/17,25/21,33/48>.

*xdrs* *xadārīs* (pl.) 'pitch-dark' <25/6> (CA *khadara* 'to conceal s.th., prevent s.th. from being seen').

*xdm* *xadīmah* pl. *xadāyim* 'halter', i.e. *risan* <7/16> (CA *khadamah* 'a plaited thong'). *tixīdām* 'showing off' <9/31>; *tixīdām al-bnayy fi l-ḥaflah* 'girls swaying their hips as they dance at a festive occasion'.

*xdn* *xadīn* 'beloved one; wife' <16/9> (CA *khidn, khadīn* 'private friend, amorous associate').

*xḏl* *xuḏlān* 'disappointment, being left in the lurch' <21/23 (CA *khidhlān*).

*xrj* *xirj* pl. *xrūj* 'saddle-bags, large leather bags with fringes and tassels carried by camels' *KhaAd*, 385; *Musil*, 581; 'double bag that can be thrown across the camel saddle and also a smaller bag of the same kind to be put on the horse saddle' *Musil*, 149 <9/22,22/3> (CA *khurj* 'a pair of saddle-bags').

*xrr* *xarr* 'to trickle down, flow down; to close (eyes)' <33h> (CA *kharra* 'to fall down, stumble').

*xrᶜ* *xāriᶜ* 'running, fleeing with bent neck; frightened to death' *KhaAd*, 255 <4/17> (CA *khariᶜ* 'anything that may be lifted; bending; supple'). *ixtirāᶜ* 'fright, mad flight', said of fleeing ostriches, *Musil*, 151. *mixrāᶜ* pl. *maxārīᶜ* 'panicky, fleeing with the neck stretched forward' <6/14>; also: 'coward, frightened man' *Su* ii, 43. *yixriᶜ ixrāᶜ* 'to scare, frighten' *Su* iii, 115.

*xzr* *taxāzar* inf. n. *tixīzār* 'to throw glances, side looks at one another; to keep a close watch on the other's movements (e.g. the sand grouse as they fly at great speed and with sudden swerves in close formation)' <9/23,19/13>; *taxāzarat al-ᶜyūn* 'the eyes looked at the eyes of the others' (CA *takhāzara* 'to look from the outer angle of the eye; to contract the eyelids, to sharpen the sight'). *xēzarān* 'cane, reed, bamboo, rattan' *Musil*, 293 <9/31> (CA *khayzarān*).

*xzrf* *xazraf* 'to embellish, decorate' <25/14> (CA *zakhrafa*). *xazraf* pl. *xazārīf* 'a kind of plant that grows in the south of Najd' <19/5> (CA *zukhruf* 'good edible plants').

*xzz* *xazz* 'to run fast, nimbly' <4/24>.

*xzn* *xazn aḏ-ḏifar* 'one's repository of courage', i.e. one's own kin on whom one can depend for assistance <30/25>.

*xzy* *xaza*, similar in meaning to *ᶜār* 'ignominy, shame, vileness' <21/25>; *xazāha* 'her (a woman's) shame' *Musil*, 609

(CA khazā 'what is despicable, ignominious').

*xsr* *xasārah* 'loss (through lavish entertainment of guests)' <15/12>. *xusrān* 'losing, damaging' <21/15>. *xassārah* 'those who suffer a loss; reckless spenders' <6/12>. *maxāsīr* 'the cost' *Musil*, 246; *illi yanṭaḥūn al-maxāsīr* 'those who do not mind incurring losses due to their generosity' *JuKha*, 84 (CA *khāsir* 'one who lost his property').

*xšm* *xašim* pl. *xšūm* 'nose; steep spur of a ridge, edge of a mesa, bluff, cliff' *Musil*, 679 <2/5,5/6,7/5,11,10/9,30/17, 31/13> (CA *khashm* 'nose').

*xṣṣ* *xaṣṣ* 'to single out, distinguish' *Glos*; *txuṣṣih* 'you address him especially' <6/34,24/10,25/2>; *xuṣṣihum li bi-s-salām* 'give them my greetings' *Musil*, 310 (CA *khaṣṣa* 'to distinguish s.o. particularly').

*xṭr* *xāṭir* 'mind' <;23>. *xaṭar* 'danger' <26/28>; *tarᶜa ba-l-xaṭar* '(the she-camels) graze in the area of danger (an expression conveying the tribe's confidence in its ability to repulse any enemy attack)' *Musil*, 550. *xaṭrin, mixṭir* 'on the brink of, in risk of, in danger of' <11/22,23/11> (CA *khaṭar* 'imminent danger, peril, risk').

*xṭṭ* *xaṭṭ* 'line; track' <11/5>; 'the breach a charging horseman opens in the enemy lines' <32/7>.

*xṭf* *xaṭaf* 'to catch one unawares'. *taxāṭifaw* 'they rushed ahead of them, cut off their escape and attacked the enemy' <19/23> (CA *takhāṭafū* 'they contended together in snatching s.th.'). *xaṭṭāf* 'a wild beast or a good hunting hound that attacks its prey without being urged' *Musil*, 548.

*xṭl* *xaṭlan* 'long (said of arms)' <2/10> (CA *khaṭil* 'long', whereas *akhṭal, khaṭlāʾ* refers particularly to long, broad ears).

*xṭm* *xṭām* 'noseband, halter' <11/11,18/15,25/1> (CA *khiṭām* 'halter, cord of which one end is fastened round the nose and jaws of a camel').

*xṭw* *xaṭṭa* 'to step, pace' *Musil*, 173, 251. *taxaṭṭa* 'to go by' *Musil*, 140. *xaṭwah* pl. *xṭa* 'step, pace'. *xaṭw* (with foll. genit.) 'some of, a certain one' *Glos* <4/12,17,11/8>; *xaṭwāt sōdan* 'a certain black she-camel' <2/8>; also *xaṭāt* 'many a one, someone, anyone' *Musil*, 180.

*xṭy* *axṭa* 'to commit an error, to do wrong; to miss (a target)'

*Musil*, 647; *la tixṭi al-ǵuwādi* 'do not commit injustice, wrong' *Hess*, 155. *xaṭa* 'wrong, offense' <15/3>. *mixṭiy* 'wrong, incorrect, at fault' <11/a>. *mixṭiyāt* (pl. f.) 'handling, treating s.o. in a cruel fashion, mauling' <33/8>; *mixṭiy w-ṣāyib* 'missing and reaching (the target)' *Musil*, 636 (*akhṭaʾa* 'to wrong, commit an offense').

*xḏb* *mxaḏḏab*, *maxḏūb* pl. *maxāḏīb* 'dyed (with henna, paint)' <12/24> (CA *mukhaḏḏab*).

*xff* *xaff*, *yxuff* 'to disperse, to chase away (when a wind blows, rain is believed to come down in smaller drops)' <13/4> (CA *khaffa* 'to diminish, decrease, to become deficient', said of rain). *inxaff* 'to become light' <5/12> (CA *istakhaffa* 'he found it light to carry'). *xafīf* pl. *xfāf* 'slim; light, not heavy with load' *Glos* <1/13,6/29,27/3>. *xuff* pl. *xafāf* 'foot, pad of the camel' <3/15,4/19,5/7,7/7, 8/7> (CA *khuff* pl. *khifāf, akhfāf*).

*xfg* *taxāfag* 'to come down with a clattering noise' <6/27>; 'to tremble, shake, quiver, lurch' <9/27>. *xafagān al-galb* 'the trembling, fluttering of the heart' (CA *khafq al-aqdām* 'the pattering of the feet').

*xfy* *yixfa* 'it is hidden' <14/7>. *ma xfi* 'what is hidden, concealed' <21/8> (CA *khafiya*). *xāfiy* 'hidden' <19/3>; *xafiyyāt* 'hidden things' *Musil*, 289.

*xlj* *xalūj* 'a she-camel whose calf is killed immediately after birth and who notices it' *Musil*, 194.

*xlṣ* *ixluṣ* 'be away! off with you!' <30/4> (CA *khalaṣa min* 'to withdraw, retire, go away'). *mixliṣ* 'real steel, *fūlāḏ*' <32/9>.

*xlʿ* *xalīʿ* 'dislocated, cast off, removed' <5/4>.

*xlf* *xalaf* 'to be different, contradictory'; *yixlif rāyik* 'he is different from what you think' <4/12>; *yixlif ḥōfih*, see *ḥwf* <4/21>; *yixlif* he goes against (the opposition of)' <5/12> (CA *khalafa* 'to become different from, contrary to what it was thought to be', said for instance of the taste of water). *taxallaf* 'to remain behind; to lag' <30/9>. *taxālaf* 'to contend; inflict on one another (the loss of)' <33/54>; 'to go in different or opposite directions' <13/16> (CA *takhālafa* 'to take a contrary position'). *ixtalaft*, 'I became confused, bad-tempered'; also 'to totter, tumble' *Glos* <12/4>; *ixtalaf galbih* 'his heart changed', i.e. 'he became insane, mad, possessed' *Hess*, 155. *mxālif* 'rebellious, wayward' *Musil*, 199. *nāgtin mixtalfin ʿagilha* 'a mad, unmanageable she-camel' *Hess*, 76. *xalfah* pl. *xilf, xalfāt* 'she-camel with a young 1-7 months old' *Hess*, 77; 'she-camels which are milked after giving birth to young, during the suckling time' *Musil*, 324, 333; 'a she-camel who gave birth this year' *IngCa*, 71 <12/11> (CA *khalifah* pl. *khalif, khalifāt* 'pregnant she-camel, a she-camel one year after giving birth and once again being impregnated'). *mixlāf* pl. *maxālīf* 'a path between two low, isolated mountains (*ḏilʿ*)' <19/22>. *xilf* 'behind' <5/11, 33/44> (CA *khalf*).

*xlg* — *xalg* pl. *xalāyiǵ*; *maxlūg* pl. *maxālīǵ* '(God's) creation, creature, people' *Glos* <9/17,12/17>.

*xll* — *xalal* 'defect, fault, flaw' <9/6>. *mistixill* 'impaired, disturbed; sad (*mištiḥin*)' <24/2> (CA *ikhtalla* 'to become defective; to become upset, disturbed').

*xly* — *xalla* 'to leave, leave behind, abandon, desert' *Musil*, 227 <26/24>. *al-mxalla* 'wounded man who is abandoned on the battlefield' <26/24>. *xāli* 'empty, vacant' <20/1, 26/7> (CA *khālī*). *xala* 'a region where the camels will find no sustenance in any particular year; all that lies beyond the camp' *Musil*, 217, 325, 679 <26/7,33h> (CA *khalāʾ*). *xalyah* pl. *xalāya* 'she-camels whose calves were taken away from them and slaughtered; she-camels producing plenty of milk' <10/11,12/11> (CA *khalīyah* pl. *khalāyā* 'a she-camel that brings forth, and whose young one is drawn away in order for her milk to continue for the use of her owners, she being made to yield her milk by means of the young one of another, which is then withdrawn from her, and she is milked'). Such a she-camel is also called *ḏīr*.

*xmd* — *xāmid* 'silent, motionless and dead (desert)' <3/9> (CA *khāmid*).

*xmṣ* — *mixmiṣ* 'narrow, lean in the waist' <17/8>. *mixmāṣ* 'one with a narrow waist' *KhaAd*, 273 (CA *khamīṣ, mikhmāṣ* 'lank in the belly').

*xng* — *xannag, yxanniǵ* 'to throttle, strangle, squeeze one's throat' <33k> (CA *khannaqa*).

*xwr* — *xūr* 'she-camels producing plenty of milk' <33/15> (CA *khawwārah* pl. *khūr* 'she-camel abounding with milk, whose milk flows easily').

*xw*ᶜ *mixwā*ᶜ pl. *maxāwī*ᶜ 'a low tract of land, a plain, depression' *JuA*, 230, 234 <6/33> (CA *khaw*ᶜ 'a low tract of land with some growth of *rimth*-bushes').

*xwf* *xāfah* 'dangerous land; land where one risks being attacked by the enemy' <32a>.

*xwy* *xāwi* 'empty' <20/1> (CA *khāwī*).

*xyr* *xēr* 'prosperity, good' <3/22,10/14,13/22>; the closeness of Dindān's outlook to that of the pre-modern bedouins is mirrored by the fact that for him *xēr* has in large measure retained the meaning of 'pasture' following abundant rains, cf. *Musil*, 674; *xēr allah* 'the Lord's bounty, providence'; *balad bha xēr* 'a good land, they use to say of a country whose inhabitants do eat and are satisfied' *Doughty* i, 248, 256. *xyār* 'the choicest part of, the best of' <28/3> (CA *khiyār*). *xīrah* 'the elite, the chosen, elect, the best men' <33c> (CA *khīrah*).

*xyṭ* see *ftg*.

*xyl* *xāl, yixīl, xayyal* 'to imagine, think, believe, suppose that'; *wēn txīl ha-l-barǵ* 'where do you place this lightning?' asked when men observe the distant flashes of lightning in an attempt to judge whether it lightens from rain clouds or not and in what territory before migrating in that direction in search of pasture, *Musil*, 146 (CA *khāla*). *maxāl* 'rain clouds' <3/11,26/10>; *xyāl, maxāyīl* 'black rain clouds' *Hess*, 67 <5/1,10/5,13/15,14/10,18/2,19/1,27/8> (CA *makhīlah* pl. *makhāyil* 'cloud showing signs of rain'). *xyālah* 'mare' <33/17>. *xēl* (coll.) 'horses; horsemen' <32e, 33/31> (CA *khayl*). *maxyūl* pl. *maxāyīl* 'a stick on which the shepherd hangs his cloak as a stratagem to prevent his flocks from wandering off in his absence'.

*xym* *xēmah* pl. *xyām* 'light white tent' *Musil* 269-270 <3/8>.

*dbḥ* *adbaḥ* 'to crouch, hunch, lean down; to curve, bow, incline'; *adbaḥan an-njūm* 'the stars began to decline' *Su* i, 139; *dōbaḥaw* 'they pressed their heads to the necks of their mares to escape the shots of the enemy' *Musil*, 173. *idbāḥ* 'running with the neck stretched low, bent forward' <4/20> (CA *dabbaḥa* 'to lower one's head during prosternation in prayer so that it is in a lower position than the back'). *midbiḥāt* (pl. f.) 'curved, bent, bowed' <30/15>.

dbr  *dabbar* 'to turn one's back and move away; to go, walk back' <8/3,25/8> (CA *dabara* 'to go away'; *adbara* 'to turn back, retreat'). *dibrah* 'ruling, decree' <12/14> (CA *dabrah* 'turn of fate')

dby  *diba, dabwa* 'young locusts whose wings are just growing; they are so numerous at times that they crawl in a long chain urging each other on and even riding one on top of the other' *Musil*, 112-113, 627; 'the later broods, born of the spring locust, sexless, or imperfect females, finding only burned-up herbage, are dry and unwholesome (as food)' *Doughty* i, 244; 'locusts before they fly' *SuFa*, 269. *diba ḥannān* was explained as 'young locusts making a humming sound as they crawl, *ḥann*' <9/4> (CA *dabā*).

djw  *dija* 'darkness, darkness of night' <12/25> (CA *dujā*).

dḥm  *daḥam* 'to push, shove, hustle; to enter by pushing one's way in' <;29> (CA *daḥm* 'hard push, shove').

dxl  *daxal ʿala* 'to seek protection from' <10/4,14/7>. *dixīl* 'one who places himself under the protection of s.o.' <9/17,10/3>. *dxālah* 'protection granted by request, e.g. when an oppressed or pursued person enters the tent, or its sacred precincts, of s.o. whose protection he desires' *Musil*, 441; *Glos*.

dxn  *duxxān* 'smoke of gunpowder' <2/16>; 'evil intent' <21/22>.

drb  *dārbāt* (pl. f.) 'trained, accustomed to' <6/7> (CA *dārib*). *darb* pl. *drūb* 'path; road; ways, manners, habits' <21/10,19>; *darb al-fasād* 'the road of sin' *Musil*, 294.

drj  *daraj* 'to roll' *Musil*, 76; 'to stream' *Musil*, 265. *darraj, ydarrij* 'to force to walk' *Musil*, 367; 'to nudge on; to walk' *Musil*, 204. *darj* 'ammunition, bullets' <22/3,31/4> (CA *daraja* 'to walk, go step by step').

drʿ  *dirʿ* pl. *druʿ* 'coat of mail, armour' *Musil*, 53; 'the best kind is called *ad-Dāyūdi* (lit. David's work, i.e. made by Jewish armourers)' *Hess*, 105 <33/24> (CA *dirʿ*).

drm  *mdarram* 'sound, unscathed' <7/7> (CA *darim* 'smooth, well-shaped'). *dirīmah* 'drumming, beating of the feet on the ground' <26/10> (CA *darama* 'to walk with short, quick steps, to hop').

*drhm* *darham* 'to trot', said of a camel, *Musil*, 356, 550 <4/3>. *dirhām* 'camel trot' *Musil*, 85, 550; 'a trot similar to *al-wakhd*, faster than *adh-dhamīl*' *Su* ii, 214 <27/6>.

*drwz* *dirwāzah* pl. *darāwīz* 'big doors, gate' <9/19> (Persian *darvāzah* 'gate').

*dry* *diri, yadri* 'to be aware, to know; to have news of; to discover' *Musil*, 217.

*dsml* *dismāl* pl. *disāmīl* 'headdress, kerchief', a word of Indian origin with the meaning of 'national produce', an inferior kind of cloth, *Fawzān*, 158; 'a red headscarf made of cotton' *Hess*, 129 <6/21>.

*dʿy* *daʿwa* pl. *daʿāwi* 'case, matter, affair' *Glos*; 'dispute' *Musil*, 501 (CA *daʿwā* pl. *daʿāwī* 'claim, demand'). *dʿiyyah* 'important matter; duty, task' <9/17,17/3>. *dʿāh* pl. *dʿa* 'imprecation, curse, malediction' *Hess*, 167 (CA *duʿāʾ ʿala*)

*dġrg* *daġārīġ* (pl.) 'copious' (CA *daġraqa* 'to pour, splash a fluid').

*dġš* *daġaš, yadġaš* 'to attack at dusk' *Hess*, 98. *madġūš* 'brave man, hero' <30/16> (CA *daġasha ʿala* 'to attack'; *tadāġasha* 'to come to blows with one another, join battle').

*dġl* *daġal* 'to cover a she-camel *bi-l-ġaṣb*, by forcing his way into her' <20/5> (CA *daġala* 'to enter a place in a suspicious way').

*dfr* *dafr* 'the thrusting, pushing' *Ḥa* <2/21>.

*dfg* *difag, daffag* 'to pour out' *Musil*, 143, 225; *yadfig as-samin yimnāh* 'his right hand pours out for the guests melted butter (an epithet for a generous man)' *Musil*, 187-188. *madfūg* 'pushed, rushed' <2/6> (CA *dafaqt ad-dābbah* 'I made the beast hasten, go quickly').

*dflj* *daflij* 'to run fast, to zip by; to run at a hurried pace when spurred on by the rider's chiding and chanting' <4/6, 6/22>; *diflāj* 'quick trot' *Musil*, 598.

*dfn* *difan* 'to bury'. *difīn* 'dust and earth clogging a well' *Glos* <16/4>. *mindifin* 'buried, clogged' (CA *dafīn*, said of a well 'partly filled up with earth or dust').

*dgg* *dagg, yidiġġ* 'to hammer, pound (powder, coffee, metal)' *Musil*, 108, 242, 519. *dagg* 'pounding, beating' <23/8> (CA *daqqa* 'to pound, crush'). *digg*, contr. of *jill*, pl. *dgāg* 'camels with gaunt, hollow bellies', i.e. *ḍāmir*, 'with a small posterior and slender legs and necks' <24/3> (CA *daqīq, duqāq* 'slender').

*dgn* — *dēgān* 'a youth overfond of dress' *Musil*, 125; 'high-spirited, brave young man' <21/12>.

*dkk* — *dakk, ydukk* 'to prod, poke, punch; to rouse, stir up s.o.' <13/10>; 'to cause pain, torture, afflict, harass, beset s.o. (worries, disasters etc.)' *Musil*, 108; *Faraj*, 208. *duwāčīć* 'worries, unrest, anguish' *Musil*, 113. *midaćć* 'ramrod' *Hess*, 148; *Glos*.

*dlb* — *dūlāb* pl. *duwālīb* 'millwheel' *Musil*, 273. Here *duwālīb* denotes 'the vicissitudes brought by the turning wheel of time' <12/2> (CA *dūlāb* pl. *dawālīb* 'a kind of water-wheel').

*dlj* — *adlaj, tidlij* 'to journey all night or part of it' <4/22, 6/23,7/5> (CA *adlaja*). *dillij* (pl.) explained as 'camels that walk for great lengths of time without *raġa*, noises of protest; obedient and persevering camels' <24/7>.

*dll* — *dall, ydill* 'to know the way to; to point out the way, to lead s.o. who risks going astray' <2/27,6/32,8/11,26/13>; *dilīl* pl. *duwālīl* 'guide, s.o. who is expert at finding his way through the desert, familiar with the watering places' *Musil*, 509; 'in distant forays they (the nomads) must hire a *dilīl* or land-pilot to ride with them; he is commonly some former exile or guest in that country of which he now will betray the hospitality' *Doughty* i, 271 <8/11>. *darb ad-duwālīl* 'the path of correctness, righteousness' <14/4>; *bi-dalālah* 'with foreknowledge' *Su* ii, 125. *dallāl* pl. *dalālīl* 'middle man who establishes contact between buyer and seller and whose *dalālah*, fee, is 2 1/2 *girš* from each side to the bargain' *Hess*, 147; 'running broker of all that is put to sale in the market' *Doughty* i, 661 <13/19>.

*dlh* — *dalah, lya jīt b-adlah* 'when I want to forget, to be diverted, free from care, not to think of' <24/12>. *tadallah* 'to move in a quiet, unrestricted way, at a leisurely gait' *Musil*, 547. *dālih* 'carefree; lighthearted' <24/13>. *dillih* (pl.) 'empty of mind, forgetful to their surroundings' <24/7> (CA *dalūh* 'a she-camel that does not yearn for her mate or young').

*dlw* — *daluw* pl. *dla, dliyy* 'a leather bucket used to draw water from a well' *Glos*; 'bucket of the bedouins; it is made of sheep skin, about 50 cm. wide and 20 cm. high' *Hess*, 64; *Musil*, 71-72, 322 <6/8,33/43> (CA *dalw* pl. *dilāʾ, dilīy*).

*dmṯ* — *damṯ* 'soft' <4/21> (CA *damt͟h* 'soft, sandy land').

*dmḥ* — *dimaḥ, yadmaḥ* 'to forgive'; *nadmaḥ* 'we disregard (one's lapses)' *Musil*, 608. *indimaḥ* 'to be forgiven, excused' <21/24> (CA *madmūḥ* 'forgiven, erased').

*dm*$^{c}$ — *madma*$^{c}$ pl. *midāmi*$^{c}$ 'place where the tears collect in the sides of the eyes; the inner and the outer angles of the eyes, sides of the eye' <8/4> (CA *madma*$^{c}$ pl. *madāmi*$^{c}$ 'part where the tears run, inner angles of the eye').

*dml* — *dāmil* 'admixing, adding (one colour to another)' <15/8>.

*dmm* — *dimām* 'round like a dome, kubba' <25/11>. *dammām* 'large drum' *Musil*, 85.

*dmy* — *dāmi, dāmyāt* (pl. f.) 'bleeding, covered with blood' <33/48>.

*dndn* — *dandan* 'to tinkle, jingle; to hum a tune' <21/6>. *dindān* 'tinkling sound; a tune, song' <4/1,21/6> (see *dnn*).

*dn*$^{c}$ — *midānī*$^{c}$ (pl.) 'curved, crooked' <6/26>; *dana*$^{c}$*, yadna*$^{c}$ 'to help oneself to s.th. without being invited'; *dinū*$^{c}$ 'one who acts in such manner' *Musil*, 613-614; 'mean person' *Ḥa* (CA *dani*$^{c}$ 'mean, vile').

*dnf* — *midinfāt* (pl. f.) 'emaciated' <24/3> (CA *danif, mudnif* 'extremely gaunt and weak because of disease').

*dng* — *dānūg* pl. *duwānīǵ* 'sailing ship' <6/26> *JuA*, 76.

*dnn* — *dann* 'to make a ringing sound' <23/7>; *dann al-jaras* 'tinkling of (camel's) bells; a bell is hung on the neck of only a valuable she-camel which is inclined to wander afar' *Musil*, 551 (CA *danna, dandana* 'to buzz').

*dny* — *dana, yadni* 'to draw near, to be imminent' <11/22,16/3, 21/15>. *danna* (imp. m. s. *dann*), *adna, istadna* (imp. m. s. *istadin*) 'to bring near, to bring, to lead to; to fetch' *Musil*, 102, 105 <12/1>; *dann li* 'bring, lead to me' *Musil*, 108, 358; *idna b-xēr* 'bring the good things, prosperity' <27/2>; *yidna* 'it is brought' <32/1>. *dāna, ydāni* 'to be near; to come near; to accept, to bear with' <21/29>. *al-adnēn* 'one's close relatives, kin' <21/29>. *danāwah* 'relatives'; *duwāni* 'relatives, fellow-tribesmen' ( = *bini* $^{c}$*amm*) *Musil*, 488 (CA *daniya* 'he was *ibn* $^{c}$*amm*, son of a paternal uncle; closely related').

*dhr* — *mass ad-dahar*, lit. 'hit by fate, misfortune' <12/8>. As in ancient times the concept of *dahar* (CA *dahr*), meaning fate, has some doubtful connotations to the orthodox Islamic ear. *Lane* writes: '*ad-dahr* was applied by the Arabs to Fortune; or fate: and they used to blame and revile it: and as the doing so was virtually blaming and reviling God, since events are really brought to pass by Him, Moḥammad forbade their doing thus.' Although Dindān is a believing Muslim in his fashion, his reference to *dahar* here is indicative of the persistence of this distinctly pagan concept among the bedouin population of the Arabian peninsula.

*dhkl* *dahāčīl* explained as *nidaf* 'soft, sandy ground; the *lhūd*, sandy slopes of an *abrag*' <10/12>.

*dhl* *midhāl* pl. *midāhīl* 'place one keeps returning to, place one frequents (because of one's preference for it); haunt, favourite place frequented by migrating beings (nomads, birds, gazelles etc.); a maze of footprints on the ground, a crisscross of traces' (i.e. an indication that the place is frequented by men or animals) <1/1,3/1,15,10/11,13/18, 23/11,26/25,29/3>; *midhāl al-ᶜarab, aṣ-ṣēd* 'the traces of bedouins, game' *Hess*, 61.

*dhn* *madhūn* 'anointed, smeared, rubbed with' <28/1> (CA *dahana*).

*dwd* *ṣanᶜ dāwūd* 'the product of David', i.e. 'steel, arms made by Jewish armourers' *Musil*, 85 <33/25>.

*dwr* *dār, dawwar* 'to search, look for, seek' *Musil*, 304; *Glos* <9/6,11/16,22/1,29/2>. *dīrah* pl. *dyār* 'territory, region, tribal homeland, tribal range' *Glos* <33/35>. *ad-duwāwīr* 'the tents pitched in circles'.

*dws* *dīsat* 'it was routed, trampled on, thrashed' <2/18>; cf. Turki ibn Ḥmēd's verse, combining the verb's literal and metaphorical meanings: *min la yidūs ar-rāy min gabil ma dīs, ᶜalēh dāsōh al-ᶜyāl al-grūmi* 'who is not quick to thrash out a sound opinion before the others do so (i.e. who rushes headlong into action or wavers), will be trampled on by fiery warriors' *KhaAd*, 361 (CA *dāsa* 'to tread, trample on; to thrash; to inflict utter defeat'). *dāsāt* (pl. f.) i.e. *madyūs* 'thrashed, thrashed out, thought out' <18/13>.

*dwf* *dāf, adūf* 'I mix, admix with water' <31/4> (CA *dāfa* 'to mix, moisten s.th. with water; steep in water').

*dwl* *dwāl* 'a large army, large numbers of armed men' <18/12,13> (cf. CA *dawlah*).

*dwn* — *dīwān* 'a kind of coin' <9/30,21/11>. *dānah* 'a pearl' <28/1> (Persian *dāneh* 'grain, berry, bead').

*dww* — *daww* pl. *diyyān, dwiyyah* 'vast desert; a large, elongated, level plain surrounded by mountains' *Musil*, 289, 366, 475, 500, 677 <4/14> (CA *daww* 'vast, waterless desert').

*dwy* — *dawa, yidwi* 'he runs, hurries, scampers'; *idwāy* 'a scamper' <4/23> (CA *dawwā* 'to travel in the *daww*, waterless desert'). *dwa* 'medicine, remedy' <9/12> (CA *dawāʾ*).

*dyd* — *dēd* pl. *dyūd* 'breast, udder' <33/49>.

*dyg* — *tidāyag* 'to beat down, pour down on' <14/17>.

*dyk* — *dīć* 'a tussock of black wool that stands erect on the place where the *šamāyil* are fastened to the *figār*, the back of the camel' <14/14>.

*dym* — *dayyam* 'to circle, rise to the sky' <20/4> (CA *dawwama, dayyama as̱ẖ-s̱ẖams fī as-samāʾ* 'the sun spun in the middle of the sky'). *dām* 'as long as' <23/15,29/6,30/6,31/11>; *ḥillin dām bāgīha* 'as long as he wishes the period to last' <21/8>. *dāyman* 'always' <1/8,25/10>.

*ḏbb* — *ḏabb* 'to climb' <1/1,2/1,3/1,8/1,10/1,19/1> (cf. CA *d̲h̲abbaba fī as-sayr* 'he exerted himself in journeying, he hastened').

*ḏbḥ* — *ḏibaḥ* 'to slaughter; to kill' <32f,33b>. *ḏabḥ* 'killing, slaughtering' <33e>; also *ḏabḥah* <24/17>. *ḏabbāḥah* 'those who slaughter much' i.e. 'generous entertainers of guests' <6/12,26/24>.

*ḏbl* — *ḏibbil* 'lips, mouth; fine and small teeth; the incisors of the upper row' *Musil*, 114, 561 <19/15>. *ḏābilah* 'a woman with fine teeth' *Musil*, 202. *ḏābil ar-rīǵ* 'a charming beauty, with whom one immediately falls in love so passionately that the saliva of the mouth dries up as if one were in a fever' *Musil*, 153 (CA *d̲h̲abala* 'to whither, lose its moisture; *d̲h̲abl* 'tortoise-shell of which bracelets etc. are made; s.th. resembling ivory').

*ḏrb* — *ḏirib, yaḏrib* 'to speak ill of' *Musil*, 384. *ḏarib* pl. *ḏarbīn*, a word used by Dindān in a positive sense, 'eloquent, clever, smart' (which does not exclude the meaning of 'clever in disparaging the enemy or adversary') <15/12, 25/18,21,26/13>; *ḏarb al-lsān* 'eloquent, strong in argument, entertaining in speech' *SuFa*, 308 (CA *d̲h̲arib* 'sharp'; *lisān d̲h̲arib* or *mad̲h̲rūb* 'a sharp, eloquent, foul tongue'; *qawm d̲h̲arb* 'sharp men').

*ḏrr* *ḏarrah* 'a speck, tiny particle' <3/6>.

*ḏrᶜ* *taḏraᶜ* 'she pushes away (the other camels) with the elbows of her forelegs (CA *d̲h̲araᶜa* 'to stretch forward, extend the arm or foreleg') <2/12>. *miḏrāᶜ* pl. *miḏāriᶜ* 'legs' <6/25, 7/6,27/10>; *ḏirᶜān* <9/21,24/5,29/8> (CA *mid̲h̲rāᶜ* pl. *mad̲h̲āriᶜ* 'the legs of a beast; parts between the knee and the armpit'). *ḏarrāᶜ* 'a tailor' <32/2> (CA *d̲h̲arrāᶜ* 'one who measures with the *d̲h̲irāᶜ*, cubit').

*ḏry* *ḥimm aḏ-ḏra* '(camels with) black humps' <1/8,33/29> (CA *d̲h̲irwah* pl. *d̲h̲urā* 'the upper part of a thing, hump'; *aḥamm* pl. *ḥumm* 'black'). *miḏāri* 'upper part of the cheeks, channel where the tears flow' <33/2> (CA *damᶜ d̲h̲arīy* 'tears pouring forth'). *ḏara* 'shelter, partition which protects the fireplace from the wind' *Musil*, 300; *Glos*.

*ḏᶜḏᶜ* *ḏaᶜḏaᶜ* 'to blow (breeze); to ululate' *Glos* <17/2> (CA *d̲h̲aᶜd̲h̲aᶜa* 'to shake, to agitate', similarly *zaᶜzaᶜa*, said of the wind).

*ḏᶜf* *ḏaᶜaf* 'filth, impurities' (similar in meaning to *ᶜaḏf, Musil*, 113) <1/3> (CA *d̲h̲aᶜf, d̲h̲uᶜāf, ᶜud̲h̲āf* 'poison').

*ḏll* *ḏall, yḏill* 'to fear, to be afraid, fearful of; to flee cowardly' *Musil*, 163 <32a>. *ḏillah, ḏill* 'fear' *Hess*, 171 <29/4, 31/5> (CA *d̲h̲illah* 'baseness, ignominiousness'; *d̲h̲ill, d̲h̲ull* 'submissiveness'). *ḏilīl* 'fearful; miserable; a coward' *Hess*, 169; 'a man who values his health and life above his honour; seeing that during a hostile attack he would have to face superior numbers he fears for his life, *hāb*, and takes to flight' *Musil*, 547 <8/12>. *ḏilūl* 'a riding camel regardless of sex, although the idea of a she-camel predominates (no plural is formed, more than one *ḏilūl* is *rćāb*)' *Musil*, 332.

*ḏnn* *ḏinīn al-ᶜabas* '(the smell, fragrance) of the urine on the camel's tail' <13/12> (CA *d̲h̲anīn* 'mucus of any sort; a thin fluid').

*ḏhb* *ḏahab* 'to perish, disappear' *Glos*. *maḏhūb* pl. *miḏāhīb* 'lost, wandering aimlessly' <12/11>; *maḏhūb* 'cursed one'. *ḏāhibah* 'a stray or lost she-camel'; *miḏhib* 'the man who lost her' *Musil*, 348; also 'a hunter who lost his falcon' *Faraj*, 187. *ḏihīb* 'fleeing, lost herd' *Musil*, 307.

*ḏwb* *ḏīb*, passive of *ḏāb* ‘to melt, to melt away, disappear’ <12/13,27>. *ḏōb* ‘something that has been melted’ <25/22> (CA *d̲h̲awb* ‘what is fluid, liquid; melted honey’). *taḏyīb* ‘melting’ <12/13>. *ḏuwāyib* ‘girl’s hair braids, long plaits of hair on the upper part of the head and above the ears’ *Musil*, 118, 553, 560, 564-565.

*ḏwd* *la tinḏād* ‘she cannot be driven away, prevented from coming to’ <2/12,4/2,18> (CA *d̲h̲āda al-ibl ʿan al-māʾ* ‘he kept back the camels from the water’). *ḏōd* pl. *aḏwād, ḏīdān* ‘a herd of 15-30 camels’ *Hess*, 75, or ‘70-80 animals’ *Musil*, 336 <32b,33g>. *ḏwēd* ‘a small herd owned by a single family’ *Hess*, 75; *Musil*, 262.

*ḏyb* *ḏīb* ‘wolf’ <4/23,5/10,18/12,22/4> (CA *d̲h̲iʾb*).

*ḏyr* *ḏāyir* ‘scared, terrified’ <6/19,7/12> (CA *d̲h̲āʾir*). *mḏayyir* ‘alarming, scaring’ *Musil*, 178.

*ḏyl* *ḏēl* pl. *ḏyūl, aḏyāl* ‘tail’ <7/8,8/6,9/26,19/11,27/12> (CA *d̲h̲ayl*).

*rʾy* *rāy* pl. *ar-rya, ar-rāyāt* ‘opinion, counsel, advice’ <18/20, 24> (CA *raʾy*). *mrāwāh* ‘hesitation’ *Musil*, 501; *Glos*.

*rbb* *rabb* ‘to frequent a place’. *marabb* ‘frequented pasture’ *Glos* (CA *arabba bi-l-makān* ‘he stayed in the place, not quitting it’). *ribīb* ‘one who stays in, cleaves to her tribal homeland’ <13/18>. *ribāb* ‘white cloud drifts seen against the pitch-black of a thundercloud’ (CA *rabāb* ‘clouds suspended beneath other clouds, sometimes white and sometimes black’). Here the word is used in the more general sense of clouds bringing rain <1/5,12/22,13/11>. *rubbān* ‘rain clouds’ <18/3>. *ribābah* ‘one-stringed violin (the string is made of the hair of the horse’s tail and the sound box of sheepskin)’ *Hess*, 143.

*rbd* *rabda* pl. *rubd* ‘female ostrich’ <7/12,8/2> (CA *rabdāʾ* pl. *rubd* ‘black with white and red specks, ashy hue’, said of ostriches).

*rbʿ* *ruwābiʿ* (pl.) ‘thoughts, opinions; pondering, musing’ <6/10>; *yigūl al-mwallaʿ wa-r-ruwābiʿ tdīrih dēr ćima dēr miʿwādin ʿala ma bağa s-sāni* ‘the infatuated poet speaks, driven in circles by his musings like a camel trained to draw water from a well goes back and forth at the driver’s directions’ *JuA*, 151. *mirbāʿ, marbaʿ* pl. *marābīʿ* ‘spring pasture' *Musil*, 78, 273 <6/18,10/12> (CA *mirbāʿ* 'place that produces herbage in the beginning of the *rabīʿ* season'). *ribīʿ* 'spring; fertility, abundance; luxurious growth of the grasses, or annuals' *Musil*, 16, 92, 338, 507 <5/1, 7/13>. *mrabbaʿ* '(a camel) fat of the spring pasture' *Doughty* i, 404; *Musil*, 181 (CA *rabīʿ* 'the spring of Arabia, the season beginning at the autumnal equinox when the rains bring forth the herbage from the earth'). *rbūʿ* 'Wednesday' <13/6> (CA *al-arbaʿāʾ*). *rabiʿ* 'fellow-tribesmen, company of men'; *rabʿi* 'my people' *Musil*, 505.

*rby* *ruwābi* 'drifting sands' <23/3> (CA *rābiyah* pl. *rawābī* 'elevated sands').

*rṯm* *raṯmah* pl. *rṯūm* 'sharp stones and the like that wound the camel's hoof' <7/7> (CA *raṯẖm, raṯẖīm* 'pebbles crushed by the feet of camels; *aḵẖfāf marṯẖūmah* 'camel's feet upon which the stones made marks'). *rṯām* 'nose, snout' <11/12> (CA *mirṯẖam*).

*rjʿ* *rijaʿ, tirjiʿ* 'she (the camel) recovers after exhaustion and loss of weight' <1/7>; 'to return (i.e. herbage after rain)' <30/2> (CA *rajaʿa ilā aṣ-ṣiḥḥah* 'he returned to health'). *rajiʿ* 'rain, the return of herbage and desert plants after rain' *Hess*, 65 <;1,;2,32a> (Koran 86:11 *wa-s-samāʾ ḏẖāt ar-rajʿ* 'by the heaven that hath rain'). *tirjiʿ ad-dār* 'the herbage returns to the tribal territory after rains' <10/6>. *rijīʿ* pl. *rijāyiʿ* 'an abandoned well of which the water has sunk below the surface and which must be dug out anew; a well that has been covered, concealed, and then was dug out anew' *Hess*, 63 <5/3>. *rijjaʿ* 'camels accustomed to turning a flush wheel'; *mirjāʿ* pl. *marājīʿ* 'a *sānyah*, a she-camel trained to draw water for irrigation purposes brought back from pasture, i.e. one with previous experience in the *masna*' *Hess*, 76; *JuA*, 57 <6/7>; also *mirjaʿān* <19/24>; hence: 'lean, emaciated', *darbin l-ahal hijnin smān w-marājiʿ*, *JuA*, 234.

*rjf* *mirjif* 'trembling, quaking, rumbling' <18/2> (CA *rajafa ar-raʿd* 'the thunder rumbled, made a confused noise in the clouds').

*rjl* *marjilah* pl. *marājil* 'manly virtue, chivalry, bravery' <6/11,22/7>; *ṣāḥib al-marjilah* 'gentleman, i.e. courageous, shrewd, experienced, far-sighted and patient'

*Musil*, 52. *rajjāl* pl. *rijājīl* 'manly, courageous man, a man to be depended upon' is stronger than *rajil* 'an ordinary man; not every *rajil* is necessarily *rajjāl*' *Musil*, 385, 472; *Doughty* i, 515 <32d>.

*rjm* — *rijim* pl. *rjūm* 'cairn, peak, heap of stones (made into a shelter or an observation post)' *Glos*; *Musil*, 191, 514; here it has the more general meaning of 'hill, mountain, mountain peak' (like CA *rajmah* pl. *rijām* i.e. 'a mountain of the *haḏbah* type', see under *hḏb*) *JuMu* i, 20-21 <1/1,2/1,5/1, 8/1,10/1,11/1>.

*rjy* — *rija, yarji* 'to hope, wish for' <15/1>. *rāja* 'to long for' *Musil*, 204. *ana b-rijāk* 'I put my hope in you' *Musil*, 217.

*rḥl* — *raḥāyil* 'strong she-camels used for long journeys, female pack camels' *Musil*, 228 <23/6>. *rḥūl* 'she-camels carrying smaller loads, especially the tent and its furniture, on the march' *Musil*, 548; *riḥlah* pl. *rḥal* 'load camels used to move camp' *Glos*. *rḥalah* 'ordinary march, lasting from eight or nine in the morning till two or three in the afternoon'; *rḥalah jayyidah* 'a forced march, from the rising to the setting of the sun' *Musil*, 76 (CA *rāḥilah*; *baᶜīr dhū riḥlah* 'a strong he-camel').

*rḥm* — *la riḥm ubūha* 'may the father (of these words) not be pardoned by God', i.e. a curse <30/4>.

*rḥy* — *rḥiyy* 'the lower end of the column-like swarm of locusts' <25/5> (CA *raḥā* pl. *ruḥīy* 'mill-stone').

*rxrx* — *raxrāx* pl. *raxārīx* 'vast spaces of soft ground; sandy plains' <9/30,26/6> (CA *rakhrākh, arḍ rakhākh* 'vast plain of soft ground').

*rxm* — *raxam* pl. *rxūm* 'vultures which feed only on dead bodies' *Musil*, 633; 'a small white carrion eagle, stiff-feathered, her white wings tipped black and bill yellowish, of which the flesh is forbidden meat' *Doughty* i, 374, 439; 'anyone who behaves in a despicable, abject fashion; coward' <6/9,31/13> (CA *rakham* 'vulture; a bird that eats human dung; a foul bird, not pursued as game, too weak to take prey').

*rxy* — *arxa* 'to loosen; to pour down' *Musil*, 355 <4/16,10/8> (CA *arkhā* 'to slacken, to let loose'; *arkhā dumūᶜan* 'he shed tears').

*rdd* — *radd, yirudd* 'to bring back (to original healthy state)'

<12/13>; 'to drive, turn back' <7/16,14/4,21/25>; 'to recapture and drive back' <32/15>; 'to answer; to mould verses, to say poetry' *Hess*, 143 <31/1>. *yiruddaha* 'he turns his mare (to renew the attack)' *Musil*, 163; *raddaw al-bill* 'they brought the camels or horses from their pasture ground (in preparation for a raid or war)'. *radd* 'yield, profit' *Hess*, 60. *rudd* 'withdrawal, flight' <33/34>. *raddah* 'return (of health), recovering' <14/18>; 'a ruse used in warfare, sudden turnabout by seemingly fleeing cavalrymen, followed by a frontal assault on the enemy' *Hess*, 99. *rdūd* 'turnabouts by galloping horsemen, followed by a charge at the enemy' <33/7>. *radd ᶜašrin* 'a few times ten' <13/7>. *radd* 'returning comrades, men who do not participate in the attack itself' *Musil*, 614 (CA *radda* 'to reverse; to turn or put back'). *mardūd* 'repeated, more than once' <25/2>. *mardūd al-xabar* 'news; news sent back in response to an inquiry' <30/24>. *maradd* 'firmly trodden footpath for the persons hauling up the water bucket' *Musil*, 362.

*rdᶜ* *ridaᶜ, yardaᶜ* 'to hit; to halt, slow down, repress' <17/6>; 'to tip, give s.th. extra' *Glos* (CA *radaᶜa* 'to keep, prevent, restrain, repel').

*rdf* *ridf* pl. *rdūf, ridāyif* 'rump, backside' <4/21,15/8,10>; 'posteriors, buttocks of a woman' <28/3>. *mardūfah* 'a she-camel mounted by two riders, one in the saddle and one behind it' <32d>. *ridīf* 'rear rider, person who sits behind the saddle, holding on to its rear knob' *Musil*, 313; *Glos*; 'a sheikh's backrider, who is also his gunbearer' *Doughty* i, 378. *mrādif* 'sitting on the camel's hips behind the rider' *Musil*, 178. *mirdif* pl. *marādīf* (pl.) '(arranged) in thick layers (e.g. of fat)' <18/2,19/12>; 'richly laden with (stalks of a palm-tree with dates)' <24/5>; *bi-ṣiniyytin yidlag ᶜalēha marādīf* 'on a tray soaked with fat' *Su* iii, 139 (CA *rawādif* 'layers of fat, overlying one another in the hind part of a camel's hump').

*rdm* *yardim ᶜagābih* 'its back towered up' <1/4> (cf. CA *ar-radm* 'that of which one part is put upon another'). *ruwādīm* (pl.) explained to me as 'coming continuously, coming in great numbers'; *al-jahām mardūm* 'the herds of camels which thronged (upon a place)' *Musil*, 80 (cf. CA *wird mur-*

*dim* 'a steady flow of people coming to water'), or *ruwādīm* could mean 'covered with fat' <12/5>; *mardūm* 'covering, covered with' *Musil*, 551.

*rdn* *ardān* 'sleeves'; *saḥḥāb al-ardān* '(a woman) whose long sleeves trail on the ground' <28/4> (CA *rudn* pl. *ardān* 'the base of the sleeve').

*rdy* *ridiyy* pl. *ridyān* 'mean, base, vile, weak; a scamp' *Musil*, 163; *Glos*; the opposite of the bedouin ideal of manliness <9/34,21/17,27>. *ridiyy an-niṣīb* 'ill-starred one, wretch' <30/4> (CA *radīʾ* 'bad, depraved, vile, mean, low, weak'). *ridiyyah* 'a common mare' *Musil*, 501. *rida* 'meanness, baseness, vileness' <21/19>.

*rzg* *marzig al-gōm* = *al-ḥalāl* 'the camels and other livestock of the tribe; means of livelihood' <5/11>.

*rzm* *arzam* 'to groan, grumble; the grumbling sound with which a she-camel calls her calf; the sound made by a camel when the fetters around its knee are untied in the morning' *Hess*, 79 <2/12> (CA *arzamat an-nāqah* 'the she-camel made a grumbling sound, groaned yearningly towards her young').

*rzn* *rizīn* pl. *rzān* 'heavy, heavy and moving slowly; resting solidly on the ground' <1/4,9/31,10/5,19/1> (CA *razīn* 'heavy, steady, motionless', said of a cloud hanging in the sky).

*rsx* *risax, yarsix* 'to be firmly rooted; to stand firm; to be fixed, steadfast' <3/21,30/5> (CA *rasakha* 'to be firm, stable, fast').

*rsm* *rsūm* 'the traces; the green and herbage that sprout up in the wake of rainfall' <23/3,27/6>; 'traces left on s.o.'s face or soul as a result of hardship or grief' *Musil*, 198 (CA *rasm* pl. *rusūm*).

*rsn* *risan* pl. *arsān* 'rein, halter of a camel' *Musil*, 354 <6/19, 24/9,26/5,7,28/2>. *risīn* explained as 'an abundant well' <6/34>.

*rṣx* *ruṣṣix* (pl.) 'firmly planted', similar in meaning to *russix* <6/29> (CA *raṣakha* = *rasakha*).

*rḏf* *marāḏīf* 'heated stones used to roast meat; stones the size of a fist that are heated and used to make clarified butter, *samn*, from *zibd*, cream' <24/13> (CA *raḏf* 'heated stones upon which meat is roasted'; *raḏafa* 'to cauterize with a heated stone; to roast on heated stones').

*rᶜy* — *rāᶜi* 'owner' <11/6>; 'inhabitant of' *Musil*, 298-299; *rāᶜi d̲ilūl* 'a camel rider' *Glos*; *rāᶜ al-ǵuwāriᶜ* 'the "owner" of verses' i.e. 'poet'. *rāᶜi* pl. *riᶜyān, rīᶜān* 'a shepherd who stays all day with the herd on the pasture ground' *Hess*, 62; *Musil*, 336 <26/25,32/3>. *riᶜiy* 'pasture; pasturing' <19/5>. *riᶜiyyah* pl. *raᶜāya* 'herd of camels; flock of 80-200 sheep' *Hess*, 62; 'a herd larger than ten camels' *Musil*, 336 (CA *rāᶜī* pl. *ruᶜāh, ruᶜyān, ruᶜāʾ, riᶜāʾ* 'shepherd, herdsman').

*rġb* — *raġāb* 'scorched land, thirsting for water' <3/12> (CA *raġāb* 'wide, sandy tract of land that takes much water before it flows').

*rfḏ̣* — *rifaḏ̣, yarfuḏ̣* 'to come down, splash down on; to become scattered' <10/9,12/22> (CA *rafaḍa* 'to scatter; to throw, cast'). *rāfiḏ̣* 'coming down' <18/5>.

*rgb* — *rgibah* pl. *rǵāb* 'neck' <1/8,7/7,8/4,9/31,24/6,30/15> (CA *raqabah* pl. *riqāb*). *mirgāb* pl. *marāǵīb* 'a high spot used as a look-out' *Glos* <7/11,14/1>; also *margib* <13/1, 24/1> (CA *marqab* 'an elevated place on which a watchman stations himself'). *marāǵīb* 'well-watched, well-guarded (camels)' <12/8>.

*rgd* — *rigad, yargid* 'to sleep, slumber' <21/1> (CA *raqada* 'to sleep'). *rāǵid, rāǵdah* 'sleeping'. *margid* pl. *marāǵid* 'sleeping place' *Hess*, 60.

*rgᶜ* — *rigaᶜ, yargaᶜ* 'to stitch a piece of tough camel hide under the scarred hoof of a camel' *Musil*, 275; *ma yargiᶜ* 'it does not help (in redressing a situation), does not provide a way out of one's predicament' <21/7>. (CA *raqaᶜa* 'to patch, to repair'). *marāǵīᶜ* (pl.) 'patches; tough camel hide pieces of the size of the hoof that are stitched under the scarred hoof', see *ḥfy* <6/29>.

*rgy* — *riga* 'to climb, ascend' <;3,6/1,13/1,33i> (CA *raqiya*). *marga* 'ascent, climb' <2/2,14/1> (CA *marqā* 'place of ascent').

*rkb* — *rićib, yarkab* 'to ride; to fit', *raćbaw* 'they mounted their horses and rode to meet the enemy' <32e>; 'to be loaded with', *raćbih ḥimiltin* 'he became encumbered with a load, became burdened with problems' <26/27>. *rakkab* 'to fix, fit, install' <16/6>. *rćāb, rikāyib* (pl.) 'riding camels of a tent or individual' *Hess*, 75; 'mounted camels' *Glos*; '*rćāb* is a plural for *d̲ilūl*, if the number is ten or less, a larger number being expressed by the word *jēš*' *Musil*, 332 <9/24,36,26/9,32/13,33/36>. *rkūb, rićb* 'riding on a camel' *Musil*, 515 <23/13>. *rukbi* 'camel on which the shepherd rides' <33i>. *rakkāb* 'rider of a camel' <8/b>. *rakb*, 'a small party of mounted men' <19/18>, dimin. *rkēb Musil*, 367 <33i> (CA *rakiba* 'to ride; to mount').

*rkd* *rikad* 'to pound softly (inside the mortar)' <23/8> (CA *rakada* 'to be stationary, motionless'). *arkād* 'heavy and moving slowly (clouds)' <2/6>.

*rkz* *tarakkaz fīh* 'became fixed therein' <3/2>.

*rkḏ̣* *rikaḏ̣* 'to run, charge, attack, lead an assault' *Glos* <2/17>. *mirkāḏ̣* 'galloping of the attacking horse riders; attack' *Musil*, 105 <2/16>. *rakḏ̣ah* 'the distance of a horse's gallop' <32/12> (CA *rakaḍa* 'to run, strike the ground with hoofs').

*rkn* *rikin* pl. *arkān* 'side (of a valley or watercourse)' <3/13>; 'pillars along the sides of a mosque' <29/1>.

*rky* *rika* 'to lean on, push (with the breast and legs)' <2/11> (CA *rakā*). *irtika, yirtići* 'to lean against, push' *Musil*, 306 <3/17> (CA *irtakā* 'to lean, rely on'). *irka* 'pressing s.th. against s.th.' *Musil*, 145. *mirtići* 'supporting one's side against a pillow when seated' *Musil*, 64. *marćiy* pl. *marāći* 'a sizable body of armed camel riders' i.e. *al-jēš* <9/8>. *mirka* pl. *marāći* 'a tanned, but not grained, piece of leather that is put in a hollow in the sands in order to water the camels or to put food on; it is used on raids or journeys and the bedouins put it on the backs of their camels and ride on it' *Hess*, 120. *marka dlāl* 'the part of the fireplace where the coffee-pots rest' *Musil*, 81, 83.

*rmḥ* *rimaḥ, yarmaḥ* 'to kick' <22/1> (CA *ramaḥa* 'to kick, strike with the hind leg'). *rimḥ* 'long horseman's lance: the beam, made of a light reed of the rivers of Mesopotamia, is nearly two of their short horse-lengths; they charge them above their heads' *Doughty* i, 332, 379.

*rmk* *rmikah* pl. *rimak* 'mature horse' *Glos*; 'a mare in her best age, a mature mare in good condition' *Raswan*, 125 <2/17> (CA *ramakah* 'a mare, particularly one of a mean breed').

*rml* *marāmīl* 'men who have exhausted their supplies' *Musil*, 321 <26/25> (CA *armal, murmil* 'a man whose travelling-provisions have become exhausted and who has become poor').

*rmy* — *rama* 'to shoot at; to throw, cast' <30/3>. *marmiy* 'shot at' <9/25>. *marāmi* 'shooting range' <11/11>. *ramyah* 'a report, shot' *Musil*, 132. *ramiy* 'shooting' *Musil*, 132.

*rnn* — *rannān* 'thundering, reverberating' <3/7>.

*rhj* — *rēhajān* 'holding much water' <19/10> (CA *arhajat as-samāʾ* 'the sky poured with rain').

*rhrf* — *rahārīf* = *ar-ragg, ragrūgah* 'a plain covered with small, crumbled stones' *Musil*, 682 <24/6>; *ragrūgah* 'a plain covered with weather-worn débris'; *rigārīǵ gāʿ* 'plains covered with coarse sand, where mirages may often be observed, mostly at noon' *Musil*, 152.

*rhf* — *marhaf* pl. *marāhīf* 'fine; sharp (teeth); sharpened, pointed' *Musil*, 561 <19/15,26/26>. *mirhifāt* 'sharp, pointed weapons' <31/7,33/18> (CA *murhaf* 'made sharp, pointed, slender'). *rihīf* 'very thin' *Musil*, 92. *bi-tarhīf* 'firmly, *bi-libābah* i.e. expertly, graciously' <24/15>.

*rhm* — *arham* 'to utter a soft, neighing sound' <4/3>.

*rwḥ* — *rawwaḥ* 'to hasten to one's night's lodgings' *Musil*, 151; 'to return in the evening; to reach the place of its night's rest (said of a camel)' *Musil*, 456, 551. *marāḥ* 'departure' <16/9,31/11>. *rēḥān, rāḥān* 'sweet basil or other scented plants thriving especially at the edges of water holes in the channels where rain-water remains for a long while. Before this water reaches the putrid stage it is pure and clear, and during that time the *rēḥānah* grows luxuriantly, its juicy twigs, *ġaḏḏāt al-ġṣūn*, rising and falling with the slightest breeze' *Musil*, 176; *Hess*, 132, 150 <24/16>; *ya-ʿūd rēḥānin* 'O fragrant flower stalk' (in poetic address of a beloved) *Musil*, 564 (CA *rayḥān* 'sweet basil; any sweet-smelling plant').

*rwd* — *rād, yirīd* 'to want, desire' <9/5,32/3> (CA *arāda*). *rād, yirūd* 'to come and go, to frequent a place, visit regularly' <33/10,33/53> (CA *rāda*). *marād* 'place one frequents' <12/24>.

*rws* — *rūs al-miḏāmi* 'the end of the *maḏma*', see *ḏmy*, <11/15> (CA *raʾs* 'the extremity of a thing').

*rwʿ* — *rawwaʿ* 'to frighten, scare, startle, alarm' <11/5> (CA *rawwaʿa*). *irtāʿ, yirtāʿ* 'to be scared, afraid' <32/11>.

*rwy* *riwi* 'to quench one's thirst, to drink, drink from' *Musil*, 145; *Glos*; *irwīk* 'quench your thirst!' *Doughty* i, 444; *yarwa* 'he is well watered, has drunk enough water' *Hess*, 119. *ruwa, yarwi; rawwa* 'to go to, bring water from a well; to water, drench' *Hess* 119; *Glos*; *ruwwēt min al-ᶜidd* 'I brought water from the well' *Hess*, 119. *arwa, yirwi* 'to give plenty of water to drink' *Hess*, 119 <26/26>. *mirwi* 'one who waters, drenches' <18/23>. *rawwāy* pl. *ruwāwi* 'he who brings water, goes to the well to fill the skins with water and returns to the camp' *Hess*, 119; *Musil*, 206 <33/47>. *rāwyah* pl. *rwiyy, ruwāya* 'water-skins made of camel leather, large receptacles made of camel skin used to hold and carry water on a camel's back' *Hess*, 119; *Musil*, 70, 249; *Glos* <33/47>. *riyyah* 'the water that is brought in the skins; the bringing of the water' *Hess*, 119; *Glos*. *rwa* 'the water supply' *Musil*, 206. *mrawa* 'watering place' *Musil*, 359.

*ryd* *rēda* pl. *rīd, ryād* 'vast desert' *Su* ii, 196 <6/27>.

*ryᶜ* *tarāyaᶜ* 'to pause and look around, turn around' <1/12, 2/19,33/8>. *rāyiᶜ* pl. *ryāᶜ* 'returning; making a turnabout' <32/6>. *marāyīᶜ* (pl.) 'returning, turning back' <6/16> (CA *tarayyaᶜa* 'he paused, waited, hesitated'). *rīᶜ* pl. *rīᶜān* 'a narrow, short defile' *Musil*, 682. <5/10,6/19>.

*ryf* *rīf* 'a territory with a good pasturage and abundant crops; in poetry *rīf* signifies a battle ground where a lone wolf finds plenty of food' *Musil*, 618; 'darling' <24/12> (CA *rīf* 'land in which are sown fields; abundance of herbage').

*rym* *rīm* 'white gazelle' *Musil*, 26 <12/21> (CA *riʾm*).

*zbr* *zibar* 'to heap up'. *zabbar* 'to collect in heaps' *Musil*, 94. *zibārah* 'sand-dune, knoll, elevation' *Glos* <15/9>. *mzabbar* 'heaped up, swelling, protruding, bulging' <15/9>; *zibīr* 'in heaps, piled up' <18/9> (CA *zabara* 'to build layer upon layer').

*zjm* *zijīm* 'stammering or humming sound made by camel during travel when the rider calls to him' <5/5> (CA *zajama* 'to mutter under one's breast').

*zḥm* *zḥām* 'mêlée, fighting, jostling' *Glos* <2/21>. *mazḥūm* 'frightened, cornered' *Musil*, 365.

*zrb* *zarb* 'dry, dead wood' <5/4>.

*zrbl* *zirbūl* pl. *zarābīl* 'a low shoe made of rough leather, with a thick sole, a stiff instep, a low and wide heel and clasps for tightening the shoe, worn by herdsmen' *Musil*, 121 <14/14>.

*zrg* *zarag* 'to throw, dart; to pass quickly, slink' *Glos*. *zirīǵ* 'speed, streaking through the air' <4/12>; *zarg rmāḥ* 'the flying of spears through the air; thrust, piercing (of a spear)' <4/18>; *zarg šōf* 'blinking of the eye, wink of an eye' <27/13> (CA *zaraqah* 'he threw at him with a *mizrāq*, javelin, a *rumḥ*, spear'; *zaraqah bi-rumḥ* 'he pierced him with a spear'). *zāriǵ* 'looking with covetous intent at s.th.' <18/16> (CA *zaraqah bi-*$^{c}$*aynih* 'he looked sharply, intently at him'). *azrag* pl. *zurg* 'blue, blue-green, greenish' *Musil*, 21 <27/4>; *zarga* 'a white she-camel with some black hairs that is notorious for its impetuousness, *ṣalf*, and unruliness and for shying at the least thing' *Musil*, 329, 334; *JuSa*, 168. These qualities make a camel unsuited for labour requiring docility and a steady, regular effort.

*z*$^{c}$*j* *za*$^{c}$*aj ṣwāt* 'he howled, screamed, wailed' *Musil*, 209. *zi*$^{c}$*ūj* 'vehement, (a wind) snatching up everything' *Musil*, 608; 'agitated' <33/5> (CA *inza*$^{c}$*aja* 'to be disquieted, disturbed, agitated').

*z*$^{c}$*jl* *zi*$^{c}$*jūl* 'strong animal'.

*z*$^{c}$*z*$^{c}$ *za*$^{c}$*za*$^{c}$ see *ḏa*$^{c}$*ḏa*$^{c}$. *za*$^{c}$*za*$^{c}$ *tizūzā*$^{c}$ 'to move to and fro; to be agitated' <24/5> (CA *za*$^{c}$*za*$^{c}$*a* 'to shake, agitate'; *rīḥ za*$^{c}$*za*$^{c}$, *za*$^{c}$*zā*$^{c}$, *za*$^{c}$*zū*$^{c}$ 'a strong wind'; *za*$^{c}$*za*$^{c}$*a al-ibl* 'to drive the camels vehemently, relentlessly'). *zī*$^{c}$*zā*$^{c}$ 'fast running of a mount spurred on by its rider' *Musil*, 151. *za*$^{c}$*ā*$^{c}$ 'a strong, vehement camel'; *za*$^{c}$*zā*$^{c}$ 'shy, easily frightened animal' *Musil*, 189. *zi*$^{c}$*zū*$^{c}$ pl. *za*$^{c}$*āzī*$^{c}$ 'a little bit, last remains, leftovers' <6/17>.

*z*$^{c}$*m* *za*$^{c}$*am* 'vehemence, powerful surge' <26/7>.

*zġf* *mizġāf* pl. *mizāġīf* i.e. *sābiǵ* 'a horse that outruns other horses' <19/23>; *an-na*$^{c}$*ām al-mizāġīf* 'ostriches fleeing at great speed' *Su* ii, 130 (the fact that this word in both instances occurs at the end of the line demonstrates that poets have recourse to these rare, poetic words mainly for the sake of sustaining the monorhyme) (CA *mizġaf* 'desirous, eager, avid').

*zġn* *zaġin* pl. *zġūn* 'the axillae; armpit' <6/24,9/29>.

*zff* *inzaff* 'to become thin, light' <5/12> (CA *istazaffah* 'he found it light to carry').

*zfg* *zafg* 'whizzing, streaking, flashing by' <27/13>.

*zlb* *azlab* 'to rush, hurry on s.o., chase away' <6/20>.

*zlzl* *zilzāl* 'quaking, shaking of the earth' <1/4,26/6>. *miḥan w-zalāzīl* or *ġarābīl* 'ordeals, hardships, difficulties' <14/7>. *mzalzilāt* 'clouds quaking with thunder' <13/15> (CA *zalzāl* pl. *zalāzīl* 'violent motion, earthquake; trials, troubles, afflictions').

*zlf* *mizālīf* 'slippery slopes, slides' <24/16>.

*zll* *zall* 'to pass; to disappear' *Musil*, 163 <13/6> (CA *zalla* 'to move away, pass'). *zallah* 'lapse, misdeed, offence, sinning' <14/4,21/24,27> (CA *zallah* 'a slip, wrong action, sin'). *zall* 'fine wool with a silky gloss, from which the prayer rugs are woven' *Musil*, 173 <9/26>. *zlāl* 'pure water (of the rain)' <18/7> (CA *zulāl* 'cool, limpid water').

*zlh* *tazlah* explained to me as 'she walks at a strong, eager pace', similar in meaning to *tisijj* <2/13> (CA *zaliha* 'to crave, strive for').

*zlwᶜ* *zalāwīᶜ* (pl.) 'travelling at a rapid pace' <6/15> (CA *zalaᶜa* 'to snatch, to take out').

*zmr* *mizmār, mizmārah* pl. *mizāmīr* 'reed-pipe, small flute made of reed' *Hess*, 139 <9/8>.

*zmlg* *zimlūg* pl. *zimālīǵ* 'flower stalk, bud at the end of a juicy twig' *Su* iii, 97; 'grass seeds, sprouting annuals' *Musil*, 225-226 <27/6>.

*zmy* *zima* 'to loom, to rise up in the distance (camels increase their pace as they try to reach the looming landmarks ahead as quickly as possible)' *Musil*, 155 <6/22>. *yazmi* 'it increases' *Su* ii, 102. *zima* 'elevated, high place' <11/10>. *zāmi* pl. *zuwāmi* 'elevations, hills, prominences' <11/10,25/3>.

*znd* *zanad* pl. *aznād* '(strong) arm' <2/21> (CA *zand* 'each of the two bones of the forearm').

*zhm* *zaham* 'to call s.o. by his name; to invoke s.o.'s help, assistance' <30/14>.

*zhy* *zaha, yazha* 'to be adorned with, to be beautiful, charming on account of' <14/14,25/21,33/30>; *tazha al-miyāriċ manāćibha* 'her shoulder blades are adorned with a cushion' *Musil*, 170 (CA *zahā* 'to make bright, gay, beautiful').

*zwd* *zād* 'to increase, become more, greater' <33/3>; 'to add to' <20/3>; pass. *zīd* 'it became greater' <25/17>; 'it was added to' <30/7>. *zāyid* 'increasing; adding to, giving extra' <6/18,11/6>; 'greater (in pride)' *Musil*, 521. *zōd* '(tribal) arrogance, pride' <18/22>; *zōdin w-nagṣāt* '(deeds of) superiority and shortcoming' *Musil*, 609. *zōdin wara* 'more than' <30/18>. *zād* 'provisions, victuals, supplies, food' <2/24,11/20,13/19>.

*zwr* *zōr* pl. *zīrān, azwār* 'breastbone of the camel; the callous stump that supports the camel's breast when it lies down' <4/19,9/29,24/6>. '*zōr* is the spot in the middle of the lower part of the breast, on which the kneeling camel leans against the ground. When kneeling, the shins of the fore-legs touch the *zōr*. To "remove the *zōr* from the shins of the forelegs" means to induce the camel to rise and start' *Musil*, 152. Doughty describes the function of the *zōr* in relation to the other parts of the body as follows: 'The great brutes fall stiffly, with a sob, upon one or both their knees, and underdoubling the crooked hind legs, they sit ponderously down upon their haunches. Then shuffling forward one and the other fore-knee, with a grating of the harsh gravel under their vast carcass-weight, they settle themselves, and with these pains are at rest; the fore bulk-weight is sustained upon the *zōr*; so they lie still and chew their cud, till the morning sun' *Doughty* ii, 290 (CA *zawr* 'breast of the camel').

*zw*$^c$ *zā*$^c$*, yzū*$^c$ 'to take flight; to lift; to leap up' *Musil*, 157, 225; 'to go forward, to depart, take off' *Musil*, 80, 247; 'to run' *Musil*, 366 <4/19>. *yzū*$^c$ *galbi* 'my heart leaps'. *inzā*$^c$ 'to rush, to storm forward' *JuA*, 57. *zō*$^c$*, zō*$^c$*ah* 'leap, jumping up; hurrying' *Musil*, 151, 225 <23/2> (CA *zā*$^c$*a* 'to drive, urge on a mount'; *zā*$^c$*a an-nāqah* 'he spurred on the she-camel by shaking the ropes of the halter'). *mizāwī*$^c$ (pl.) 'fast, in a hurry, rushing' <6/20>;

*zwf* *zāf* 'to blossom, flower' <30/21>.

*zwl* *zōl* pl. *azwāl* 'the indistinct outline, silhouette, form of a figure (of a man or animal) observed from afar' *Musil*, 189 <4/6,11/11,24/12>; *azwāl rabdan* 'the silhouettes of fleeing ostriches' *Musil*, 154 (CA *zawl* pl. *azwāl* 'a form, a figure one sees from a distance').

*zwy* *zāwi, mzawwi* 'covering, putting on (fat) in layers' *Musil*, 170; 'fat on all sides of the body' <27/3> (CA *zawwā* 'to invest, deck, adorn s.o. with s.th.'). *zuwiyyah* 'curls, tresses' <17/8>.

*zyl* *mzīl* 'crafty; vicious' <8/11> (CA *mizyal* 'clever, ingenious; shifty').

*zyn* *zān* 'to become good, nice, healthy' <3/3,9/7,21/14> (CA *zānah* 'it graced him', contr. of *s̲h̲ānah*). *zayyan* 'to make good, nice' <21/14, 26/28>. *zēn* pl. *zyān, azyān* 'good, fine, well' *Glos* <9/12,33a>. *mazyūn* 'beautiful' <28/3>. *ya-zīnha* 'how beautiful they (pl. f.) are!' <1/10,3/22,6/16,22,7/4,12/26,23/14,24/8>.

*sbb* *tisābīb* 'the causes, roots of things, life' <12/17>. *isābīb* 'life; connections, ties' <21/22>; *d̲āg suww asbābha* 'he tasted the bitterness of defeat, got the worst of it' <30/19>. *ḥbāl al-asbāb* 'the ropes of chance, opportunities for success' *Musil*, 364-365 (CA *tasbīb*, 'making available or preparing the means or cause of attaining something'; *qaṭa$^{c}$a allāh bih as-sabab* 'God cut short his life'). *sibīb* 'hair of the horse's tail, manes; horse' *Musil*, 159, 307 <33/11> (CA *sabīb* 'hair of the forelock, the tail or the mane of a horse').

*sbr* *sibar* 'to reconnoiter'. *sabir* pl. *sbūr* 'a group of 4-10 camel riders who reconnoiter the country ahead of the raiders' *Hess*, 100. *sabrāt an-niḏar* 'guns with long barrels, allowing the marksman to take aim at the target with precision; guns' <2/24,30/15> (CA *sabara* 'to probe, measure, determine by conjecture or by the eye distance or depth').

*sb$^{c}$* *sabi$^{c}$* pl. *sbā$^{c}$* 'animal of prey, such as a lion, wolf' *Musil* 273, 615 <7/2> (CA *sabu$^{c}$* pl. *sibā$^{c}$* 'predatory animal').

*sbg* *sibg* 'unrivalled speed, outstripping all others' <27/13> (CA *sabq*).

*sby* *sibiyyah* pl. *sibāya* 'what brings booty, spoil winners, i.e. horses or fearless cavalrymen, fighters whose task it is to capture the herds of the enemy' *Musil*, 80, 554; *Glos* <33/16>; also 'captured she-camels' *Musil*, 633; *hal as-sibāya* = *hal al-xēl* 'horse riders who throw themselves on the herds and then drive them away as their booty' *Musil*, 545; *ḏʿār as-sibāya* 'one who fills even heroes with fear' *Musil*, 526; *Glos*; *sard as-sibāya* 'group of raiders, plunderers' *Musil*, 147 (CA *saby, sabīy* 'what is made captive, captive').

*sjj* *sajj* 'to run without rest, to keep up a brisk pace over long distances' *KhaAd*, 390 <6/26>.

*sḥr* *saḥar* 'time a little before daybreak' <31/13> (CA *saḥar* 'last part of the night').

*sḥg* *sḥūg* 'pouring rain' <2/5> (CA *saḥīqah* 'violent rain'; *munsaḥiq* 'pouring forth').

*sḥm* *asḥam* pl. *siḥm* 'black, dark brown' (also said of jackals, wolves etc.) *Musil*, 21 <5/7,7/2>; *siḥm aḏ̣-ḏ̣uwāri* 'black animals of prey' *Musil*, 634. *msaḥḥam* explained as 'black with a reddish hue' <7/10>.

*sḥn* *saḥan* 'to crush, pound, grind (medicine etc.)' <9/12> (CA *saḥana* 'to crush, pound; to rub').

*sdd* *sadd* pl. *sdūd* 'what one conceals inside his breast; the secrets of the heart' <5/3,16/1,17/5,33/3>; 'excuses' *Musil*, 203 (CA *sadda* 'to close up; to bar'). *fi sadd liḥyiti* 'by the honour of my beard' *Hess*, 97 (see *lḥy*). *sdād* 'pledgets, tampons' *Hess*, 150. *rāy sidīd* 'wise, good counsel, judgment, opinion' <31/2> (CA *sadīd* 'hitting the mark; right; heading in the right direction').

*sds* *sidas* pl. *sidis, sidsān* 'a camel in its seventh year when it has grown its teeth called *sidāsiyyāt*, an age at which riding camels are at the peak of their strength' *Hess*, 74, 76 <6/15,27/3> (CA *sadas* pl. *sudus*).

*srb* *sarrab* 'to pour water' <8/8> (CA *sarraba al-qirbah* 'to pour water into the water-skin'). *sarāb* 'mirage' <7/15, 20/2> (CA *sarāb* 'semblance of water at midday, making everything appear as if cleaving to the ground', see *lāl*). *msarrib* '(the heat of summer) creating the *sarāb*, the mirage'. *surbah* pl. *sirab* 'horse riders; troop of about 10-30 horse riders' *Musil*, 515; *Hess*, 99 <32/5,33/9> (CA *surbah* pl. *surub* 'a collection of *khayl*, i.e. horses or horsemen, from ten to twenty').

*srbl* *sarbal* 'to run at a calm, steady pace' <23/14>. *sarbalat lil-haḏīl* 'it picked up the pace from a steady gait to a fast trot' <8/9>. *sirbāl* 'a steady pace of a camel' <6/24>;

*msarbil* 'one who pulls (the rope) steadily' *Musil*, 343.

*srj* — *sarj* pl. *srūj* 'saddle of a horse' <33/24> (CA *sarj* pl. *surūj*).

*srjf* — *sirjūf* pl. *sarājīf* 'side of the breast, left side of the breast between the first rib and the shoulder, the soft spot of the side under the ribs' *JuA*, 162; *Musil*, 585 <19/2> (CA *s͟hurs͟hūf* 'the extremity, head of the rib next to the belly').

*srḥ* — *saraḥ* 'to roam; to pasture at pleasure; to set out in the morning' <4/11,16/7,26/11,33/48>; *aṭ-ṭarš as-sāriḥ* 'the herd being driven to the pasture in the morning' *Musil*, 336. *sāriḥ* pl. *sarārīḥ* 'herdsman' *Musil*, 212 (CA *saraḥa* 'to pasture in the morning; to send in the morning to pasture'). *sarḥah* pl. *srāḥ* 'a kind of tree; *Cotoneaster nummularia, Maerua uniflora, M. crassifolia*' <26/11,33i> (CA *sarḥ* pl. *sirāḥ* 'a certain kind of tree, of great size and tall, used for its shade; a tree with spreading branches beneath which men alight in the summer').

*srr* — *sarr* 'to gladden s.o.' <3/9>; *sirrhum* 'gladden them!' <30/24>. *misarrah* 'luck, joy, pleasure' *Musil*, 364 (CA *sarra* 'to gladden, rejoice s.o., make s.o. happy'). *istarr* 'to be delighted, happy at' <10/13>. *mistarr* 'gladdened, happy, joyful' <3/22>.

*sry* — *sara, yasri* 'to travel by night' <33/47>. *sāri* 'one who travels by night'. *siriy* 'flowing' <17/7> (CA *sarīy* 'rivulet, brook'). *saryah* 'journey by night' <33/42> (CA *saryah*). *sarāya, suwāri* 'troopers' *Musil*, 556 <33/38>; *d̲īb as-siriyyah* 'wolf of a picked troop' *Musil*, 289 (CA *sarīyah* pl. *sarāyā* 'a portion of an army; about four hundred horsemen').

*sʿd* — *saʿd, sʿūd* 'happiness, prosperity' <33/41> (CA *saʿd, suʿūd*).

*sfr* — *sifar* 'whiteness of dawn, daybreak' <30/13>; *sifar aṣ-ṣibḥ* 'the first dawn' *Hess*, 169 (CA *safar*). *asfar aṣ-ṣibḥ* 'dawn, the sky pales in the East, but all stars remain visible' *Hess*, 69. *wajhin misfir* 'an open, pleasant face' *Hess*, 169.

*sff* — *sifāyif* (pl.) 'many-coloured camel's hair ribbons, about a metre and a half long by ten centimetres wide, that are tied to the rear cone of the saddle and flutter to the right and left with each movement of the camel on the march' *Musil*, 142, 292, 353, 475 <6/31,9/22> (CA *safīfah* pl. *safāʾif* 'a thing woven').

*sgf* *sigāyif* (pl.) 'broad pieces of wood, planks; ceiling beams' <6/17> (CA *saqāʾif*).

*sgm* *sigim* 'hostility, enmity, state of war' <33f> (CA *saqīm ʿala* 'full of rancour, malice against').

*sgy* *siga, yissi, tassi* for *yisǵi, tasǵi* (in the Dōsiri dialect the *gāf* of *siga* in the imperfect is assimilated to the *sīn*, which is geminated) <3/15,9/27,10/11,12/23,13/12,18/5,19/14, 29/3,33/1> (CA *yasqī*). *yissinnih* 'they (pl. f.) irrigate it' <5/1>. *masga* pl. *misāǵi* 'watering place' <3/20,19/4> (CA *masqā*). *sga* pl. *siǵyān* 'skin in which sour milk is rocked until it turns into butter milk' *Hess*, 115.

*slb* *yaslib al-ʿagil* 'it is enchanting' <12/25> (cf. CA *salabah fuʾādah wa-ʿaqlah* 'he despoiled him of his heart and his reason'). *aslāb* 'clothes' <12/11,30/3>.

*slf* *sālfah* pl. *suwālif* 'story, narrative' <32f>.

*sll* *sall* 'to draw forth, unsheathe'. *slāl, salāyil* 'swords' <22/6>.

*slm* *salm* pl. *slūm* 'customs, manners, established norms' *Glos*; *slūmih* 'the period of its (the season's) rule' <25/4>.

*smḥ* *simāḥ* 'smooth' <17/8>; 'a hard plain, a plain covered with coarse sand (where there are no impediments to the swift movements of the horses)' *Musil*, 517, 558, 683. *samḥāt al-ǵbāl* 'presenting a beautiful sight as they (she-camels) approach' <27/6> (CA *samḥ* 'submissive, easy, gentle', said of a camel).

*smr* *sāmir* 'staying up at night' <18/7> (CA *sāmir* 'holding a conversation at night; waking at night'). *asmar* 'brown, dark' (said of the wings of a falcon) <1/1,15/7>; *sumr al-wḥūš* 'dark-winged birds of prey' <3/1>. *samra* pl. *sumr* 'a dark-coloured she-camel' <20/2>; 'any rusty black berg of hard stone in the desert; and in the great plutonic country from hence (al-Qaṣīm) to Mecca the *sumr* are always basalt; the same, when any bushes grow upon it, is called *ḥazim*' *Doughty* i, 668. *simārah* 'darkness; dark spot' <22/1>. *simār al-lēl* 'the dark of night' <19/22>. *simāri* 'the hoofs, pads of a camel' <6/29,26/10>. *umm al-misāmīr* lit. 'mother of the nails' i.e. a gun.

*smm* *simūm* 'scorching, hot wind' <27/7> (CA *samūm* 'violent and intensely hot wind').

*smn* *samin* 'melted butter' *Musil*, 187; 'this butter is the poor nomads' money, wherewith they may buy themselves clothing and town wares' *Doughty* ii, 306 <25/22>.

*smy* *misma* 'so called, so named' <14/12> (CA *musammā*).

*snd* *sanad, sannad, ysannid* 'to go up, to move to higher ground, to travel in south-westerly direction' (because the Arabian peninsula slopes up in that direction); *sannad*, '"to go up", is used for travelling in a westerly direction, whereas *ḥadar*, "to go down", means that one is going towards the east' *Musil*, 182 and *Hess*, 61 <30/21,33/33> (CA *sanada* 'to ascend'). *sannad* 'to hold back one's mare on meeting a much stronger enemy' *Musil*, 536. *sānid, msannid* pl. *snūd* 'going up, travelling to higher ground'<27/5>. *misnād* 'movement away from the prey or enemy; turning up and away (before attacking again)' <2/16>; 'movement to higher ground, upper part of the valleys (in search of good pasture)' <13/18>; *sinūd* 'the upper parts of a valley' *Musil*, 520, 683. *snād* '(camel) with a big, firm body' <2/8,13/12> (CA *sinād* 'strong, tall in the hump, long in the legs', applied to a she-camel). *snād* 'a definite course' *Musil*, 589.

*sndr* *sawwaw fīhum sanādir ad-dinya* 'they beat the hell out of them' <32f,33k> (CA *sandara* 's.th. done quickly, expeditiously'; *sandarīy* 'quick, bold, strong, vehement').

*snʿ* *sannaʿ* 'to steer in the right direction; to make, do right' <6/1,6>; 'to take care of, manage, fix' *Glos*. *sānaʿ, ysāniʿ* 'to perform s.th. well'. *sanaʿ* '(right) direction; purpose, aim' <21/12>. *ʿala ġēr tasnīʿ* 'clumsily, incompetently, wrongly' <6/8>. *asānīʿ* 'clear, well-trodden roads' <6/23>.

*snf* *snāfi* f. *snāfiyyah* 'a gentle, charming, adroit young person' <;17>.

*snn* *sann, ysinn* 'to pierce, thrust; to sharpen, whet' <30/18> (CA *sannah bi-r-rumḥ* 'he thrust him with the spear'). *sinīnah* 'a sharp sabre' *Musil*, 217. *snān* 'spear-head' <19/23> (CA *sinān*).

*sny* *sana, yasni* 'to draw water from the well'. *sannāy* 'man pulling the rope of the bucket' *Musil*, 339. *sana* 'brilliance, glistening, sparkle' <5/8> (CA *sanā*). *misniy* 'affected by intense drought' <3/12> (cf. CA *sanah* 'drought'). *asna* 'drought-stricken' <18/4>; *sanāwi* 'wadi that did not flow for a long time'. *sāni* pl. *suwāni* 'camel used to draw water from a well for irrigation purposes' <3/19,9/27> (CA *sāniyah* 'a camel upon which water is drawn from a well by a man riding or leading it away from the well, having the two extremities of a long rope tied to the saddle, and the upper end of the well-rope being tied to the middle of the former rope').

*shl* — *shēl* 'Canopus'; the disappearance of Canopus in June signals the beginning of the *gēḍ* 'the hot and dry season, extending over four months to about the first days of October'.

*shy* — *tashi lṯāmih* 'she lowers the veil as if in a moment of forgetfulness' <11/14> (*sahā* 'to be unmindful, inadvertent').

*swg* — *sāg, yisūg* 'to drive; to pay compensation, ransom, dowry (e.g. horses or camels)' <33b>; to pass, hand over, to deliver a gift' *Hess*, 92; *Glos*. *insāg* 'to be driven' *Musil*, 108. *sōg* 'the act of driving on, urging on' <1/7>, also *sāgah Musil*, 367; 'the gift offered as ransom'; *sōg ar-rgibah* 'paying the ransom (lit. of the neck)' *Hess*, 92. *syāg* 'number of she-camels, sheep, or mares given in compensation to the father of the girl whom a man wishes to marry' *Musil*, 139-140, 193; 'the price paid for a mare' *Musil*, 378. *masyūg* 'driven, urged on' <1/11,2/16>. *miswigah* pl. *misāwīǵ* 'stick used to urge on an animal' (CA *sāqa* 'to drive cattle; to send a dowry, s.th. in exchange'). *sāgah* 'rear (of a group of raiders, army)' <8/8> (CA *sāqah* 'the rear of an army', pl. of *sāʾiq*, 'who drives on the army from behind and guards it'). *sūg* 'market, market town' <2/23>; also 'market of death, battle' <2/17>.

*swm* — *sām, yisūm* 'to offer a price, bargain' *Glos*; *Hess*, 147; *sīm* pass. 'it was bargained for' <12/24,28/1>. *sōm* 'being for sale' <27/14>. *misāmah* 'a saddle to which the water bags are tied' *Musil*, 354 <11/5>. *msīm* 'enduring difficulty' *Glos*; *lēlih msīm* '(marching) all night long' <5/12> (CA *sāmah* 'he kept to it').

*swy* — *sawa, yiswa* 'to be worth, equal to' <21/11>. *sawwa* 'to do s.th.; to inflict' <30/14,32f,33k>. *istiwa* 'to be ready; to become fully fledged' <23/2>. *miswi* 'making, creating' <14/13>. *suwan asnān* 'equal in teeth', i.e. 'of one age' <9/21>. *swāt* 'like, as' <21/31,30/20> (CA *sawīy* 'equal, uniform').

*syb* — *sīb* 'a rivulet', similar in meaning to *ġēl*, i.e. 'water running on the surface of the earth in rills' <12/5> (CA *sīb*).

*syḥ* — *sāyiḥ* 'flowing, running' <12/5> (CA *sāʾiḥ*).

*syr* — *sēr* 'march, regular pace' <9/25>. *misyār* 'visit' <29/6>. *sayyar ᶜala* 'to pay a visit' *Glos*.

*syᶜ* — *mistisīᶜ* 'wild, agitated' <5/5> (CA *sāᶜa* 'to be in a state of commotion'; *asyaᶜ* 'exceedingly agitated').

*syᶜb* — *sayᶜab, tsēᶜib* 'she walks with a swinging, arrogant gait, as if to challenge the other camels' <2/14> (perhaps from CA *saᶜaba, musaᶜᶜab lih* 'a liberty permitted to him, a liberty he arrogates').

*syl* — *sāl* 'to flow, stream' <1/3,6/6>. *sayyal* 'to cause to stream, to create a torrent, to indundate' *Musil*, 5 <18/4>. *sēl* 'torrent, the streams that rush through the wadis after heavy rains' <3/12,6/5,10/7,13/15,18/9>. *siyāl* 'acacia-trees; a species of acacia, *Acacia raddiana, tortilis*' <6/14> (CA *sayālah* pl. *sayāl* 'a species of mimosa or acacia; certain trees with white thorns'). *malḥi as-siyāl*: camels like to rub themselves against the bark of the *siyāl*-trees and as a result these trees often present a planed-down appearance <6/14>.

*šʾn* — *mištān* 'out of sorts, upset; feeling bad, angry' <9/36, 21/7> (CA *i<u>sh</u>taʾana*).

*šbb* — *šabb, šabbab* 'to light, kindle (a fire, war)'. *šabbibaw nīrānhum* 'they lit their fires'. *šabb li-l-ḥarb nārih* 'he started a war'. *šbūb* 'the kindling of a fire' <6/2>; *šbūb al-ḥarb* 'those who unleash, start a war' <22/7>; *šbūb al-lāl* 'the simmering of the mirage' <6/17> (CA *<u>sh</u>abba* inf. n. *<u>sh</u>ubūb* 'to kindle'; *<u>sh</u>abba al-ḥarb* 'to kindle war').

*šbḥ* — *šibaḥni* 'he looked at me intently' <17/10>. *šabḥih ṭifūḥ* 'his gaze skips over; he does not look at, disregards.'

*šbr* — *šibir* pl. *šbūr, ašbār* 'span between the thumb and the little finger' *Hess*, 123 <4/19,31/7>. *ṭwāl aš-šbūr* 'those whose reach is long, far' (lit. 'those whose span reaches far') <26/21> (CA *<u>sh</u>ibr*). *šibriyyah* 'short and narrow dagger' *Musil*, 133.

*šbk* — *šibak, yašbuk* 'to grasp at, intertwine with, join' <25/12>. *šabkah* 'mêlée, scuffle' *Glos* (CA *<u>sh</u>abaka* 'to insert, intertwine'). *ištibak* 'to become intertwined, mingled' <30/16>.

*šby* *šiba* 'point of a sword or spear' <26/26> (CA *s̲h̲abāh* 'the point of the extremity of anything').

*štt* *šattān* 'dissolved, separated, disunited' <29/7> (CA *s̲h̲attān*).

*štr* *ad̲-d̲yūl aš-šitr* 'short tails without much hair' <7/8>; *id̲ān šitr* 'prick-eared' *Su* i, 127 (CA *as̲h̲tar* 'slit, crooked', said of an eyelid or lip).

*šty* *šatta* 'to graze in the winter' *Musil*, 78. *aš-šta* 'winter; forty nights' rule of the star Sirius, from December to about 20 February' *Musil*, 8 <25/4>. *šitwi* 'rain of that period' *Musil*, 8 (CA *s̲h̲itāʾ*). *mašta* pl. *mišāti* 'winter pasture' *Musil*, 77. *mišti* pl. *mišāti* 'a she-camel that gives birth at the beginning of the winter' *Hess*, 77.

*šḥḥ* *šaḥḥ* 'to be niggardly, greedily desirous' <28/7> (CA *s̲h̲aḥḥa*). *šaḥḥ bi-* 'to spare one's life' *Glos*. *šāḥḥ* pl. *šāḥḥīn*, and *šiḥīḥ* pl. *šḥāḥ* 'sparing, niggardly, parsimonious with, clinging jealously to s.th.' <31/9>; *ašḥāḥ* 'misers' *Musil*, 482.

*šḥm* *šaḥam* 'unmolten fat' *Musil*, 97; *Hess*, 115 <6/17,19/12>. *mašḥūm* pl. *mišāḥīm* 'fattened' <12/27>.

*šḥn* *ištaḥan* 'to be depressed, gloomy, angry' < ;5 >. *šaḥḥan* 'to threaten s.o.'. *šaḥnah* 'fear'; *minšiḥin* 'anxious, fearful' *Musil*, 421 (CA *s̲h̲aḥana* 'to bear rancour, malice, spite against').

*šxtr* *šixtūr* pl. *šaxātīr* 'water that comes down continuously, in streams; rain or other fluid coming or cascading down in a continuous flow, stream' <14/12,32/4>. *ḥijrin dmūʿih šaxātīr* 'an eye shedding tears in streams' *JuA*, 226.

*šxṣ* *yašxaṣin* '(the eyes) become frozen in a stair' <10/4> (CA *s̲h̲axaṣa* 'to become fixedly open', said of eyes). *mišxaṣ* pl. *mišāxīṣ* 'a coin made of gold' *JuA*, 160 <20/3> (CA *mas̲h̲k̲h̲aṣ* pl. *mas̲h̲āk̲h̲iṣ* 'dinars, pieces of gold').

*šxl* *šaxal, yašxal* 'to sieve through a piece of cloth, e.g. a piece of an old mantle' *Hess*, 121 <18/8>. *šixlūl* pl. *šaxālīl* 'water pouring forth in floods, cascading down' *Musil*, 322 (CA *s̲h̲ak̲h̲ala* 'to purify, sieve').

*šdd* *šadd, yšidd* 'to saddle; to move the camp' *Glos*; 'to load the tent and other luggage on the camels in order to start a journey; to wander, roam' *Hess*, 59. *šadd* 'saddling' *Musil*, 292. *šdād* pl. *išiddah* 'saddle' *Glos* <25/10>. *šidd, šaddah* pl. *šdūd* 'day's march; the distance covered in a day's march by a caravan, i.e. 30-40 kilometers' <33/35>.

*šdy* *yašda, yšādi, yšād* 'he resembles, he is like' *Musil*, 177, 482 and *Glos* <6/17,23,25,26,8/6,7,9/19,24/7,9,26/8,32/2, 33/5> (CA *shadā* 'to assimilate, liken to').

*šḏb* *mašḏūb* 'peeled off, pruned, stripped of its bark' <7/7> (CA *shadhaba*).

*šrb* *širib, yašrab* 'to drink'. *širīb* 'one who drinks from a well, camps near a well with others' <22/9>. *mašrab* pl. *mišārib* 'place of watering' <2/27,33/55> (CA *sharīb* 'one who drinks with another'; *mashrab* 'place of drinking').

*šrd* *šarad, yašrid* 'to run away, flee, escape' *Musil*, 115. *širīdah* pl. *šarāyid* 'remains; remnants, survivors (of a battle, calamity etc.)' <3/13,18/10> (CA *sharīdah* pl. *sharāʾid* 'a remainder of anything'). *šurrid ar-rīm* 'fleeing gazelles' <12/21>.

*šrr* *minšarr* 'spread out, covering' <3/8> (CA *sharrah* 'he spread it').

*šrᶜ* *šarraᶜ, yšarriᶜ* 'to water animals'; *arwēt al-bill w-šarraᶜat fi l-mašraᶜah* 'I brought the camels to the water and they drank from the watering place' *Hess*, 63. *šāriᶜ* pl. *širrāᶜ* 'entering into, bending to water to drink; drinking' *Musil*, 204; 'attacking' <32/10>. *mašraᶜ* pl. *mišāriᶜ* places with abundant and good water, where, besides watering the herds, the women also get all the water needed in the camp' *Musil*, 565 <33/25> (CA *shāriᶜ* 'entering water, lowering one's head in order to drink'; *mashraᶜ*). *šarᶜah* 'law, source of authority; favourite, maiden of the lover's choice' <11/19,13/18>.

*šrf* *šarraf* 'to climb to a summit, ascend a mountain; look out from a high place' <18/1,23/1,27/1>. *mašraf, mišrāf* pl. *mišārīf* 'elevation, a high vantage point, summit' *Musil*, 227 <19/1,24/1>. *šrifah* 'a high place' *Glos* (CA *ashrafa* 'to be high; to look upon, view from above'; *mashraf* 'a place from which one overlooks').

*šrh* *šarh* 'one who feels slightly offended, entertains an ambition or hope' *Glos* <19/24>. *tišrah ᶜala* 'she begins to yearn for' *Musil*, 548. *rāᶜ al-jaḥaš šarhin ᶜala jadᶜ xayyāl* 'the rider of a donkey who entertains the ambition of throwing a horseman from the saddle' *Su* ii, 87. *ᶜalēh šarhah* 'he was depended on'; *kunt mašrūhin ᶜalēh* 'I depended on him' *Musil*, 552.

*šṭr* — *šuṭrah, šiṭīr, šiṭīrah* '(a weapon) with a sharp point or blade; sharp, cutting; a sword' <32/9>; *sēfin šiṭīr* 'a sabre with a cutting edge' *Musil*, 360.

*šṭṭ* — *šaṭṭ* 'hump' <15/10> (CA *shaṭṭ* 'the side of a camel's hump').

*šᶜb* — *šiᶜīb* pl. *šiᶜbān* 'a main valley or watercourse of an intermittent stream' *Musil*, 683 <7/3> (CA *shiᶜb* pl. *shiᶜāb* 'watercourse').

*šᶜf* — *šaᶜaf* pl. *šᶜūf* 'the upper part of the hump' <12/10> (CA *shaᶜaf* 'the upper or uppermost part of the hump of the camel'). *mišᶜāf* pl. *mišāᶜīf* 'a camel with long thick hair on the hump' *Musil*, 548 <19/11>. *šaᶜfah* 'an elevation not necessarily high, but prominent' *Musil*, 682.

*šᶜl* — *išᶜāl* 'a blazing fire' <6/2>; *šaᶜāl* 'glitter, sparkling light' <18/6,21,20/3> (CA *shaᶜala* 'to burn brightly'; *ashᶜala an-nār* 'he made the fire burn fiercely'). *mišᶜal* pl. *mišāᶜīl* 'torch, used by the bedouins to follow the traces of the robbers at night; it consists of a kettle filled with firewood carried by two men holding the chains fastened to the kettle's handles while the fire is kept burning by a third man who picks up dead wood on the way' *Hess*, 102 <2/5,14/17> (CA *mashᶜal*).

*šᶜml* — *tišᶜimāl* 'shine, glitter, lustre; glistening, pulsating light' <1/11,20/3> (cf. CA *ishtaᶜala*); *an-nūr ytišaᶜmal* 'a bright, pulsating light'.

*šff* — *šaff* 'wish, desire' <18/1,23/15>; *šaffi* 'my wish, desire is for' <9/1,20/6,33/39>. *bi-š-šaff* 'as one may like or fancy'; *b-šaffi* 'it looks good to me' *Musil*, 166, 387.

*šfg* — *šifag, yašfig ᶜala* 'to be anxious, worried about' <21/13>. *tišaffag* 'to be anxious, keen' *Glos*. *šafgān* 'being in a state of anxiety; keen, desirous, anxious' (CA *mushfiq ᶜalā* 'fearful, cautious on account of'). *mašfūg* 'anxious and desirous (here it means that the captured camels are longing to return to their rightful owners while they are driven away by the enemy)' <2/19>. *bi-l-ašfāg* 'what is liked best' *Musil*, 109. *šifūg* 'kind, tender mother' *Musil*, 192. *šifag* 'the paling sky, following the *ṣufrah*, the red glow in the western sky after sunset' *Hess*, 70 <26/8> (CA *s̲h̲afaq* 'mixture of the light of day with the blackness of night at sunset').

*šfy* — *šifa* 'a little; a beginning of' <9/3>; *šifāti* 'my healing, desire' *Musil*, 318 (CA *s̲h̲afā* 'extremity, edge; a little, somewhat'). *šifah* pl. *šifāya* 'lip' <24/15> (CA *s̲h̲afah* 'lip'). *šifa* 'a flat top of a long ridge, upland' *Musil*, 113, 151, 683; 'high desert, steppe' <26/8,32/4>.

*šgḥ* — *ašgaḥ* 'fair, white tinged with rose'. *šugḥ al-banāt* 'fair maidens' <15/6>. *šagḥa* pl. *šigḥ* 'a white she-camel with a shade of pink colour' *Musil*, 334; *šugh al-bkār* 'young she-camels of that hue' <33/30> (CA *as̲h̲qaḥ* 'what is not of a pure white hue').

*šgr* — *ašgar* pl. *šugr* 'fair, reddish, reddish brown' *Musil*, 31 <29/8>. *šagra* 'a gold sorrel horse; mare of a chestnut colour' *Raswan*, 127; 'light yellow mare' *Musil*, 373; 'fawn she-camel' *IngCa*, 73 <33b,33/16,39>.

*šgg* — *šagg, šaggag, yšaǵǵiǵ* 'to cleave, cut, split; to tear, shred, rend' <1/6,13/4,29/5,33/21>; 'to erupt, break through' <9/24> (CA *s̲h̲aqqaqa* 'to cut s.th. lengthwise; to rend, rip, slash').

*šgy* — *šigiyy* 'miserable, suffering the torments of love, pained, distressed' <17/5> (CA *s̲h̲aqīy* 'unfortunate, unhappy, miserable').

*škl* — *mišāčīl* 'men of importance, enjoying prestige, having great self-esteem and high aspirations' *Glos*. *ahl aš-šikālah* 'men carrying themselves with a decorous, dignified air' <18/25> (CA *s̲h̲ākilah* 'a particular way of conduct').

*šlf* — *šalfa* pl. *šilf* 'broad blade of a spear' *Musil*, 133 <33/26>.

*šlg* — *yašlig al-ma* 'he (lifts the bucket that has been hoisted from the well and) splashes the water (in the trough)' (CA *s̲h̲alaqa* 'to beat'). *mašlūg* 'splashed; split, rent' <2/12>.

*šll* — *šall* 'to take, carry; to take away; to snatch' *Glos*; 'to drive' *Musil*, 5; 'to take far away' *Musil*, 205 <8/5,22/6>. *šallah* 'far journey' *Musil*, 205 (CA *s̲h̲alla* 'to urge on, drive'). *šilīl* pl. *šalāyil* 'a pace of camels or horses' <8/5>; *ya-l-hijin šillan bina šallah* 'camels, take us on a fast ride' *SuFa*, 494; *wallah ʿala markab sibūg aš-šalāyil* 'I wish for a riding camel that travels at a fast pace' (CA *s̲h̲ullah* 'the place one aims to journey to'). *šilīl* 'hem (of a mantle)' *Musil*, 360; 'horse's tail and the hairs of the tail' *Musil*, 513, 554.

*šly* *šāla, yšāli* ‘to suit s.o., to be of avail to s.o., conducive to one’s health or mental state’ <26/1>. *ašla* = *afḍal* ‘better, more suitable’ <20/6>. *mitšāli* ‘feeling, doing fine; being in good spirits and health’ <29/3> (CA *ishtalā* ‘to save from harm’).

*šmx* *šimmax an-nīb* ‘(camels) with long eye-teeth; camels’ <30/20> (CA *shāmikh* ‘high, lofty’).

*šmšl* *šimāšīl* = *hamālīl* ‘(local) rains’ <13/5>. *šimšūl* ‘a few, some’; *šimšūl ḏōd* ‘a small herd of 15-20 camels’ *Hess*, 62 (CA *waqaʿa fī al-arḍ shamalun min maṭarin* ‘a little rain fell on the earth’).

*šml* *ašmal* ‘to travel north’ <29/7> (CA *ashmala* ‘to go into the direction of the wind blowing from the north’). *šimlūl* ‘a herd of 8-10 camels’; *šimlūl ḏōd* ‘a small herd’ *JuA*, 164. *šimālīl*, synonym of *šimāšīl*, ‘twigs growing luxuriantly in the top of the palm-tree from which, later on, bunches of dates will hang’ *Musil*, 322; here the meaning is ‘date bunches’ <8/6,9/26> (CA *shamālīl* ‘shoots that divaricate at the heads of the branches, like the fruitstalks of the raceme of the palm-tree’). *mišāmīl* ‘camels with a *šamlah, šmālah* pl. *šimāyil*, a bag-netting, a thick net made of camel wool, placed on the udders and tied across the hip and under the tail’ *Musil*, 88; *Hess*, 78; *Doughty* i, 370 <10/11, 14/12> (CA *shamlah* ‘waist-wrapper’).

*šmm* *šmām* ‘instantly, forthwith’ <25/4>; *min šmām* ‘just, very recently’.

*šnb* *šanab* pl. *ašnāb* ‘moustache; teeth (of a carnivorous animal)’ <30/14> (CA *shanab* ‘sharpness of the canine teeth’).

*šng* *šanag* pl. *ašnāg* ‘side; direction’; here the ‘wings’ of the ostrich are meant <11/9,10>. *šanag* ‘one half of a slaughtered animal cut lengthwise’.

*šnn* *šannah* pl. *šnūn* ‘dry, old water-skin; piece of an old, thoroughly dried hide’ *Musil*, 142; *Glos* <8/8,33/5> (CA *shannah* ‘a skin, an old and worn out water-skin’).

*šhb* *ašhab* pl. *šihb* ‘of a grey, dusty colour, grey with a tinge of blue’ *Musil*, 21 <5/2,14/16,30/16>; *ašhab aḍ-ḍahr* ‘camel with a bald or grey back’, i.e. ‘a pack camel’ *Musil*, 510; *ašhab al-wāwi* ‘the grey wailer’, i.e. ‘a wolf’ *Musil*, 163; *ašhab al-milḥ* ‘dark-grey salt’, i.e. ‘gunpowder’ *Musil*, 632;

*ašhab al-lāl* 'the grey quivering air on a hot day' *Musil*, 147-148 (CA *ashhab*). *mišhāb* pl. *al-mišāhīb* 'kindling, a dry, long piece of wood that is kindled in one fire in order to light another or to be used as a torch' *Hess*, 123 <7/10,12/12,30/17>.

*šhr* — *šahar, yašhar* 'to be vociferous, to trumpet, to announce in a loud voice' <21/27,23/8>. *bi-tašhīr* 'in a loud voice, noisily' (CA *shahara* 'to make apparent, commonly known; to divulge, render notorious'). *mištahar* 'loud, audible to all, announcing at the top of one's voice' <30/26>.

*šhg* — *šihgūg* 'a lofty mountain' <1/1>; *šāhig* pl. *šhūg, šihǵān, šawāhiǵ* 'high, steep mountains; the highest summit of a range' *Musil*, 224, 365, 682 (CA *shahaqa*).

*šhl* — *šihlūl* pl. *šahālīl* 'sweet, limpid (water)' <31/4> (CA *shuhlah* 'a blue or greenish hue').

*šwb* — *šōb* 'what is mixed with s.th. else', i.e. 'gunpowder' <30/16> (CA *shawb*).

*šwr* — *šārah* 'a striking appearance, outstanding beauty' <15/6> (CA *fulān ḥasan ash-shārah* 'such a one is good, beautiful in appearance'). *šōr* 'decision reached in the *majlis*, the tribal assembly, concerning the course the tribe is going to follow; forecast of the next journeys of the tribe, whereof a kind of running advice remains in the mind of the tribesmen' *Doughty* i, 290; 'good advice' *Musil*, 482.

*šwf* — *šāf, yišūf* 'to see'. *šūftin* '(a thing) clearly visible' <11/15>.

*šwg* — *šōg* 'longing, desire; a coveted thing of which one is worthy' <2/25>; 'sweetheart; husband' *Musil*, 561.

*šwl* — *šōl* has the same meaning as *bill*, 'camels collectively', *Musil*, 141, 344 <1/8>; *šuwāyil* (pl.) 'good milch camels' *Su* iii, 141 (in CA *shāʾil* pl. *shuwwal* means 'she-camels raising their tails to the stallion as a sign that they have conceived'; and *shawl, shawāʾil* 'she-camels whose milk has dried up', whereas the vernacular *šōl* has the connotation of 'rich in milk').

*šwm* — *šāmi* pl. *šuwāmi* 'made in Syria (e.g. paper, swords, coffee-pots)' *Musil*, 81, 112 <18/18>; 'Syrian' <25/11>.

*šwy* — *šawa* 'to grill, to roast, to broil' <13/19> (CA *shawā*). *šwa, šwiyyah* 'entrails, intestines' *Musil*, 613. *šuwiyy* 'roasted, broiled, fried' <17/4> (CA *shawīy*).

*šyb* — *šīb, šiyyāb* (pl.) 'grey' <1/9,12/10,13/12>. *šāyib* pl. *šībān* 'grey beard, old man' <15/1>. *šīb al-ġawārib* 'camels with grey or white hair; from continuous sweating the hair covered by the cushion on which the rider rests his feet becomes white' *Musil*, 308.

*šyx* *šēx* pl. *šīxān* 'chief, head of a tribe' <33c>.

*šy*$^{c}$ *šāya*$^{c}$ 'to call a herd of camels with a short drawling song' *Musil*, 379; *mašyā*$^{c}$ 'the ditty sung by the herdsman to keep the returning herd of camels together' *Musil*, 337; *mšāyi*$^{c}$ 'one who calls to his animals in a singing voice' *Musil*, 347. *šī*$^{c}$ 'good reputation, fame' <6/13>; *tašyī*$^{c}$ *ṭībih* 'spreading the reputation of his goodness' *Musil*, 366 (CA *s͟hay*$^{c}$ 's.th. that becomes spread, known to all').

*šym* *šāmah* pl. *šāmāt* 'beauty spot' <25/15>; 'hills of different colours; dark undulating country covered in some places with rose-tinged sand' *Musil*, 683 (CA *s͟hāmah* 'a mole'). *šīmat ḥamulah* '(she is) the boast of her kin' *Musil*, 192.

*šyn* *šān* 'to become, be bad, ugly, in a bad condition' <9/2, 11/20,21/14,26/28>. *šēn* 'ugly, bad' contr. of *zēn* 'good, beautiful' (CA *s͟hayn* and *zayn*). *ya-šēn* 'O rascal!', an expression used in jest even with a person dear to one, *Musil*, 300, 615.

*šyy* *šin* = *šayyin* 'anything, something' <9/13>.

*ṣbb* *ṣabb, yṣubb* 'to pour, pour forth' *Musil*, 106; *Glos* <19/8, 25/11>. *ṣibīb* 'pouring, splashing' <2/12>. *ṣubb, mṣabbab* 'what is poured' i.e. 'lead, bullets' <30/5,31/4>; *mṣabbab ad-darj* 'the ammunition, bullets in the magazine of the rifle'.

*ṣbḥ* *ṣabbaḥ* 'to attack at sunrise (when the left forelegs of the resting camels of the enemy's camp are unfettered)' *Musil*, 523 <30/13>.

*ṣbr* *ṣibir* pl. *aṣbār* 'the rim of a copper mortar in which coffee beans are pounded' <23/8> (CA *ṣubr, ṣibr* pl. *aṣbār* 'the sides of a vessel').

*ṣby* *ṣibiyy* pl. *ṣibyān* 'youth, lad' <16/8,30/24> (CA *ṣabīy* 'a youth').

*ṣḥṣḥ* *ṣiḥṣāḥ* 'sandy, flat plain shut in by rocky ridges'; also *ṣaḥṣaḥ* 'a plain shut in by low but steep bluffs' *Musil*, 683 <4/22>. (CA *ṣaḥṣaḥ, ṣaḥṣāḥ* 'barren plain strewn with small pebbles, smooth tract of land').

*ṣxf* *miṣāxif* 'tender parts' (CA *sak̲h̲īf* 'thin in texture').

*ṣdr* *ṣidar* 'to move away from the well, watering place' <30/19>. *ṣaddar* 'to hoist the bucket by moving away from the well while pulling the rope'. *ṣidir, ṣidīr* 'camels just turning back from water' *Glos* <13/17>. *ṣdūr wrūd* 'those coming from the watering place, those heading towards it; coming and going' <33/50>. *hi mṣaddrah* 'she is driving the herd away from the watering place towards the pastures' <33g>.

*ṣdm* *ṣaddām* 'bumper of a car' <16/11>.

*ṣrr* *ṣarrah* 'clamour, din, confused cries' <3/19> (CA *ṣarrah* 'vociferation, vehemence of grief or anxiety').

*ṣr*$^{c}$ *miṣrā*$^{c}$ pl. *miṣārī*$^{c}$ 'reins' <32/1>; in <6/21> *miṣārī*$^{c}$ apparently means '(the two halves of) the saddle'.

*ṣrf* *ṣirīf* 'grating, creaking noise (e.g. of the wooden saddle)' <26/9> (CA *ṣarīf* 'creaking, grating').

*ṣrm* *ṣaram* 'to cut off, harvest (dates)' <24/16>. *ṣarām* 'harvesting, cutting off (the fruit, bunches of dates)' <11/22, 18/11>. *miṣārīm* (pl.) 'cut off' <12/6> (cf. CA *ṣarama* 'to cut, cut off the fruit of the palm-trees'; *maṣrūm* 'cut off, having the fruit cut off'). *ṣarāyim* (pl.) 'the *xṭām*, noseband or halter of a camel' <6/21,7/5,9/28>.

*ṣ*$^{c}$*fg* *ṣi*$^{c}$*fūg* 'the crest of a spur of sand ($^{c}$*irǵ*)' <1/6>.

*ṣ*$^{c}$*g* *ṣa*$^{c}$*ag* 'to strike, hit, destroy; to stun' <11/4>. *ṣā*$^{c}$*ūg* 'summit, pinnacle' (perhaps the association is with thunderbolts striking the peak, cf. CA *ṣa*$^{c}$*aqa*) <2/2>.

*ṣġy* *ṣāġa, yṣāġi* 'to obey, listen to' <32/1> (CA *aṣġat an-nāqah* 'the she-camel inclined her head towards').

*ṣfr* *ṣfiri* pl. *ṣifāri* 'autumn'; *ṣfiri*, one of the five seasons known to the bedouins, 'ninety nights from the beginning of October to the beginning of January; autumnal rains' *Musil*, 8 <5/5>. *ḥill aṣ-ṣifāri* 'in the days of autumn' <14/20>. *miṣfār* 'autumnal camping grounds' *Musil*, 632. *maṣfar* 'autumn pasture' *Musil*, 78 (CA *ṣafarīy* 'the period of the auroral rising of Canopus; autumnal season when the fruit of the palm-tree is cut off'). *ṣufrat aṣ-ṣibḥ* '4-6 o'clock in the morning' *Hess*, 69. *aṣ-ṣufrah* 'dusk, red twilight after sunset when Venus becomes visible' *Hess*, 70. *aṣ-ṣufritēn* '(time of rest) before sunrise and after sunset' *Musil*, 368. *miṣāfīr* (pl.) 'travelling at the time of *aṣ-ṣufrah*'; the bedouins use it with the meaning 'the latter third of the night'

<26/12>. *mṣaffir* 'one who goes to sleep again after the dawn prayer until the time work starts'; *ṣaffarna* 'we slept at sunrise' *Musil*, 413. *ṣafra* 'a pure white mare without any other colour or shade, preferred by bedouins' *Musil*, 251, 373 <32/1,2,3,4> (CA *aṣfar* fem. *ṣafrāʾ* 'yellow'). *ṣifārah* 'white colour' <15/8>.

*ṣff* — *ṣaff* 'to run in a row' <6/31>; 'to draw s.th. close together' *Musil*, 61. *ṣifīf* 'a row; camels running side by side' <8/a,26/9>.

*ṣfg* — *ṣifag, yaṣfiǵ* 'to strike, slap, hit' *Musil*, 204; *Glos* <2/1, 10/7>; 'to push in the wrong direction'. *taṣfiǵ brūgih* 'its lightning flashes' <1/4>; *yaṣfig as-simm* 'dripping with poison, poison flashing between its jaws' <30/7>. *tiṣṭifiǵ* 'she flaps, flutters' <11/9>. *ṣaffag* 'to stamp noisily' *Musil*, 200-201. *tiṣāfag* 'to bump into one another, jostle for space' <3/18> (CA *ṣafaqa* 'to strike, slap; to beat with an audible noise', said of a bird's wings or the wind). *ṣafǵ* = *ṣalf* 'a strong, sudden gust of wind' *Musil*, 561 (CA *ṣafq*). *maṣfūg* '(as if) hit, slapped' <1/13>. *iṣṭifāg* 'clashing' *Musil*, 293.

*ṣfy* — *ṣifāh* 'rocks, boulders; slabs of stone, ground rock, flat rock' *Musil*, 271 <5/4,27/9> (CA *ṣafā* 'smooth stones').

*ṣgr* — *aṣgar* 'more clever, intelligent, sly' <8/11>.

*ṣgᶜ* — *ṣigaᶜ* 'to hit, strike' <23/8>. *ṣugᶜ al-hḏāb, mahāḏīb* 'the smooth peaks of conical granite or basalt mountains' <12/21,27/9>. *ṣugᶜ al-ḥzūm* 'the tops of stony hills' <8/9>. *aṣgaᶜ* 'bareheaded' (CA *ṣaqaᶜa* 'to strike s.o. on the top of his head'; *aṣqaᶜ* f. *ṣaqᶜāʾ* pl. *ṣuqᶜ* 'white on the top of the head'; *ṣawqaᶜah* 'top, uppermost part of s.th.; hollow made in upper part of a dish of crumbled bread').

*ṣgl* — *maṣgūl, mṣaggal* 'polished, burnished (swords)' <16/12, 17/9,18/6,33/18> (CA *ṣaqala* 'to polish').

*ṣkk* — *ṣakk* 'to lock, shut, collide; to press, press s.o. hard' <13/19>; 'strike, pound' <23/9>. *ṣakk ᶜala* 'to surround, encircle, press around' *Glos* <6/4>. *ṣićć* (pass. 3 m. s.) 'he was locked in, shackled, fettered' <2/22>. *mṣakkik* 'closed, shut' <7/9>.

*ṣlb* — *miṣlāb* pl. *miṣālīb* 'the wooden structure upholding the leather water trough' <3/21>; 'the wooden crosspieces connecting the boards of the front and hind parts of the camel saddle' *Musil*, 350 <4/7>; 'thick stake used for poking the fire' *Musil*, 107. *ṣilīb, as-ṣōt aṣ-ṣilīb* 'loud, severe voice; shouted commands' <7/12>; *ar-rāy aṣ-ṣilīb* 'firm, hard opinion, determination' <22/6>. *ṣilīb al-xadd* 'the hard, firm ground' <33/28> (CA *ṣulb, ṣalīb* 'hard, firm; stony, rugged'; contr. of *layyin* 'soft'; *ṣalīb al-ᶜaṣā* 'severe in his treatment of camels'). *mṣōlbāt, mṣālbāt* (pl. f.) 'indefatigable, keeping up an unflagging strong pace' <7/5, 8/5>. *ṣillāb* 'hardiness, endurance' <30/23>. *ṣulb jadd* pl. *jiddān* 'kinsmen on father's and grandfather's side' <16/8,28/7,30/14,31/2>; *ṣulb at-tarāyib* 'the marrow of the man and the loins of the wife', i.e. 'offspring, children'; *ṣulb al-ᶜarab* 'the Arab's stock' *Doughty* i, 327 (CA *ṣulb* 'the backbone, loins'; *hāʾulāʾ abnāʾ ṣilabatihum* 'these are the sons of their loins', because the sperm of the man is held to proceed from the *ṣulb* of the man, hence *ṣulb* also signifies *ḥasab* 'rank, quality; power, strength').

*ṣlf* — *ṣalf* = *ṣafǵ* 'a strong, sudden gust of wind' *Musil*, 561 <5/1>.

*ṣlfg* — *ṣalfag* explained as 'to move with a swinging gait, with slight zigzags' <6/21>.

*ṣly* — *ṣala, yaṣla* 'to roast'. *iṣṭala, yiṣṭili* 'to burn, to be ablaze' <5/8>. *ṣāli šaᶜālih* 'the blaze of its fire, its leaping flames' <18/21> (CA *ṣalā* 'to roast, broil, burn').

*ṣml* — *ṣimīl* pl. *ṣimlān* 'skin for water or milk, leather sack for sour milk' *Hess*, 118; *Musil*, 71 <8/b,20/4>; 'sour milk-skin which the women rock on their knees to make butter' *Doughty* i, 262, ii, 83. *ṣiml aṯ-ṯōb* 'worn, old, tattered garb' <29/5> (CA *samal* 'old and worn out', said of clothes; 'having ragged wool'). *mṣammil* 'determined (to attain his objective, to carry out an attack)' <33/15>. *ṣammalaw* 'they came to a firm decision, were determined to' *JuA*, 52. *ṣamlah* 'determination, courage' *Hess*, 88.

*ṣnd* — *ṣindīd* pl. *ṣanādīd* 'valiant, courageous man' <33/12> (CA *ṣindīd* pl. *ṣanādīd* 'courageous lord; chief eminent among his people because of his noble virtues').

*ṣnᶜ* — *min ṣanᶜ* '(arms) made by (Jews, Christians)' <33/17, 25>. *ṣāniᶜ* pl. *ṣanāniᶜ* 'craftsman, farrier' <6/30>.

*ṣwb* — *ṣīb*, pass. of *ṣāb* 'to hit' <12/16,31/6>. *ṣōb* 'in the direction of, towards' <11/17,18/11,19/13,26/23,30/24>(CA *ṣawb* 'course, direction, bearing').

*ṣwt* *ṣīt* 'fame, high reputation' <9/20>. *w-gad ištahar ṣītih* 'he was famous all over the desert' *Musil*, 593 (CA *ṣīt* 'fame, reputation').

*ṣyḥ* *ṣāḥ aṣ-ṣayyāḥ, ṣāyiḥ* 'in the case of an enemy attack occurring and their herds being taken, one or more of the tribesmen cry out so that the others are alerted and rush to the scene of battle in order to retrieve their captured animals' *ʿUbūdī*, 711; *Musil*, 80, 518-519, 525 <33/11>. *ṣyāḥ* 'crying, shouts, screams of alarm' <19/5>.

*ṣyd* *ṣēd* 'quarry, game (mostly referring to gazelles)' *Glos* <1/8,6/19,7/3,8/9,26/3,27/5> pl. *ṣyūd* <33/8> (CA *ṣayd*, used in a sing. and pl. sense; pl. *ṣuyūd*); 'aim, intent, purpose' *Glos*; *ṣēdak* 'your goal, aim' *Musil*, 318 (see also *gnṣ*).

*ṣyf* *ṣēf* 'summer' for the bedouin denotes the period from the middle of April to the beginning of June. It is followed by the hot and dry season, *al-gēḏ*, cf. *Musil*, 8. *ṣēf, ṣēfi* 'rain in that season' <7/13,32/4>; 'the grasses refreshed by copious summer rain wither more prematurely than in its absence because the scorching sun absorbs all their sap in a few days' *Musil*, 8-9, 16. *miṣyāf* 'period of pasturing on the green produced by the *ṣēfi* rains'; here, metaphorically, 'the fat accumulated during that period' <19/6>. *maṣyaf* 'pasture in the season of *ṣēf*' *Musil*, 78.

*ṭbx* *ṭabxah* 'cooking, boiling; a brew of coffee' <6/20>.

*ṭḥf* *ṭuwāḥīf* explained as *bwārdiyyah* 'gunmen' <19/19>.

*ṭrb* *yaṭrib* 'he is happy, merry, joyful' <6/16>. *ṭarab* 'joy, happiness' <;7>. *ṭarbān, miṭribāni* 'merry, happy, joyful' <19/8,21/4,23/9,24/13>.

*ṭrḥ* *ṭaraḥ, yaṭraḥ* 'to throw down; to throw off the saddle; to fell' *Glos*; *Musil*, 646 <30/26>; 'to take down the tent'; *ṭirīḥ* pl. *ṭraḥa* 'a warrior rolling on the ground, thus thrown from his saddle' *Musil*, 263, 531, 542; 'a robber who has been caught in the act', *jīt aḥūf w-allāh ṭaraḥni* 'I came in order to plunder and God has thrown me down' *Hess*, 97 <2/20,33/8> (CA *ṭaraḥa* 'to cast, throw, fling').

*ṭrd* *ṭarad* 'to chase, chase away' <32b>. *ṭard, ṭrād* 'duelling on horseback, in which one man attacks another trying to outflank him' *Musil*, 104, 554 <33e>; 'hand-to-hand fight of warriors on horseback; mock battle in which the struggles of a real battle are imitated; cavalry play' *Musil*, 245, 561, 577; 'movements of attack and defense in a fight' *Musil*, 152. *ṭarrād* 'one chasing s.o. else' <2/18>.

*ṭrr* — *ṭarr* 'to rend, tear apart'; *yṭurrih* 'he shoves him away, hits him' <3/12,20,13/11,30/12> (CA *ṭarra* 'to cut, slit, rend; to drive away; to slap'). *ya ṭarr jēbi ṭarrāh* = *ya fari jēbi faryāh*, an exclamation of woe, despair, 'Ah, that thing which made me tear the slit opening at the upper part of my garment'.

*ṭrš* — *ṭaraš, yaṭriš* 'to travel without tent and women, e.g. for some business'. *ṭāriš* pl. *ṭrūš*, also *miṭrāš* pl. *miṭārīš*, 'traveller' of this kind, *Musil*, 162; *Hess*, 61. *ṭarš* 'camel herds spread out in pasture' *Glos*; 'the herds of an entire camp' *Hess*, 62 <3/19,33c>.

*ṭrᶜ* — *ṭarᶜāt* explained as 'good camels' <26/26>.

*ṭrf* — *ṭārif* 's.th. at the far end of s.th., hem' <3/20,6/21>; 'leading camel of the *jēš*, the mounted troop' <6/22>. *ṭārif nābha* 'the point of her fang' <30/12>. *ṭwārif* 'the tents pitched at the edge of the camp where the greatest danger threatens' *Musil*, 78.

*ṭrg* — *ṭārūg* 'road, way' <1/3,2/27>. *ṭurgi* pl. *ṭarāģi* 'wayfarer' *Hess*, 61 <14/18>; *ṭurgiyyah* 'an expedition of a few men, wayfaring peacably in the desert' *Doughty* i, 523. *ṭarg al-ēmān* lit. 'the treading of legs on the ground; the movement of the legs' <6/22> (CA *ṭarq* 'the track in which camels follow one another'). *miṭrig, miṭrāg* pl. *miṭārig* 'stalk; stick; branch' *Musil*, 127 <24/16> (CA *miṭraq* 'rod, stick, small staff').

*ṭry* — *ṭara* 'to occur to one's mind' <9/9>; *ma niṭri* 'we don't think of, the thought does not occur to us' <31/6>; *taṭri ᶜalayy* 'I think of her' *Musil*, 225; *la ṭrēt ana l-bōg* 'I never thought of treachery' *Musil*, 219. *ṭarra* 'to mention' <5/3, 9/9>; *ma tṭarra, la tiṭra* 'it is not mentioned; (the thought) does not occur, present itself to s.o.' <26/6,27/14>. *ṭāri* 'mention, word of, news, notion' <13/18,21/12,19>; *ṭāri al-ḥarāyib* 'news of war' *Musil*, 513. *ṭarāt* = *ḥalāt* 'the best, choicest, most pleasing parts of' <32/13>.

*ṭᶜn* — *ṭaᶜan* 'to thrust with a spear or other weapon' <33/26>. *ṭiᶜīn* 'wounded by the thrust of a weapon'. *mṭāᶜanah* 'a contest with spears' *Musil*, 564 (CA *ṭaᶜana* 'to smite and pierce with the spear; to thrust, poke, goad; to attack').

*tfḥ* — *ṭifaḥ* 'to splash, spurt' *Musil*, 88; 'to bubble up' *Musil*, 108. *ṭāfiḥ* 'spurting' *Musil*, 108; *ṭiffaḥ* (pl.) 'running fast as if floating over the ground, flying' (CA *ṭāfiḥ*).

*ṭfg* — *maṭfūg* 'hasty, coming or going in a rush' <2/8> (CA *ṭafiqa*).

*ṭfl* — *ṭifal* explained to me as *ribāb* 'rain cloud' <3/8>; 'dew' ( = *ṭall, nida*) *Musil*, 17 (in CA *ṭifl* also has the meaning of 'small clouds'; *ṭafal* 'rain').

*ṭgg* — *ṭagg, yṭigg* 'to hit, strike; to flee, make off; to scram' <33f>. *ṭiǵīǵ* 'helter-skelter flight, rush to escape' <33f>. *ṭagg ᶜṣiyyhum* 'tapping with their sticks (on the she-camels' necks to make them kneel on the ground before a tent or house, where the riders are to be guests)' *Musil*, 469.

*ṭlb* — *ṭalab, yiṭlib* 'to supplicate, ask for, request'. *ṭallab* 'to search for' *Musil*, 578. *aṭlab* 'to go in pursuit of' *Musil*, 578; *Glos*. *ṭalab* 'camel riders pursuing raiders' *Musil*, 514; 'object of pursuit; the person sought after for revenge' *Glos* <26/22>. *miṭlib* 'pursuer' *Musil*, 84. *al-xēl al-maṭlūbah* 'mares that are the envy of all' *Musil*, 577.

*ṭlḥ* — *mṭalwaḥ* 'long and lean' <8/4> (CA *ṭalaḥa* 'to be lean, emaciated by reason of fatigue or disease'; *ṭalīḥ* 'a she-camel rendered lean by journeys'). *ṭalḥ* (coll.) 'a species of acacia, desert acacia (*Mimosa gummifera*)' *Doughty* i, 425-426 <19/7>.

*ṭlᶜ* — *ṭalaᶜ* 'to go out, come out, emerge, appear' *Glos*; *iṭlaᶜu* (imp. pl.) 'get out!'; *ma ḥinna b-ṭālᶜīn* 'we will not get out' *Hess*, 160. *ṭālaᶜ* 'to see, see and notice, descry, spy, look out over' *Musil*, 358. *ṭalᶜ al-ḥabil* 'the length of the cords of the halter', similar in meaning to *ya ṭūl rsanah* 'he was knocked down from the back of his horse and was flung away the length of its halter' *Sow*, 269 <2/20> (CA *ṭalᶜ* 'the amount' synonym of *miqdār*).

*ṭlg* — *ṭallag, aṭlag* 'to let go, let off, loosen, discharge' <24/16>; *yṭalliǵhin* 'he (the herdsman) unties the camels (by loosening the cords fettering their legs above the knee)' *Musil*, 337 (CA *aṭlaqa*).

*ṭmᶜ* — *ṭimiᶜ* 'to hope for, desire gain'. *ṭimaᶜ* 'gain; coveted object'

*Glos*; 'price paid to the father of the bride' *Hess*, 135; *ᶜala ṭimaᶜ* '(on the attack) for booty' *Musil*, 356; *aṭāmīᶜ*, *ṭimāyiᶜ* are plurals with the same meaning <6/11,21/11>. *ṭimāmīᶜ* 'raiders craving booty' (CA *ṭamaᶜ* 'coveting; a thing that is coveted').

*ṭmm* — *ṭamm* 'to cover; to rise high' <25/3> (CA *ṭamma* 'to be abundant, rise high, choke up, cover', said of water). *ṭumām* <11/10> explained as *ṭāmim* 'the wide plain, the distant land one looks upon when coming over a ridge'.

*ṭmn* — *ṭamman* 'to bend, lower; to slope down, be lower' <9/32>. *ṭāmin, ṭimāni* 'going, moving downward' <19/21> (CA *ṭāmana* 'to bend, lower').

*ṭws* — *ṭās* pl. *ṭwis* 'helmet made of steel' *Hess*, 105 <33/24>. *ṭāsah* 'kettle with two rings' *Musil*, 70 (CA *ṭās* 'drinking cup').

*ṭwᶜ* — *ṭōᶜ* 'obedience' *Musil*, 227. *mṭawwiᶜt al-ḥarīb* 'subduers of the enemy' <22/7,26/21>. *miṭwāᶜ* 'obedient camel' *Musil*, 151.

*ṭwg* — *ṭōg* 'peak, highest prominence' <2/1> (CA *ṭāq* pl. *aṭwāq* 'a prominence projecting from a mountain, a ridge or ledge in a mountain' = *qunnah*).

*ṭwl* — *ṭōlah* 'pride, power, prestige' <9/35> (CA *ṭawl* 'excellence, power, superiority').

*ṭwy* — *ṭawa* and *ṭāwa* 'to fold, wrap up'; *ṭawa, yaṭwi* 'to fold, take down the tent' *Hess*, 59; *ṭawwaw w-rawwaw* 'they took down their tents and filled their water-skins' *JuA*, 61; *yaṭwi* 'he folds up; covers the distance rapidly' <4/14>. *tiṭwa* 'it is covered, plastered, made firm on the inside (e.g. the walls of a well with stones)' <33/28>. *tiṭāwa* (3 f. s. imperf. of the VI form of the verb) = *tadraᶜ* 'they (the she-camels) walk slowly' <13/14>. *mṭawwa* '(a well) covered on the inside with stones'. *bīrin maṭwiyyah* 'a well with stone-covered walls; *aṭ-ṭayy* 'the casing, the stone-covered walls of a well' *Hess*, 63 (CA *ṭawā* 'to fold, fold up; to traverse'; *ṭawā al-biʾr*, inf. n. *ṭayy*, 'to case the well with stones').

*ṭyb* — *ṭīb* 'virtue, goodness; well-being, good, health' *Musil*, 461 <9/2,21/24>; 'perfume' <12/24>. *ṭayyib* 'a man of honour' *Musil*, 182.

*ṭyḥ* — *ṭāḥ* 'to fall down' <4/4,12,32a,33/8> (CA *ṭāḥa* 'to perish, to fall').

*ṭyr* — *ṭayyar* 'to scare, stampede' <19/19>. *ṭāyir* pl. *ṭiyyār* 'lively, alert' <12/10,27/12>; *ṭāyrāt ᶜyūnih* 'rolling his eyes in a frenzy' *Musil*, 447. *ṭēr* 'bird of prey, trained falcon' *Musil*, 570 <2/20>. *ṭār* pl. *ṭīrān* 'drum' *Musil*, 304 <3/10>; 'brim of the mortar in which the coffee is pounded' *Musil*, 467.

*ṭyf* — *aṭ-ṭāyif* 'the spectre; depressive mood'.

*ḍbb* — *ḍabb ᶜala* 'to surround s.th. tightly and completely'. *ḍbāb* 'brass rings clasping s.th. tightly and keeping it together' (CA *ḍabba ᶜalā* 'to seize, grasp s.th. violently, firmly').

*ḍbr* — *ḍibar* 'to amass, pile up'. *tiḍibbār* explained as '(the act of) covering s.th. completely' <10/10> (CA *ḍabara* 'to collect together, pile up').

*ḍbs* — *ḍubbis* (pl.) explained as 'dry, brittle', i.e. *yābis* as dry planks and the like <6/17>.

*ḍby* — *ḍabiy* pl. *ḍba, ḍabyān* 'gazelle' *Hess*, 85; *Glos* <24/4>.

*ḍḥy* — *ḍaḥa* 'time in the morning, after the passing of the dew' *Musil*, 4, 537; '8-10 hours in the summer, 9-10 in winter' *Hess*, 70 <6/1,10/1,13/1,26/11>; *yḍaḥḥīhin* 'he watches the herd pasturing in the morning' *Musil*, 336; *Hess*, 62 (CA *ḍuḥā* 'early part of the forenoon').

*ḍdd* — *ḍaddatih* 'she opposed him, turned him away' <3/20> (CA *ḍaddath*). *ḍidd* 'enemy, adversary, opponent' <33/33, 37>. *ḍadd al-ḥāl* 'adverse circumstances' <6/11> (CA *ḍadd*).

*ḍrb* — *ḍarab* 'to cross, traverse, to ride' *Musil*, 222; *Glos* <32c>; *ḍārbāt* (pl. f.) 'she-camels crossing the desert' <6/33>. *ḍarāyib* (pl.) 'the offspring, descendants of' <8/8> (CA *ḍārib* pl. *ḍawārib* 'she-camel that has been covered by a stallion'). *tiḍrāb* pl. *tiḍārīb* 'pounding, beating, palpitating' <12/3>. *miḍrāb* 'paw (e.g. of a lion)' <30/11>. *ḍarbah* 'blow, stroke' <33/37>.

*ḍrs* — *tiḍarras, ytiḍarras* 'to gnash its teeth, molars' <5/10>.

*ḍry* — *ḍāri, mḍarra* 'trained to, accustomed to' *Glos* <6/20>; *mḍarrīha* 'training her (the she-camel)' *Musil*, 365 (CA *ḍārī* 'habituated to, devoted to' e.g. the animal of prey to the chase).

*ḍᶜf* — *aḍᶜaf* 'to render weak; to ruin' <33b>. *miḍᶜif* 'ruining, routing' <18/19>. *ḍiᶜīf* pl. *ḍᶜūf* 'poor fellow-tribesmen whose supplies have been stolen by the enemy; they go from tent to tent and feed as guests' *Musil*, 90.

*ḏ̣ᶜn* *aḏ̣ᶜān, ḏ̣iᶜnān, ḏ̣aᶜāyin, ḏ̣ᶜūn, ḏ̣aᶜānīn* 'camels which carry the tents, clothing, household goods, women and children of a migrating clan; small groups of camels which carry the property of moving bedouins' *Musil*, 286, 625 <29/7,33c, 33/35,38>. *nahār aḏ̣-ḏ̣iᶜīn* 'the day on which the tent with all its contents is loaded on camels for removal to another camp' *Musil*, 286 (CA *ẓaᶜīnah* 'camels carrying the litters in which the women ride').

*ḏ̣fr* *ḏ̣āfir* pl. *ḏ̣afrān* 'brave youth' <16/8>; *rajjālin ḏ̣āfirin gāṭiᶜ* 'a brave, merciless fellow' *Hess*, 102 (CA *ẓāfir* 'successful, victorious'). *ḏ̣ifar* 'victory' <30/25> (CA *ẓafar*).

*ḏ̣fḏ̣f* *ḏ̣ifḏ̣āf, ḏ̣ifīf* explained as 'a pace not slow and not fast; a moderate pace' <23/14>.

*ḏ̣ff* *ḏ̣aff* 'to take all, round up' *Glos*; 'to fold together, press inward' <11/10>. *istiḏ̣aff* 'to hold, fold, press together' *Musil*, 592 (CA *ḍaffa* 'to collect, to close together; to press').

*ḏ̣fy* *ḏ̣ifa, yaḏ̣fi* 'to spread over; to be abundant' *Glos*; *Musil*, 142 <31/13>. *ḏ̣āfi* 'abundant, ample' <33/21>; *garnih ᶜala l-matin ḏ̣āfi* 'her tresses reach below the waist' *Musil*, 103 (CA *ḍafā* 'to become full, ample; be much in quantity').

*ḏ̣lᶜ* *ḏ̣alaᶜ, ḏ̣ālaᶜ, yḏ̣āliᶜ* 'to limp' *Musil*, 211 <33/30>. *ḏ̣āliᶜ* 'limping, walking on one foot rather than on the other' (CA *ẓalaᶜa, ḍaliᶜa* 'to limp, walk with a halting step', said of the camel). *ḏ̣ilᶜ* pl. *ḏ̣lūᶜ, ḏ̣ilᶜān* 'rib' <23/8>; 'low mountain' *Glos*; 'an isolated, rugged mountain, usually of granite' *Musil*, 684 <;8> (CA *ḍilᶜ* 'a small mountain, extending lengthwise, not high').

*ḏ̣lf* *ḏ̣alf* pl. *ḏ̣lāf* 'the lower parts of the boards, fashioned like shovels, that are the supports of a camel saddle' *Musil*, 68, 350 <9/33> (CA *ẓalif*). *miḏ̣ālīf* '(camels or cranes that) remain standing in a fixed position with their necks curved downward' <19/4,24/9>.

*ḏ̣ll* *ḏ̣ill* pl. *ḏ̣lāl* 'shade' <6/31,18/11,22/1> (CA *ẓill* pl. *ẓilāl*). *miḏ̣ālīl* '(running, walking) in a direction away from the sun' (hunters approach their prey in the late afternoon with the low sun in their back, so that the ostriches flee in the other direction), also <13/16> (cf. CA *qad waradat tamshī ᶜalā ẓilālihā* 'they came to the water walking upon their shadows'). *mistiḏ̣ill* 'a *wagir*, a cavity in the rocks holding rain-water' <11/12> (CA *istaẓallat al-ᶜuyūn* 'the eyes, of a camel, sank in the head'). *ṭirīg al-miḏ̣ālīl* 'the ways of evil' <14/8> (CA *maḍallah* 'going astray, deviation from the right path').

*ḏ̣lm* *ḏ̣ilīm* 'male ostrich' <5/9> (CA *ẓalīm*). *ḏ̣alām* 'darkness' <18/5,25/6,12>; also *ḏ̣alma* <6/32,8/11> (CA *laylah ẓalmāᵓ* 'a night intensely dark').

*ḏ̣mr* *ḏ̣imīr, ḏ̣āmir* pl. *ḏ̣imāyir* 'bosom, one's inner self' *Musil*, 167 <6/2>. *b-agṣa aḏ̣-ḏ̣imāyir* 'in the innermost entrails; in the depth of my soul' *Musil*, 167, 569.

*ḏ̣my* *ḏ̣ma* 'thirst' <19/6>; *ḏ̣ma al-bill* 'the day on which the camels become thirsty' *Glos* <3/19>; *ḏ̣ma al-bill wišuh?* 'how long have the camels thirsted, not been watered?' *Musil*, 338. Bedouins of ᶜTēbah described to me the stages of the *ḏ̣ma*, the days the camels pasture in the desert without being watered, as follows: at night the camels are watered at the well, *al-bill txammar ᶜala l-bīr*; the next morning they are watered again, *tiṣbiḥ*, and then are driven to the pasture, *nahār aṣ-ṣidir*; the next day is *nahār al-ġibb*; then *nahār ar-ribiᶜ*; then *nahār al-xams*, 'the fourth day of *aḏ̣-ḏ̣ma*'. *miḏ̣mi, ḏ̣imāni* 'thirsty' <19/16,23/13>; also *ḏ̣amyān* <3/20,9/11> (CA *ẓamaᵓ*; *ẓamᵓān* 'thirsty'). *maḏ̣ma* pl. *miḏ̣āmi* 'waterless desert' <11/15,33d,33/53> (CA *maẓmāᵓ*).

*ḏ̣nn* *ḏ̣ann, yiḏ̣inn* 'to think, expect' *Musil*, 81. *miḏ̣ann* 'what one thinks, surmises, suspects, expects, anticipates' <2/7>. *ḏ̣anniti* 'I think, expect' *Musil*, 80.

*ḏ̣ny* *ḏ̣ana* 'offspring, progeny, child; calf, young; descendants = *ḏirriyyah*' *Musil*, 50, 328, 609; *Hess*, 136 <24/4> (CA *ḍanᵓ, ḍinᵓ, ḍanw, ḍinw* 'offspring of anything').

*ḏ̣hr* *aḏ̣har, yiḏ̣hir* 'to bring forth, into the open; to show, make public' <3/9,21/25>; 'to rescue' (CA *yuẓhir*). *miḏ̣hir* 'demonstrating, showing, manifesting' <9/20>. *miḏ̣hirah* 'what brings (the young) forth, progenitors' <27/14>. *ḏ̣āhir* pl. *ḏ̣āhrīn* 'coming, getting out of' <32a>.

*ḏ̣wḥ* *ḏ̣āḥ, ḏ̣ōḥ* 'lightning; brilliance, luminosity' <31/12> (CA *waḍaḥ* pl. *awḍāḥ*).

*ḏ̣wn* *ḏ̣ān* (coll.) 'sheep' <26/24>.

*ḍww* *ḍaww* see *wḍy*.

*ḍyr* *ḍīr* pl. *ḍyāra* <15/10> 'a camel whose cub is killed and is then trained to let the cub of another female suck her. Thus she does not lose her milk with fretting, while the mother of the living cub continues to treat it in the same way. In this way both she-camels adopt the cub, both feed it, and the owner can milk both of them' *Musil*, 22. 'The mother of the living calf is also called *ḍīr*, i.e. they are both *ḍyāra*. If the living calf also dies, its skin is stuffed (*baww*) so that both mothers continue to produce milk. In that case they are *ḍyāra ᶜala baww*' *Hess*, 78 (see *bww*). A camel whose cub dies and after her first grief (*xlāj*) has been spent is then trained by her owner (*yḍayyirha*) to feed the cub (*ḥwār*) of another camel. This is done as follows. The owner stitches and sews together nostrils and anus of the animal with sharp pegs and thread, so that she can only breathe through the mouth. After three or four hours, the nostrils are unstitched and then, if she shows signs of affection towards the cub, the anus is opened as well. She has thus become *mḍayyarah* (an informant of al-Ġanānīm of ar-Rūgah of ᶜTēbah). The process is also described in *Lane* under *ẓaʾara* and *Musil*, 87, *yḍīrūn ᶜalēha ḍyār* 'they trick her into accepting another camel's calf'. Yet another way of deceiving the mother is called *jrār*, *Musil*, 87 and *Lane* under *jarūrah* (CA *ẓiʾr, ẓīr* pl. *ẓuʾār* 'she-camel made to incline to and suckle the young one of another, or that keeps close to the stuffed skin of a young one').

*ḍyᶜ* *ḍāᶜ* 'to get lost' <32/4>. *ḍāyiᶜ* pl. *ḍīᶜ* = *hamal* 'camels pasturing freely, without being watched' <;16>.

*ḍyg* *ḍāg* 'to be, become narrow; to be distressed, dejected' <6/1,12/3>. *ḍayyag* 'to make narrow; to press through' <6/5>. *ḍīġ* 'narrowness, narrow place; difficult situation, distress' *Musil*, 219 <32/15>. *ḍāyiġ, maḍyūg* 'distressed, dejected, anguished, uneasy' <1/12,21/4, 26/1>. *miḍīġ* pl. *miḍāyiġ* 'narrow place, mountain pass' <12/4,27/9> (CA *maḍīq*).

*ḍym* *ḍām, yḍām* 'to contain, hold back s.th.' <25/3>. *ḍām, ḍāyam* 'to hurt, injure; to wrong, treat unjustly' <33/49>; *la yḍām ḍiᶜīf* 'no weak person should be wronged' *Musil*, 465. *ḍēm* 'unjust treatment, violence, oppression' *Musil*,

476. *maḏ̣yūm* 'suffering injustice' *Musil*, 80. *ḏ̣aymāt* (pl. f.) 'hurting, causing pain or injury' <33/47> (CA *ḍāma* 'to wrong, to treat unjustly, tyranically; to harm, injure, hurt').

*ʿbb* — *ʿabbāb* 'a well with plenty of water' (CA *ʿubāb* 'abundance of water').

*ʿbr* — *ʿābir* 'rim' <3/21> (CA *ʿibr* 'bank, side'). *ʿibār* 'wailing, sobbing' <9/7,15/2>; *nijrin lya ḥirrik tizāyad fī ʿibārih* 'a mortar that wails when its insides are stirred by the pestle'. *ʿabrah* pl. *ʿabāyir* 'sobs, repressed tears' <24/2> (CA *ʿabrah* 'tear, sobbing'). *min gidīmin miʿtibar* 'of old fame (said of gunpowder)' <31/4>; *iʿtibār* 'fame' *Musil*, 540.

*ʿbs* — *ʿabas* 'dried urine on the tail of a camel' <13/12> (CA *ʿabas* 'urine and dung that have clung to the tails of camels, drying thereon').

*ʿbl* — *ʿabal* f. *ʿibla* 'a rock made up entirely of white flints, mostly a hillock standing in isolation or a conical steep rock, of the sort frequently found in the highlands of Najd' *JuMu* i, 23 <5/7,13/9> (CA *ʿablāʾ* 'rock; white, crystal-like hard rock or hill covered with white stones').

*ʿtš* — *ʿataš* 'a bend in a watercourse' <3/13> (CA *ʿatas̲h̲a* 'to bend').

*ʿtg* — *ʿawātiǵ* (pl.) 'the part of the camel's neck next to the cheeks' <6/24,27/12> (CA *ʿawātiq* 'lateral, adjacent parts').

*ʿty* — *ʿāti* 'arrogant, disobedient' <31/5> (CA *ʿatā*). *ʿatāwah* 'oppression; arrogant, lawless behaviour'.

*ʿṯbr* — *ʿaṯābīr* 'mishaps, problems'.

*ʿṯkl* — *ʿaṯākīl* 'clusters of leaves or flowers in a tree; the curling ends of women's hair' <10/13> (CA *ʿit̲h̲kāl* pl. *ʿat̲h̲ākīl* 'raceme of a palm-tree, a stalk with a bunch of dates').

*ʿṯn* — *ʿiṯnūn* pl. *ʿaṯānīn* 'some long hairs that grow behind the camel's ears on the neck', according to ad-Dindān <1/9, 9/19,13/12> (CA *ʿut̲h̲nūn* pl. *ʿat̲h̲ānīn* 'small long hairs under the part beneath the lower jaw of the camel; the portion of the beard that extends beyond the two sides of the cheeks') .

*ʿjb* — *yiʿjib* 'he pleases, makes s.o. marvel at' <4/15,27/6> (CA *aʿjaba*). *taʿājīb* 'wonderful things'; in this context it means 'artful, entertaining discourse' <12/1,26>. Similarly, *ʿjūbi* 'someone who entertains a company with his tales' *Su* i, 82.

*ʿjj* *ʿajj* 'to whirl, to approach in a violent motion (used alike for a violent passion, for rising dust, and for an approaching throng of raiders)' *Musil*, 614. *ʿajj, ʿajjah, ʿajāj* 'dust and sand caught up by a whirlwind which runs like a pillar through the desert; columns of dust and sand enveloping the cavalry, whose horses raise up the dust with their hoofs' *Musil*, 515, 567 <2/17,4/18,19/19,32/4>. *ʿajājah* 'strong wind that raises clouds of dust and sand' *Musil*, 19 (CA *ʿajāj* 'dust raised by the wind').

*ʿjz* *ʿajūz* pl. *ʿajāyiz* 'old woman' <6/10>; *la hum mšāwirt al-ʿajāyiz* 'they consult not old women' *Musil*, 128-129. *ʿajzān* 'powerless, weak' <21/24>.

*ʿjl* *ʿajjal* 'to hasten; to urge to speed' *Musil*, 514 <2/22>. *ʿajal* 'the wheel of a car with the tyre' <16/6>.

*ʿjm* *ʿajmah* pl. *ʿjām* 'a *šiʿīb*, watercourse; a steep ravine or crevice in the side of a mountain' <11/2,18/4>. *ḥanīn al-ʿjām* 'the noise made by a *sēl*, a torrent that comes thundering down from the mountains through a steep watercourse'. *ʿajim* 'solid, hard, presenting an impregnable surface' <25/11> (CA *ʿajmah* 'hard rocks protruding in a valley'; *aʿjam* 'in which there is no opening so that the sound does not issue from it').

*ʿdd* *ʿadd, yiʿidd* 'to count, number' *Musil*, 304; 'to tell, recount' *Musil*, 271 <2/7,30/13>. *b-ġēr ʿaddād* 'countless, innumerable' <2/22>. *ʿaddi* 'I feel like (= *ćanni*)' *Musil*, 164; *ʿaddha* 'they (pl. f.) are counted, reckoned (to stem from)' <9/20> (CA *ʿadda*). *ʿidd* pl. *ʿdūd* 'a well with plenty of water, a well that is never empty' *Glos*; 'a well with spring water which never dries up' *Musil*, 485, 677; *Hess*, 63 <13/15,33/55>.

*ʿdl* *mʿaddal* pl. *maʿādil* 'the point of the *masna*, the sloping path on which the camel drawing water goes back and forth, that is next to the reservoir into which the water is poured from the bucket; at the *mʿaddal* the *sānyah* turns around and starts pulling the rope of the bucket on its way down towards the opposite point, the *maṣabb*' *JuSa*, 53-54 <19/13> (CA *maʿdil* pl. *maʿādil* 'place of turning away or back'). *bi-l-ʿadāl* 'well-balanced, well-shaped' <27/10>.

*ʿdm* *ʿadām* 'annihilation, extinction' <18/16,25/9>. *ʿadāmah* pl. *ʿadām* 'sand-hills; small knolls of sand blown around an obstacle' *Glos* <3/12,11/a,18/6>. *ʿadīm* pl. *ʿdāmi* 'unequalled in courage, champion' *Glos*; *ʿadīm al-wiṣāyif* 'matchless, peerless in regard to her qualities, beauty' <28/7>.

*ʿdw* *ʿada* 'to run; to attack'; *ʿadāna* 'we attacked' <32/10>. *ʿadda* 'to drive out, away; to exceed, go beyond' *Musil*, 534; *Glos*. *taʿadda* 'to cross; to pass, go beyond, surpass' *Glos* <2/26>. *ʿaduww* pl. *ʿidwān* 'enemy, adversary' <9/16, 21/22,24/14>; other plurals are *al-ʿda*, *al-aʿādi* <33/12, 36,45>. *mʿādi* 'aggressor, attacker' <22/2>. *ʿawādi* = *sillah* 'the attacking men'. *ʿādi* 'running' <7/2>. *ʿadāwi* 'camels having pastured on good herbage, fat camels' *Hess*, 76 (CA *ʿudwīy, ʿudawīy* 'camel pasturing on the herbage called *ʿudwah*'; however, I was informed by S.A. Sowayan that among the bedouins the word is associated with *ʿidwah*, meaning 'elevation, knoll', to which the hump of a well-fed camel is likened).

*ʿd̲b* *ʿd̲āb* 'sweet-tasting saliva' <12/25> (CA *ʿad̲h̲b* pl. *ʿid̲h̲āb* 'sweet water or beverage'; *nisāʾ ʿid̲h̲āb at̲h̲-t̲h̲anāyā* 'women sweet in respect of the front teeth'). *kalām al-ʿad̲b* 'sweet, charming chatter' <12/26>.

*ʿd̲r* *ʿad̲āra* (always used in the plural) 'all young women, whether virgins or not' *Musil*, 197 <6/28,30/3,33/22> (CA *ʿad̲h̲rāʾ* pl. *ʿad̲h̲ārā*).

*ʿd̲l* *ʿad̲d̲āl* 'censurer, rebuker, critic; the stock character who blames the poet for abandoning himself to his passion' <24/14> (CA *ʿād̲h̲il, ʿad̲h̲d̲h̲āl* pl. *ʿud̲h̲d̲h̲āl*).

*ʿd̲y* *ʿad̲iy* 'pure, clean, sweet, healthy', said of water, air and the like, *Musil*, 289, 500 <17/12>; *bilād ʿad̲iyyah* 'districts in which the atmosphere is clear and salubrious' *Musil*, 666 (CA *ʿad̲h̲ā al-balad* 'the country was remarkable for its good, pleasant air').

*ʿrb* *ʿarrab* 'to speak, pronounce clearly' <25/20>. *ʿarab, ʿirbin* 'bedouins, tribesmen' <;23>. *ʿarībāt, ʿarāba* (pl. f.) 'she-camels of a noble race, good she-camels' <9/20,14/12, 33/46,49> (CA *ibl ʿirāb* 'camels of pure Arabian race'). *ʿirb* 'good and strong camels but not of a thoroughbred race' *Hess*, 75.

*ʿrš* *ʿarš* 'God's throne; heaven' *Hess*, 155 <25/12> (CA *ʿarsh*).

*ʿrḏ* *ʿaraḏ, yʿariḏ* 'to appear, to come into s.o.'s way' *Glos*; 'to defile before the tribe's chiefs' *Musil*, 526. *ʿāraḏ* 'to come across; to meet and join' <32b>. *miʿtarḏitin* '(a woman) stretched out on the saddle, the legs wound around the *ġazāl*, the upright cones at both ends of the saddle' <33h> (CA *iʿtaraḍa* 'to lay across, transversely, sideways'). *ʿirḏ* 'honour, sense of honour' <16/13,27/1> (CA *ʿirḍ* 'a man's honour or reputation which he preserves from impairment and blame'). *ʿrēḏiyyah* 'men dancing in the *ʿarḏah*' <9/31>. *ʿarāḏah* 'the warriors defile before the standing chief, assure him of their fidelity, and by uttering their war cry raise one another's spirit' *Musil*, 561; also *ʿarḏah* 'defile on horseback, parade' *Musil*, 81, 526, 578; 'a war dance in which two lines of men face each other and make small steps while singing and balancing their swords'. *ʿarūḏ* '(a cloud) blocking, filling the horizon' <2/7,13/8,14/17>.

*ʿrf* *ʿirfah* 'a lush, isolated patch of pasture only frequented by gazelles and other game' <13/17> (CA *ʿurfah* 'open, elongated track of land with herbage').

*ʿrg* *ʿirǵ* pl. *ʿrūg* 'long spur of sand' <1/6,13/9,25/6> (CA *ʿirq*). *ʿargāh* pl. *ʿarāǵi* 'the wooden crosspieces fastened over the mouth of the elongated bucket to which the rope, *ar-rša*, is attached' *Musil*, 72 (CA *ʿarqāh*).

*ʿrgm* *al-ʿarāǵīm*, the meaning of this word was explained to me as follows: in times of drought, when good pastures are lacking, the bedouins feed their camels with cut branches from *al-wahaṭ* (CA *waḥṭ* 'groups of *ʿurfuṭ*, mimosa-trees, with broad leaves and sharp, curved thorns, which is eaten by camels, particularly the upper extremities of its branches'), a shrub not unlike the *samr* (*Acacia raddiana, tortilis* and *laeta*), with long thorns and broad leaves; the cut branches have been charred in a fire to dull their thorns and to give them *nakhah*, the taste and smell that makes them palatable to the camels <12/9>.

*ʿrk* *ʿawārić* 'the sides of the belly' <9/29>; *ʿark* 'rubbing' *Musil*, 362 (CA *ʿārik* pl. *ʿawārik* 'a camel that rubs its sides with its elbows so as to cut through the skin'). *maʿāric* 'battles' <33/12>.

*ᶜrn* ᶜ*irn* ‘the wood of the *samr*-shrub’ <5/8>; ‘a gnarled stub of massy wood, resembling the stool of ling-wort, tan wood’ *Doughty* i, 268, 426 (CA ᶜ*irn* ‘a species of thorn-tree’). ᶜ*irnūn* pl. ᶜ*arānīn* ‘the upper part, ridge of the nose; nose’ *Musil*, 115 <9/28> (CA ᶜ*irnīn* pl. ᶜ*arānīn* ‘bridge of the nose, hard part of the bone of the nose’).

*ᶜrw* ᶜ*irwah* pl. ᶜ*ra*, ᶜ*arāwi* ‘loops, button-loops, single bow knots (of the tent ropes, which can be loosened or tightened according to the strength of the wind), loop-shaped handles (e.g. of a water-skin)’ *Musil*, 263; *Hess*, 118 <2/3> (CA ᶜ*urwah* pl. ᶜ*urā*).

*ᶜry* *maᶜāri* ‘blemishes, faults; shame’ <21/25>. ᶜ*aryān* ‘naked, without clothes’ <29/5>; ‘devoid of herbage’ <3/14> (CA *maᶜārī* ‘parts that are visible, of a woman’).

*ᶜzr* ᶜ*izrān* ‘ᶜIzrāʾīl, the angel of death’ <21/32,25/16>.

*ᶜzz* ᶜ*izz* ‘pride, glory’ <30/10>. ᶜ*izzāh*, ᶜ*izzita*, ᶜ*izzi likum* ‘O, what a pity!’ *Glos* <9/3,13,16/2,33/11>. *wa-*ᶜ*izzāh*, *ya-*ᶜ*izzāh* ‘Alas!; O, dear me!’. ᶜ*izz allah* ‘by God!’ <21/27>.

*ᶜzl* *ribābin lih ti*ᶜ*izzāl* ‘clouds that are apart, arriving at intervals’, i.e. the rain comes in showers, intermittently <1/5> (CA ᶜ*azala*). *ta*ᶜ*āzīl* ‘distinctive features, the outlines that set one part of the body apart from the other’ <9/29>; ᶜ*ūdin zaha līnih bi-zēnih w-ta*ᶜ*āzīl* ‘a twig (i.e. a slender young woman) whose tenderness is enhanced by beauty and a well-shaped figure’ *Faraj*, 199. *ma*ᶜ*āzīl* ‘high mountains, soaring peaks’ <13/1>. *m*ᶜ*azzal* ‘set apart from, distinct; well-marked in outline’ <27/11>; ‘(a camel) with a lean belly’ *Musil*, 293.

*ᶜzw* ᶜ*itiza*, *yi*ᶜ*tizi* = *intaxa* ‘to shout a battle cry’ *Hess*, 170. ᶜ*izwah* pl. ᶜ*azāwi* ‘kinship on father’s side’ *Musil*, 263, 310 <2/19>; *yi*ᶜ*za min āl Flān* ‘he hails from such-and-such a kin’ *Musil*, 263. Hence ᶜ*izwah* pl. ᶜ*azāwi* also has the meaning of ‘shout to one’s kin in battle, battle cry’ <2/19> (CA ᶜ*izwah* ‘the assertion of a relationship, i.e. of a son to a father’).

*ᶜsbl* ᶜ*asābīl* ‘the teats of a camel’s udder’ <13/13>.

*ᶜsr* ᶜ*isr* ‘hardship, want, poverty due to natural causes’ <13/20>. ᶜ*asrin* ᶜ*ala* ‘difficult, hard, burdensome’ *Musil*, 84 <25/13>.

*ᶜsf* ᶜ*asaf*, *y*ᶜ*asif* ‘to break in, train’ <;20>. ᶜ*asīf* pl. ᶜ*asāyif*, also *mᶜasūfah* 'a trained, broken in she-camel' *Musil*, 176; *Glos*. 'A camel that has not been broken in and is refractory is called *ṣaᶜab* pl. *aṣᶜāb*' *Hess*, 72.

*ᶜsm* *ᶜasām* 'clouds of dust' <18/17>.

*ᶜšb* *ᶜišb* 'herbage; spring forage' *Doughty* i, 260; 'grasses, annuals (as distinct from *šijar*, perennials)' *Musil*, 9 <32a>. *ᶜišbat as-sōda* 'black herbs' <3/3> (CA *ᶜu<u>sh</u>bah*).

*ᶜšr* *ᶜašir* 'the ten fingers' <12/26>. *ᶜašīr* 'friend; woman one loves, sweetheart' <25/21>. *ᶜašīrah* 'tribe, tribal section'.

*ᶜšš* *ᶜišš* dimin. *ᶜšēš* 'nest; shelter' <33i> (CA *ᶜu<u>sh</u>ay<u>sh</u>*).

*ᶜšg* *ᶜaššāg, maᶜšūg*, it was explained to me that bedouins love sprightly she-camels that come to their owner at a trot as soon as they hear his voice or see him, without waiting for their calves, knowing that they will rejoin them later <2/13>.

*ᶜšy* *ᶜašša, yᶜašši* 'to rest in the afternoon, after the time of *ᶜaṣir*' *Hess*, 99; *yᶜaššin* 'they (the camels) graze in the late afternoon till supper time' *Musil*, 337. *mᶜašša* pl. *maᶜāši* 'the place where one alights in the evening for supper' *Glos* <33/5>; 'place where the locusts alight after sunset and stay for the night' <9/4> (CA *ᶜa<u>shsh</u>ā* 'to pasture the camels in the evening'). *ᶜašiyy* 'evening' <6/27>. *ᶜašiyyah* pl. *ᶜašāya* 'week' <33/43>. *ᶜšāwah* 'by sheer force' (CA *ᶜa<u>sh</u>iya ᶜala* 'to wrong s.o.').

*ᶜṣr* *miᶜṣīr* pl. *maᶜāṣīr* 'dust-raising winds; whirlwind, believed to be an evil spirit who sometimes tears away the tents' *Hess*, 159 <5/2> (CA *iᶜṣār* pl. *aᶜāṣīr* 'whirlwind of dust, dust raised into the air by the wind in the form of a pillar'). *ᶜaṣir* 'time midway between the noon and sunset, middle of the afternoon' *Musil*, 4, 406. *ᶜṣēr* 'late afternoon, time before sunset' *Musil*, 4 <7/4>.

*ᶜṣrf* *ᶜiṣrūf* pl. *ᶜaṣārīf* 'the protruding parts of the *miṣālīb*, the upper horizontal sticks of the *ćitab* saddle to which the driver of the *sānyah*, the camel used for drawing water for irrigation purposes, joins the end of the rope by which the elongated bucket, *ġarb*, is hoisted from the well' *JuSa*, 45 <24/17>.

*ᶜṣy* *ᶜṣiyy, ᶜiṣyān* = *miṣālīb* 'the crosspieces connecting the front and hind parts of the camel saddle' *Musil*, 350; 'the main poles forming the frame of a camel litter' *Musil*, 68

<9/33> (CA *ʿaṣā* pl. *ʿuṣīy, ʿiṣīy* ‘stick, staff, rod’).

ʿṭr *miʿṭār* ‘a good, strong she-camel with a hump that quickly raises itself when the camel grazes on good pasture’ <10/13> (CA *miʿṭir, muʿṭir* ‘a beautiful she-camel, as though there were a dye upon her fur; strong and beautiful, or red camel’).

ʿṭy *ʿaṭa* ‘to give, bestow’. *ʿaṭa maʿ* ‘to embark boldly upon, to go at a good speed’ <5/9> (CA *taʿaṭṭā* ‘to hasten’). *ʿaṭni allah* ‘give me God, promise me by God’ *Musil*, 529.

ʿḏ̣d *ʿaḏ̣d* pl. *ʿḏ̣ūd* ‘elbow joint, upper arm, upper half of the arm or foreleg’ *Musil*, 115; *Glos* <7/6,27/10,33/29> (CA *ʿaḍud*).

ʿḏ̣ḏ̣ *ʿaḏ̣ḏ̣, yʿuḏ̣ḏ̣* ‘to bite’ <30/14>.

ʿḏ̣m *ʿaḏ̣im* pl. *ʿḏ̣ām* ‘bone’ <11,4,7,25/17,30/1,12>.

ʿḏ̣y *ʿaḏ̣a* ‘limbs, parts of the body’ <13/14> (CA *ʿuḍw* pl. *aʿḍāʾ*).

ʿfr *ʿafra* pl. *ʿifr* ‘a white she-camel, pinkish white’ <11/15>. *ʿafār* ‘pinkish white colour’ <15/8> (CA *aʿfar* f. *ʿafrāʾ* ‘of a whitish dust-colour’). *ʿifri* ‘gazelle, white beneath its belly and yellowish on its back’ *Musil*, 26; *Doughty* ii, 164.

ʿfrt *ʿifrīt* ‘demon, imp, afreet’ <8/10>.

ʿff *ʿeff* ‘exemption (from hard work); health’ <5/7>; *nāgtin mʿaffāh* ‘a mount that for some reason is spared from hard work’ *Hess*, 76 (CA *ʿiff* ‘abstinence, virtuousness’).

ʿfn *ʿafin* ‘rotten state of mind (following betrayal by the beloved one)’ <11/22>; ‘egoist devoid of all virtue’ *Musil*, 487.

ʿgb *taʿāgab* (this may also be the 3 f. s. imperf. of the VI form of the verb, instead of *titaʿāgab*, cf. *Proch*, 48, *taxānag*; in the Najdi dialects the 3 f. s., 2 f. s. and 2 pl. personal prefixes of the V and VI forms of the imperf. verb are elided, *Proch*, 45.) ‘to come one after the other, in successive waves’ <2/6,9/4,13/5,14/12> (CA *taʿāqaba*). *ʿagābih* ‘his back, the part at the back’ <12/21>. *ʿugib* <11/13,22,12/7,26/8,30/19>, *min ʿugb* ‘after’ <6/16,21/13>. *ʿāgib fi* ‘s.o. who works no good; a failure, flop, loser’ <21/17>. *ʿgāb* pl. *ʿuggab* ‘a small black or brown eagle’ *Doughty* i, 374 <8/11> (CA *ʿuqāb*).

ʿgd *ʿagad* ‘to knot, tie’ <22/8>. *ʿaggad* ‘to fasten, tie’; *ʿaǵǵidih* 'fasten it!' *Musil*, 355. *ᶜaǵīd* pl. *ᶜgida* 'the leader of a raid' <18/20> *Hess*, 99; *Musil*, 506, 641.

*ᶜgrb* *mizintin ᶜagribiyyah* 'a raincloud making its appearance during the reign of Scorpio' <33/23>.

*ᶜgg* *ᶜagūg* 'a cloud heavy with rain' <3/7> (CA *ᶜuqqat as-saḥābah* 'the cloud was rent by the wind and poured forth its water', hence *saḥābah ᶜaqqāqah*).

*ᶜgl* *ᶜagal* 'to tether, hobble' *Glos*; *yᶜagil, yᶜaǵǵilhin* 'he fetters the camels' left legs with a short rope above the knee' *Musil*, 337, 367. *maᶜgil* pl. *maᶜāǵil* 'part of the leg in which camels are bound with the rope called *ᶜgāl*' <8/6> (CA *maᶜqil* pl. *maᶜāqil*). *mᶜaggal* 'hobbled' <33/29>.

*ᶜlb* *ᶜilba* pl. *ᶜalābi* 'the tendons, sinews of the neck, the two fleshy parts of the back of the neck; neck' *Musil*, 115 <19/23>; *mitīn al-ᶜalābi* 'one with a stiff neck; one who, disliking to bend his neck or to salute, is full of conceit' *Musil*, 470, 487 (CA *ᶜilbāʾ* pl. *ᶜalābīy* 'the tendons of the neck').

*ᶜlg* *ᶜallag* 'to attach to, throw on, hang on' <8/b>. *ᶜlāg* 'the gear that is loaded on the camel's back' <4/14> (CA *ᶜilāq* 'a thing that is hung, suspended'). *ᶜalāyiǵ* 'provisions and gear loaded on the camel' *JuA*, 164. *ᶜalīǵ* 'food bag' *Musil*, 585. *iᶜlāg* 'the fastening of the noose at the other end of the rope holding the bucket to the *ćitab*, the saddle of the *sānyah*'. *ḥirbah ᶜōligiyyah* 'a blade made in Hadramaut' <33/26>.

*ᶜlm* *ᶜilm* pl. *ᶜlūm* 'report, news' *Musil*, 523; see also *Doughty* ii, 294 <6/34,21/32,30/24>; 'reputation' <15/11,12, 21/28>; 'words of advice' <14/5>. *ᶜalāmah* 'sign, memento' <23/4>; 'distinguishing mark, colour' <11/7>; 'landmark' *Musil*, 676. *bīr ᶜēlimiyyah, ᶜēlam* 'a big well holding much water' <17/6,19/10,33/50> (CA *ᶜaylam* 'a well having much water').

*ᶜmd* *ᶜamad* 'to do s.th. on purpose, intentionally'; *la ᶜamadna xaṭan* 'if wrong is purposefully committed against us' <18/18>. *ᶜammad* 'to proceed on a straight course' *Musil*, 162; 'to dispatch' *Glos*. *ᶜamūd* pl. *ᶜimdān, ᶜimmād* 'tent pole; column; pole to which the motherless foals are tied' <33/27>; 'pillars of dust; whirling columns of locusts' *Doughty* i, 380-381 <2/17,3/2>.

*ᶜmr* *ᶜumr* pl. *ᶜamār* 'body' <6/29,9/31> (CA *ᶜumr* pl. *aᶜmār*). *ᶜāmir* 'brand-new, in excellent condition' <16/7>. *maᶜmūr* 'building, edifice' <25/15> (CA *ᶜāmir* 'in a state of good repair'). *miᶜtimir* 'one who is making a religious visit, performs the *ᶜumrah*; one who is aiming to make such a visit' <16/10> (CA *muᶜtamir*).

*ᶜms* *ᶜmōmas* 'to become clouded over, murky' <8/1> (CA *ᶜamasa* 'to be obscure, unclear, recondite'). *ᶜmōmas ar-rāy* 'the mind became clouded, shrouded in darkness, confused' <12/14>.

*ᶜml* *ᶜammāl* 'continuously, incessantly' <6/26>. *bi-l-ᶜamālah* 'on purpose, intentionally' <18/18>. *ᶜimliyyah* 'a tried riding camel' *Musil*, 358.

*ᶜmm* *ᶜamm* pl. *ᶜamām* 'uncle; the family whom a black slave serves and whom he calls his uncles' *Musil*, 82-83 <11/4>.

*ᶜnd* *ᶜanūd* 'leader of the gazelle herd' *Glos* <33/34> (CA *ᶜanūd* 'a she-camel that pastures aside from the herd; that precedes, leads the others').

*ᶜndl* *ᶜandal, ᶜandaliyyah* = *iṣīl* 'thoroughbred mare' *Musil*, 552; 'a pure-white mare of noble descent' *Raswan*, 112 <33/39>; 'a slender, graceful woman with a luscious bosom' *Su* ii, 186 (CA *ᶜandal* 'a she-camel with a big head; big-bodied she-camel').

*ᶜnz* *ᶜanz* pl. *ᶜnūz* 'the old she-gazelle which leads and guards a herd of gazelles. She takes her post on a height, scenting the enemy. If she scents something suspicious, she looks eagerly in that direction and stamps her foot angrily when she cannot at once discover the cause of her fears. On catching sight of the enemy she flees, with the other gazelles following her in a long line which wavers to the right or left according to the direction taken by the old doe' *Musil*, 201 <8/3>.

*ᶜng* *ᶜung* pl. *ᶜnūg* <1/8,7/15,11/11> and *maᶜānig* <6/25> 'neck'. *maᶜnūg* 'long-necked (camel)' <2/10>.

*ᶜnn* *ᶜnān* pl. *ᶜinnah* 'reins' <2/15,19/19,32/2> (CA *ᶜinān* pl. *aᶜinnah*). *xirj ᶜnēni* 'a saddle bag woven of colourful strands of wool' <6/30>.

*ᶜny* *ᶜāni* 'one who is looking for support, protection' <21/21>. *ᶜāniyyah* 'material support, subsidy (e.g. to kinsmen in difficulty)' <9/36>. *mᶜanna* 'suffering, troubled, distressed, grieving' *Musil*, 501 <11/3> (CA *ᶜannā* 'to hurt, to make suffer'). *iᶜtana* 'to observe s.th. scrupulously; to attach importance to s.th.' <18/25> (CA *iᶜtanā* 'to be anxious about s.th.; to be careful to do s.th. well'). *ᶜana* 'because of, for the sake of' <17/8,32/14,15> (CA *ᶜanāʾ* 'difficulty, trouble').

*ᶜhd* *ᶜahad* 'truce'; *ᶜihdin* 'a truce' <23/6>; 'covenant, solemn promise' <33i>; *ᶜaṭni ᶜihd allah* 'promise me by God', said to a travel companion about whose intentions one harbours some doubts, *Hess*, 155; *ᶜalāk ᶜahad allah w-imān allah inni ma axūnik* 'I give you God's covenant and peace, security, that I will not betray you' *Hess*, 155 (CA *ᶜahd* 'covenant, compact, agreement').

*ᶜwj* *ᶜāj* 'camel saddle' <6/30>. *ᶜūj* (pl.) 'curved, crooked' <7/4> (CA *aᶜwaj* pl. *ᶜūj*).

*ᶜwd* *ᶜādah* pl. *ᶜawāyid* 'customs, habits, manners' <21/32, 30/11>. *ᶜādi* 'customary, by tradition and right belonging to' <2/26>. *ᶜōd, ᶜōdah* pl. *ᶜyād* 'big, old, of things and people' *JohnEa*, 245; *ᶜōd* 'old stallion, old man' *Musil*, 225, 375; *ᶜōdah* pl. *ᶜyād* 'old horse' *Glos*; here the reference is to palm-trees (probably with the connotation that these tall palms need big amounts of water, thereby exhausting their owner and the camels that draw the water) <1/7,24/5> (CA *ᶜawd*). *ᶜaydān* 'tall palm-trees, so called when the stumps of their branches have fallen off and they have become bare trunks from top to bottom' *SuFa*, 674 <9/26> (CA *ᶜaydān*). *ᶜūd* pl. *ᶜūdān* 'shaft of the spear' *Musil*, 133 <26/26,33/26>; *ᶜūdān* also means 'sticks, beams, poles' <9/27,24/3>; *ᶜūd* 'branch, twig' <11/22>, 'slender figure' <33/19>. *mᶜīd, miᶜwād* pl. *maᶜāwīd* 'a camel trained to draw water'.

*ᶜwz* *ᶜayzān* 'helpless, powerless' <21/25> (CA *ᶜāyiz* 'poor, needy').

*ᶜwṣ* *ᶜūṣ l-anḏa* 'strong, rugged and enduring camels' <20/6, 24/8,26/25> (CA *ᶜawṣāʾ* 'difficult, hard, rugged').

*ᶜwṭ* *ᶜawwaṭ* 'to utter a lowing sound' <1/12>.

*ᶜwn* *ᶜān* 'to help, aid assist'; *ᶜinna* 'help us!' <21/19> (CA *aᶜāna*). *ᶜānat allah* 'the help of God' <18/23> (CA *ᶜawn*).

*ᶜwy* *ᶜawa* 'to howl, cry loudly, wail' *Musil*, 202 <18/12,22/4, 23/9>. *ᶜwiyān* 'howling, crying' <23/8> (CA *ᶜawā*).

*ʿyd* — *ʿīd* 'feast; place where weary travellers find hospitality and a warm welcome' <6/33>.

*ʿyr* — *ʿērah* pl. *ʿayrāt, ʿērāt* (often used in conjunction with *l-anḏa*) 'hardened camels, strong camel mounts' *Musil*, 156; *Glos* <6/31,27/4,30/23> (CA *ʿayrān* 'camel resembling the wild ass, *ʿayr*, in quickness and briskness; hardy').

*ʿyʿy* — *ʿāʿa* 'to crow, as a cock' *Musil*, 273; *yʿāʿaw lha* 'they called, shouted to them (the horses)' <32e>.

*ʿyf* — *ʿāf, yiʿīf* 'to dislike, loath, feel disgust for s.th.; to have enough, be fed up with; to turn away from' *Musil*, 183 <19/8,30/19>. *ʿīf*, pass., 'it is disliked' <24/11> (CA *ʿāfa*).

*ʿyl* — *ʿāl, yiʿīl* 'to attack, transgress' <8/10>; 'to lose the way; to go wrong; to transgress' *Glos*; *Musil*, 487; *ʿāl ʿala flān* 'to hurt, attack s.o., do wrong' *Musil*, 225. *ʿaylāt* 'transgressions, acts breaching the peace, evil deeds, daring attacks' <2/25>. *ʿāyil, ʿayyāl* pl. *ʿiyyāl* 'transgressor, violator, wrongdoer' *Musil*, 344, 487 <6/13,18/18,26/21> (CA *ʿāla fī al-arḍ* 'he went round about in the land'; *ʿayyāl, muʿīl* 'seeking after prey', said of lions). *ʿyāl* 'children; young men, sons of' <6/32,18/12,26/13>. *ʿayyil* 'baby boy, child' *Musil*, 243.

*ʿyn* — *iʿtān* 'to take aim at; to catch sight of'.

*ʿyy* — *ʿayya* 'to refuse; to be obstinate' *Glos* <32b,33c>; 'to be obstinate in the defence of, not to give up' <33/18>.

*ġbb* — *ġabbab* 'to postpone to the morrow'. *ġabāb* 'the following day' <12/19>. *ġibb* 'after, following' <10/6,18/9, 33/42> (CA *ġibba* = *baʿda* 'after').

*ġby* — *ġabba* 'to cover, conceal' <19/22,21/27> (CA *ġabbā*). *ġābiy, ġabiyy* 'hidden, obscure, unknown' <6/32,14/7>.

*ġṯr* — *ġaṯīr* 'the traces, leftovers; drizzle, misty rain following the downpour' <12/19>.

*ġdr* — *ġadīr* 'a pool of water left by a torrent; place, e.g. a hole in a channel with steep banks, where rain-water stagnates and remains for a long time (but not until the summer)' *Musil*, 682 <1/3> (CA *ġadīr*). *ġadāri* 'pitch-black clouds; moonless nights' <18/8>. *ġadra* 'a dark rainy night' *Musil*, 18; *lēl ġadra* 'a night without moonlight' (CA *ġadrāʾ* 'darkness').

*ġdy* *ġada* ‘to be, to become, turn into’ <12/8,10,13/6>; ‘to get lost’ *Glos*. *ġada bi-* ‘to take, to take away’ *Musil*, 552. *ġādi* ‘gone; lost; one who lost his way’ <2/13,27>. *min ġādi, ġād* ‘beyond, the part that extends farther than, away from; elsewhere’ *Musil*, 166 <2/5> (CA *ġadā* ‘to go, depart early’).

*ġḏy* *ġaḏa* ‘to raise, nurture’ *Glos*. *ġaḏḏa* ‘to feed, nourish with’; *tġaḏḏa* ‘she (the mare) is fed’ <33/12> (CA *ġad̠h̠ā*).

*ġrb* *ġārib* pl. *ġawārib* ‘shoulder blade; nape’ *Musil*, 96, 298 <7/11,13/13,24/7> (CA *ġārib* pl. *ġawārib* ‘fore part of the hump’). *ġarb* pl. *ġrūb, ġawārīb* ‘large, elongated bucket drawn by the *sānyah*; streams (of water, tears)’ <6/5> (CA *ġarb* ‘tears flowing, *masīl*, from the eye’).

*ġrbl* *ġirbāl* pl. *ġarābīl* ‘adversities, difficulties’. *miḥan w-ġarābīl* ‘trials and adversities’ <10/4> (CA *ġarbala al-qawm* ‘he slew, crushed the people’).

*ġrṯ* *ġirṯān* ‘having a slim waist’ <15/5> (CA *ġart̠h̠ān*).

*ġrd* *ġarrad, yġarrid* ‘to sing, warble’ <;17>.

*ġrr* *ġarr* ‘not to keep an appointment, not to honour a promise’ <24/16,33/40>. *ġarrar b-* ‘to lead, go astray with, cause s.o. to take a wrong course’. *min ġarrih* ‘because of its deception, deceived by it’ <3/1>. *ġirrah* pl. *ġirrāt* ‘unawareness, inadvertency’ (CA *ġirrah*). *ġarīr* ‘darling’ *Musil*, 168; ‘inexperienced youth’ K̲h̲aAd, 279. *ġarīrah* ‘inexperienced, young lady’ *Su* ii, 176 <24/16> (CA *ġarīr* ‘beguiled, deceived’). *šāt al-ġrēri* ‘white antelope’ *Musil*, 190. *ġurr al-mzūn* ‘clouds with white spots in the front parts’ <31/12> (CA *aġarr* pl. *ġurr* ‘white, having a white spot, blaze on the forehead, face’).

*ġrs* *ġars* pl. *ġrūs* ‘plantation of trees, date palms’ <12/23, 18/11,19/14>.

*ġrf* *maġrafah* pl. *maġārīf* ‘big, wooden spoon for taking meat from the kettle’ <19/9> (CA *miġrafah* pl. *maġārif* ‘a ladle for scooping up water or food’).

*ġrg* *ġarg* pl. *ġrūg* ‘crevices, watercourses through the rocks’ <2/1> (CA *ġariqa*).

*ġrml* *ġirmāl* ‘singing of camel songs’ <6/16>. *ġirmūl* pl. *ġarāmīl* ‘sand-dunes; a knoll in the sand where grass grows in abundance’ *Musil*, 682; *Glos* <10/10,13/10,14/16>.

*ġrng* *ġarnūg* pl. *ġarānīġ* ‘a crane’ *Musil*, 108 <24/9> (CA *ġurnūq* 'an aquatic bird, long in the neck and in the legs, white or black; stork; Numidean crane; a comely, beautiful youth').

*ġzl* *ġazāl* pl. *ġizlān* 'gazelle' <26/4>.

*ġzy* *ġazuw* pl. *ġizwān* 'raid, a party of men setting out to capture booty' *Hess*, 99 <33i>. *ġazzāy* 'raider' <33/49>.

*ġšy* *taġašwa* 'to cover completely' <19/1> (CA *taġashshā* 'to cover, conceal'). *iġtiša* 'to cover, wrap up, envelop' <18/15>.

*ġṣn* *ġuṣin* pl. *ġṣūn* 'branch, twig' <3/2,10/13,12/3,6,30/2>.

*ġṭrf* *ġaṭraf* 'to sing boastful songs, to ululate' <11/2,14/2,17/1, 21/6>. *ġaṭārīf* 'the boastful songs and cries of men returning from a successful raid', close in meaning to *zaġārīt* 'ululation' <19/20,24/8> (CA *taġaṭrafa* 'to magnify oneself, be proud; to walk in a haughty manner').

*ġṭṭ* *ġaṭṭ* 'to dip in; to touch'. *ġaṭṭ* here means 'whirling clouds of dust (that envelop the traveller)' <20/2> (CA *ġaṭṭa* 'to immerse, plunge in').

*ġṭy* *ġaṭṭa* 'to rein in, restrain' <4/15> (CA *ġaṭṭā* 'to cover'). *taġaṭṭa* 'to cover o.s.' *Musil*, 164. *ma yinġaṭṭ* 'he is not to be restrained, does not slacken his pace, effort' <4/15>.

*ġḍḍ* *ġaḍḍ an-nahad* 'with firm and supple breasts' <17/8>; *ġaḍḍāt al-ġṣūn* 'juicy twigs' *Musil*, 176 (CA *ġaḍḍ* 'fresh, juicy, sappy, moist, not flaccid').

*ġḍy* *aġḍa* 'to avert one's gaze, refrain from looking at' <29/2> (CA *aġḍā* 'to contract one's eyelids, to close one's eyes in order not to see a thing, by reason of shame; to connive'). *ġaḍa* 'a kind of shrub, offering good firewood; *Haloxylon Persicum*' *Musil*, 66, 113 <33/44,52> (CA *ġaḍā* 'a shrub, a kind of Euphorbia with a wooden stem, five or six feet high, and many twigs forming a large feathery tuft, affording shelter to the travellers and food to his camels').

*ġfl* *ġaffalōha* 'they did not attend to it', i.e. 'they left the she-camel sterile, not impregnated' <9/18> (CA *ġafala* 'he neglected it, intentionally'; *aġfala ad-dābbah* 'he left the beast unbranded').

*ġltm* *mġaltimāt al-maxāyīl* 'pitch-black clouds' <10/5> (cf. *mḥaltimāt ar-rʿūd* 'clouds rumbling incessantly with thunder' *JuA*, 45; *Faraj*, 195).

*ġll* *ġall* 'to cause to grief' *Glos*. *ġalīl, ġull* 'fretting; brooding anger, rancour, spite; unsatified love' *Musil*, 172, 576 <8/1,23/7,33/45>. *zaʿlān min ġull* 'burning with rage; s.o. who cannot show his hatred' *Musil*, 589. *ġallah* 'suffering' *Musil*, 204 (CA *ġill, ġalīl* 'latent rancour, spite'). *maġlūl* pl. *maġālīl* 'very thirsty; furious' <13/21> (CA *maġlūl, ġalīl* 'burning of thirst; burning inside from thirst, or anger and vexation'). *mġill* 'seething with frustrated desire' <19/16> (CA *muġill* 'rancorous, spiteful'). *miġtall* 'filled with unsatisfied passion, love, desire' *Musil*, 172 (CA *muġtall*).

*ġlm* *ġlām* pl. *ġilmān* 'young man of 15-30 years old' *Hess*, 139; 'young but valiant man' *Musil*, 265 <25/20>. *ġlayyim* 'youth of about ten years old' *Hess*, 139. *ġilma* 'youths from eighteen to twenty years of age, who are ever making raids' *Musil*, 537 (CA *ġulām* pl. *ġilmah, ġilmān* 'a young man, one whose moustache is growing forth').

*ġly* *aġla* 'to make expensive, to raise the price' <13/19>. *ġala* 'high esteem; high price' *Musil*, 309; 'passion of love' *Musil*, 217.

*ġmr* *ġimir* 'valiant, brave youth; a guy, fellow' <16/8,25/8, 33/11> (CA *ġumr* 'inexperienced, ignorant boy or man'). *ġamīr* 'the scum, algae and dirt floating on stagnant, warm water' <19/9> (CA *ġamīr* 'a certain plant; herbage growing at the root of other herbage'). *ġamir* synonym of *ġaṭṭ* 'dust clouds' <20/4> (CA *ġamr* 'much, abundant', said of water, dust etc. that covers him who enters into it).

*ġml* *ġimlūl* pl. *ġamālīl* 'a rather narrow valley with dense vegetation' <13/4> (CA *ġumlūl* pl. *ġamālīl* 'a narrow valley with many trees and luxurious vegetation; low tracts of land covered with herbage').

*ġnm* *ġannam, yġannim* 'to give part of the booty to s.o. who did not participate in the raid' *Hess*, 101 (CA *ġannama* 'to give spoil, a free and disinterested gift'). *mitġānim, ġānim* pl. *ġānmīn* 'having obtained, gained, acquired; taker of spoil, successful raider; able, worthy man' *Glos*; *Musil*, 286 <9/11,33/10>. *ġanīmah* pl. *ġanāyim* 'spoil, plunder, booty; acquisition of s.th. without difficulty' *Musil*, 286 <33/25, 37> (CA *ġanīmah* pl. *ġanāʾim*).

*ġwr* *ġār* 'a precipice; crevice; canyon' *Musil*, 682. *ġōr* 'depression, confluence of water' <13/4> (CA *ġawr* 'the bottom, lowest part of anything; low, depressed ground').

*ġwy* — *aġwa* 'to cause to err, lead astray, mislead, seduce; to lust after' <29/2> (CA *aġwā*). *ġāwi* 'bungling, doing s.th. wrong' <7/1> (CA *ġawā* 'to err, act ignorantly'). *ġawyān* 'a man lusting for sexual intercourse' *Musil*, 560; *bint ġawyānah* 'a girl who is fond of dress' *Musil*, 124.

*ġyb* — *ġayyab* 'to cause to disappear, be absent' <21/23>. *ġāyab, yġāyib* 'to be absent, one person from another; to go away' <3/21,32/8> (CA *ġāyaba*). *miġīb* 'direction of sunset, the west' <5/2>.

*ġyr* — *ġār* 'to sink in, fall in; to seep away, to dry up' <10/14>. *aġār, yġīr* 'to charge at the enemy (by mounted men); to attack at once, launch an attack' *Musil*, 578; *Hess*, 99; *Glos* <9/8,25/9>. *ġārah* 'attack, assault' *Musil*, 523; *Glos* (CA *ġārah* 'raid, sudden attack'). *ġayyar ʿala* 'to bring in a bad, angry mood; to upset, rouse anger' <24/1>. *taġayyar* 'to be angry, out of sorts, peevish' <331>.

*ġyl* — *ġēl* pl. *ġyūl* 'thicket' (CA *ġīl* 'water running on the surface of the earth, rivulets, streamlets for irrigation, water running amid stones in a valley'; hence 'dense vegetation in a valley'). *miġyāl* pl. *maġāyīl* same meaning as in CA: '(a valley with) abundant vegetation and many thickets due to the perennial presence of water' <8/7,13/8>.

*ġym* — *ġēm* pl. *ġyām* 'clouds; thin or small clouds' *Musil*, 5 <3/16, 11/12,18/2> (CA *ġaym* pl. *ġuyūm, ġiyām* 'clouds, overcast sky'). *maġāyīm* '(clouds) covering the sky' <12/20> (cf. CA *ġayyamat as-samāʾ*).

*fʾl* — *fāl* 'destiny; good omen' <18/20,26/28>; *ṭayybīn al-fāl* 'men smiled upon by fortune' <6/32>. *ʿala fālihum* 'as destiny would lead them' *Glos* (CA *faʾl* 'a good omen').

*ftr* — *fattar, yfattir* 'he tires, wears out' <2/21> (CA *fattara* 'to make to flag, render weak, faint').

*ftg* — *ftūg* 'rents, slits, openings between clouds' (CA *fatq* pl. *futūq* 'a gap of the clouds'); *xāyiṭ ftūgih* 'its rents are sewn up' i.e. 'clouds without gaps, a seamless cover of clouds' <2/4>. *maftūg* 'sharp, a sharp weapon, dagger' <2/15, 18/18> (CA *maftūq, fatīq* 'sharp in the two edges, sharp').

*ftl* — *fital* 'to twist, plait' *Glos*.

*fty* — *fita* 'young man' <21/16> (CA *fitā* = *s̲h̲ābb*). *fitāt al-*

*ḥayy* 'the most beautiful, noble maiden of the tribe' <33/40>.

*fjj* *fajj* pl. *fjūj* 'gap, mountain pass; a hollow of some width between two hills, with a road running through it' *Musil*, 678 <4/2,10/2> (CA *fajja* 'to cleave; to rip open'; *fajj* 'a wide road between two mountains'). *fajj* 'wide, spacious, broad' *Musil*, 318 <7/6,8/5,30/23>.

*fḥj, fjḥ* *faḥḥaj, tfaḥḥij* '(the she-camel) spreads her hind legs' *Musil*, 333. *fajḥan* 'wide apart' <3/15> (CA *afḥaj* f. *faḥjāʾ* 'having the front parts of the feet near together and the heels wide apart, having the legs wide apart, having bowed legs').

*fḥm* *faḥam* 'charcoal' <1/9>. *faḥḥām* pl. *al-faḥāḥīm* 'charcoal burner'; the men look like charcoal burners because they are charring the *wahaṭ*-branches, see $^{c}$*arāǵīm* (under $^{c}$*rgm*).

*fxt* *fāxat* 'to miss the right direction, take a wrong turn, go astray from' (CA *fak͟hata* 'to stride with the body swaying from side to side').

*fxḏ* *fixḏ* pl. *fxūḏ* 'thigh, limb between *sāg*, the shin, and the *waŕ*, the haunch' <7/8,27/11>.

*fdy* *fida* 'to be ransom for' <9/34>. *fda* 'ransom'; *ya-na fda* 'may we be ransom for (one we love more than we love ourselves)' <22/6> (CA *fadā*, *fidā* 's.th. or a captive, who is given for a man, who is therewith liberated').

*frḥ* *firiḥ, yafraḥ* 'to rejoice; to be glad' *Glos* <1/7>.

*frx* *farx* 'the young one of a bird, a falcon' <23/2>.

*frr* *minfarr* 'twisted, torn' <3/2>; *farrah* 'dispersion, disruption, being rent' <3/2> (cf. CA *farfara* 'to break, rend, tear s.th.').

*frs* *farras, yfarris* 'to spank, worst; to maul, beat up, pummel' <331> (CA *farasa* 'to seize and break the neck of').

*fr*$^{c}$ *fara*$^{c}$, *yafra*$^{c}$ 'to chase away, separate, disperse (e.g. the other camels from the water trough)' <2/12>; *gāydin yafra*$^{c}$ *l-idāmi* 'the dominant female rushes to the fore from among the gazelles and takes the lead in the herd's escape' <11/8>. *farra*$^{c}$ 'to loosen' *Musil*, 204; 'to separate'. *farrā*$^{c}$ 'one who separates two parties, stands as a barrier between them' <32/8> (CA *fara*$^{c}$*a* 'to make a separation; to interpose, intervene as a barrier between; to smite'). *far*$^{c}$ pl. *frū*$^{c}$ 'the starting point of a gully or valley; a branch gully of a side valley; watershed' *Musil*, 638, 677 <14/16>.

*frg* *fārag* 'to separate o.s. from, leave, abandon'; *fārǵīna* 'leave us alone! (said to a woman)' <32b> (CA *fāraqa*). *mfārig* 'departing, parting, leaving' <5/4>. *firīǵ* pl. *firǵān* ' a group, party' <4/11,;23>; 'a camp of 5-10 tents' *Hess*, 59; 'a camp with less than ten tents; a partition of a tribe, households of close kin wandering together' *Musil*, 77; *Doughty* ii, 250. *farāǵīn* 'small camps, less than ten tents' *Musil*, 361-362.

*fry* *fara, yafra* 'to rip open; to cut wide open' *Glos* <18/5>. *allāh yafra baṭnih* 'may God slit his belly' *Hess*, 168; *anti farētīni* 'you have destroyed me'; *ya-mifriyyat al-jēb* 'who makes me rend the shirt on my breast' *Musil*, 200-201. *infara* 'to be shredded, cut, rent' <17/5> (CA *farā* 'to slit, cut lengthwise'; *infarā* 'to become slit, cut'). *iftara, yiftiri* 'to discover, to rummage and bring to light' <29/4>.

*fzz* *fazz* 'to spring up in fear' *Musil*, 396. *fazzāt* 'leaps, bolts' <4/5,24> (CA *fazza* 'to be frightened', said of a gazelle; *fazzah* 'a leap with fright'). *tafzīz rabda* 'the fastest gait of an ostrich, during which it flaps its wings' *Musil*, 626.

*fz*$^{c}$ *fiza*$^{c}$ 'to ride in answer to a cry for help; to give aid, render assistance, to rush to the aid, rescue of' *Glos* <33/11>. *ifza*$^{c}$*u, rab*$^{c}$*akum wixḏu* 'come out to our help quickly, your comrades have been robbed!' *Musil*, 525. *fazza*$^{c}$ 'to rally, incite; to call for help' *Glos*. *afza*$^{c}$, *istafza*$^{c}$ 'to cry, ask for help' *Musil*, 646, 579. *faz*$^{c}$*ah* 'cavalry making the counter attack in order to rescue the captured animals and to drive the raiders back' *Musil*, 524-525 (*faza*$^{c}$*a* 'to aid, succour'; *faza*$^{c}$*a ilā* 'to seek, demand aid, succour').

*fṣl* *faṣṣal, yfaṣṣil b-tafṣīl* 'to compose, mould; to polish, refine (poetry)' <9/1,21/5> (CA *faṣṣala* 'to string beads; to cut cloth to measure').

*fṭr* *fāṭir* pl. *fiṭīr, fiṭṭar* 'a she-camel older than twenty years' *Musil*, 334, or 'older than 14 years' *Hess*, 74 <9/18,12/8, 26/7,27/14,30/20>. Nowadays, however, any she-camel older than nine or ten years is called *fāṭir*, my own informants and *Su* ii, 196 (CA *fāṭir* 'a camel whose *nāb*, tush, is coming forth').

*fṭm* *fṭām* 'weaning' <11/6> (CA *fiṭām*).

*fṭn* *fiṭin* 'to remember, to realize all of a sudden; to think of' *Musil*, 326; 'to understand' *Musil*, 200. *fiṭin l-* 'to mind, look after' *Glos*. *fiṭin ᶜala* 'to remember' *Musil*, 168. *ifṭin al-Jadiy* 'keep an eye on the Pole Star!' *Musil*, 355. *faṭṭan* 'to call to mind, remind of' *Musil*, 188. *faṭṭān* 'perspicacious, intelligent, discerning person' <21/3,29/4> (CA *faṭina* 'to be intelligent, knowing').

*fḏ̣y* *fiḏ̣a* 'to penetrate, pierce, go through' *Glos* <6/8>; 'to defeat' <18/13>; *fḏ̣āhum* 'he penetrated, went through them; defeated them' <33f>. *tifaḏ̣ḏ̣aw* 'they were defeated, they fled' <33f>; *tifaḏ̣ḏ̣a bāli* 'my mind was cleared' *Musil*, 343. *afḏ̣a* 'to let loose, let go, flow; to divulge, reveal' <19/2,21/3> (CA *afḍā* 'to make known'). *fiḏ̣a* 'a plain and wide expanse of land, vast plain' *Musil*, 259 <3/14> (CA *faḍāʾ* 'a wide, spacious tract of land'). *fiḏ̣a bāl* 'a clear mind, good conscience' *Musil*, 261. *afḏ̣a* 'calmer' *Musil*, 405.

*fᶜm* *fiᶜm* 'a torrent that sweeps everything in its way, a torrent that fills its channel' <1/6> (CA *faᶜm* 'full, filled'; *sayl mufᶜam* 'a full torrent').

*fgr* *figir* 'bottom of a well, the *kōkab*, the point in a well from which water issues and gushes out' <5/3,16/4,17/6> (CA *faqīr* 'hollow dug in the ground, well, mouth of the well'). *figār* 'the back of a camel' <7/9,13/13,19/12, 31/9> (CA *faqār* 'the vertebrae of the back').

*fkk* *fakk, yifukk* 'to untie, loosen' <9/33,12/13,18/20,21>; 'to deliver, rescue, save, recover' *Glos*; 'to liberate; to free and recover persons or possessions captured by the enemy' *Musil*, 578 <32f>. *yāma fakkēna* 'how many times have we freed (our captured herds)' *Musil*, 526.

*flj* *mfallij al-milḥ* 'the bullet fired by the ignition of the powder, *milḥ*' <9/25> (CA *mufallaj* 'split, cleft').

*flg* *falag* 'to hit on the head, cause a head injury' *Glos*. *maflūg* 'cleft, cut in two halves' <2/24> (CA *falaqa* 'to split, divide lengthwise').

*flk* *falkah* 'the bit; iron ring of the bridle' <32/1> (CA *falkah* 'spindle; anything hemispherical, circular').

*fll* *maflūl* 'a coward, wretched person' <21/2> (CA *maflūl* 'broken, notched in the edge').

*fnjl* *finjāl* pl. *fanājīl* 'small, earless cup, made of white porcelain or stoneware, in which the coffee is poured' *Musil*, 101 <6/12>.

*fnd* — *fand* pl. *fnūd* 'twig' <4/13,27/10> (CA *fand* 'branch of a tree').

*fny* — *fāni* 'vast and empty' <3/9>. *fāni* pl. *fuwāni* 'ceasing to exist, transitory, mortal' <21/13,23/3,11> (CA *fānī* 'coming to an end'). *fana* 'open space' <25/16>.

*fhd* — *fahad* pl. *fhūd* 'leopard' <33/8,25>.

*fhg* — *mafhūg* 'wide, set apart' <2/9> (CA *fahaq* 'anything that is wide'); 'forced backwards and forewards (said of locks and bolts), bent (neck)', *Musil*, 109, 112.

*fhm* — *tifahham* 'to understand, to fathom' <9/8> (CA *tafahhama* 'to understand, one thing after another', namely speech or language).

*fwḥ* — *fāḥ, yifūḥ* 'to boil over, bubble up' *Musil*, 108; 'to flow (a well)' <5/3,9/9,16/4> (CA *fāḥa* 'to pour forth, to boil'). *fōḥ* 'the bubbling up, welling forth' <5/3,9/9,16/4> (CA *fawḥ*). *fayḥa* pl. *fīḥ* 'good-tempered, enduring she-camels, camels fit for riding' *Musil*, 475 <23/13>.

*fwd* — *fād, fawwad, afād* 'to gain, bring booty' *Musil*, 566 <18/22>. *tfīd* 'you capture booty' *Musil*, 538. *fōd* 'booty' *Musil*, 566; *Glos* (CA *istafāda* 'to gain, acquire property').

*fwᶜ* — *fāᶜ* 'to vault, pounce' *Glos*. *fawwaᶜ* 'to spout up, to bubble up' <17/7> (*fawᶜat an-nahār* 'the rising, first appearance of the day').

*fyḏ̣* — *fāḏ̣* 'to overflow, pour forth; to be abundant' <17/5, 25/3>; 'to appear, come out' *Glos*. *fayyaḏ̣* 'to let down, lower into' *Musil*, 339; 'to go downstream' *Glos*. *fēḏ̣ah* pl. *fyāḏ̣* 'a fertile depression, the point where the wadi becomes wide and shallow' *Glos*; *Musil*, 678 <26/11> (CA *fāḍa*).

*fyy* — *fayy, fayyah* 'shadow' <5/9,9/22,31/3> (CA *fayʾ*).

*gbb* — *gabb* 'to become inflated, to blow up; to spring up and dash away' *Sow* (1981), 67. *gibb aḏ̣-ḏ̣lūᶜ* 'with arched, bulging ribs' *Musil*, 318. *gabba* pl. *gubb* 'horse with arched ribs, big-chested horse, fine horse' *Glos* <2/15,18/17> (CA *qabbāʾ* pl. *qubb*; *qubbun baṭnuh* 'the horse's belly was firmly compacted, so as to have a round form').

*gbl* — *agbal, yiǵbil* 'to appear, approach, come forward' <1/11,

3/17,8/3,10/2,33/9>. *ǵbāl* 'in front of, ahead of; front part' <18/8>. *miǵbil* pl. *migābīl* 'coming, approaching' <8/3,21/7>. *ǵiblah* 'direction of the *qiblah*, Mecca'. *ǵibli* 'in the direction of Mecca' <33/51>. *gibīlah* pl. *gibāyil* 'tribe' <33/14,33e>.

*gbw* *gabuw, gabwah* 'cloud (of ashes, dust etc.)' *Su* iii, 60 <33e> (CA *qabā* 'to vault').

*gḥṣ* *guḥṣ al-xēl* 'energetic thoroughbred horses' <2/18> (cf. CA *qaḥaza* 'to jump').

*gḥgḥ* *guḥguḥ* 'an ʿ*ibla* of white pebbles, flint' <26/10>.

*ǵid* particle with following perf. which indicates the termination of an action <4/4,12/10,11,32/4> (CA *qad*).

*gdd* *gadd* 'to rend, tear'. *ǵidīd, ǵidd* 'a leather thong, sometimes twisted around a strong rope made of palm fibre, with which the rope of the bucket is tied to the saddle of the camel drawing water from a well for irrigation, strap' *JuSa*, 49 <19/6,24/17> (CA *qidd* 'thong cut from untanned skin').

*gdm* *gidam* pl. *aǵdām* 'foot; foreleg' *Musil*, 367 <12/12,28/4>. *migdim, miǵdim* 'front, head of' <3/18>; 'the leader' *Musil*, 367. *migādīm* 'coming, lying ahead' <12/15, 18/3>; *fi migādīm* 'in the front, forefront of' <11/15>. *ǵiddām* 'up front, ahead' *Musil*, 367.

*gdy* *ǵida, ǵadda, yǵaddi* 'to direct, lead, show the way' *Glos* <3/5,18,14/8>; 'to lead, to steer in the right direction; to indicate and prepare the way' *Musil*, 81; 'to do s.th. well' <21/6>. *igtida, yiǵtidi* 'to be guided by, find one's way with the help of, serve as a beacon for' <25/15>. *ǵida* 'sensibleness, reasonableness' <21/1>. *ǵādi, miǵdiyāt* 'the right direction, course' <2/25,15/3>. *la tixṭi l-ǵuwādi* 'do not commit any injustice, wrong'; *ihrij bi-l-ǵādi* 'speak the truth!' *Hess*, 155 (CA *aqdā* 'to return from a journey; to be steadfast in the path of righteousness').

*grb* *garrab, yǵarrib* 'to bring near; to run so well as to make the distance seem short' <9/30,11/10>. *migrāb* explained to me as 'four to five days of grazing in pastures without water in the hot season before returning to the watering place', see *ḏmy* <1/7>; *garab* 'when the camels going to be watered spend the first night far from their pasture, reach the water the following noon, stay there over night, approach the tents on the third day, and do not return till the fourth day from the time when they set out' *Musil*, 338 (CA *qaruba* 'to be near').

*grb*$^{c}$ *garba*$^{c}$, *yigarbi*$^{c}$ 'to make a noise by knocking into s.th. accidentally' *JohnDoii*, 92; 'to rattle s.o., make s.o. uneasy, nervous'. *girbā*$^{c}$ 'one who is set on edge by the slightest noise (in the dark)'. *girba*$^{c}$*ah* 'rattling, clatter, clanking' *Ḥa* <5/12>.

*grḥ* *ǵāriḥ* pl. *girraḥ* 'sheep and goats in their fifth year' *Hess*, 83. *garāḥ* 'pure, sweet water; fresh water, good drinking water' *Musil*, 562 <10/8,30/2,31/4,33/10> (CA *qarāḥ* 'clear, pure water').

*grdb* *girdūb* 'the highest point of a *ḥazim*, stony hill' <19/18, 21>.

*grd*$^{c}$ *girdu*$^{c}$ pl. *garādī*$^{c}$ explained as 'lengthwise extended, rugged rows of hills, partly covered with stones, lower than the *ḥazim* type' <6/27> (CA *qardad* pl. *qarādīd* 'high, rugged ground; the middle of a man's back').

*grr* *garr* 'to rest, remain, reside; to be firmly established' <30/8>. *garrah* 'motionless, fixed position' <3/21>. *garār* 'steadiness'; *ḥāmi garārih* 'his unflagging, hot pace' <15/5> (CA *qarr, qarār*). *magarr li-l-farāǵīn wa-n-njū*$^{c}$ 'a watering-place with room for camps both small and large' *Musil*, 361. *mistigarr* 'base, abode, residence' <30/17>.

*grṣ* *gurṣ* 'disk; round, flat form' <5/7>.

*gr*$^{c}$ *gara*$^{c}$, *yagra*$^{c}$ 'to hold back, check, stop s.o. from doing s.th.'. *ǵāri*$^{c}$ 's.o. who holds back, checks, restrains, prevents' <4/18>. *girī*$^{c}$ 'sound of things knocking together' <5/12> (CA *qara*$^{c}$*a* 'to knock, hit, beat, strike'). *ǵuwāri*$^{c}$ 'heads (not covered by a scarf)' <6/4> (CA *aqra*$^{c}$ 'bald-headed'). *rā*$^{c}$ *al-ǵuwāri*$^{c}$ 'poet, maker of verses' <21/5,6> (CA *qawāri*$^{c}$ *al-qur*$^{\text{ɔ}}$*ān* 'verses of the Koran that are recited as protection against *jinn* etc.'). *garāyi*$^{c}$ 'the select, the best; choice camels, camels of a noble breed' <u>*KhaAd*</u>, 483 <33/29> (CA *qāri*$^{c}$ 'choice part'; *qarī*$^{c}$*at al-ibl* 'thoroughbred, excellent camels').

*grg*$^{c}$ *ǵirǵi*$^{c}$ 'to burn and crackle (in the fire)' <17/4>; *kiṯr al-garga*$^{c}$*ah yaftaḥ al-bāb* 'if you rattle the door long enough in the end it will open' $^{c}$*Ubūdī*, 1007 (CA *qarqa*$^{c}$*a* 'to make harsh sounds like that of steel beating on steel'). *flān mgarga*$^{c}$

*ar-rās* lit. 'he rattles with the head', i.e. 'his head is hollow, he is hare-brained, stupid' *Hess*, 171.

*grn* *ǵarn* pl. *grūn* 'strands of hair, tresses; curls, plaited locks' *Hess*, 129; *Musil*, 109 <12/24,28/3>; 'horns, antlers' <33/43,44> (CA *qarn* pl. *qurūn* with the same meaning). *ǵūrān* 'a pace in which the camel puts its left hind leg next to its right foreleg and so on' <9/25>; *igrān* 'a long, fast pace of the camel' *Musil*, 286 (CA *qarn* 'a fast pace'). *magrūn* 'connected, hitched together' <28/5>.

*gry* *gara, yagra* 'to still the hunger of s.o.; to be of use to, to bring advantage, to benefit' <14/5>. *agra, yiǵri* 'to feed a guest'; *ǵra* 'the food served to a guest'. *migra* 'the vessel from which the guest has eaten' *Hess*, 145 (CA *qarā aḏ̣-ḏ̣ayf* 'he fed the guest'). *gara* 'back' *Musil*, 273; 'the ridge of a hill' *Musil*, 680; *gara al-ḥazim* 'the back, plateau of the high, rugged desert' <18/14>; *šīb al-gara* 'camels with grey hair on their back' <1/10,10/13>; *nābi garāha* 'a fat camel whose hump resembles a bulging knoll, cone' *Musil*, 626 (CA *qarā* 'the middle of the back').

*gsm* *magsūm* pl. *migāsīm* 'what is destined, ordained by God, fated' *Glos* <12/16>.

*gsy* *migsiy* 'resisting, struggling against' <5/11> (CA *qāsāh* 'he struggled, contended with s.o., s.th.'). *gāsi* 'hard, merciless, relentless' <30/12>.

*gšl* *gašlah* 'villa; large house surrounded by a wall' <25/11>.

*gšm* *gišīm* 'hot coals, *jamr*' (*qishm* 'flesh that has stewed to a dark-red colour').

*gṣb* *giṣab* 'cane, reed' <9/31> (CA *qaṣab*).

*gṣd* *gṣād* '(the act of) coming down straight at, hitting fully' <13/10> (CA *iqṣād* 'hitting s.th. with full effect').

*gṣr* *gāṣar* = *jāwar* 'to be, become a neighbour of another tribe' *Hess*, 94 <33a>. *giṣīr* pl. *gṣara* 'neighbour; a member of another tribe who has left his kin for some reason and who, for a time at least, desires to make his home in a different territory. He comes to an agreement with the host tribe that they will be neighbours, and as such will protect each other against harm from the other tribe' *Musil*, 267; *Hess*, 94 <32f,33a,33/15>. *tigiṣṣār* 'moderation, taking things in modest portions' <10/2>. *gāṣir* 'falling short of, unable to attain' <21/28>.

*gṣṣ* — *gaṣṣ, ygiṣṣ* ‘to cut, cut off’ *Musil*, 316 <2/24>.

*gṣf* — *tigaṣṣaf* ‘to come in loud claps (thunder)’ <13/6> (CA *raᶜdun qāṣifun* ‘a lound thunderclap’).

*gṭb* — *giṭab* ‘to fill; to complete; to tie up, wrap up’ *Glos*; ‘to seize mentally, to understand’ <21/12>. *gaṭṭab* ‘to gather, draw together’; *ygaṭṭib aṭ-ṭēr* ‘he sews up the eyelids of the falcon’ *Musil*, 32 (CA *qaṭaba* ‘to collect, gather, draw together s.th.’). *giṭīb* ‘firm, drawn together firmly’ <2/3>. *migṭib* ‘knowing for certain’ <2/18>.

*gṭr* — *migṭir* ‘dripping, leaking’ <33/36>.

*gṭᶜ* — *giṭaᶜ* ‘to cut; to stop, interrupt, suspend; to be interrupted’ <6/34,25/4>; ‘to cross, traverse’ *Glos*; ‘to tire (riding animal)’ *Musil*, 367. *gaṭṭaᶜ* ‘to break, cut; to pass through’ <26/7>; *yagṭaᶜin* ‘they (pl. f.) cross, traverse’ <27/13>. *gaṭᶜah* ‘crossing of a desert’ <9/24>; *migāṭīᶜ* (pl.) ‘major desert crossings, traverses’ <6/22> (CA *maqṭaᶜ* pl. *maqāṭiᶜ* ‘a place of traversing’). *mgaṭṭᶜāt* ‘(she-camels) cutting through, traversing (the desert)’ <24/6>. *giṭīᶜ* pl. *giṭᶜān* ‘a herd’ *Musil*, 84, 336 <19/4> (CA *qaṭīᶜ* ‘a herd of between 10-40 sheep and the like’).

*gṭm* — *giṭam* ‘to clip’. *guṭm al-xafāf* ‘clipped of hoof’, i.e. ‘their hoofs are round as though they have been clipped’ <8/7> (CA *qaṭama* ‘to bite with the front teeth; to cut’).

*gṭn* — *giṭan, yigṭin; al-ᶜarab gṭanaw* ‘the bedouins camp for a longer period at the well (generally in the summer)’ *Hess*, 60; *Musil*, 247. *migṭān* pl. *migāṭīn* ‘a place where the bedouins make a prolonged stay in summer time’ *Musil*, 247 <9/18>. *giṭīn* ‘the camp; the bedouins who camp near the well’ *Hess*, 60. *gāṭin* ‘one who camps near the well for a considerable length of time’ *Musil*, 649 (CA *qaṭana* ‘to stay, sojourn in a place’).

*gṭy* — *giṭāh* pl. *gṭiyāt* ‘sand grouse’ *Musil*, 328, 363; *Glos* <9/23, 27/4,32/5,33/10>; ‘the flight of sand grouse is very noisy, somewhat resembling the sound of the wind, *farr*, to fly with a buzzing sound’ *Musil*, 363 (CA *qaṭāh*).

*gḏ̣b* — *gaḏ̣ḏ̣ab* ‘to grasp, clasp, hold tight’ <4/8,6/19,24/9>. *tigaḏ̣ḏ̣ab* ‘to seize, grasp, grip, take by force’ (CA *qabaḍa*, through transposition of the consonants). *migḏ̣āb* ‘handle, grip’ <30/16>.

*gḏ̣ḏ̣* *gaḏ̣ḏ̣, yguḏ̣ḏ̣* 'to pierce, to tear up, to break into pieces, crush, demolish' <25/17,30/11> (CA *qaḏḏa*).

*gḏ̣*$^{c}$ *giḏ̣ī*$^{c}$ 'fastened upon, having a firm grip on' <5/6> (CA *qaḏa*$^{c}$*ah* 'he held him in check, subdued him').

*gḏ̣m* *giḏ̣am, tagḏ̣am* 'she champs (the bit), chews on, snaps at with the teeth' <2/15>; *giḏ̣īm* 'biting with front teeth' <5/10> (CA *qaḏima al-faras* 'the mare bit with the front teeth'; *al-qaḏm* 'biting and chewing with the front teeth and molars, in particular on s.th. tough and dry').

*gḏ̣y* *giḏ̣a* 'to finish, to end; to be ended, terminated, to be exhausted, finished, obliterated; to fulfil, accomplish' <9/2, 23/4,26/20>. *ingiḏ̣a* 'to be finished, settled, accomplished' <16/1,26/23>. *mingiḏ̣i* 'finished; extinct, dead' <;23>. *giḏ̣a* 'recompense, compensation' *Glos.*

*g*$^{c}$*d* *ga*$^{c}$*ad* 'to remain, sit, stay'. *ma ga*$^{c}$*ad wādi* 'not a wadi remained (without rain)' <2/7,14/18>. *ag*$^{c}$*ad* 'to prevent from moving; to tie down, keep at bay' <30/18>; 'to cause to sit up, to awaken' *Musil*, 549; *yiǵ*$^{c}$*id an-nīm* (pl. of *nāyim, nēm*) 'he makes the sleeping sit up' <12/25,16/3> (CA *yuq*$^{c}$*id*). *gi*$^{c}$*ūd* pl. *ǵi*$^{c}$*dān* 'young male camels for the first six years, until their eye-teeth, *nībān*, become fully developed' *Musil*, 334 <32c,33/5,40,46> (CA *qa*$^{c}$*ūd* 'a young male camel, a camel on which the shepherd rides'). *gi*$^{c}$*īd, g*$^{c}$*adah, ǵi*$^{c}$*dah* 'the leading animal on which the herdsman mounts and rides at the head of his herd' *Musil*, 269, 336, 337, 660 <33h> (CA *qu*$^{c}$*dah* 'a camel on which the shepherd rides'; *qa*$^{c}$*adah, qa*$^{c}$*īdah* 'a beast of carriage').

*gfz* *magfizi, magfiziyyah* 'a kind of palm-tree producing white-coloured dates' <17/9>.

*gfgf* *tamši gifāgīf* 'they trudge, plod along; walk with a faltering gait' <19/7> (*taqafqafa* 'to shudder, tremble, shiver').

*gfl* *giffal, giffāl* (pl.) 'lean and fit camels and horses with taut bellies' <6/23> (CA *qāfil* 'a slender horse'). *gaflah* pl. *ǵfāl* 'the width of a finger (the smallest measure of length)' *Hess*, 123; *arba*$^{c}$ *ǵfāl* 'the width of four fingers pressed against one another' <27/12> (CA *qufl* pl. *aqfāl* 'lock, padlock').

*gfy* *gifa, agfa* 'to turn back, move away; to make an escape, retreat' *Musil*, 219 <3/11,33/9>; *tiǵfi* 'she turns away, moves away' <6/28,19/11>; inf. n. *igfa, igfāh* 'the return; turning back, fleeing' *Glos* <6/16>. *tigaffa* 'to follow in the traces of' <3/11,14/10>. *tigāfa* 'to move away one following in the steps of the other' <33/35> (CA *qafā, taqaffā*). *gāfi* 'consequence, result' <21/2>. *miǵfi* 'turning one's back, turning away, moving away' <21/7>; *miǵfīn* 'those going back' *Musil*, 165. *miǵfīn b-* (pl.) 'moving away, departing with (booty etc.)' <32d>. *gāf* pl. *ǵīfān* 'rhyme', generally used with the metonymical meaning of 'rhymed verse, poetry' *Musil*, 175, 283 <6/1, 4,9/8,35,11/1,12/1,2> (CA *qāfiyah*).

*glb* *gālab* 'to turn over, to change one's fortunes for the worse', said of the *dinya*, 'world, destiny' <12/2> (CA *qallaba* 'to turn over'). *tigallab* 'to turn, turn around' <19/13>; *tigallab ʿala* 'to turn against, in one's disadvantage' <21/12>. *ǵilīb* pl. *gilbān* 'a well, whether walled and deep or unwalled and wide' *Musil*, 684 <6/7,7/6,33d,e,33/50> (CA *qalīb* pl. *qulbān* 'a well in the desert').

*glt* *ǵaltah* pl. *ǵlāt* 'a deep, rocky crevice filled with rain water; a water hole among the rocks, at least one metre deep' *Glos*; *Hess*, 64; *Musil*, 684 <9/23> (*qaltah* 'a hole in the hard rocks').

*glṭ* *galaṭ* 'to step forward; to be first; to go ahead of' *Glos*. *gallaṭ* 'to push forward' *Musil*, 355; 'to send ahead' *Glos*. *gallāṭ* pl. *glūṭ* 'scout, s.o. sent ahead of the main party; the man who precedes the camels to the well in order to prepare the ropes, the bucket and the water trough' <2/13>.

*glʿ* *galaʿ* 'to uproot, pluck' *Glos*; *glaʿat b-* 'she eloped with, ran away with' <33h>. *glāʿah, ǵilīʿ* pl. *galāyiʿ* 'a captured horse whose owner was thrown from the saddle during the fight' *Musil*, 434, 556; *Palva*, 98; *Glos* <2/20>. *gilīʿin midāh* 'his is a long journey, a road stretched out far' *Musil*, 158. *miglāʿ* pl. *migālīʿ* 'a utensil to pull out s.th., pincers' <6/3>.

*glfʿ* *galfaʿ* 'a kind of *ḥazim*, rugged hills covered with flat, scaled stones' <18/7> (CA *qilfiʿ* 'ground of a depression that becomes chapped after the pool of water left by the rain has dried up and its bottom has been baked by the sun').

*gll* *gall ʿala* 'to be stingy with, give but little' <32f>. *gullihum* 'their fewness, small numbers' <32e>. *tigallal* 'to set out on a journey, carrying a burden (a camel train, caravan)' <33/38> (CA *aqalla, istaqalla* 'to lift up s.th. and transport').

*gm*$^{c}$ — *yagma*$^{c}$ 'he bridles, curbs, subdues' <18/18> (CA *qama*$^{c}$*a*).

*gnb* — *ginīb* 'barking, howling' (CA *qānib* 'a howling wolf').

*gnd* — *mgannad* 'spiced, perfumed' <6/12> (CA *qand* 'a perfume, aromatic').

*gnz*$^{c}$ — *ganāzi*$^{c}$ 'heads' <26/26> (CA *qanza*$^{c}$*ah* pl. *qanāzi*$^{c}$ 'a forelock; hair; long parts of the hair, hair in the middle of the head').

*gnṣ* — *gannāṣ* 'hunter; stalker of great ground game (*ṣayyād* is the light hunter with hawk and hound, to take the desert hare)' *Doughty* ii, 116 <33/48>.

*gn*$^{c}$ — *ganna*$^{c}$ 'to cover, envelop'. *tiganna*$^{c}$ 'to veil, conceal, cover one's face; to be covered, enveloped' <10/9,14/17>. *mitganni*$^{c}$ 'covering, enveloping; covered, enveloped in' <3/8> (CA *taqanna*$^{c}$*a* 'to be veiled').

*gnf* — *ǵinīf* pl. *gnūf* 'big cloud, cumulus' <1/11,13/9,14/16> (CA *qanīf* 'clouds carrying lots of rain').

*gnn* — *gunn* 'a person who lacks any ambition, sluggard; slave' <13/13,21/18> (CA *qinn* 'slave').

*gny* — *ǵanāh, ganāh* pl. *ǵinyān* 'spear, javelin; the bedouins' short loaded club-stick, heavy cane ending in a knob' *Doughty* i, 443; *Musil*, 127 <2/23,24/5,33/31> (CA *qanāh* 'stick, spear', usually one with a hollow shaft).

*ghr* — *gahar* 'to repel, ward off' *Glos*; 'to stop, rein in'; *ighar gi*$^{c}$*ūdak* 'stop your camel' *Musil*, 561; *yaghark* 'he will tame you' *Musil*, 364 (CA *qahara*). *maghūr* pl. *miǵāhīr* 'halted, stopped (by one who puts himself in the way)'; synonym of *ḥīrān* 'camel calves' *JuA*, 227 <12/22>.

*gwd* — *gād, yigūd* 'to lead' <2/7>; 'to be led away' <13/17> (CA *qāda* 'to lead'). *ingād, yingād* 'to be swept along; to be led away; to follow; to be stirred up' <2/20,32/4>. *mingād* 'led, led on, coming in uninterrupted waves' <2/4, 13/8>; 'direction' <2/9> (CA *munqād*). *istigād* 'to be led, to obey' <18/15>. *gāyid, gāydat al-jimīlah* 'the leader of the gazelle herd' *Glos* <11/8,24/12> (CA *qā*$^{\supset}$*idah* 'a she-camel that precedes the other camels or leads them on').

*gwr* *mgawwar* 'a conical mountain with a round top' < 13/1 >; *gārah* pl. *gūr, gwār* 'an isolated table mountain; a mesa' *Musil*, 680; 'conical rocky outcrops' < ;8 > (CA *muqawwar* 'cut in a round form'; *qārah* 'a small isolated black mountain').

*gws* *agwās* '(curved like) bows' i.e. 'camels with hollow, lean bellies' < 20/6 > (CA *qaws* pl. *aqwās*).

*gw*$^{c}$ *gī*$^{c}$*ah, gā*$^{c}$ pl. *gī*$^{c}$*ān* 'a flat plain where the rain-water forms no brooks' *Musil*, 680 < 10/8 > (CA *qā*$^{c}$, *qī*$^{c}$*ah* pl. *aqwā*$^{c}$, *qī*$^{c}$*ān* 'a wide, flat tract of land without rocks, stones or trees, which lies lower than the surrounding ground and where the rain-water accumulates').

*gwl* *gīl* 'words; poetry' < 8/1 >.

*gwm* *gām* + imperf. 'to begin to, start doing s.th.' < 2/6,;17, 21/6,12,33/30 >; *gāmat tigallab* $^{c}$*ala* 'she (the world) became fickle, began to change, turn against' < 21/12 >. *gāmah* pl. *gāmāt* 'a man's height' *Hess*, 124 < 11/1,25/8 > (CA *qāmah* 'stature; fathom; measure of length, six feet'). *gyām* 'measure, size, width' < 25/13 >. *gyāmah* 'resurrection; tumult, upheaval' < 11/20 > (CA *qiyāmah*). *guwāmah* 'support, undercarriage, legs' < 25/9 >. *gōm* pl. *gīmān* 'enemies, warriors, armed following, troop' *Musil*, 316; *Hess*, 102 < 5/11,32d,33e >. *gōmāni* 'enemy, s.o. from an enemy tribe' *Musil*, 116, 223, 359, 505. *ḥalāl al-gōm* 'may he be the *ḥalāl* (possession of) *al-gōm* (enemies, raiders); may he be captured and taken away as booty by the enemy'; $^{c}$*asāk li-l-gōm* 'may you fall in the hands of your enemies' *Hess*, 168.

*gyd* *gēd* pl. *gyūd* 'fetters, shackles, chains' < 33/17 > (CA *qayd* pl. *quyūd*).

*gys* *gēs, gēsah* 'measure' < 4/19 > (CA *qāsa* 'to measure'). *gyās* 'measure, size' < 27/12 >.

*gyḏ̣* *gēḏ̣* 'the hot and dry season, extending over four months from about the beginning of June to about the first days of October, when the bedouins encamp in the settled territories' *Musil*, 8, 164, 338 < 19/7,20/4 > (CA *qayẓ*). *migīḏ̣* 'place where the bedouins and their herds spend the hot season' *Musil*, 78.

*gyl* *gayyal* ‘to rest in the shade at midday’ <33i>. *mgayyil* ‘taking a rest in the shade at noon’ *Musil*, 209 <;17,33i>. *gāylah* ‘noon, midday’ *Hess*, 70 <6/26>; *bi-l-gāylah* ‘between one and three in the afternoon, the hottest part of the day’ *Musil*, 189, 562; ‘time when the sun rises towards noon’ *Doughty* i, 399. *migyāl* pl. *migāyīl* ‘noon rest, pause in a shady place’ <6/20,10/6,13/10,17,26/11,31/3>. *ḏ̣hūrhinnah migāyīl* ‘their backs are exposed to the midday sun’ i.e. ‘the riders spend the *gāylah*, the time of the greatest heat, on the back of their mounts and do not rest in the shade’, a metaphor for ‘hard riding’ <8/b>.

*kbb* *kabb* ‘to shake, spill, pour into, cast aside’ *Musil*, 101, 325. *kabbab* ‘to become fat, to thicken, bulge’ <6/18> (CA *kabba* ‘to be weighty, heavy’).

*kbd* *ćabd* pl. *ćbūd* ‘liver (an organ thought to be the seat of passion, especially of burning feelings like hate, spite, malice etc.); the entire area of the stomach, entrails’ *Hess*, 149; *Musil*, 115 <13/21,33/45>; *yangaᶜ ᶜala ćabdi liḏīḏ al-garāḥ* ‘clean, sweet water filled my entrails (after revenge was taken)’ *Musil*, 575 (CA *kabd, kibd*).

*ktb* *ćitab* pl. *ćitbān* ‘pack-saddle, saddle to which the ropes of the bucket are attached when the *sānyah* starts drawing water’ <21/31> (CA *qatab*).

*kṯḥ* *ćaṯḥ an-njūm* ‘the time marked by the position of the stars when the hot winds of summer begin to blow and stir up, *ćaṯḥ*, clouds of dust’; *ᶜajāj w-simūm b-sitt liyāl gidm an-njūm tiṭlaᶜ* ‘the clouds of dust and the hot storms six nights before the appearance of the stars (i.e. *aṯ-ṯrayya*, the Pleiades, *al-mirzim*, Sirius, *al-jōza*, Orion, and *shēl*, Canopus)’ *Hess*, 66 (CA *kathaḥa* ‘to blow s.th. away’).

*kḥl* *kuḥil* ‘antimony, kohl’ <22/6> (CA *kuḥl*).

*kdd* *kadd* ‘to toil’ <12/12>. *kaddah* ‘(an attack) by all together; an all out attack’ (cf. *katt* ‘to come together all at once’ *Glos*) <32/6> (CA *kadkada ᶜala* ‘to attack’; *makdūd* ‘vanquished’).

*kḏb* *ćiḏbān* ‘liars’ <24/11> (CA *kadhaba* ‘to lie, tell a lie’).

*krsᶜ* *kirsūᶜ* pl. *karāsīᶜ* ‘elbow of the camel, joint of the foreleg’ <4/19,6/24> (CA *kursūᶜ* pl. *karāsiᶜ*).

*krᶜ* *karaᶜ* ‘to drink from a water-hole’ <u>KhaAd</u>, 207. *kurrāᶜ* (pl.) 'drinking in one row with the necks lowered to the water; flying in close formation with the gaze fixed in one direction' <32/5> (CA *kāriᶜ* 'drinking', as a designation of palm-trees standing at the edge of the water; *mukraᶜ* 'standing at the edge of water').

*krnb* *karānīb* <12/23>, explained to me as synonymous with *karab* 'the thick bases of the fronds used in Mesopotamia and Upper Arabia as fuel' *PhilHe* ii, 171, but the context makes it clear that what is meant in this line are the yellow stalks from which the date bunches hang. In the north the word *kirnāfah*, pl. *karānīf* (CA *kirnāfah*) occurs, meaning 'the underside of the *krubah*, the place where the bases of the fronds are broken off' (in CA *karnīb* has the meaning of 'dates with milk').

*ksr* *kisar* 'to swing around; to break; to defeat' *Glos* <18/20>. *kāsrin ᶜungih* 'lowering, curving its neck downward' <11/11>.

*ksy* *maćsiy* 'clothed, dressed' <9/26>; *ćāsyāt* (pl. f.) 'dressing, enveloping in, draping on' <33/20> (CA *kasā* 'to clothe, dress').

*kfx* *kifax* 'to shake, flutter, palpitate vehemently' <6/21>; *galbi kifax* 'my heart pounded' *JuK̲h̲a*, 33 (CA *kafak̲h̲a* 'to beat').

*kff* *ćaff* pl. *ćfūf* 'foot of camel' <4/22,11/11> (CA *kaff* pl. *kufūf*).

*kfl* *fi ćfālih* 'in his protection, care; under his leadership' <18/14> (CA *kafālah* 'protection, care, support').

*kfy* *kifa, ćifa* 'to spare, save from; to be sufficient' <23/12>; 'to perform s.th. well on behalf of s.o. else, to be equal to the task' <30/9>; *ćifōna* 'they did well on our behalf'; *ćifīna* 'may satisfaction be obtained for us!' <26/21>; *al-lah yićfīna* 'may God spare us all' *Glos*. *ćifāk al-ᶜōg* 'may God save you from an obstruction'; *ćifāk aš-šarr* 'may God save you from evil' *Musil*, 114 (CA *kafā* 'to suffice, to be enough; to obtain satisfaction for a person, to save s.o. the trouble of having to do s.th.; to defend, protect, save s.o. or s.th.; to perform s.th. in an appropriate, competent manner'). *kāfa* 'to protect, save, spare' *Glos*; 'to be equal to, to be able to stand up to, to measure up to' <33k> (CA *kāfaʾa* and *kāfā* 'to be equal, of equal value to; to measure up to'). *kafuw*, said in praise of a man to indicate that he was capable and equal to the task, *Glos*.

*klb* *ćalb* pl. *ćlāb* 'dog' <16/7>. *ćlēb* 'dog' (reflex of the CA diminutive *kulayb*).

*kll* *ćall* 'to get tired' *Musil*, 343 (CA *kalla* 'to become tired, weary; to be dim, dull'). *ćilīl* 'a little remaining *jamr*, red-hot coals' <14/3> (CA *sanā barqin kalīlin* 'the dull, faint flicker of a lightning').

*klm* *kalām, ćalām* 'words; poetry' *Musil*, 318 <6/6,7/1,9/2, 11/a,18/1,25/5>.

*kly* *ćālyāt* (pl. f.) 'to find grass, green fodder' (CA *kalaʾa*).

*ćam* 'how many', often used in boastful sections as the equivalent of the formulas *wa-rubba* or *wa-qad* introducing the *fak̲h̲r* sections of classical poetry, see also *yāma*, <2/23,;8, 18/20,21/28,23/4,33/40> (CA *kam* 'how much, how many').

*ćima* 'like, as', a conjunction used in similes, often as a synonym for *mit̲il* (CA *ka-mā*).

*kmm* *makmūm* pl. *mikāmīm* 'covered', said of the spadix, that later grows into the bunch of dates, when it is covered after the spathe has burst open in order to protect it from the heat, birds, locusts etc.; 'every cluster, which had enclosed in it a spray of the male blossom, was lapped about with a wisp of dry forage; and this defended the sets from early flights of locusts' *Doughty* ii, 466 <12/23> (CA *kimām* 'covering which is wound round the date panicle to protect it from drying and from birds'; *kamma* 'to provide a palm with a *kimām*').

*kmn* *ćiman, yaćmin* 'to be hidden, concealed' <31/5>. *aćman* 'to lie in ambush'. *ćimīn* 'ambush, reserve' *Glos* (CA *kamana* 'to conceal oneself, to hide; to be hidden; to lay in ambush for s.o.').

*ćan* 'as if, as though', a conjunction frequently used in poetry to announce a simile. In many cases it takes a pronominal suffix, referring to the comparison's subject (CA *ka-anna*).

*kns* *kinnas* 'strong camels' *Glos* (the closest CA equivalents are perhaps *kināz* 'solid, compact, strong', said of camels, or *qinʿās* 'a big, fleshy camel').

*knn* *ćann* 'to hide, conceal; repress'; *ćannēt* 'I have hidden' <19/2,29/4>. *ćinīn, ćnān* 'what is hidden; concealment;

what one hides inside his breast, the feelings and thoughts one dissimulates' <6/3,16/2,19/2,23/2> (CA *kannana* 'to hide, veil'; *kinān* 'cover, covering'; *kanīn* 'concealed'). *ćannah* 'the period of the eclipse of the Pleiades in late May and early June'. *maknūn* 'hidden, concealed' <28/6>. *mistićinn* 'concealed, hidden; dense, deep (shadow)' *Musil*, 294 <18/11> (CA *mustakinn* 'concealed, well-preserved').

*kny* *ćana* 'to conceal; to suppress; to endure, bear' <21/31>; *aćnāh* 'I conceal, repress my feelings; I bear it, endure it'; *aćmāh* has the same meaning, *Faraj*, 167 <19/3> (CA *kamā* 'to cover, conceal s.th.'). *ćāni* 'hiding, concealing, suppressing' <23/7>. *maćniy* 'suppressed, concealed' <9/7> (CA *takannā* 'to hide, cover o.s.').

*khb* *ćahhab* 'to pour down, come down in torrents' <18/6>. *akhab* 'to lean over'; *akhab ʿala l-bīr* 'he leant so far over the edge of the well as almost to fall in'. *kawhab* 'to go down to' *Su* ii, 160. *mićāhīb* 'falling, coming down to' <12/22>.

*kwd* *kūd* 'difficulty' *Glos*; 'hardness; (excessive) pride; unruliness, recalcitrance' <33/13>.

*kwr* *kār* 'pride', i.e. 'ʿ*izz*, s.th. one puts great store by, aspiration; labour, work' *Musil*, 271 <20/6>. *ḏabḥ as-suwāri kārna* 'the killing of troopers is our sport' *Musil*, 556 (Persian *kār* 'work, business, task, affair'). *kūr* pl. *akwār* 'the saddle of a camel' <25/10,26/9> (CA *kūr* pl. *akwār*).

*kwn* *aćān* 'to attack, assault, wage war on' <33g>. *ćāyin* 'attacking, assaulting' <32d>. *kōn* 'battle, fight' *Glos*. *yikūn* 'as long as' <3/21>. *ya-kūn, kūn* 'except for, unless' <;23,23/13>.

*kyr* *ćīr, ćīrah* 'a heap of red-hot coals; smith's forge' *Musil*, 321 <7/10,18/21> (CA *kīr* 'bellows, smith's forge with bellows, blast-furnace').

*kyl* *ćāl, yćīl* 'to load supplies' *Musil*, 521; 'to load a gun' *Hess*, 106. *ićtāl* 'to receive as one's portion, apportionment, allotment; to be showered with, receive in great quantity' <u>*KhaAd*</u>, 347; *min gaddam al-jūd yićtāl* is a proverb similar in meaning to *min gaddam al-ḥisna tigāḏa al-jimāyil* 'who performs good deeds, will receive a similar good treatment from others' ʿ*Ubūdī*, 1444 <26/22> (CA *iktāla*). *ćyāl* (pl.) 'a measure, a load' <2/24>; *ćēl* 'measuring' *Musil*, 70

(CA *kayl* pl. *akyāl*). *mikyāl* pl. *mikāyīl* 'measure of capacity (for grains, liquids etc.)' <18/19>.

*la, lya, lē, lēn* *la, lya* subordinate conjunctions corresponding to CA *i̲dh̲ā*, 'if, when'; *la, lya* are also used with the meaning of CA *ilā*, 'to, towards, as far as, until'. Combined with the particle of negation *la* these conjunctions may also introduce a hypothetical conditional clause, *lya la, lāla* 'if not, if it weren't for' (< *lōla* < CA *law lā*). The particle *lē* introduces a nominal clause in the same way as CA *inna*; like *ya* and *lya* it sometimes conveys an idea of suddenness and surprise, 'and then, and all of a sudden, lo and behold', but more often it functions as a syndetic particle introducing the main clause following a subordinate clause introduced by the conjunction *yōm* 'when'. *lēn* 'until, till' (CA *ilā an*). Cf. *JohnEa*, 16; *JohnDoii*, 93-95; *Sow*, 65-72.

*lbb* *labbah* 'sands at the foot of an *ʿirǵ*, a high sand-hill' <14/15> (CA *labbah* 'upper part of the chest, low neckline'; *labab* 'the sand at the foot of a dune, the underside of its slope').

*ljj* *lajj* 'to make a noise as if in protest or dismay, to clamour; to tinkle, ring' *Musil*, 173 <6/7,22/5> (CA *lajja al-qawm* 'the people uttered confused cries'). *lajjah* 'noise, din, shouting, noise, clamour' <19/4,10>.

*ljlj* *lajlij* 'to make a tumultuous, confused din' <6/7,23/8>; *lijlāj ahal sūg* 'the uproar of people in a market place' *JuA*, 100 (CA *lajlāj* 'stammering speech'; *lajlaja* 'to speak with an indistinct utterance, to stammer').

*ljy* *lājiyy* 'taking refuge in; being stored, amassed, contained in; being carried around in' <33/45> (CA *lajaʾa* 'to seek refuge').

*lḥḥ* *laḥḥ* 'to be close, next to, rub against' *Glos*. *alaḥḥ* 'to press s.o., to urge s.o. persistently' <13/3>.

*lḥd* *liḥd* pl. *lḥūd* 'grave' <33/28> (CA *laḥd* pl. *luḥūd* 'burial niche in the grave').

*lḥz* *milḥāz riʿ* 'the narrow part of a defile' <5/10> (CA *malḥaz* pl. *malāḥiz* 'narrows, defile', synonym of *maḍīq* pl. *maḍāyiq*).

*lḥf* *ʿūj al-luwāḥīf* 'the slanted poles supporting the draw-wheels suspended above the well'.

*lḥg* *liḥiǵ, yalḥag* ‘to catch up, reach, overtake’ <2/16,3/9,8/8, 19/20,21/31,32e,33/10>. *alḥag, yilḥiǵ* ‘to rescue; to enable s.o. to attain, reach, overtake’ *Musil*, 513 <13/13>. *malḥūg* ‘overtaken’ <2/14>.

*lḥm* *talāḥam* ‘to interlock so as to form one unbroken whole’ <14/10> (CA *talāḥama* ‘to be joined together, to cohere’). *lḥām* ‘solder’ <18/21> (CA *liḥām*).

*lḥy* *liḥyah* pl. *liḥyān* ‘beard’ (symbol of manhood, ‘to shave a man’s beard is the greatest punishment among the Rwala’ *Musil*, 589); ‘man; (number of) men’ <9/10,32f,33/54>. *lāḥi* ‘halter of the camel’ <4/2>. *liḥiyy* pl. *luwāḥi* ‘cheeks, jaws’ <7/10,9/19,32/2> (CA *laḥy* ‘jawbone’). *malḥi* ‘peeled off; stripped of its bark, leaves etc.; tapered’ <6/14,9/21,24/3,27/7>. *mlāḥi* ‘rubbing against’ *Musil*, 365 (CA *laḥā* ‘to peel, strip’; *liḥāʾ* ‘bark’). *talāḥa* ‘to sing, hum a tune to one another, strike up a tune in response to another singer’ <9/8,14/2> (CA *talāḥā* ‘to rail at, jeer at one another’).

*ldd* *aladd* ‘fierce, obstinate, difficult to deal with’ <11/21> (CA *aladd* ‘quarrelsome, obstinate, dogged’).

*lzm* *lizim, yalzam* ‘to hold on to, not let go’ <4/8,28/2>; ‘to reach’ <21/32>.

*lṭm* *laṭṭāmah* ‘those who smite, strike forcefully’ <6/13> (CA *laṭṭama* ‘to slap much, violently’). *laṭm* ‘slapping, striking’ <22/2>. *liṭīm* ‘contender, rival, enemy’.

*lḏ̣y* *talaḏ̣ḏ̣a* ‘to burn’ <33/26> (CA *laẓiya* ‘to burn brightly, be ablaze; to burn with rage’; *tatalaẓẓā al-manīyah fī rimāḥihum* ‘fate is burning in their spears’).

*lʿb* *laʿab* ‘to play; to sing poetry’ <21/4,6,24/8>. *laʿʿāb* pl. *laʿāʿīb* ‘merrymaker, player; singer, poet’ <3/10,22/1> (CA *laʿʿāb* pl. *laʿāʿīb*). *liʿb* ‘song’ <5/10,21/6>; ‘playful, dancing movements’ <7/15>; also ‘the composition of a poem’, *liʿbat flān* ‘one’s poem’ *Maws* i, 74. *liʿb al-afkār* ‘the play of thought, free association of thoughts’ <10/1>.

*lʿj* *iltaʿaj* ‘to flash’ <13/8>. *mišxaṣin yalʿaj tgādiḥ ḥamārih* ‘a gold coin flashing with red sparkles’ *JuA*, 181. *lāʿij* ‘flashing’ *Musil*, 190 (CA *laʿaja* ‘to burn, to cause burning pain’; *iltaʿaja*)

*lʿz* *talaʿwaz* ‘to become angry, upset’ <;23>. *laʿwaz* ‘to become wrinkled, contracted, convulsed’; *laʿāwiz* ‘wrinkles in the face’ *Ḥa*.

*lġf* — *laġaf, yalġaf* ‘to hit, strike, scour (said of the effect of the hot wind on a rider’s face)’ <5/2,11,27/7> (CA *laġifa* ‘to lick’).

*lft* — *talāfat* ‘to become aware of, attentive to’ <2/19>. *iltifat* ‘to pay attention to, to heed’ <21/15>.

*lfy* — *lifa* ‘to come to; go to, head for; arrive at’, also *alfa* <9/2, 36,24/10,26/18,30/24>; *malfa* ‘addressee, the one for whom the poem carried by the messenger is destined’ *Musil*, 180; *malfāk ᶜala flān* ‘you will go to this or that one’; *min hu malfāk* ‘to whom shall I deliver this?’ *Musil*, 180. *lāfi* ‘s.o. who enters a place, arrives’ *Musil*, 204 (CA *alfā* ‘to come to’).

*lgy* — *iltiga* ‘to meet (in battle), to encounter’ <33/14> (CA *il-taqā*). *mlāga* ‘encounter, armed clash, battle, duel’ *Musil*, 528 <33/22>. *lga* ‘battle’ <33/24>. *laggāy* ‘the man who receives the bucket once it is drawn up from the well and pours the water into the trough’.

*lmm* — *lamm* ‘to assemble, group together’ *Musil*, 517. *iltamm* ‘to be gathered together’ *Musil*, 113. *lammah* ‘group; gathering, assembly’ <4/11,24/8>; *lammat al-ᶜirbān* ‘the assembly, gathering of the tribesmen (e.g. to repel an attack)’ *Musil*, 264 (CA *lammah*).

*lhb* — *lahab, yalhab* ‘to burn’ <12/7>. *lahīb* pl. *luwāhīb* ‘flames’ *Musil*, 306 <12/9,19/16,23/13>. *lihbūb* pl. *lahābīb* ‘ravine, gap between two mountains’ <12/4> (CA *lihb* pl. *alhāb, luhūb, lihāb*).

*lhd* — *lhadah* pl. *lhūd* ‘callous spots or blisters on the camel’s back and flanks caused by the heavy, unequally distributed load or by uneven saddles whether for freight, *ḥdājah*, or for riding, *šdād*. If these callous spots disappear, well and good; if they become blisters and open, suppurating sores, *dabrah* pl. *dbūr*, are the consequence’ *Musil*, 262, 370 <33/36> (CA *lahdah* ‘blister’, *al-lahīd min al-ibl*).

*lhm* — *iltaham* ‘to remember nostalgically, with regret’ <11/20, 23/11,30/26> (CA *iltahama* ‘to swallow in one piece’).

*lhy* — *talahha* ‘to be distracted, to amuse o.s.’ *Musil*, 118. *miltihi* ‘distracted; occupied by, busy with s.th. else’ <26/19>.

*lwb* — *lābah* ‘kith and kin’ *Glos*; ‘one’s own group, clan’, synonym of *xuṣlah*, ‘tribal section’ *Hess*, 90 <22/2,26/26,28/7, 30/25,32/11,33/18>.

*lwḥ* — *milwāḥ* pl. *malāwīḥ* 'cloth pieces waved by the falconer when he wants to coax a falcon to return to him, the decoy swung by a falconer when trying to lure a falcon towards him, *lawwaḥ aṭ-ṭēr*' *Musil*, 475, 485 <4/10> (CA *milwāḥ* pl. *malāwīḥ* 'a kind of decoy-bird').

*lwḏ* — *talāwaḏ* 'to mount quickly, to jump on the horse's back' <32e> (CA *lāwaḏha* 'to cling to, seek refuge with').

*lw*$^{c}$ — *lā*$^{c}$ 'to hit, strike, scorch', said of hot winds, <12/7>. *lō*$^{c}$*āt* 'torments' *Musil*, 181 (CA *lā*$^{c}$*a* 'to burn, torment, cause burning pain')

*lwl* — *lāl* 'mirage; a level plain glistening in the sun, quivering of the air on a hot day' *Musil*, 148, 680 <6/17,20/2,4> (CA *āl* 'mirage in the period between sunrise and the time when the sun is very high, i.e. during *aḍ-ḍuḥā*, in appearance raising figures seen from a distance', see *sarāb*).

*lwy* — *luwa* 'to bend, twist, turn' *Glos* <21/15,24/17>; *luwāni* 'he pulled me' *Musil*, 183. *ilwih* 'make it, twist it tight!' <5/6>. *lāwa, ylāwi* 'to bend, to move back and forth, to twist, to move around' <33/27>; *lāwītih* 'I squeezed, pressed it' *Musil*, 564 (CA *lawā* 'to twist, turn, crook, bend, distort, pervert s.th.'). *ad-dīn al-luwiyyah* 'the false oath' *Musil*, 430. *layy* 'bending, twisting'. *mlāwāt* 'contortions, twisting, swerving' <4/5>; *mlāwyāt al-*$^{c}$*nān* 'twisters of the rein' i.e. 'spirited mares' <19/19>. *malāwi* 'twisting (sand-hills)' <33/51>.

*mār, mēr* — 'but', a word that indicates an opposition to what precedes it <11/21,21/28>.

*mtn* — *matin* pl. *amtān, mtūn* 'upper back' *Glos* <3/17,9/15,22, 25/13,28/3> (CA *matn* pl. *mutūn, mitān* 'half or side of the back; back'). *mitīn* pl. *mtān* 'firm, strong, thick' <9/19>.

*mṯl* — *miṯil* pl. *amṯāl* 'something similar, resembling' <1/9>. *amṯāl, amāṯīl*, also *timāṯīl*, 'landmarks, elevations' <6/22, 8/10,10/1,20/4> (CA *amṯhāl* 'mountains resembling one another'). *timāṯīl* 'verses, poetry' <10/2,13/2>; 'scored rock-inscriptions' *Doughty* i, 260, 479 (CA *timṯhāl* pl. *tamāṯhīl* 'picture, image').

*mḥṣ* — *miḥṣ* pl. *mḥūṣ* 'strong ropes' *Glos* <13/17>.

*mḥg* — *amḥag* 'most fierce, violent' <11/21> (CA *māḥiq aṣ-ṣayf* 'the fiercest summer heat'). *mamḥūg* 'crushed, defeated' <2/18> (CA *maḥaqa* 'to wear down, grind').

*mḥl* *maḥal* 'barrenness, drought' *Glos* <10/6>; 'absence of pasture owing to the lack of good rain'; *yōm al-maḥal, yōm ad-dahar, yōm al-ġullah* 'the period of want and misery caused by light and irregular rains. At such times the younger camels cannot even sufficiently nurse their sucking young and give no milk for use of the owner's family, thus compelling him to sell camels in order to buy barley or wheat for himself and his children' *Musil*, 10, 533, 549.

*mḥmḥ* *timaḥmaḥ* 'to be depleted, worn away, reduced to almost nothing' <6/17> (CA *maḥḥa* 'to be threadbare, worn out'; *maḥmāḥ* 'nothing left').

*mḥy* *maḥa, yamḥa* 'to wipe out, delete' <3/6>.

*mdd* *madd, yimidd* 'to go, go on, to set out, ride out, depart' *Musil*, 79, 289, 318; *Glos*. *madd* pl. *mdūd* 'provisions, supplies' <3/5,27/2>. *midd* pl. *amdād* 'a measure for grain etc., a *midd* being two *nṣēf* and about a third of a *ṣāᶜ*' *Hess*, 124 <18/19> (CA *mudd* pl. *amdād* 'a measure for corn, equal to five *arṭāl* or a quarter of a *ṣāᶜ*').

*mdr* *midar* 'towns, regions' <18/16> (CA *madar* 'towns, villages, tracts of cultivated land').

*mrj* *timarwaj*, inf. n. *timirwāj*, 'to strut, to walk with a swinging, haughty gait' <24/4>. *tamrij* 'said of a riderless mare running about the battle field' *Musil*, 637 (CA *marija* 'to go, move at will, random').

*mrḥ* *amraḥ, yimriḥ* 'to spend the night, lie down for the night' *Musil*, 366; *taᶜaššᶜind yahūdi, amriḥ ᶜind naṣrāni* 'have supper with the Jews and spend the night with Christians' (a saying) *Hess*, 170. *marraḥ* 'to let the animals rest at night'; *ymarriḥhin bi-l-mrāḥ* 'he makes each animal kneel down in the place allotted to it (to rest at night)' *Musil*, 337, 641. *mrāḥ* 'place near the tent where the camels rest at night' *Glos* <;23,29/7,31/10>; *miriḥ* 'places near the tents where the herds rest' *Hess*, 62 (CA *murāḥ* 'the nightly resting-place of camels, sheep or goats').

*mrr* *murrah* 'bitter and burning herbal medicine' <3/3> (CA *murrah* 'myrrh; a certain medicine for scorpion stings, intestinal disease etc. that is sucked, applied as a plaster or swallowed in a dry state'). *murr...murr* 'now... then, one time...and another time' <33/39>.

*mrs* *māras* 'to walk at a strong pace, to run at full speed'

<6/23> (CA *mārasa* 'to exert oneself'). *amras* 'to slip off the pulley reel (said of the rope holding the bucket)' (CA *imrās*).

*mrṭ* — *mrāṭ aš-šimālīl* 'a raceme from which most dates have dropped' <8/6>; the Duwāsir say *ma ʿād fīha illa mrāṭ* 'there is only a little left in it' (CA *mariṭa* 'to have little, thin hair'; *nak̲h̲lah mumriṭ* 'a palm-tree dropping its ripe dates in a juicy state').

*mry* — *māriyyah* pl. *muwāri* 'slender slabs of stone put up to mark the location of a well', also *māriyyat niṣib*, *Hess*, 63; 'sign by which a place can be recognized' *Hess*, 161 <9/28,33/1>; in <13/16> it means 'freshly trodden camel paths'.

*mzz* — *mazz, yimizz* 'to suck' *Musil*, 109. *mazz* 'sucking, sipping' <24/15> (CA *muzz* 'delicious wine'; *mazza* 'to suck, sip').

*mzn* — *mizin* (coll.), sing. *miznah* pl. *mizin, mzūn* 'clouds bringing rain' <2/5,6,3/14,13/6,31/12,33/23>; *miznah* 'a small cloud, originally white, which is joined by many other similar clouds' *Musil*, 5 (CA *muzn* coll. 'clouds bringing rain'; *muznah* 'white cloud') .

*mzy* — *miza* 'virtue, healthy situation, good standing, good reputation' <29/5> (CA *mazīyah* 'virtue, merit, excellence, anything perfect').

*mss* — *mass* 'to grip, tighten, fasten' <19/22>; 'to become tight (a knot)' <5/6>; *yimiss* 'he exercises a steady and equal pull on the rope (of the bucket)' *Musil*, 347. *mass* 'grip' <4/7>. *ma ymiss mass* 'he does not grasp (the rope) firmly' *Musil*, 346.

*mšš* — *miššah* 'the marrow' <22/4> (CA *mas̲h̲s̲h̲ā* 'to suck the marrow').

*mšʿ* — *maššaʿ* 'to unsheathe; to bring out, take out s.th.' <30/15>; *mišaʿ* 'to pull s.th. with one's hand' (CA *imtas̲h̲aʿa as-sayf* 'he rapidly drew his sword').

*mṭy* — *miṭiyyah* 'riding camel' <17/2> (CA *maṭīyah*).

*mḏy* — *māḏi faʿālih* 'a resolute man, one who accomplishes what he has set out to do' <18/17> (CA *maḍā fī al-amr maḍāʾan* 'he carried out the affair').

*mkn* — *māćan maʿ* 'to become enraged; to render furious' <331>. *mićān* 'place' <3/22,23/10> (CA *makān*). *mićnān* 'a plant with yellow flowers' <3/22> (CA *maknān* 'a favourite part of the camel's diet in spring, producing rich and copious milk'). In *Flora of Saudi Arabia* by A.M. Migahid, Riyadh 1978, I found *mit͟hnān*, *Arthrocnemon glaucum* 'succulent, leafless perennila with dense branches and spikes that grows in salty places'. Perhaps the Egyptian author took the affricated *kāf* for a *t͟hāʾ*.

*mlḥ* — *malḥa* 'a black she-camel' *Musil*, 147 <3/15,14/13>; *malḥa ġrābiyyah* 'glossy like a raven' *Musil*, 335 (CA *amlaḥ* f. *malḥāʾ* 'a white colour admixed with black'). *milḥ* pl. *malāḥ* 'gunpowder' <2/24,18/15,27/13,30/16,31/3,4>. *amlaḥ* 'black, grey' <18/12>; *amlaḥ ad-darj* 'gunpowder' <22/3>. *malāḥ* 'small hailstones' <17/12>. *milḥ* 'attractiveness, charm' i.e. it is *milīḥ, mamlūḥ* 'charming, beautiful' <28/1> (CA *malīḥ*).

*mll* — *milīlah* pl. *malāyil* 'red-hot coal' *Musil*, 579 <33/4>. *mallah* 'red-hot soil' *Musil*, 204 (CA *mallah* 'hot ashes, live embers').

*mlh* — *tamlah* explained to me as '*tġaffil*, the she-camel momentarily forgets about her calf (and rushes to the shepherd when she sees him approaching or hears his voice)' <2/13> (CA *malīh, mumtalah* 'crazy, out of one's senses').

*mly* — *mala, yamla* 'he fills' <12/19>. *mamliyy* 'filled' <9/23> (CA *malaʾa* 'to fill').

*mnʿ* — *manaʿ* 'to grant *manʿ*, a pledge by the pursuer to spare the life of the pursued and protect him from others; the pursued in turn surrenders his mount and weapons to the pursuer' *Glos*; *imniʿūna* 'spare us!' <331>. *imnaʿ ya-xayyāl* 'give pardon, O rider!' *Musil*, 529. On details concerning the practice of *manʿ* see *Musil*, 529-530.

*mnn* — *mann* 'to take away the strength of, to exhaust, to weaken' <19/6> (CA *manna* 'to render weak, exhaust', e.g. by constant travelling).

*mny* — *min mnāha* 'it wishes for, longs to, likes to' <6/15,24>. *minwah* 'what one desires, likes, longs for' <16/9,19/16> (CA *munyah* pl. *munā* 'wish, desire').

*mhr* — *muhrah* pl. *mhār* 'a mare between her first and tenth year' *Musil*, 375 <33/27> (CA *muhr* 'foal, colt'; *muhrah* 'filly').

*mhl* — *ṭūl l-amhāl* 'a long life span' <1/10,26/20>.

*mhy* — *mahāh* 'wild cow' <9/25,13/17> (CA *mahāh*).

*mw* — *māw* 'copper; bullet, cartridge' <30/5,8,31/5>.

*mws* *mūs* 'knife, razor' *Musil*, 112, 341 <32/2>.

*mwṣ* *māṣ* explained as 'electrified iron' <25/11> (cf. Egyptian *mās*; CA *miġnāṭīs* 'magnet').

*myḥ* *māḥ* 'to descend into the well in order to scoop up the water into the bucket when the well holds only little water'; *bīrin ma tmāḥ* 'a well that does not need a man to climb down into it', i.e. it has plenty of water and the bucket fills itself when it is lowered into the well <17/7>. *mayyāḥ* pl. *mayyāḥīn* 'a man who climbs down in the well and scoops away the sand with a *ṣhalah*, a metal bowl' *Hess*, 64; 'the man who climbs down into the well to scoop up the water if there is only a little of it at the bottom; or who pulls the rope of the bucket to ascertain whether it has filled with water' *JuSa*, 98-99 <19/9> (CA *mayḥ* 'when a man descends into the well if it holds little water and fills the bucket with his hands').

*myl* *mayyal* 'to apply kohl with a *mīl*, also *ġaṭrūf*, a small knife for rubbing on the eye black' *Musil*, 193 <9/12> (CA *mīl*).

*nbt* *nabt, nibāt* 'plants, herbage' <6/18,7/13>.

*nb*$^{c}$ *nibābī*$^{c}$ explained as 'hollows holding surface water that quickly evaporates, similar to *ṯimad*, a cavity in which the rain-water collects and from which men drink during the two months of spring, but which fails when the summer comes' <6/34>; *nab*$^{c}$ 'spring water' *Musil*, 681; *nabbā*$^{c}$ pl. *yanābī*$^{c}$ 'dripping hole, water trickling from a hole in the rocks' *JuMu*, 28 (CA *nab*$^{c}$ 'water that wells from the earth, dripping hole').

*nbnb* *nibnūb* 'stalk, a smooth twig' *K͟haAd*, 201; 'young, beautiful woman with a gracious figure' *JuA*, 150, also *binībah* <28/3>.

*nbh* *nibah, yanbih* 'to push upwards' <26/2>. *nabbah* 'to tell, notify, remind, alert' *Glos*; *nabbah* $^{c}$*ala* 'to call on' *Musil*, 653.

*nby* *niba* 'to rise up, to be elevated, to protrude from' (CA *nabwah, nabw* 'high ground'; *nabā, naba*ʾ*a* 'to be high, elevated'). *niba* pl. *nibyān* 'elevation, isolated dome-shaped hillock' *Musil*, 681 <6/19>. *nābiy* 'protruding, high, prominent, bulging' *Musil*, 318, 365 <31/9>. *nabba* 'to answer; to say *naᶜam*, yes, in response to a call' <29/1> (CA *nabbaᵓa* 'to inform, advise, communicate'). *niba* 'words; report, message; memory' *Musil*, 130 <26/28>.

*njb* *nijībah* pl. *nijāyib* 'a she-camel of a pure race; a pure-blooded, noble she-camel, because both her sire and dam were recognized as thoroughbreds' *Musil*, 367 <7/8,20/5, 26/25>; *ar-rćāb al-manjūbah* 'female riding camels without blemish' *Musil*, 577 (CA *an-nājib min al-ibl* 'strong, fleet camels').

*njḥ* *anjaḥ* 'to do s.th. to the extreme, in full'; *anjaḥ miṣāxifhin bi-rūs al-misāwīǵ* 'he saturated the tender parts of the animals' bodies with the tips of his sticks' *JuA*, 105. *nijāḥ* '(the state of being) done, cooked to perfection, overcooked' <16/3,17/4>.

*njr* *nijir* pl. *njūr* 'mortar for pounding coffee-beans' *Musil*, 84 <23/7>.

*njm* *najim* 'star; falling star' <4/12>; 'star-stone, meteorite' *Doughty* i, 412; 'lamps used for the decoration of a building's facade' <25/14>.

*njy* *najja* 'to rescue, save s.o. from perdition' <8/12> (CA *najjā*).

*nḥr* *naḥar* 'to head for, go straight to' *Glos*; *Musil*, 162, 186; *naḥar* pl. *nḥūr* 'upper part of the breast; breast, front part' *Hess*, 167; 'part of the camel's breast directly under the throat' *Musil*, 600 <3/20,8/5,9/19,18/2,19/23,24/6, 30/23,31/9>. *manḥir* 'the lower part of the throat from where an animal is killed' *Glos* <28/6>, pl. *manāḥir* 'the two sides of the throat where it joins the breast' *Musil*, 96, 318.

*nḥz* *naḥaz, yanḥaz* 'he hits the ground hard with his feet' <7/3> (CA *naḥaza* 'to hit, beat; to push').

*nḥl* *niḥīl* pl. *niḥḥāl* 'thin, lean, skinny, emaciated' <26/2> (CA *naḥīl, nāḥil* pl. *nuḥḥāl*).

*nḥy* *naḥa* 'to push in a certain direction' *Glos*; 'to come at, to come, to go in the direction of' <19/20> (CA *naḥā* 'to go, move in the direction of'). *nāḥa* 'to attack, charge, chase s.o.; to engage s.o. on horseback' <17/1,33/31>. *anḥa, yinḥi* 'to run, move in a downward direction' <10/5, 12/21>; *anḥa ᶜala* 'to come down, beat down on' <10/7, 10,14/15>. *anḥēt* 'I descended, returned' <3/2>; *anḥa maᶜ ar-rīᶜ* 'to make off quickly down the defile'. *intaḥa* 'to move in the direction of' <18/11> (CA *anḥā ᶜalā = aqbal ᶜalā*; *anḥā ᶜalayh ḍarban* 'he moved to him and hit him'). *nuwāḥi* 'directions, quarters' <17/11> (CA *nāḥiyah* pl. *nawāḥī*). *manāḥi* 'directions'; *ᶜala gadd al-manāḥi* 'as fancy dictates, according to his liking' <17/2> (CA *manḥā* 'aim, goal; behaviour, mode of conduct'). *naḥāwi* 'aiming at; eager to' <9/24>.

*nxy* *naxa* 'to call for help; to invoke s.o.'s honour in an appeal for his assistance' *Glos*; *Musil*, 503 <21/9,33/22>. Dindān's *nxawah* pl. *naxāwi*, 'battle cry, the war cry of a kin', would be: *ya-ālād ibn Ḥarāršah, ya-ᶜyāl ubūy*. *intaxa* 'to shout one's war cry' *Hess*, 170; *Glos*; 'when a warrior shouts his war cry before the chief or his comrade to prove that he will not desert them' *Musil*, 503.

*ndb* *andab* 'to delegate; to send after s.o.' *Glos*. *nidīb* 'messenger, envoy' <4/1,25/1,27/3,30/23>.

*ndᶜ* *nidīᶜ* 'worn away, damaged, impaired' <5/7>.

*ndf* *nidaf* 'the sand that piled up on top of an *abrag*' <10/10>; *rūs an-nidaf* 'the crests of the sand-hills'.

*ndy* *nāda* 'to call, to shout' <;29> *Musil*, 218, 251; *nādīni* 'call me' *Musil*, 219 (CA *nādā*). *mnādi* 'crier, one who summons, commander' *Musil*, 312.

*nḏl* *naḏil* pl. *anḏāl* 'wretch, coward; low, base, mean, despicable person' *Musil*, 260 <6/5,26/24> (CA *na<u>dh</u>l* pl. *an<u>dh</u>āl* 's.o. of a despicable character').

*nzḥ* *nizaḥ* 'to be distant, far off; to dash along, run away' *Glos*. *nazzaḥ* 'to exhaust, to empty (a well)' <6/7> (CA *nazaḥa, anzaḥa al-biʾr* 'he drew water from the well until he had emptied it'). *an-nāziḥ* 'a long distance; a depleted well' <9/24> (CA *nāziḥ* 'a well that has been emptied'; *nazzaḥat ad-dār* 'the land lies far away'). *mnazziḥāt* 'camels that cover large distances'. *mintiziḥ* 'far, far-flung' <9/30> (CA *muntazaḥ*).

*nzz* *nazz* 'to bound away' <4/24> (CA *nazza* 'to run sprightly, nimbly; to leap, jump, bound', said of a gazelle).

*nzl* *tinizzāl* 'descending, falling in great quantity and with force' <1/6,26/10>. *nzili* 'one belonging to a *nazil* pl. *nzūl*, encampment composed of many smaller groups' *Hess*, 59 <32b>; 'a camp with more than thirty tents' *Musil*, 77, 170.

*nsf* *nisaf, yansif*, also *nassaf* inf. n. *tansīf*, 'to throw, toss; to push aside' *Glos*; *Musil*, 91 <3/13>; 'to let down (hair)' *Musil*, 175. *tansfih* 'she pushes him away, sweeps him aside' <3/20> (CA *nasafa* 'to scatter').

*nsm* *nisam* 'breeze, blowing of the wind' <13/4>.

*nsns* *nisnās* 'a light, moist wind which cuts the face and penetrates the clothes to the bone' *Musil*, 470 <16/11,20/5, 31/14> (CA *rīḥ nasnās* 'a cold wind').

*nšd* *nišad, naššad, ynaššid* 'to ask, inquire, question' *Glos* <26/13,23>. *yinšdūn* 'they ask, inquire about' <33/50>. *anšdik* 'I ask you' (formula introducing a riddle) <25/7>. *naššād* 'singer, poet' <6/1,10/1,13/1, 25/19>. *nišīd* (coll.), *nišīdah* (n. un.) 'poem, song' *Hess*, 143 <32/13>.

*nšr* *nišar, yanšir* 'to set out with the intention of spending the entire day on the pasture ground' *Hess*, 63; *inširu* = *imšu* 'run!' *Musil*, 286. *našir* 'a herd on the pasture ground'. *anšār* 'long journeys' *Musil*, 286.

*nšf* *nišaf, yanšif tanšīf* 'to suck up' <19/16> (CA *nas̲h̲afa* 'to suck up, absorb'). *manšūf* pl. *manāšīf* 'dried out, dried up' <19/6> (CA *nas̲h̲ifa* 'to dry, become dry').

*nšy* *niša, yinši* '(the cloud) rises and appears at the horizon' <3/14,26/16,31/13> (CA *nas̲h̲aʾa*). *našša, ynašši* 'to bring into being, give rise to, engender (e.g. rain clouds)' *Musil*, 467 <3/6,18/10>. *mnašši* 'creator, originator' (cf. CA *ans̲h̲aʾa allāh al-k̲h̲alq* 'God originated the creation'). *manša* pl. *manāši* 'the place where the clouds appear on the horizon, originate' <14/11> (CA *mans̲h̲aʾ* 'place where s.th. or s.o. arises, originates from'; *nas̲h̲aʾa as-saḥāb* 'the clouds arose and appeared, made their first appearance'). *našuw* 'growing up, emerging, coming into existence; pregnant' *Musil*, 176; *taww al-bint našwin bha ummha* 'her mother had just conceived the girl' <33/19>; *mnaššin bha* 'she is pregnant, carries a foetus in her womb' <33e>.

*nṣb* *niṣīb* 'fate, destiny' <3/5,6/15,30/4>.

*nṣr* *naṣrāni* pl. *niṣāra* 'Christian' <33/17>.

*nṣm* *nṣūm* 'hoofs of a camel' <27/8> (CA *mansim* pl. *manāsim*).

*nṣy* *niṣa, yanṣa; tanaṣṣa* 'to head for, go straight to' *Glos* <8/12, 9/34>. *naṣṣa* 'to steer to, direct towards (a mount)' <11/13,22/2,25/2>; 'to address (greetings) to' <26/14,

15>. *nuwāṣi* 'forelocks, fore parts of the head' <3/10, 18/8,> (CA *nāṣiyah* pl. *nawāṣī*).

*nṭḥ* *niṭaḥ, yanṭaḥ, naṭṭaḥ* 'to meet, encounter; to charge at, advance on, attack; to face, confront' *Glos* <2/22,30/19>; *naṭṭaḥ* 'to meet s.o. with s.th., rush s.th. to s.o.' *Glos*; *Musil*, 252, 595 <16/11>. *tanāṭaḥ* 'to fight (a duel)' *Musil*, 528, 595; *naṭḥah* 'attack; ability to attack, take on an enemy' *Musil*, 520 (CA *naṭaḥah* $^{c}$*anh* 'he pushed, thrust him away from him').

*nḏy* *niḏuw* pl. *niḏa, inḏa, anḏa* 'lean, gaunt camel' *Glos* <4/1, 6/31,33,9/28,36,20/6,24/8>; 'camel whose hump lost its fat because of incessant traveling' (CA *niḍw* pl. *anḍā*ʾ, *niḍwān* 'a lean, emaciated camel'; *niḍw safarin* 'lean, emaciated by journeying'). $^{c}$*ayrāt an-niḏa* 'she-camels used for raids to distant places' *Musil*, 475.

*n*$^{c}$*t* *bi-l-iṣūl mna*$^{cc}$*atāt* 'excellent, of a pure breed' <7/14> (CA *na*$^{c}$*ata* 'to describe s.th. by naming a characteristic'; *na*$^{c}$*t* 'anything excellent').

*n*$^{c}$*r* *man*$^{c}$*ūr* pl. *manā*$^{c}$*īr* 'brave, daring and proud men' *Su* i, 40 <6/11,15/12>. *nā*$^{c}$*ūr* pl. *nuwā*$^{c}$*īr* 'waterwheel, wooden sheaf of a pulley, i.e. *maḥālah*' <7/6,9/21>; *nā*$^{c}$*ūr* = *migām* 'water hoist' *Musil*, 339; synonym of *markūz* pl. *marākīz* 'two stout poles planted in the ground at the sides of a well that has not been covered on the inside with stones in order to support the roller on which runs the rope' *JuSa*, 71 (CA *nā*$^{c}$*ūrah* 'any rotary machine to raise water').

*n*$^{c}$*m* *na*$^{c}$*ām* 'the wooden structure on which the roller of the water hoist is mounted' <9/27> (CA *na*$^{c}$*āmah* 'the wooden poles of the water hoist or the crosspiece placed on the *zarānīq*, the two posts on the sides of a well to which the pulley is suspended'). *nā*$^{c}$*im* 'smooth, firm of texture' <12/24,27/10>. *manā*$^{c}$*īm* 'well-watered, juicy' <12/7> (cf. CA *nā*$^{c}$*im, munā*$^{c}$*im*). *na*$^{c}$*āmah* pl. *na*$^{c}$*ām* 'ostrich' <6/14,8/2,11/9,25/1,26/8,27/5>.

*n*$^{c}$*y* *n*$^{c}$*āh allah* 'may God curse him! may God blacken his face, blame him!' <21/4> (CA *na*$^{c}$*ā* 'to announce the death of s.o.'; *na*$^{c}$*ā* $^{c}$*alayh* *dhunūbah* 'he mentioned, divulged his faults, blamed him').

*nfj* *mnaffij* 'wide apart, spacious' <6/24,24/6,27/10> (CA *intafaja janbā al-baᶜīr* 'the flanks of the camel bulged, were big').

*nfḥ* *nāfaḥ tinīfāḥ* 'to walk with swinging, dancing movements' <6/28> (CA *yanfaḥ* 'he gestures, sways').

*nfd* *nifūd* 'sand-hills' <33/51>. *nifād* 'exhaustion, extinction' <12/18> (CA *nafād*).

*nff* *naff, yniff* 'to blow; to carry away (e.g. a torrent sweeping away everything in its way)' *Musil*, 551 <1/3>.

*nfl* *nifal* 'to exceed; to outdo; to excel'. *naffal* 'to show preference; to bestow extra praise or reward on' *Glos* <32/7> (CA *tanaffala* 'to do more than is required'). *nfāl* 'what is done in excess of duty, praiseworthy deeds' <18/22>; *tanāfīl* 'what is in excess of, superior' *Faraj*, 199; 'deeds beyond what might be expected of s.o.' *Glos* (CA *nāfilah*).

*ngd* *mangūd* pl. *manāgīd* 'a blemish, shortcoming; faultfinding, criticism of one's moral qualities' <16/13>.

*ngḏ* *nigaḏ, naggaḏ* 'to loosen (hair), to unplait, unbraid' *Musil*, 176 <33/20> (CA *naqaḍa* 'to tear apart, take apart, undo'). *mnaggaḏāt* 'loosened, unplaited (hair)' <15/8>. *nāgiḏat al-jidāyil* 'woman unbraiding the hair on her temples' *Musil*, 227 (CA *naqḍ*).

*ngᶜ* *niǵīᶜ* explained as 'a thorn that enters the foot of the camel and hurts it' <5/11> (cf. CA *naqaᶜa*).

*ngy* *intiga* 'to pick, select'; *mintiǵi* 'having chosen, selected' <16/6>; *yantigin* 'they (pl. f.) extract, pull out' <6/3> (CA *intaqā* 'to extract; to select'). *niga* 'purity; integrity, honesty, good faith, fairness' *Musil*, 505-506, 614; *Glos* <22/8>. *majrūd an-niga ᶜalēkum* 'the honesty in our relations has been removed', *raddēna an-niga ᶜalēkum* 'we have returned the *niga*'. 'As soon as this is done, they may attack without injuring their honour in the least, *lya raddēna an-niga ngīr ᶜala waḏḥ an-niga* i.e. their face will remain white, their honour unstained, because war has been declared openly, fairly' *Musil* 504-506. *ᶜilm nigāwi* 'war report' *Musil*, 617, because the war has been declared openly, fairly, *ᶜala waḏḥ an-niga*.

*nkb* *mankib* pl. *manāćib* 'shoulder' <9/21,15/9,27/9> (CA *mankib* 'the joint of the shoulder and the upper arm').

*nkr* *nāćar* 'to deceive, delude' *Musil*, 206. *inkiri* 'a strong one; s.o. scheming and wily, deceiving' <17/1>; *yḏākir w-*

*ynākir* 'he mixes repeating God's name with bad acts' *ᶜUbūdī*, 1715 (CA *munkar*).

*nks* — *nikas* 'to come back, to return home' *Musil*, 529; *Glos*. *intikas* 'to stoop, lower, bend one's head' <2/20> (*intakasa* 'to be turned over, inversed; to drop forward').

*nkᶜ* — *nuwāčīᶜ* 'sharp stones jutting out from the inside of a well' <6/8>; 'as some of the wells are as much as a hundred metres deep, the drawing of water is very fatiguing, especially on account of the bulges in the rocky sides which impede the bucket in coming up: the right hand must not only hold the rope firmly, but must shake it most of the time so as to keep it in the centre' *Musil*, 347 (*nakaᶜa* 'to beat back, prevent', e.g. cattle from drinking).

*nkf* — *ankaf* 'to come back, return from a raid' *Glos*. *rakb al-manākīf, manāčīf, nikāyif* 'mounted men returning from a raid' (also *maᶜāwīd*) *Musil*, 105, 158, 642 <19/18>. *inkāf* 'the return from a raid' *Musil*, 228. *nakkāf* 'returning' *Musil*, 204.

*nkl* — *nikāl* 'punishment, by way of setting an example' <33c>. *ynakkilūnih tankīl* 'they give him a sound thrashing' *Musil*, 454 (CA *nakāl* 'exemplary punishment, warning example'; *nakkala* 'to punish severely').

*nmr* — *nimir* 'leopard' *Doughty* i, 373 <5/5>. *namran* 'a group of tigers, leopards; courageous warriors' *KhaAd*, 351; 'a strong, numerous army' <33/13>.

*nhb* — *nāhab* lit. 'to snatch, to seize (the earth)', synonym of *xamm*; 'to run at a strong pace' <24/9> (CA *tanāhaba al-arḍ ᶜadwan* 'to race along at a tearing pace').

*nhj* — *nahaj, yanhaj* 'to hurry, hasten' *Musil*, 151; 'to set out on a journey' *Musil*, 630.

*nhš* — *nahaš* 'to snatch, snap away' <33/4> (CA *nahasha* 'to bite, snap, grab with the teeth').

*nhl* — *nhāl* (pl.) 'thirsty', i.e. camels when they have arrived at the well and start to gulp down the water <6/4> (CA *ibl nawāhil, nihāl*; *nahal* 'the first drink').

*nhm* — *naham* 'to call for assistance; to urge on (a camel) with shouts, to chide' <5/5,11/9> (CA *nahama* 'to scold and threaten, to chide a camel'; *nahamt al-ibl* 'I shouted at the camel encouraging it to pick up its pace'; *nahīm* 'chiding of camels'; *ṭarīq nahhām* 'a road where is heard a chiding of camels'). *nāhim* 'one who calls for aid; one who is far from home and longs to return' <16/9>.

*nhy* *naha, yanha* 'to forbid, prohibit, interdict; to restrain, prevent from'; *nihōni* 'they forbade me' <14/4,15/2,16/3, 24/11,14> (CA *nahā*).

*nwb* *nuwāyib* 'grave duties (like taking revenge)' <21/4>. *nōb* 'commission, charge, order; duty, task performed on behalf of s.o.' <26/20> (CA *nāba* 'to act on s.o.'s behalf').

*nwx* *nawwax* 'to make a camel kneel down in order to dismount' <33i>. *manāxah* 'place near house or tent where camels are made to kneel down' <26/25>. *manāx* 'regular battle, i.e. when the men dismount and engage in a pitched battle' *Musil*, 506.

*nwd* *nūd* pl. *anwād, nuwāyid* 'wind, breeze' <1/3,13/4> (perhaps from CA *nāda, yanūd idhā ḥarraka raʾsah wa-kitfayh, tamāyala*).

*nwr* *nawwār, nwār* 'blossoms, pasture' *Musil*, 478 <10/11> (CA *nuwwār, nawr* 'blossoms').

*nws* *nawwas* 'to move, to be far away' <11/13>. *nawwāsah* 'those having a long reach, who strike at the enemy regardless of the distance between them' <6/13>.

*nwṭ* *nūṭ* 'long'; *nūṭ ar-rǵāb* 'having long necks' <8/4,19/12, 21> (CA *nāṭa* 'to suspend, to hang').

*nwf* *nāf, yinūf* 'to surpass; to tower above' *Musil*, 601-602. *nāyif* 'lofty, high, soaring' <3/1,15/7,24/1> (CA *nāfa* 'to be high, lofty').

*nww* *naww* 'the rains that come with the appearance of certain stars; heat, hot winds, rain, as phenomena connected with the appearance of certain stars' *Hess*, 65 <;3,11/14,12/21, 25/3> (CA *nawʾ* pl. *anwāʾ* 'setting star; the setting of one of the stars which compose the Mansions'; the ancient pagan Arabs used to attribute rains, winds, heat and cold to the setting and rising of certain stars, and so did the bedouins until only recently).

*nwy* *nawa, nuwa l-* 'to intend, to intend for s.o.; to aim at; to resolve to' *Musil*, 318 <3/5,18/4,16>. *nawwa* 'to head, aim for' <29/7> (CA *nawā* 'to intend, to head for'). *intawa* 'to purpose to travel to a certain place' <33/35>. *mintuwi* 'one who has conceived an intention, a desire to do s.th.' <21/7> (CA *intawā* 'to propose, intend, purpose').

*niyyah* 'an intention, plan, desire to do s.th.' *Musil*, 485; 'a project (especially to travel, raid etc.)' *Musil*, 510 <9/3, 5,16>. *rabbak nāwi lak* 'your Lord intends for you' *Musil*, 364. *naww* 'intention, ambition' (CA *an-nawā*).

*nyb* — *nīb* 'camels in the age when the eye-teeth, *nāb*, pl. *nībān*, break through, i.e. in the eigth year' *Hess*, 74; *Musil*, 334 <7/16,9/24> (CA *nāb* pl. *nīb* 'eye-tooth of a camel; old she-camel'). *nāb* pl. *anyāb* 'fang' <30/7,12>.

*nyḥ* — *nāḥ, yinīḥ* 'to wail, bemoan; to coo' <17/1> (CA *nāḥa*).

*nyr* — *nīrah* i.e. *ad-dahar* 'a time of drought and want' <10/11>.

*nys* — *nayyas al-ʿilm* 'to obtain reports of an enemy who is far away'. *nāyis* 'far away, distant' <11/17> (perhaps from CA *naʾas̲h̲a*). *nēs* 'layers of sand in a *baṭḥa*, the sandy middle part of a wadi' <17/6>.

*nyl* — *nīl* 'indigo' <3/16,8/4,14/13,28/5,30/15>.

*nyy* — *nayy* 'fat' <1/9,13/14,26/2> (CA *nayʾ* 'meat in a raw, uncooked state').

*hbb* — *habb* 'to blow', said of the wind <12/4>. *al-habāhīb, habāyib* 'the winds' <5/12,9/14,12/6> (cf. CA *habūb* 'wind that raises the dust'). *hābbat rīḥ, hābbat ar-rīḥ* 'a favourable wind; a good omen for success, booty' *Musil*, 217; 'a *snāfiyyah*, a lovely girl of excellent character' <33j>; *habb luh saʿad* 'the wind of luck blew in his direction' *Glos*; *lya habbat ryāḥik* 'when the winds of success blow towards you' *Musil*, 475, 479.

*hbl* — *mhabūl* pl. *mahābīl, hbāl* 'crazy, mad, stupid' <14/5, 18/15> (CA *mahbūl* 'stupid, idiotic; a fool').

*hby* — *haba* 'to be afraid' *Musil*, 360 (CA *habā* 'to run away, bolt'). *habba* 'to die down' <5/8> (CA *habā* 'to die down', i.e. when the flames disappear and the fire turns into glowing coals or ashes).

*hjj* — *hajj* 'to flee, to run away; to run fast; to stampede, scare away' <1/13,6/19,32b,33d,33/33>. *hajjaj* 'to drive out, away' *Musil*, 533. *hajjāt* 'rapid movements' <4/6>. *hajīj* 'a panic, helter-skelter flight' *Musil*, 536 <1/13,18/3, 26/8>. *mihjāj* 'a narrow, a pass between two mountains' <4/24> (CA *hajīj* 'a deep valley, chasm in a mountain').

*hjd* — *hajad, yhajid* 'to attack at night' *Hess*, 98. *mihjād* 'from appr. 10 o'clock at night until 3 o'clock in the morning'

<13/7> (CA *hajada* 'to sleep'; *hajjada* 'to wake up; to pray at night').

*hjr* *ahjar*, 'to force to go away, to take away' <12/7>. *hajir* 'strength, life force' <19/9>. *mhajjar* 'tied with the *hijār*, rope tying together one hind leg and one foreleg on one side of the animal' <33/9>.

*hjs* *hōjas* 'to think of, consider, give thought to' <31/11>. *hajs*, *hūjās*, *hājūs*, *hājis* pl. *hawājīs* 'idea, notion, thought; worry, anguished thought' *Glos*; *Musil*, 286 <21/7> (CA *hājis* pl. *hawājis* 'a thought coming at random, bestirring itself in the mind', i.e. *k͟hāṭir* 'anything occurring to the mind').

*hjf* *tahajjaf* 'to become thin, worn, exhausted' <19/5>. *hajaf* 'weakness, thinness, exhaustion' *JuA*, 229. *ar-rćāb al-hjāf* 'thin and worn camels' *Musil*, 103. *hajfa* 'a camel with a flaccid, sagging hump'. *hjāfa* 'tired, worn and hungry camels' *Su* ii, 120 (CA *hajfah* = *ʿajfah* 'exhaustion, thinness'; *inhajafa* 'to be broken by hunger and disease to that the bones stand out', said of man and animal).

*hjl* *hajlah* pol. *hjāl*, *mahājīl*, i.e. *ġadīr* 'a wide and deep pool where the water of the streaming wadis remains a long time after the rain has ceased' *JuMu*, 26 <13/7> (CA *hajl* pl. *hijāl*, *ahjāl* 'a fertile depression in the ground').

*hjm* *hajmah* 'a herd spending the night far from the camp; it is also called *ʿazīb*; *hajjamna* is equivalent to *mraḥna*, we spent the night' *Musil*, 550 <33/15>.

*hdb* *hidb* (pl.) 'curved, bent' <12/23,19/14> (CA *hadibat* 'it bends, hangs down', said of branches heavy with fruit and leaves). *mahādīb* (pl.) 'hanging down; (rain) coming down in sheets' <10/9>; *mahādīb al-xyāl* 'downward slanting clouds' <27/8>; *lēlah hēdibiyyah* 'a dark and rainy night' *JuA*, 54 (CA *haydab* 'clouds hanging down like the fringes of a cushion'). *hdibah* pl. *hadab* 'lashes, tassels, fringes' *Glos*; *Musil*, 119; 'tattered fringes of clouds descending towards the earth'. *hadab* 'the tassels ornamenting the *mīrakah*, the cushion on the camel's shoulder blades' *Musil*, 353.

*hdd* *hadd*, *yhidd* 'to urge on, urge (e.g. a falcon to pursue its prey)' *Musil*, 621; 'to lead in a she-camel to the stud'; *yhaddūn al-jmāl fi l-bill* 'they let the stud camels cover, serve the she-camels' *Hess*, 76 <33/46>; *mita thaddūn b-ebāᶜir-kum* 'when are you going to lead in your she-camels?' *Musil*, 332. *hadād* 'mating season of camels' *Hess*, 76.

*hdf* *mahādīf* (pl.) 'with their necks held low and stretched forward' <24/3>. *hidf* 'curved, crooked, slanted'; also said of coffee-pots, 'leaning slightly forward' in the hearth.

*hdm* *mahādīm* (pl.) 'broken, hanging down despondently' <12/10>.

*hdml* *hadmūl* pl. *hadāmīl*, 'rags, pieces of cloth' that scare camels if they are thrown at them (CA *hidmil* 'a tattered dress').

*hdy* *hada*, *ahda*, *yahdi* 'to bestow on' <2/27,21/20,24/17, 28/1>. *hadda* 'to lead, to lead the way to' <33/38>.

*hḏb* *haḏīb* 'a fast trot'. *haḏbāt* (pl. f.) 'prancing' *Musil*, 515. *haḏḏāb* 'a she-camel which trots as fast as a mare' *Musil*, 631.

*hḏl* *haḏal*, *yihḏil* 'to trot at a fast pace' <5/10>. *haḏīl*, *hḏāl* explained to me as 'the fast trot of camels that follow one another in one line' <4/20,7/5,8/9,26/9> (CA *hawd̲h̲ala* 'to run in an agitated manner'; *had̲h̲ālīl* 'running in one line, one following the other').

*hrb* *harab* 'to flee, run away' <33/12>. *hārib* 'fleeing, running at great speed' <2/14>. *harrābah* 'a she-camel that plunges forward through the herd when hurrying to the watering place' <3/17>.

*hrj* *haraj*, *yharij* 'to talk'; *ihriju* (imp. pl.) 'speak!' *Musil*, 139. *harjah* 'words; talk; offensive words, slander, calumnies' <21/2,30/3>; *al-harj ma lih zibdah* 'chatter without butter', i.e. 'empty talk, gossip' *Musil*, 635. *harrāj* 'a babbler, s.o. who talks too much' *Musil*, 582.

*hrkl* *hrēćlān* explained as 'pacing steadily, trotting calmly' <23/14> (CA *harkalah* 'a slow, conceited, swaggering pace').

*hzz* *hazz*, *yihizz* 'to move, shake' *Musil*, 109, 315. *nhizz as-slāḥ* 'we brandish our arms' *Musil*, 571. *hizz al-figār* '(camels) with quivering humps (because of the accumulated fat)' <19/12> (CA *hazza* 'to shake').

*hzf* *hazaf* 'to become thin' <5/12> (CA *hazafa* 'to find s.th. light').

*hzl* *mihzil* pl. *hzāl*, *hizzāl*, *mahāzīl* 'lean, gaunt, worn, emaciated (camels); poor, robbed of its strength and resources'

*JuA*, 209 <1/7,3/9,6/33,10/14,13/14,14/18,18/10> (CA *mahzūl*). *hazil* pl. *hazāyil* 'poor, lean' *Musil*, 386-387.

*hzm* *inhazam* 'to flee, to run for it' *Musil*, 217, 534, 578. *minhazim* 'fleeing, making an escape after defeat' <2/18>. *ahzam* 'to rescue, deliver' *Glos*.

*hšš* *hašš*, *yihišš* 'to leak, ooze out, seep; to flow copiously (tears)' <19/2>. *nāgtin haššah* 'a she-camel that is easy to milk, of which the milk flows easily and in good quantity' *Hess*, 77. (CA *hashsh* 'everything that is loose and soft'; *qirbah hashshāshah* 'a skin from which the water leaks').

*hšl* *hašal* 'to scatter at random; to cut in pieces'. *hašlah* 'a herd of no more than ten camels' (pl. *hšal*) *Musil*, 336. *hāšil* pl. *huwāšīl* 'coming down in streams, gushing down (rain)' <13/6>. *šannat al-hōšiliyyah* 'the leaking skin, skin pouring with water through its holes' <33/5>.

*hšm* *haššam* 'to break, snap, crush, destroy' <12/2>. *tahaššam* 'to pour, splash down (rain)' <13/7>; *lya gām rubbān as-saḥāb ytahaššam* 'when the rain starts pouring down from the rain clouds' *JuKha*, 50. *hašīm* 'dry herbage, broken twigs and other plant debris' <3/13,5/4,19/7,27/7,30/2, 33/44> (CA *hashīm* 'dry, broken plants; brushwood collected by the wood gatherer').

*hḏb* *haḏbah* pl. *hḏāb* 'a group of rocky mountainous outcrops standing apart from other such groups, usually of a brownish or reddish colour' *JuMu*, 22; 'an extensive but isolated rocky hill, isolated knoll' *Musil*, 661, 679 <27/9, 32/12>; *mahāḏīb* <12/21>. These mountainous formations dominate the landscape south of ad-Dixūl, which is therefore called Haḏb ad-Duwāsir <18/4,22/4> (CA *haḏbah* pl. *hiḏāb*).

*hḏʿ* *mahāḏīʿ* (pl.) explained as 'bent, bowed', i.e. similar in meaning to *mahānīʿ* <6/25>.

*hff* *haff* 'to pierce through, run through; to go and not return' *Glos*; 'to rush, plunge downhill and speed away; to disappear' *Musil*, 646 <19/21>. *šaffaw w-haffaw w-ittigaw ʿigb l-iʿrāḏ* 'they went uphill, plunged down over the crest and disappeared from view (after they had been before my eyes)' *JuA*, 62. *haffah* 'a gallop as fast as a gale, during which the wind resounds in the ears' *Musil*, 149 (CA *haffa* 'to run fast').

*hgw* *haga* 'to reckon, presume, imagine'. *hagwah* 'assumption, guess, surmise' *Glos. hagwiti* = *ḏ̣anni* 'my guess, surmise'. *la yihga bha* 'it is inconceivable, presumptuous (to think that she ever will fall in strange hands, will be conquered)' <30/8>. *wiš hagwitik* 'what do you think, surmise?' *Su* i, 103. *w-la tāxiḏ ad-dinya xrāṣin w-hagwāt* 'take not the world so lightly (at your guess) or as fancy dictates (as you surmise)' *Musil*, 294, 297. *tara yihga bik hagwat al-falāḥi* 'salvation, prosperity is expected from you' *Musil*, 482.

*hll* *hall* 'to loosen' *Musil*, 565; 'to stream, pour down' <33/23>. *hallal al-miṭar* 'the rain is pouring in streams' *Musil*, 5. *yihill al-ma* 'the water, tears stream' <14/16> (CA *halla* 'to pour, stream down with force', said of rain, tears). *istahall* 'to pray for rain' *Musil*, 5. *mhallil* pl. *mahālīl* 'curving down, stooped over' <8/5> (CA *muhallal* 'bent, curved'). *mihlāl* pl. *mahālīl* 'steep mountain' <6/1,14/3> (CA *hilāl* 'crescent-shaped object; layers of stones or bricks').

*hlm* *halīmah* pl. *halāyim* 'a starved, emaciated camel' *Sow* (1981), 66; 'a lean, older she-camel (whose flesh cannot be properly boiled, always remains tough and has no taste)' *Musil*, 97.

*hmz* *hamaz* 'to hit; to wound' <6/29> (CA *hamaza* 'to press; to push; to strike, beat').

*hml* *hammal* 'to let the camels wander at random, at will, in the desert' <33h>. *tahammal* 'to pasture without a shepherd'. *hāmil* pl. *hamal, hāmlāt* 'camels left to roam the pasture ground at will, unattended' <7/13,13/10> (CA *ahmala al-mās̲h̲iyah* 'he sent the cattle to pasture by themselves'; *ibl hamlā, muhmalah*). *mihmilah* pl. *mihmilāt* = *hāmil* <15/10>. *la hāml wla marʿi* 'whether on the loose or tended' *Glos* (CA *hāmil*). *himlūl* pl. *hamālīl* 'a downpour which irrigates a small territory' *Musil*, 6, 323 <10/7,14/9>.

*hmm* *hamm* 'to be concerned, care about' <31/6>. *hamām* 'passionate love, desire' <11/19>. *ṯamha hamāmah* 'her mouth is gobbling, gulping down, eating voraciously' <25/10>.

*hmy* *hamiyyah* 'stray she-camel; unattended she-camel, wandering alone in the desert' <331 ,33/6> (CA *hamat an-nāqah* 'the she-camel went, strayed alone, without a shepherd').

*hnd* *hindi* 'sabre made of black steel' *Musil*, 133 <2/24,18/6>.

*hnᶜ* *mahnūᶜ pl. mahānīᶜ* 'bent, bowed' <6/4> (CA *baᶜīr mahnūᶜ* 'a camel standing with its neck lowered'). *hānūᶜ* 'gently bending forward' *Ju<u>Kh</u>a*, 92.

*hwz* *hāz, hāwaz* 'to make a playful jab at, feint at; to stab, jab at, pierce' <4/8>. *yihūzik* 'he feints at you, challenges you in a playful way' <17/10>; *ᶜēnih yihūzik* 'her eye pierces you'. *yhāwizin* 'they (pl. f.) shy at' *Musil*, 318; *hōz* 'a jest, feint in duelling' *Musil*, 129-130. *hōzah* 'a shake, nod at' *Musil*, 275.

*hwš* *hāš, yihūš* 'to fight, tussle' *Glos* <32/9>. *tahāwaš* 'to altercate, quarrel, fight' *Musil*, 288, 496. *hōš* 'fight, fighting, battle, mêlée; bravery in battle' *Musil*, 212, 288 <33/22>. *hōšah* 'pandemonium, fracas, rough and tumble' (CA *hā<u>sh</u>a* 'to panick'; *tahāwa<u>sh</u>a* 'to become intermingled in a mêlée').

*hwl* *hōl* 'terror, fright, alarm' <23/9> (CA *hawl*).

*hwn* *ᶜala hūn* 'easily, calmly, gently, leisurely' <28/4> (CA *ᶜala hawn*).

*hwy* *hawa, yihwi* 'to go down, come down' *Glos*; 'to plunge down' <4/10>. *hawa* pl. *hwiyah* 'air, wind, draft' <5/12,8/b> (CA *hawāʾ* pl. *ahwiyah*). *hawa* 'love, passion' *Musil*, 158-159 <24/11,14>; *hawāh* 'his, her love; man or woman one desires' *Musil*, 513. *irᶜi hawāć* 'graze at will! (said to a she-camel)' *Musil*, 547. *hawiyyah* 'dagger' <17/10>.

*hyj* *hāj, yihīj* 'to rut', the rutting period of camels is the coldest season of the year, from 11 December to 21 January, *Musil*, 332. *hāyij* 'rutting; wild, furious' <6/23,7/11>.

*hyḍ* *hāḍ, yihīḍ* 'to be roused, stirred; to bring s.o. in the mood for saying, composing poetry' *Hess*, 143 <14/2,30/3>; 'to well up, surge (tears, grief, anxiety etc.)' <9/1, 26/1>. *hayyaḍ* 'to rouse, stir up, inspire emotion' <2/2, 4/5,10/1,11/2,23/1,27/1>; *tahayyaḍ* 'to be stirrred; to well up (grief)' <6/2> (CA *hāḍa al-ḥuzn al-qalb* 'grief affected the heart time after time'; *hayyaḍah* 'he roused, excited, provoked it', i.e. the heart; *tahayyaḍah al-ġarām* 'vehemence of desire returned to him a second time').

*hyᶜ* *mihyāᶜ* pl. *mahāyīᶜ* explained as 'a confluence of wadis or a valley between mountains' <6/5>; 'broad road, passage, pass' *Ju<u>Kh</u>a*, 111 (CA *ṭarīq mahyaᶜ* wide, spacious and clear road'; *hayᶜah* 'what is poured on the ground and runs in streams').

*hyf* — *mahāyīf* (pl.) 'inclining, bent over' <19/10,24/7>. *maᶜ az-zarāj mhāyfin li-l-mitāwīǵ* 'on a land covered with hillocks that slopes toward the higher elevations' *JuA*, 165 (CA *hāfa* 'to fall', said of leaves).

*hyg* — *hīg, hīǵ* 'male ostrich' *Musil*, 583 <4/9,17,11/11> (CA *hayq* 'very tall and slender', said of the ostrich).

*hyl* — *hēl* 'cardamom' <13/12>.

*hym* — *hīm* (pl.) 'crazed with thirst' <12/8>. *hyām* 'ruin, utter despair caused by unfulfilled desire' <11/22> (CA *hīm* sing. *hāʾim, hāʾimah*: *al-ibl al-ᶜiṭās̲h̲* 'camels afflicted by the disease called *al-huyām*', also 'madness, the state of one crazed by love').

*wbr* — *sūd al-wubar* 'camels with black wool' <1/9> (CA *wabar* 'wool of camels, rabbits and the like').

*wbl* — *wabil* 'heavy rain; a downpour for several days, inundating whole plains' *Musil*, 11 <1/6,9/23,10/6,18/4,29/3> (CA *wabl*).

*wṯg* — *māṯūg* 'firm, stable, fast, strong' <2/3> (CA *mawt̲h̲ūq*).

*wṯn* — *waṯna* (f.), pl. *wṯān* 'tame, docile, good-tempered, quiet (camels) that do not kick when they are being milked' <9/33> (CA *wāt̲h̲in* 'steady, still, tranquil'; *al-mawt̲h̲ūnah* 'the submissive, docile wife').

*wjb* — *wajbah* pl. *wjāb* 'half astronomical day, the unit used by the bedouins in their calculation of time; five *wjāb* is two times twenty-four hours plus one night' *Hess*, 70 <19/4> (CA *wajbat as̲h̲-s̲h̲ams* 'sunset'; *al-wajbah* 'one meal during the day and one at night').

*wjd* — *wājid* 'plenty, a lot of' <33a>. *wijūd, wajd* 'pain, sorrow, grief' *Musil*, 142, 147; *wā-wajdi* 'alas!' *Musil*, 84.

*wjᶜ* — *awjaᶜ, yūjiᶜ* 'to hurt, cause pain' <21/21>; *al-ᶜamal yūjiᶜ ar-rajjāl* 'witchcraft, sorcery makes a man ill' *Hess*, 161. *wajᶜah* 'pain, disease, suffering, hurting; every sickness' *Doughty* i, 298 <21/21>. *wajᶜān* 'grieved, ill' *Musil*, 91, 186 (CA *wajaᶜ* 'pain, ache; ailment').

*wjf* — *wājaf, ywājif* 'to run at great speed, so that the tassels of the saddle swing to and fro' <26/7>. *mūjif* pl. *muwājīf* 'swift' <19/21>; *mūjfāt* (pl. f.) 'fast she-camels' <7/3> (CA *al-*

*wajf* 'speed'; *wajīf* 'a fast, agitated pace of camels').

*wjn* *wajna* 'strong, big-bodied, hardy camel' <25/9> (CA *nāqah wajnāʾ* 'a perfect she-camel, sturdy and strong').

*wjh* *ōjah, awjah* 'to turn to face, to run in the direction of' *Glos* <33/7>. *wajh* pl. *wjīh* 'face; countenance, honour, protection; direction' *Musil*, 438-441, 55, 270; *Glos* <9/28, 12/10,27/12,33/23>. *ma lih wajh* 'he has no honour' *Hess*, 169.

*wḥš* *wḥūš* (pl.) 'predatory animals or birds' <3/1> (CA *waḥsh* pl. *wuḥūsh*).

*wḥy* *ōḥa, āḥa, yūḥi* 'to hear, listen, perceive' <2/12,19,5/10, 6/16,22/1,24/2>; 'to hurt' <4/21,21/21> (CA *awḥā* = *awmā* 'to make signs, speak secretly to'; *waḥy* 'secret sound, voice'; in modern usage the meaning has been transferred from the emitting end of sound to the receiving one).

*wdʿ* *waddaʿ* 'to take away, carry away' <12/6>.

*wdm* *see ʾdm*.

*wdn* *waddān* 'persistent downpour' <3/16,26/16,31/14> (CA *wadana* 'to moisten s.th. until it becomes soft'; *widān* 'well-irrigated places fit for agriculture').

*wdy* *wadda* 'to bring, convey, transport'. *mwaddi* 'bringing, transporting' <8/7> (CA *addā*).

*wrd* *wirid* 'to come to the water; to come at, rush at' *Glos*; *al-bill wardat* 'the camels have moved to the water' *Musil*, 341. *nird* (CA *nawrid*) 'we go to the water, rush at' <21/32>. *warrad* 'to go to the well, water' <2/14,33/10>; 'to water, give to drink, drench' <2/15>; 'to bring to the water, to one's destination' <20/2>. *warrād* 'the man watering the camels' <2/14>. *wird* 'watering party; animals or people hurrying to the water, the well' <17/7,19/5>. *wārid* pl. *wrūd* 'coming, going to the water; rushing, charging at (like herds of camels running to the water)' *Musil*, 167 <3/19,9/23,30/18,19,32/5,33/9,24,50>; or the pl. *ārād* (< *awrād*) <3/17,13/17>. *yōm l-ārād* 'the day on which the camels are watered' <2/11>. *mārūd, mārad* 'watering place, well' *Musil*, 186; *Glos* <3/18> (CA *mawrid* pl. *al-mawārid* 'watering place, well', also 'the pool of death', hence the image of attacking warriors as if thirsty for the taste of it and rushing to it, <21/32,30/18>; *wird*, *awrād* 'camels or birds coming to the water'; *īrād* 'the bringing to the water').

*wrʿ* — *wiriʿ* pl. *wirʿān* 'child; child of less than five years of age' *Hess*, 139; 'child up to its seventh year' *Musil*, 244 <28/7> (CA *waraʿ* 'weak, without the means to fend for o.s.').

*wrg* — *warg* 'doves' <14/2,18/9,27/4> (CA *warqāʾ*).

*wrk* — *warć* pl. *wrūk* 'haunches' <7/9,9/26,27/11> (CA *warik* 'what is above the thigh; hip, haunch'). *mīrakah* pl. *muwārik, myārić* 'leather cushion stuffed with wool or camel's hair on which the camel rider crosses his legs; it hangs from the front knob of the saddle, resting on the camel's shoulder blades, and is ornamented with a fringe, *hadab*' *Musil*, 171, 291, 353 <6/30,9/22> (CA *mawrik, mawrikah, mīrakah* pl. *mawārik* 'the place in front of the saddle on which the rider folds his feet').

*wry* — *wara* 'why' <14/4>; *warāk* 'for what cause, wherefore you' *Musil*, 216.

*wzn* — *māzūn* 'weighed, ready; beautiful, fine' <11/a,22/3, 28/2> (CA *mawzūn* 'weighed; of full weight').

*wzy* — *wiza* 'to gather in a place, to take refuge' <12/9> (CA *wazā*).

*wsʿ* — *wassaʿ, yissiʿ* (cf. *Proch*, 73, *yirriṯ*) 'to remove; to stay at a remove' <22/9>.

*wsg* — *wisig* pl. *wsūg* 'the top of the back, the spine' (CA *wasq* 'a camel load'); 'the rounded top of a mountain, full of crevices and hollows' <1/5>.

*wsm* — *wasm, wasmi* pl. *wsām* 'the autumnal rains, the rains of Canopus, the Pleiades, and Gemini' *Musil*, 8 <11/14, 13/15,18/10> (CA *wasmī* 'the rains of early spring', so called because in its traces the annuals shoot up later in the season).

*wsn* — *ṭuwāh al-wsāni* 'the stench did him in' i.e. he fainted; *yūnis* 'he faints' <19/9>. *mūsin* 'giving out a ghastly smell' (CA *asana* 'to become altered for the worse in odour when it has stood too long', said of water).

*wšm* — *wušīm* 'the howling of the wind' <5/1> (CA *wash̲īmah* 'vituperations, loud altercation'). *wašim* pl. *wšām* 'tattoos' <11/5,25/21> (CA *wash̲m* pl. *wish̲ām*).

*wṣy* — *waṣṣa* 'to bequeath, counsel, advice, entrust s.o. with one's last will' <21/20>; *wiṣṣīna bha* 'we were entrusted with it, bequeathed' <30/9> (CA *waṣṣā* 'to bequeath, decree by will'). *wiṣāh* 'bequest' <21/20>; 'message' *Musil*, 318.

*wṭf* *waṭfit al-jurrah* 'leaving large traces, footprints' <3/15> (CA *waṭafa* 'to come down in abundance', said of hair hanging down from the eyebrow, rain from the clouds etc.).

*wṭn* *wiṭan* has the same meaning as *dīrah* 'region, country, territory belonging to one of the tribes' *Musil*, 250, 555 <16/7,23/3>.

*wṭy* *wiṭa* 'to walk on, step on, tread on; to step, walk' <1/2>; 'to happen to, afflict' <23/5,24/16> (CA *waṭiʾa* imperf. *yaṭaʾ* 'to tread upon, to step on') . *yāṭa* 'he walks, treads with his feet' <4/2> (cf. *Proch*, 69-70: *wiṣil* imperf. 3 m. s. *yāṣal*). *waṭṭa, ywaṭṭi* 'to step on, to kick (the neck of the camel in order to make him go faster); to strike at' <19/21,23>; 'to lower, cause to lower, pull down' <25/1>; *ma twāṭa* 'she does not let herself be reined in; she is indomitable' <26/5>. *muwāṭi* 'feet, hoofs, hoof pads' <6/25,29,9/30,14/14,27/11>. *wiṭa* 'the ground, surface on which one walks; desert' *Musil*, 86 <9/30, 24/9>.

*wḏ̣h* *wḏ̣ēhi* 'Arabian oryx' <33/34,43>.

*wḏ̣y* *yūḏ̣i* 'it illuminates, shines' <31/8>; *yāḏ̣i* 'it shines' *Musil*, 108. *mūḏ̣i* 'luminous, white, fair' *Glos* (CA *aḍāʾa* 'to shed light'). *ḏ̣aww* 'fire, light of a fire' <30/17,33/42> (CA *ḍawʾ*).

*wʿy* *waʿa, yāʿi* 'to remember; to be aware, conscious' <32/14>. *min gabil yāʿi* 'before he can use his reason, becomes aware' *Musil*, 152 (CA *waʿā, yaʿī* 'to pay attention, heed; to perceive, hear; to become aware').

*wfy* *wifa* 'to be complete' <1/7>. *āfa, ōfa* 'to make full, complete; to pay in full (debt)' *Glos* <11/6>. *wāfi* 'ample, plentiful' <7/6> (CA *awfā* 'to give to the full'). *twaffāni ʿala dīnik* 'let me die in Your faith' <21/10>.

*wgt* *wagt* 'period of drought' <;1,;3>. *mūgtīn* (pl.) 'people suffering the effects of drought' <;12> (CA *waqt* 'a portion of time').

*wgd* *wigad* 'to catch fire' *Musil*, 177. *waggad* 'to fuel, keep burning' *Musil*, 306; *ǵdat* for *awgidat* 'it was lighted' <33/42>.

*wgūd* 'burning (of a fire)' <33/3>; *wigūd* 'fuel' <33/42> (CA *waqada* 'to take fire, burn'; *waqqada, awqada* 'to kindle, ignite, light'; *wuqūd* 'ignition, burning of the fire'; *waqūd* 'fuel').

*wgf* *wigaf, yāgaf* 'to stop, halt' *Glos. wǵāf* 'halting' *Musil*, 227. *wgūf* (pl.) 'standing (in fixed position); bending over' *Musil*, 346 <24/9> (CA *wāqif* pl. *wuqūf*). *wagfah* 'stand, taking up position' <33/54>.

*wgm* *wagm* 'about, approximately' <7/16>.

*wgy* *wiga, wagga* 'to protect (from being touched, hurt)'. *wala waggat al-liḥyān* lit. 'there was nothing between the jaws, nothing that prevented the jaws from touching', i.e. the morsel was so small that it could not even be chewed, <9/10>. *māgiy* 'protected against damage or harm' <9/29>. *mittiǵi* 'hidden (from view)' *Musil*, 168 (CA *waqā*; *mawqīy* 'well-preserved, protected').

*wkd* *wakkad* 'to assure, confirm; to become certain of s.th.' <19/19,26/8> (CA *akkada*).

*wkn* *wićan* 'to lean on for support' <26/20> (CA *tawakkana* 'to lean on for support'; *wākin* 'leaning on').

*wld* *walad* pl. *ālād* 'sons; young, warlike men' <2/15,25> (CA *awlād*).

*wlᶜ* *wallaᶜ* 'to ignite, kindle' <30/17>. *mwallaᶜ tōlīᶜ* 'inflamed (with passion); kindled' <6/2>. *wilīᶜ* 'burning fiercely' <5/8>. *mūliᶜ* 'shining' *Musil*, 108 (CA *wallaᶜa*).

*wlf* *mīlāf* 'a she-camel that dotes on her young'; such a riding camel is loath to part from her young or herd and *tiḥinn ᶜan walaf*, moans and murmurs grievously; 'given to, affectionate' *Musil*, 227, 349. *muwālīf* (pl.) 'affectionate, attached to s.o. by ties of affection, tender love' <24/4, 14>; *al-glūb al-muwālīf* 'the affectionate, tenderly loving hearts' <24/14> (CA *alifa* 'to like, be fond of'; *maʾlūf* 'familiar').

*walla* 'or, otherwise, or else' (CA *wa-illā*).

*wlm* *wallam, ywallim* 'to prepare, make ready' *Musil*, 362. *wālim* pl. *wālmāt* 'what is handy, ready; ready for use, consumption' *Musil*, 320 <7/16>. *al-wālmah* 'what is ready (e.g. coffee left from the day before)' *Musil*, 468.

*wly* *wala, yāla* 'to make s.th. (rain) continuous, to bring *wiliyy* rains' <14/19> (CA *walīy* 'the rains following those of the *wasm*'; *wuliyat al-arḍ walyan*). *walla* 'to go away, turn away'; *wall* 'away with you!' *Glos* <15/2,16/3>. *wāla* 'to come next to; to come in the way of' *Glos*. *wiliyy* 'God, the Lord' <9/17,10/2,12/14,15,31/12>; also *wāli* <11/a, 21/13,26/29>.

*wmr* — *wimar* see *ʾmr*.

*wmy* — *ōma, yūmi* 'to gesture at, to flutter, to wave; to make inviting, welcoming signs with one's arms; to rock, go with a rocky movement, to sway back and forth' <26/25>. *tuwāma* 'to sway back and forth, to flutter' <6/31>; *titwāmi rūshum* 'their heads nodded, moved up and down' *Musil*, 188 (CA *awmaʾa* 'to make signs with the hand or the head').

*wnd* — *wnād* (pl.) 'trudging along, dragging themselves' <13/14>; *an-nāgah winūd* 'the she-camel walks quietly'; *wandāt* 'shuffling, slowly walking women' *Su* iii, 103.

*wnn* — *wann, ywinn* 'to moan, lament, groan' <6/2,23/9>. *wannah, winīn* 'lament, wailing, moaning' <3/3,11/4,16/3, 5> (CA *annā* 'to moan, cry'; *anīn* 'moaning, wailing').

*wiyya* — 'with, in the company of' <;17>.

*yāma, yama* — 'how much! how often! how many! how many a time!' *Glos* <10/12,13/16,19/3,24/15,29/4,33/16,26,37> (sometimes used with the meaning of *ćam*, the equivalent of *wa-rubba* or *wa-qad* in boastful sections, *mufākharah*, of classical poetry).

*ybs* — *yābis* pl. *yibbās* 'dry, dried out' <7/4,20/4>.

*ytm* — *ētam* 'to orphan, deprive one of his parents' <33/27>. *yitīm* 'orphan' <11/4> (CA *aytama*).

*yd* — *yad, īd* 'hand; foot of an animal'. *īdēh* 'both his forelegs' <4/16>.

*ysr* — *īsār* 'to the left' <10/5,26/12>. *mityāmnin mityāsir* 'to the left and the right, everywhere; in abundance, plentiful, superabundant' <32a>.

*ygn* — *ēgan, yīgin* 'to be sure, certain of' <21/14> (CA *ayqana*). *īgān* 'certainty, certitude, conviction, steadfastness of faith' <21/19,24/17>.

*ymm* — *yamm* 'at; to, towards, in the direction of' *Glos* <33/36> (CA *yammama* 'to betake o.s., go to; to head for').

*ymn* — *yimīn* pl. *ēmān* 'right hand, hand; forefeet, legs of camel or horse' <6/22,9/20,30/16>; *aymān* 'to the right' <26/12>. (CA *yamīn* pl. *aymān*). *yimna* 'right hand, hand' <21/16,26> (CA *yumnā*). *mityāmin*, see *mityāsir* under *ysr* <32a>.

# APPENDIX OF PLACE NAMES

The names of places, mountains, wells, desert areas and other geographical features which occur in the poetry and narrative parts are listed according to the Arabic alphabet together with a reference to the narrative section or poem and verse where they occur and any relevant additional information I have been able to gain from available geographical works and other sources. The abbreviations for these sources are:

Ḥm — Ḥmēr, ᶜAbdallah Sāyir ad-Dōsiri, *Wāḥat ash-shiᶜr ash-shaᶜbī*, ii, Riyadh 1988.

JuMu — Junaydil, Saᶜd ibn ᶜAbdallah ibn, *al-Muᶜjam al-juġrāfī li-l-bilād al-ᶜArabīyah as-Suᶜūdīyah, ᶜĀliyat Najd*, Riyadh 1978.

KhaMu — Khamīs, ᶜAbdallah ibn Muḥammad ibn, *al-Muᶜjam al-juġrāfī li-l-bilād al-ᶜArabīyah as-Suᶜūdīyah, muᶜjam al-Yamāmah*, Riyadh 1980.

Musil — Alois, *The Manners and Customs of the Rwala Bedouins*, New York 1928.

In some cases the names of places that do not occur in the text, but are mentioned in the description given by these sources, have been transliterated according to the system used for literary Arabic. The names have been arranged according to the order of their consonants in the Arabic alphabet, while initial *a* is regarded as *alif*.

al-Abrag — <10/9> Abrag al-Miġārīn is meant, an *abrag* (see glossary under the root *brg*) west of al-Xamāsīn and north of Xašim Jwēl on the road from Wādi ad-Duwāsir to Taṯlīṯ; north of it lies the well of al-Manjūr. It belongs to the tribe of al-Ḥarāršah (Dindān's tribe) of ar-Rijbān of ad-Duwāsir, *JuMu*, 58 and *Ḥm*, 166.

al-Aflāj — <2/23> a fertile area with many wells, wheatfields and palm-trees in the southern part of al-Yamāmah between al-Xarj and as-Slayyil in the area of al-Biyāḏ̣; its main town is Layla, *KhaMu* i, 95.

al-Biyāḏ̣ — <26/12> the desert between Yabrīn on the northern edge of the Empty Quarter and al-Yamāmah; a desert on the fringe of the Empty Quarter, running in a north-south direction from the southern part of al-Xarj in the north; it is bordered in the south by the Empty Quarter, in the east by the sands of ad-Dahna and in the west by the road between al-Xarj and al-Aflāj; into it run the southern wadis of the al-ᶜĀriḏ̣ mountains between Ṭalḥah in the north and as-Slayyil in the south as well as all wadis that cross al-Aflāj, *KhaMu* i, 188-191.

al-Bēḏ̣a — <14/9> the white al-Jazla on the south-western border of the Wādi, *Ḥm*, 179.

Jabjib — <14/10,30/21> a large wadi that reaches Wādi ad-Duwāsir from the south, *Ḥm*, 180.

al-Jibal — <26/12> the mountain of al-ᶜĀriḏ̣, i.e. Ṭwēġ, *Ḥm*, 144.

al-Jazlāt — <2/6,12/20,13/9,30/5,31/3,7,8> mountains about 55 km south-west of the Wādi on the borders of the tribal land of the Duwāsir, *Ḥm*, 129. Al-Jazlāt or al-Jizil, two mountains (*hḏāb*), one called al-Jazla al-Bēḏ̣a and the other al-Jazla as-Sōda, in the upper reaches of Wādi ad-Duwāsir, west of the village of al-Farᶜah, *JuMu*, 305 and mentioned in *KhaMu*, i, 448.

al-Janbah < 14/11 > a well about 45 km north of the sand-dunes bordering the Wādi on the north, *Ḥm*, 180.

Ḥibir < 33/46 > a high black peak west of ᶜAfīf and aš-Šiᶜb and south of Ḥaslāt in the western upper reaches of Wādi Jirīr in the land of ar-Rūgah of ᶜTēbah, *JuMu*, 357.

al-Ḥaṯāmīl < 10/9 > a hilly country west of Wādi ad-Duwāsir in the same area where the Jazla mountains are situated.

al-Ḥarrah < 3/7 > presumably the *ḥarrah* between Ranyah and al-Xurmah on the road to Ṭāᵓif is meant.

al-Ḥazim < 1/5,33/45 > a large area in the Haḏb ad-Duwāsir stretching eastwards from aḏ-Ḏīrēn to aṣ-Ṣaxrah and as-Suwādah mountains, *Ḥm*, 147. A large tract of land north-east of the red mountains of Haḏb ad-Duwāsir and separated from it by the wadis of al-Ḥamal and al-Ḥmēl; it is a high desert with many mountains and wells and belongs entirely to the tribe of the Duwāsir; on the northern edge of the Ḥazim lies ar-Raqqāsh mountain, *JuMu*, 371.

al-Ḥala < 10/9 > a group of *abrag*s about 35 km west of Wādi ad-Duwāsir, named Ḥala al-Manjūr, *Ḥm*, 166 (see glossary under the root *brg*).

al-Ḥumr < 10/5 > reddish mountains and rocks south of the well of Abu Ćaᶜab which drain into Wādi al-Gamra, *Ḥm*, 165.

Ḥammat al-Murrah < 3/16 > a black mountain in the northern part of the Haḏb ad-Duwāsir; al-Murrah is a well south of as-Suwādah mountains holding brackish, bitter water, *Ḥm*, 174. *Ḥammah* is the name given to mountains so-called because of their black colour among other mountains of a reddish or white hue, *KhaMu* i, 345.

Wādi ar-Rmah < 11/18 > the largest wadi of Najd; it originates from the mountain ar-Rās al-Abyaḏ east of Khaybar and runs in a north-easterly direction to al-Qaṣīm, see al-ᶜUbūdī, Muḥammad ibn Nāṣir, *al-Muᶜjam al-juġrāfī li-l-bilād al-ᶜArabīyah as-Suᶜūdīyah, bilād al-Qaṣīm*, Riyadh 1979, 2474-2502.

Sdēr < 27/1 > a group of mountains, Sdēr al-Abyaḏ and Sdēr al-Aswad, *KhaMu*, i, 448; they are about 95 km south of Wādi ad-Duwāsir, *Ḥm*, 147.

Sarḥat aṯ-Ṯōr < 26/11 > a shady tree in one of the valleys of al-ᶜĀriḏ, *Ḥm*, 143.

as-Sirrah < 3/11 > a wadi whose *sēl*, torrent after rains, flows to the east and west of al-ᶜAlam in the High Najd, *Ḥm*, 172. A well-known wadi which runs east and south of al-ᶜAlam; its upper reaches are in the land of aš-Šiyābīn of ᶜTēbah and the administrative district of al-Khāṣirah, its middle part in that of al-ᶜṢimah of ᶜTēbah and its lower reaches in that of Ghaṭān and the district of al-Quwayᶜīyah, *JuMu*, 686-687.

as-Slayyil < 2/23 > an area rich in water, gardens of date palms and wheat-fields, dotted with many villages, between Wādi ad-Duwāsir and al-Aflāj; it lies east of al-ᶜĀriḏ mountain on the edge of the Empty Quarter, *KhaMu* ii, 33.

Sinḥ < 2/5 > a mountain 200 km south of Wādi ad-Duwāsir in the tribal area of Yām, *Ḥm*, 129.

Bini Sanāmah <;8,18/7 > red-hued mountains (*hḏāb*) in the desert west of al-Xamāsīn, *JuMu*, 711; 65 km south-west of Wādi ad-Duwāsir on the road towards at-Taṯlīṯ and the ᶜAsīr, *Ḥm*, 186. This mountain is one of Dindān's favourite haunts and on its top he composed many of his poems.

Šiḏuw — <30/17,18> there are a number of places in Najd called by this name, for instance a well near al-Xurmah, but this mountain seems to be part of the Jazlāt.

aš-Šagg — <1/6> Šagg Dxayyin near the village of al-Xāldiyyah and the *hijrah* (settlement) of Abu Hayya, *Ḥm*, 147; (*šuggah* 'ravine').

aṣ-Ṣuwwān — <1/2> a small white mountain north of al-Jazla as-Sōda, south-west of Wādi ad-Duwāsir, *Ḥm*, 146. *Ṣuwwānah*, 'tract or hill covered with flints', *ṣuwwān*, *Musil*, 683; see also *JuMu*, 857-858.

Ṭifīl — <5/2> two mountains, facing one another from east to west, in the *xabt* of Tihāmah, not far from Jedda, al-Bulayhid, Muḥammad ibn ᶜAbdallah, *Ṣaḥīḥ al-akhbār*, iv, 52-53.

Ṭwēǵ — <14/17> the foremost mountain of al-Yamāmah, an escarpment that begins in the sands north of az-Zilfi and ends in the Empty Quarter in the south, a distance of 1000 km; dozens of wadis run from its slopes, *KhaMu* ii, 117.

Ḍida — <18/9> a big mountain about 120 km south of Wādi ad-Duwāsir, *Ḥm*, 186.

Ḍāᶜin — <10/8,14/11> a well in the Haḏb, west of Wādi ad-Duwāsir, whose *sēl* flows into Wādi al-Faršah, *Ḥm*, 180. A big, black mountain north of al-Faršah, west of Wādi ad-Duwāsir and east of Ranyah in the land of the Duwāsir; on its south is a well with the same name, on its north a well with bitter water called ar-Rayyāniyyah, *JuMu*, 889.

ᶜIblah — <13/9> an elevation among the Jazlāt mountains, *Ḥm*, 176. *ᶜIblah*, 'any wide tract of land scattered with small, mostly white, rocky outcrops', *KhaMu* ii, 135. *ᶜAbal*, 'a small, isolated outcrop covered with white flint', *JuMu*, 23.

al-ᶜŌd — <26/12> the quarter of Ḥallat al-ᶜŌd in Riyadh, east of al-Baṭḥa and west of al-Xarj street, south of what is called al-Ḥallah al-Xārjiyyah, *KhaMu* i, 494.

al-Ġarābah — <33/46> a black mountain of the *haḏbah* type west of Šiᶜb al-ᶜIsībiyyāt between Ḥibir mountain and the *hḏāb* of Ḥaslāt; it is often mentioned in conjunction with Ḥibir for its proximity to it and because both mountains are of the same black colour, *JuMu*, 1014.

Ġaḏya — <14/15> a place near al-Manjūr with many *ġaḏa*-bushes, *Ḥm*, 181. Perhaps the name refers to the same place as the following item, Ġḏayy.

Ġḏayy — <13/7> a tributary of Wādi al-Faršah, so called because of its many *ġaḏa*-bushes; it runs to the south of Wādi al-Faršah, *Ḥm*, 176. A wadi 30 km from as-Slayyil in the land of al-Widāᶜīn south of that town, *KhaMu* ii, 35.

Ġāyir — <32/11> a big, black mountain in the north-western part of Haḏb ad-Duwāsir in the *fēḏah*, depression, of Sigmān, west of the *haḏbah* of Umm ᶜAmīrah and 25 km north of Šiṯīr, *JuMu*, 1007.

al-Faršah — <10/7,13/7,14/10> a wadi in the Haḏb which is reached by the *sēls* of Wādi Bīšah and Wādi Taṯlīṯ and those running down from the mountains of the Haḏb; all these *sēls* flow into the western part of the sand-dunes bordering Wādi ad-Duwāsir on the north, *Ḥm*, 176. A vast desert east of Ranyah and south of Haḏb ad-Duwāsir, *JuMu*, 190-191. *Faršah*, 'a funnel-like pit in the sand', *Musil*, 677. A *faršah* is a wide expanse of land at the lower end of a wadi into which its *sēl* empties itself; or a confluence in the upper reaches of a wadi where the smaller watercourses congregate and form the beginning of the wadi; a particular *faršah* is known by the qualifying entity term annexed to it, hence Faršat Slayyil and so on, *KhaMu* ii, 247 (CA *farsh* 'a wide plain of soft ground, unobstructed by mountains').

al-Gṭayyiᶜ <14/15> an area west of Wādi ad-Duwāsir, parallel to its sand-dunes, *Ḥm*, 181.

Gamra <12/20> a vast tract of land in the western Haḏb in the area of the *hijrah* known as al-Hamjāt bi-ṭ-Ṭuwārīf; in the middle of Gamra is the mountain Īḥāmir, about 15 km south of Ṯarbān and Abu Ćaᶜab, *Ḥm*, 170. A vast desert in the middle of which lies the small mountain called ᶜḎēdah in the land of the Duwāsir, north of the lower end of Wādi Ranyah, *JuMu*, 1082.

Ǵimra <13/11> a wadi which runs from west to east along the as-Suwādah mountains, *Ḥm*, 177. A well-known valley in the southern High Najd between Wādi ar-Rika and Ḥazm ad-Duwāsir; its upper reaches are in the land of aš-Šiyābīn of ᶜTēbah and its lower reaches in that of the Duwāsir, *JuMu*, 1085.

Ǵīᶜat al-Ġār <10/8> an area on the road from Wādi a-Duwāsir to Wādi Taṯlīṯ.

al-Kōkab <3/11> a place near Najrān.

al-Ldām <18/14> an old town and the former capital of Wādi ad-Duwāsir inhabited by the tribe of ar-Rijbān, *KhaMu* ii, 317 and H.St.J.B. Philby, *Southern Nejd*, 50.

al-Mijālīb <12/20> a place in Wādi Taṯlīṯ.

al-Maḥābīl <10/8> hills or small outcrops north of Abrag ibn Fhēr, near the white and black Jazlāt, *Ḥm*, 165.

al-Murrah <18/9> some wells east of the Haḏb, *Ḥm*, 186, see Ḥammat al-Murrah.

al-Mīᶜāl <1/5> mountains south of Wādi ad-Duwāsir, south of al-Wḥayyah and Sdēr, *Ḥm*, 147; see also Muwāᶜīl.

Muġmād <13/11> a *ṯimad* (see glossary) north of the Wādi and aṣ-Ṣaxrah mountains, not far from the Suwādah mountains, *Ḥm*, 177.

al-Manjūr <14/15,18/5> a well about 30 km from Wādi ad-Duwāsir, on its western border, belonging to the Ḥarāršah (Dindān's tribe), west of the village of al-Farᶜah, about 10 km from the *hijrah* of Abu Hayya, *Ḥm*, 181, 185. Several wells and *ṯimads* in this part of the country are named al-Manjūr, *JuMu*, 1233.

al-Muwāᶜīl <14/11> a group of mountains about 70 km south of Wādi ad-Duwāsir, *Ḥm*, 180 and *KhaMu* i, 448.

al-Inćīr <2/5> a mountain in central Najd in the tribal area of Gḥaṭān, 600 km from Sinḥ, *Ḥm*, 129. A big grey mountain south-west of al-ᶜIrḍ, west of as-Sirdāḥ, not far from the Ṣabḥa *hḏāb* towards the east, in the land of Gḥaṭān and the administrative district of al-Quwayᶜīyah, *JuMu*, 180-181.

an-Nuwāṣif <1/5> two wadis running towards al-Jazlāt, north-west of the Bini Sanāmah outcrops which run parallel to the road from the Wādi to the ᶜAsīr, *Ḥm*, 147.

al-Hajlah <13/9,14/12> the confluence of Wādi al-Faršah, Wādi Bīšah and Wādi Taṯlīṯ, north-west of Wādi ad-Duwāsir, *Ḥm*, 176. A *hajlah* is a large and deep pool of water fed by rain-water; the water remains in it for a long time and is frequented by the bedouins and their herds, *JuMu*, 26, 1317. Perhaps this particular *hajlah* is Hajlah Mxaṭmiyyah, 90 km west of Wādi ad-Duwāsir between sands, *KhaMu* ii, 451.

Haḏ̣b — Haḏ̣b ad-Duwāsir, also called Haḏ̣b Āl Zāyid, see glossary under the root *hḏ̣b*.

al-Wādi — < 2/23 > short for Wādi ad-Duwāsir, a fertile area in southern Najd with many forests of date palms and wheatfields inhabited by the tribe of the same name.

Wāsiṭ — < 33/51 > perhaps the name refers to the old agricultural wells 80 km south of ad-Dawādmi, *JuMu*, 1297.

# SOURCES OF REFERENCE

Abbreviations

BSOAS  Bulletin of the School of Oriental and African Studies
ZAL    Zeitschrift für arabische Linguistik

This is not a comprehensive bibliography of works relevant to the subject, but rather a listing of the principal sources used as references in the course of preparing this edition. For a more general orientation one might consult the bibliographies of Sowayan (1985 and 1992), Ingham (1982 and 1986), Prochazka (1988) and others.

Abboud, Peter Fouad, *The Syntax of Najdi Arabic*, unpublished dissertation, Austin, Texas 1964.
Bulayhid, Muḥammad ibn ʿAbdallah ibn, *Ṣaḥīḥ al-aḵẖbār ʿammā fī bilād al-ʿArab min al-āṯẖār*, 2nd ed., 5 vols., Riyadh 1972.
Caton, Steven C., *'Peaks of Yemen I Summon'. Poetry as Cultural Practice in a North Yemeni Tribe*, University of California Press 1990.
Doughty, Charles M., *Travels in Arabia Deserta*, republication of the third ed. in 1936 by Jonathan Cape, 2 vols., Dover Publications, New York 1979.
al-Faraj, Ḵẖālid ibn Muḥammad ad-Dōsirī, *Dīwān an-Nabaṭ*, 2 vols., Maṭbaʿat at-Taraqqī, Damascus 1952.
al-Fawzān, ʿAbdallah Nāṣir, *Raʾīs at-taḥrīr: Ḥumaydān asẖ-Sẖuwayʿir*, Muʾassasah al-Juraysī li-t-Tawzīʿ, Riyadh 1988.
al-Fiṣām, Maḥbūb ibn Saʿd ibn Mudawwis ad-Dōsirī, with notes and commentary by Abū ʿAbd ar-Raḥmān ibn ʿAqīl aẓ-Ẓāhirī, *Min asẖʿār ad-Dawāsir*, 2 vols., Maṭābiʿ asẖ-Sẖarīf, Riyadh 1989-90.
Gelder, G.J.H. van, *Beyond the Line. Classical Arabic Literary Critics on the Coherence and Unity of the Poem*, E.J. Brill, Leiden 1982.
——, *The Bad and the Ugly. Attitudes towards Invective Poetry (Hijāʾ) in Classical Arabic Literature*, E.J. Brill, Leiden 1988.
al-Ḥaqīl, ʿAbd al-Karīm ibn Ḥamad ibn Ibrāhīm, *Alfāẓ dārijah wa-madlūlātuhā fī al-Jazīrah al-ʿArabiyah*, Maṭābiʿ al-Farazdaq, Riyadh 1989.
Hess, J.J., *Von den Beduinen des Innern Arabiens*, Max Niehans Verlag, Zürich-Leipzig 1938.
Ḥmēr, ʿAbdallah Sāyir ad-Dōsiri, *Wāḥat asẖ-sẖiʿr asẖ-sẖaʿbī*, ii, Maṭābiʿ al-Farazdaq, Riyadh 1988.
Ibn Manẓūr, *Lisān al-ʿArab*, Dār al-Maʿārif, Cairo (n.d.).
Ingham, Bruce, *North East Arabian Dialects*, Kegan Paul, London 1982.
——, *Bedouin of Northern Arabia. Traditions of the Āl-Dhafīr*, Kegan Paul, London 1986.
——, 'Notes on the Dialect of Mutair in Eastern Arabia', *ZAL* 2 (1979), 23-35.
——, 'Camel terminology among the Āl Murrah bedouins', *ZAL* 22 (1990), 67-78.
Johnstone, T.M., *Eastern Arabian Dialect Studies*, Oxford University Press, London 1967.
——, 'Some characteristics of the Dōsiri dialect of Arabic as Spoken in Kuwait', *BSOAS* xxiv, 2 (1961), 249-297.

——, 'Further studies on the Dōsiri dialect of Arabic as spoken in Kuwait', *BSOAS* xxvii, 1 (1964), 77-113.
——, 'The Affrication of "kāf" and "gāf" in the Arabic Dialects of the Arabian Peninsula', *Journal of Semitic Studies*, viii, 2 (1963), 210-226.
Junaydil, Saᶜd ibn ᶜAbdallah ibn, *al-Muᶜjam al-jugrāfī li-l-bilād al-ᶜArabīyah as-Suᶜūdīyah, ᶜĀliyat Najd*, 3 vols., Dār al-Yamāmah, Riyadh 1978.
——, *Min aᶜlām al-adab ash-shaᶜbī, shuᶜarāʾ al-ᶜĀliyah*, al-Maktabah as-Suᶜūdīyah, al-Jamᶜīyah as-Suᶜūdīyah li-th-Thaqāfah wa-l-Funūn, Maṭābiᶜ al-Farazdaq, Riyadh 1980-81.
——, *Khawāṭir wa-nawādir turāthīyah*, al-Maktabah as-Suᶜūdīyah li-th-Thaqāfah wa-l-Funūn, Maṭābiᶜ al-Farazdaq, Riyadh 1987.
——, *as-Sānī wa-s-sāniyah*, al-Maktabah al-ᶜArabīyah as-Suᶜūdīyah, Jāmiᶜah al-Imām Muḥammad ibn Suᶜūd al-Islāmīyah, Riyadh 1987-88.
al-Kamālī, Shafīq, *ash-Shiᶜr ᶜind al-badw*, Maṭbaᶜat al-Irshād, Baghdad 1964.
Khamīs, ᶜAbdallah ibn Muḥammad ibn, *al-Muᶜjam al-jugrāfī li-l-bilād al-ᶜArabīyah as-Suᶜūdīyah, muᶜjam al-Yamāmah*, 2 vols., Maṭābiᶜ al-Farazdaq, Riyadh 1980.
——, *al-Adab ash-shaᶜbī fī Jazīrat al-ᶜArab*, 2nd ed., Maṭābiᶜ ar-Riyāḍ, Riyadh 1982.
Kurpershoek, Marcel, *Diep in Arabië* (*Deep Inside Arabia*), Meulenhoff, Amsterdam 1992.
——, 'De Slag van al-Muᶜtala: Orale Literatuur als Bron voor de Geschiedenis van Saoedi-Arabië' ('The battle of al-Muᶜtala: Oral History as a Source for the History of Saudi Arabia'), *Sharqiyyāt* 3/1 (1991), 39-65.
——, 'Heartbeat: Conventionality and Originality in Najdi Poetry', *Asian Folklore Studies*, 52/1 (1993), 33-74.
——, 'The Ghost of a Bedouin Knight,' *Icarus* 10 (New York, 1993), 72–94.
——, 'Between ad-Dakhūl and ᶜAfīf: Oral Traditions of the ᶜUtaybah tribe in Central Najd', *ZAL*, 26 (1993), 28-65.
Lane, Edward William, *An Arabic-English Lexicon*, Williams and Norgate, London, 1863-1893.
Migahid, A.M., *Flora of Saudi Arabia*, 2nd revised ed., 2 vols., Riyadh University Publication, Riyadh 1978.
Musil, Alois, *The Manners and Customs of the Rwala Bedouins*, American Geographical Society, Oriental Explorations and Studies No. 6., New York 1928.
Palva, Heikki, *Narratives and Poems from Ḥisbān*, Acta Universitatis Gothoburgensis, Orientalia Gothoburgensia 3 1978.
——, 'The Descriptive Imperative of Narrative Style in Spoken Arabic', *Folia Orientalia*, 18 (1977), 5-26.
Philby, H.St.J.B., *Southern Nejd*, Government Press, Cairo 1919.
——, *The Heart of Arabia*, 2 vols., Constable and Co., London-Bombay-Sydney 1922.
——, *Arabian Highlands*, Cornell University Press, Ithaca, New York 1952.
Prochazka, Theodore, *Saudi Arabian Dialects*, Kegan Paul, London-New York 1988.
Raddās, ᶜAbdallah ibn Muḥammad ibn, *Shāᶜirāt min al-bādiyah*, 6th and 4th ed., 2 vols., Maṭābiᶜ al-Bādiyah, Riyadh 1984-85.
Raswan, Carl R., 'Vocabulary of Bedouin Words concerning Horses', *Journal of Near Eastern Studies*, 4 (1945), 97-129.
as-Saᶜīd, Ṭalāl ᶜUthmān al-Mazᶜal, *al-Mawsūᶜah an-nabaṭīyah al-kāmilah*, 2 vols., Dhāt as-Salāsil, Kuwait 1987.
Sbayyil, Muḥammad ibn ᶜAbd al-ᶜAzīz ibn, *Dīwān Ibn Sbayyil*, Maṭābiᶜ al-Farazdaq, Riyadh 1988.
Sowayan, Saad Abdullah, *Nabaṭi Poetry: The Oral Poetry of Arabia*, University of California Press, Berkeley-Los Angeles-London 1985.
——, *The Arabian Oral Historical Narrative. An Ethnographic and Linguistic Analysis*,

Otto Harrasowitz, Wiesbaden 1992. References to its glossary are marked with *Glos.*

——, 'A Poem and its Narrative by Riḏa ibn Ṭārif aš-Šammari', *ZAL* 7 (1982), 48-73.

——, 'al-Muᶜānāt wa-l-ibdāᶜ fī naẓm al-qaṣīdah an-nabaṭīyah', *ad-Dārah* 23 vol. 1 (1987), 73-103.

as-Suwaydāʾ, ᶜAbd ar-Raḥmān ibn Zayd, *Faṣīḥ al-ᶜāmmī fī s̲h̲amāl Najd*, 2 vols., Dār as-Suwaydāʾ, Maṭābiᶜ al-Farazdaq, Riyadh 1987.

——, *al-Alf sanah al-ġāmiḍah min taʾrīk̲h̲ Najd*, Dār as-Suwaydāʾ, Riyadh 1988.

——, *Min s̲h̲uᶜarāʾ al-Jabal al-ᶜāmmīyīn*, 3 vols., Dār as-Suwaydāʾ, Maṭābiᶜ al-Farazdaq, Riyadh 1988.

at̲h̲-T̲h̲umayrī, Muḥammad ibn Aḥmad, *al-Funūn as̲h̲-s̲h̲aᶜbīyah fī al-Jazīrah al-ᶜArabīyah*, al-Maṭbaᶜah al-ᶜUmūmīyah, Damascus 1972.

al-ᶜUbūdī, Muḥammad ibn Nāṣir, *al-Amt̲h̲āl al-ᶜāmmīyah fī Najd*, 5 vols., Dār al-Yamāmah, Riyadh 1979.

——, *al-Muᶜjam al-juġrāfī li-l-bilād al-ᶜArabīyah as-Suᶜūdīyah, bilād al-Qaṣīm*, 6 vols., Dār al-Yamāmah, Riyadh 1979.

Wagner, Ewald, *Grundzüge der klassischen arabischen Dichtung*, 2 vols., Wissenschaftliche Buchgesellschaft, Darmstadt 1988.

# STUDIES IN ARABIC LITERATURE

SUPPLEMENTS TO THE
JOURNAL OF ARABIC LITERATURE

EDITED BY

J. E. MONTGOMERY, University of Oslo
R. M. A. ALLEN, University of Pennsylvania

ISSN 0169-9903

1. KHOURI, M.A. *Poetry and the Making of Modern Egypt (1882-1922)*. 1971. ISBN 90 04 02178 7
2. SOMEKH, S. *The Changing Rythm*. A Study of Najīb Maḥfūẓ's Novels. 1973. ISBN 90 04 03587 7
3. SEMAH, D. *Four Egyptian Literary Critics*. 1974. ISBN 90 04 03841 8
4. CANTARINO, V. *Arabic Poetics in the Golden Age*. 1975. ISBN 90 04 04206 7
5. MOREH, S. *Modern Arabic Poetry, 1800-1970*. 1976. ISBN 90 04 04795 6
6. JAYYUSI, S.K. *Trends and Movements in Modern Arabic Poetry*. 2 pts. 1977. ISBN 90 04 04920 7
7. KURPERSHOEK, P.M. *The Short Stories of Yūsuf Idrīs*. A Modern Egyptian Author. 1981. ISBN 90 04 06283 1
8. GELDER, G.J.H. VAN. *Beyond the Line*. Classical Arabic Literary Critics. 1982. ISBN 90 04 06854 6
9. AJAMI, M. *The Neckveins of Winter*. 1984. ISBN 90 04 07016 8
10. BRUGMAN, J. *An Introduction to the History of Modern Arabic Literature in Egypt*. 1984. ISBN 90 04 07172 5
11. MALTI-DOUGLAS, F. *Structures of Avarice*. The Bukhalāʾ in Medieval Arabic Literature. 1985. ISBN 90 04 07485 6
12. ABDEL-MALEK, K. *A Study of the Vernacular Poetry of Aḥmad Fuʾād Nigm*. 1990. ISBN 90 04 08933 0
13. STETKEVYCH, S.P. *Abū Tammām and the Poetics of the ʿAbbāsid Age*. 1991. ISBN 90 04 09340 0
14. HAMORI, A. *The Composition of Mutanabbī's Panegyrics to Sayf al-Dawla*. 1992. ISBN 90 04 09366 4
15. PINAULT, D. *Story-Telling Techniques in the Arabian Nights*. 1992. ISBN 90 04 09530 6
16. AL-NOWAIHI, M.M. *The Poetry of Ibn Khafājah*. A Literary Analysis. 1993. ISBN 90 04 09660 4
17. KURPERSHOEK, P.M. *Oral Poetry and Narratives from Central Arabia*. 3 volumes.
    Vol. I. *The Poetry of ad-Dindān*. A Bedouin Bard in Southern Najd. An Edition with Translation and Introduction. 1994. ISBN 90 04 09894 1